IVY

by Sarah Oleksyk

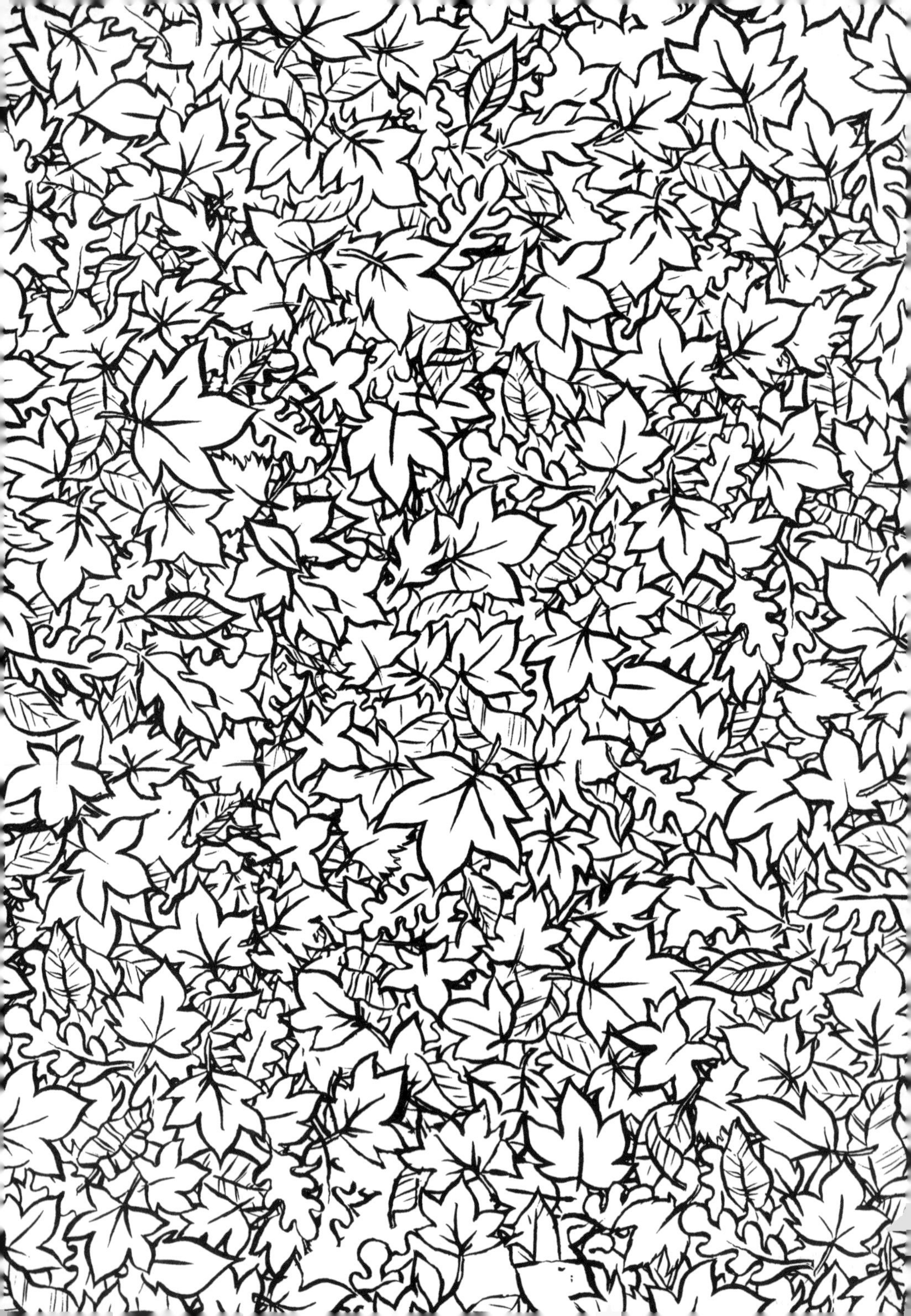

IVY

by *Sarah Oleksyk*

DESIGN BY TONY ONG • EDITED BY CHARLIE CHU

IVY

By Sarah Oleksyk

Published by Oni Press, Inc.
publisher, Joe Nozemack
editor in chief, James Lucas Jones
director of marketing, Cory Casoni
art director, Keith Wood
operations director, George Rohac
associate editor, Jill Beaton
associate editor, Charlie Chu
production assistant, Douglas E. Sherwood

onipress.com
saraholeksyk.com

ONI PRESS, INC.
1305 SE Martin Luther King Jr. Blvd.
Suite A
Portland, OR 97214
USA

First edition: January 2011

ISBN 978-1-934964-59-0

1 3 5 7 9 10 8 6 4 2

PRINTED IN U.S.A. By Lake Book Manufacturing.

High school sucks.

It's the time when you're still stuck in the orbit of people who determine the course of your day-to-day existence and are pushing hard to determine its future, while you're chafing to get out and figure out for yourself who you'll be. You're trapped between hope and helplessness, between self-awareness and obliviousness. You're surrounded by people who are in the same fix, whose drives and agendas might intersect with your own for a little while, but rarely for long. High schoolers can be horribly cruel to each other, but their cruelty is often a kind of armor against the way everyone around them is acting at cross-purposes.

Ivy is a perceptive, unsparing story about that vicious bind, the way it can shape someone, and what might be a way out of it, or at least through it. Ivy Stenova is angry for reasons she doesn't totally understand--in other words, she's in high school. She's mean, short-tempered, inattentive, deceitful; her sense of humor is as bitter as burnt coffee. Sarah Oleksyk makes us root for her anyway, because this is the moment when the spark and gifts in her can either flourish or be crushed. (The adults in this book, aside from Ivy's mom, are slightly broader caricatures than Ivy and her peers: they've assumed their final, immutable forms.) Ivy's about to become someone; we get to see the progression of her emotional state as that happens, and that's a rare and amazing thing to see on the page.

And Oleksyk makes us see it--the heart of this book is the way she draws Ivy's journey. It's a story full of silences: most of these characters' relationships to each other are spelled out less in what they say than in how they react with their faces and bodies to each other's presence. They're responding to their environment moment by moment, too. One of the things I love about Oleksyk's comics is her knack for staging, and how neatly she establishes a sense of place. (The abandoned railroad overpass that's Ivy's favorite retreat is practically a character itself.) This is the kind of cartooning whose craft serves its flow, but there's always more going on than the story spells out: impressionistic suggestions of what Ivy's feeling, or images that move away from the characters to show us something about what's happening around them.

Sarah Oleksyk's been making 'zines, prints and comics for more than a decade now; she's kind of a local legend here in Portland. *Ivy* first appeared as a series of five photocopied mini-comics. Every once in a while, Oleksyk would show up at small-press comics conventions with a new one, and there'd be an excited murmur from people who follow rising stars of art comics: did you see that new *Ivy*? Man, I wish there were a way for more people to see Sarah's stuff. Now there is, and now you get to see it too.

DOUGLAS WOLK
Portland, Oregon, 2010

Douglas Wolk is the author of Reading Comics: How Graphic Novels Work and What They Mean. *He writes about comics for* Techland, The New York Times, The Believer, *and elsewhere.*

for
LYNDSY
♡

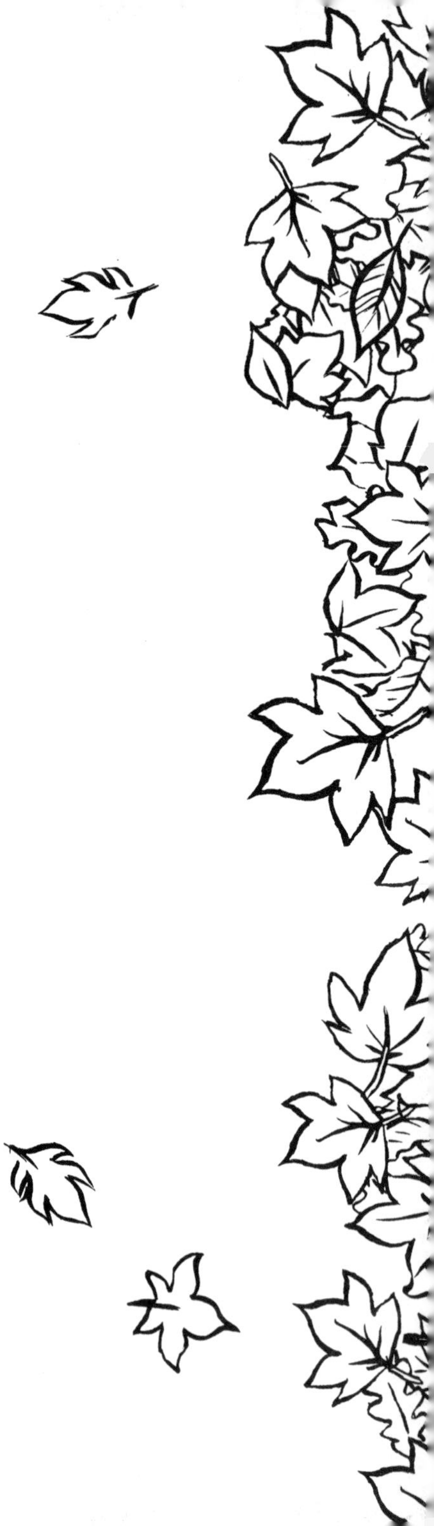

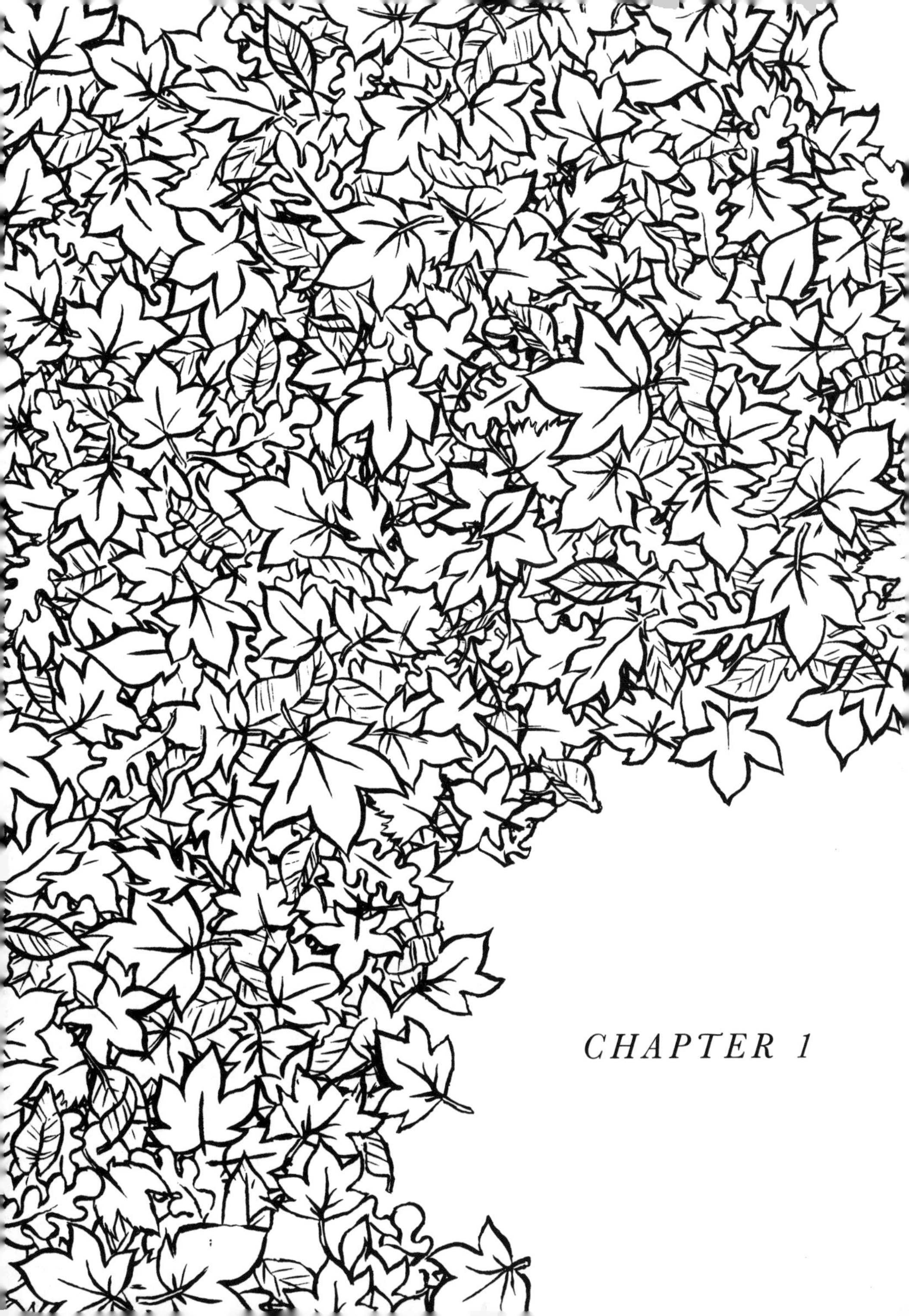

CHAPTER 1

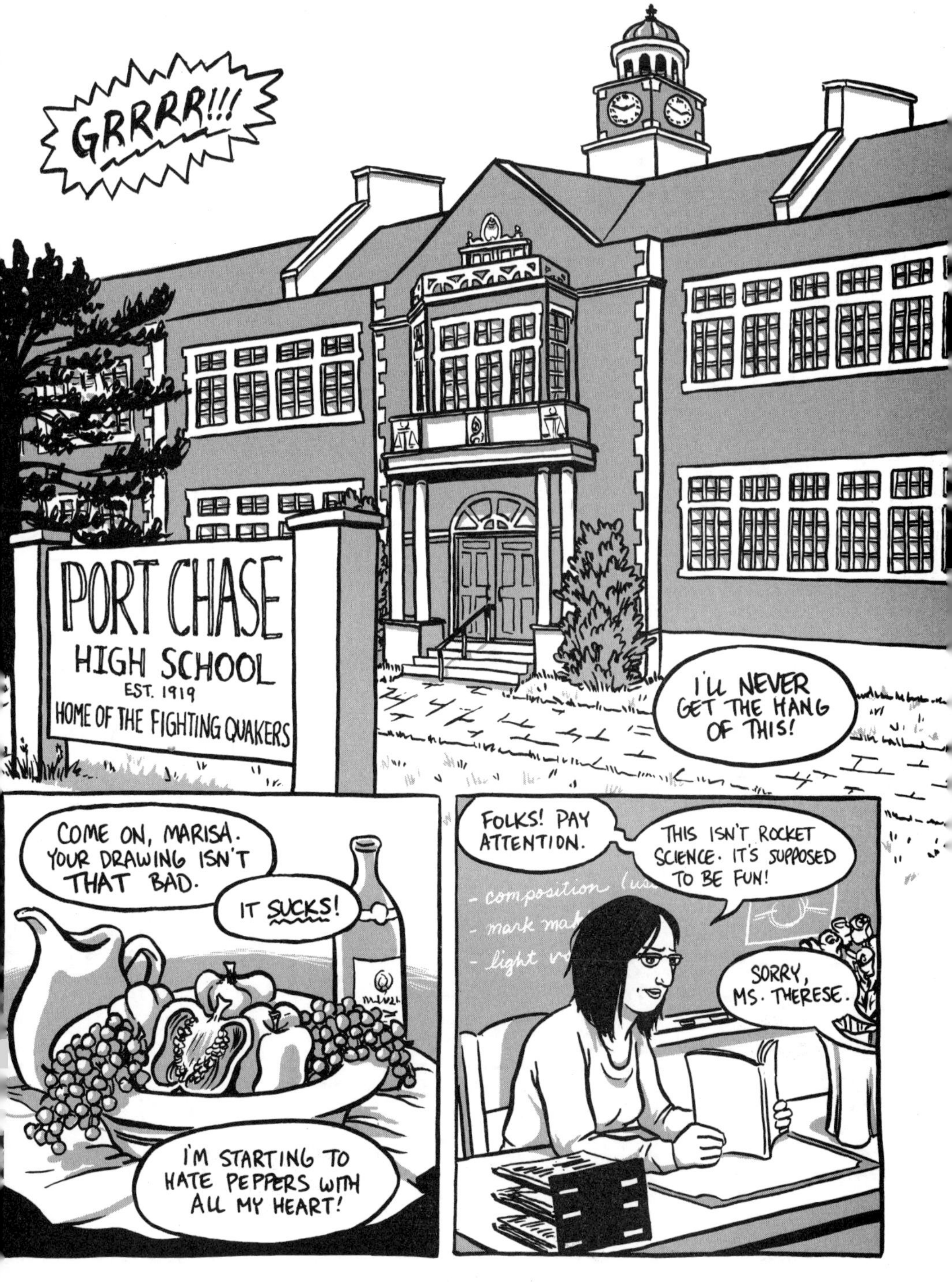
GRRRR!!!
PORT CHASE
HIGH SCHOOL
EST. 1919
HOME OF THE FIGHTING QUAKERS
I'LL NEVER GET THE HANG OF THIS!
COME ON, MARISA. YOUR DRAWING ISN'T THAT BAD.
IT SUCKS!
I'M STARTING TO HATE PEPPERS WITH ALL MY HEART!
FOLKS! PAY ATTENTION.
THIS ISN'T ROCKET SCIENCE. IT'S SUPPOSED TO BE FUN!
SORRY, MS. THERESE.

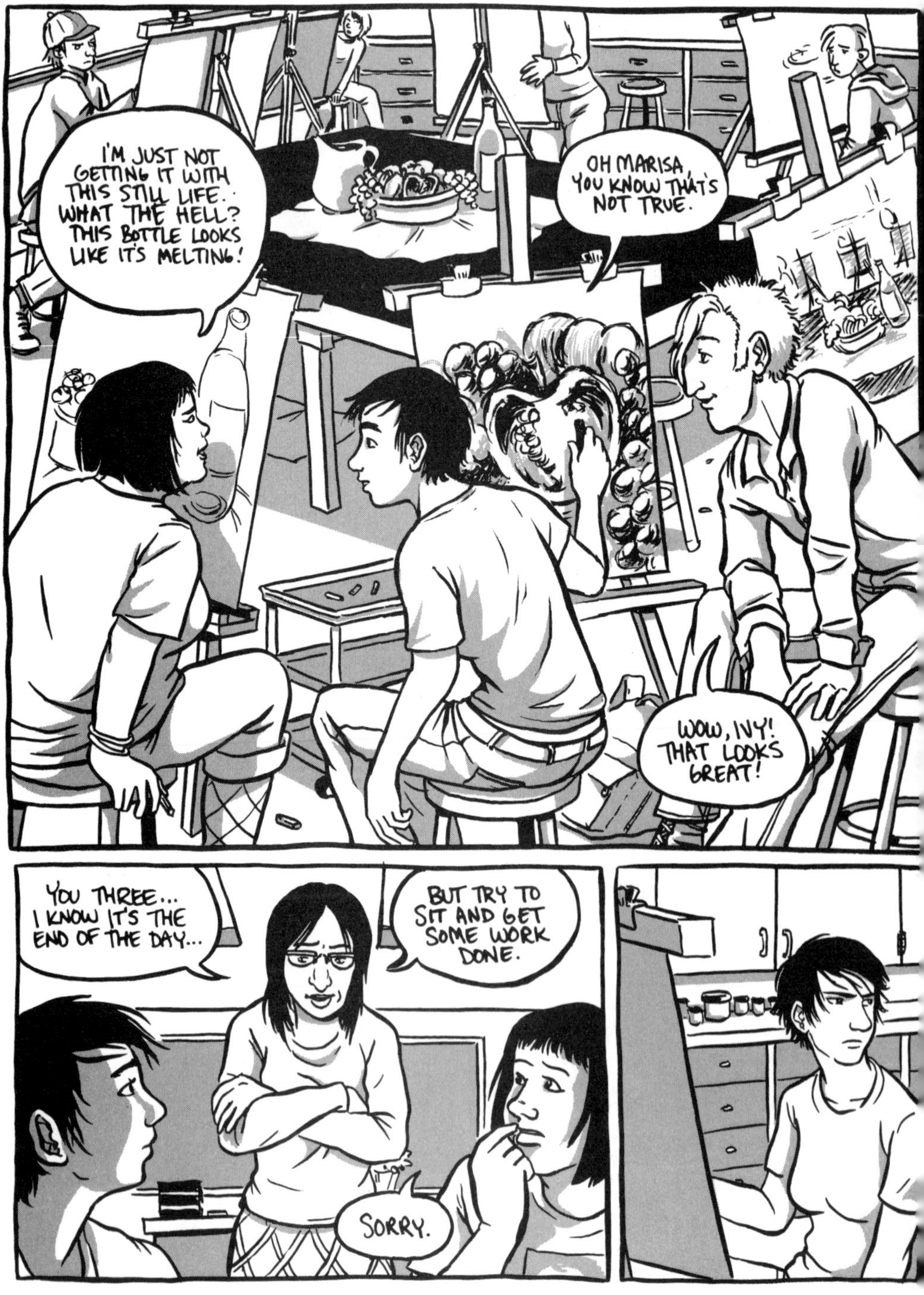
I'M JUST NOT GETTING IT WITH THIS STILL LIFE. WHAT THE HELL? THIS BOTTLE LOOKS LIKE IT'S MELTING!
OH MARISA, YOU KNOW THAT'S NOT TRUE.
WOW, IVY! THAT LOOKS GREAT!
YOU THREE... I KNOW IT'S THE END OF THE DAY...
BUT TRY TO SIT AND GET SOME WORK DONE.
SORRY.

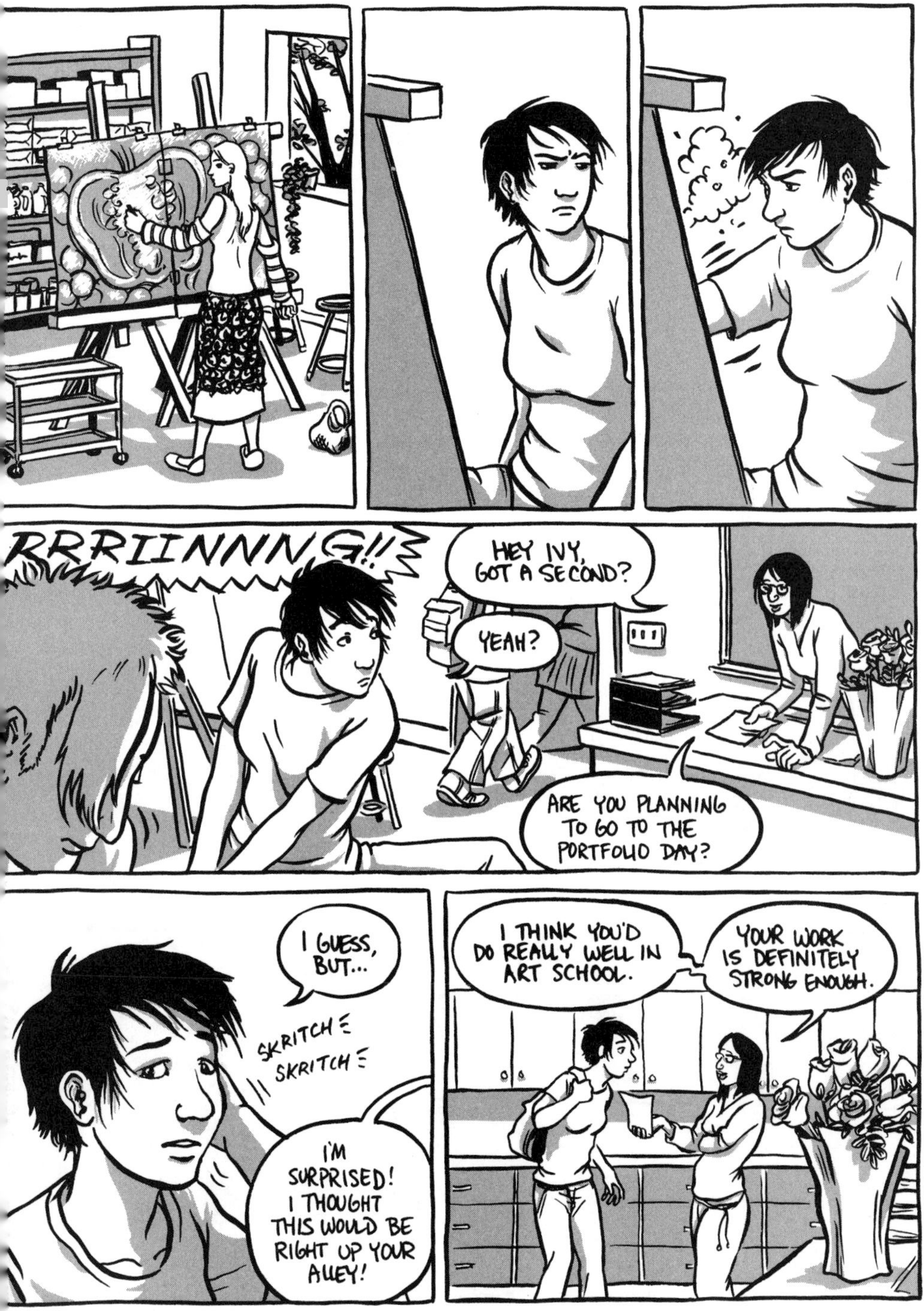
RRRIINNNG!!
HEY IVY, GOT A SECOND?
YEAH?
ARE YOU PLANNING TO GO TO THE PORTFOLIO DAY?
I GUESS, BUT...
SKRITCH
SKRITCH
I'M SURPRISED! I THOUGHT THIS WOULD BE RIGHT UP YOUR ALLEY!
I THINK YOU'D DO REALLY WELL IN ART SCHOOL.
YOUR WORK IS DEFINITELY STRONG ENOUGH.

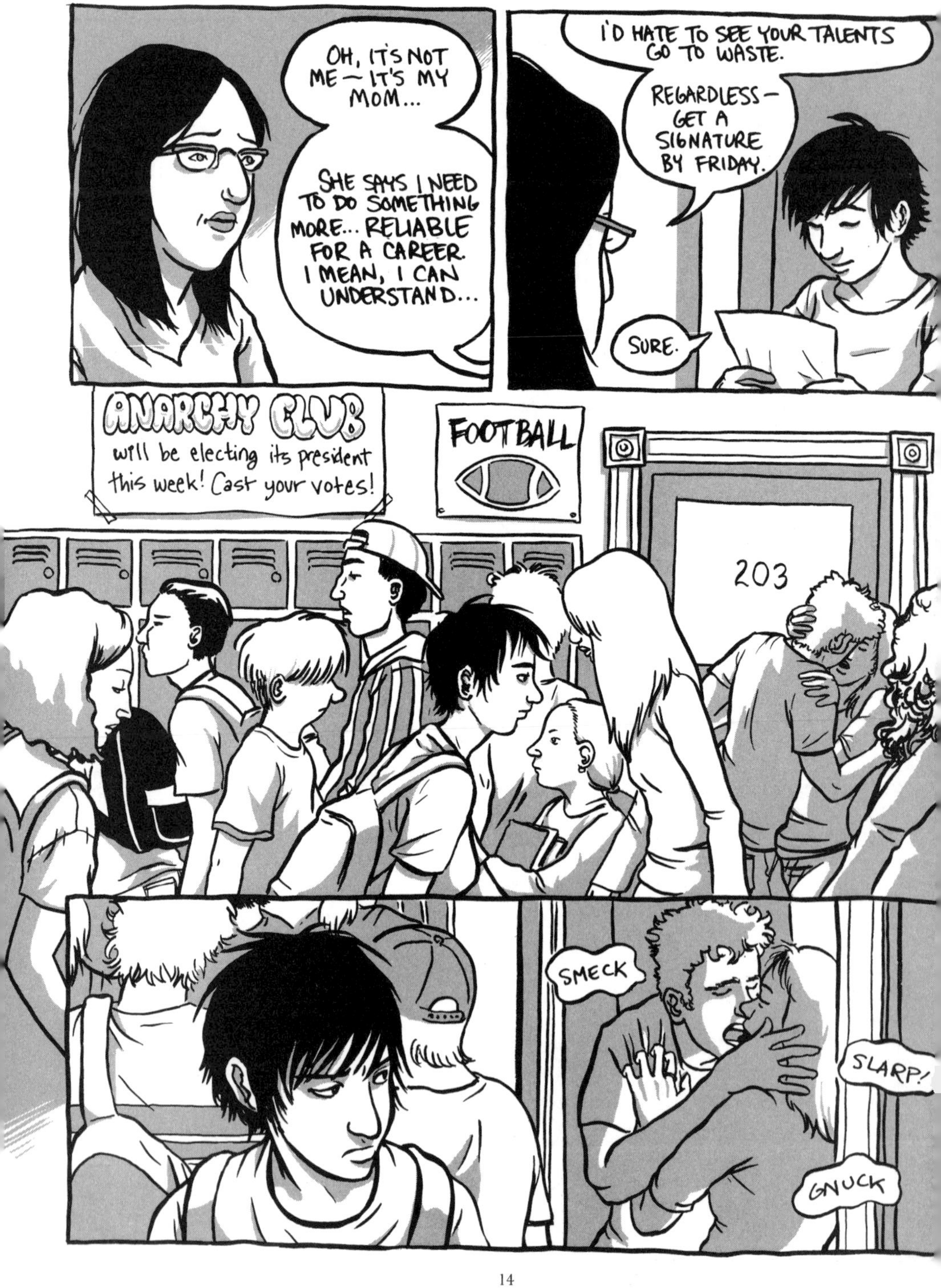
OH, IT'S NOT ME — IT'S MY MOM...
SHE SAYS I NEED TO DO SOMETHING MORE... RELIABLE FOR A CAREER. I MEAN, I CAN UNDERSTAND...
I'D HATE TO SEE YOUR TALENTS GO TO WASTE.
REGARDLESS — GET A SIGNATURE BY FRIDAY.
SURE.
ANARCHY CLUB
will be electing its president this week! Cast your votes!
FOOTBALL
203
SMECK
SLARP!
GNUCK

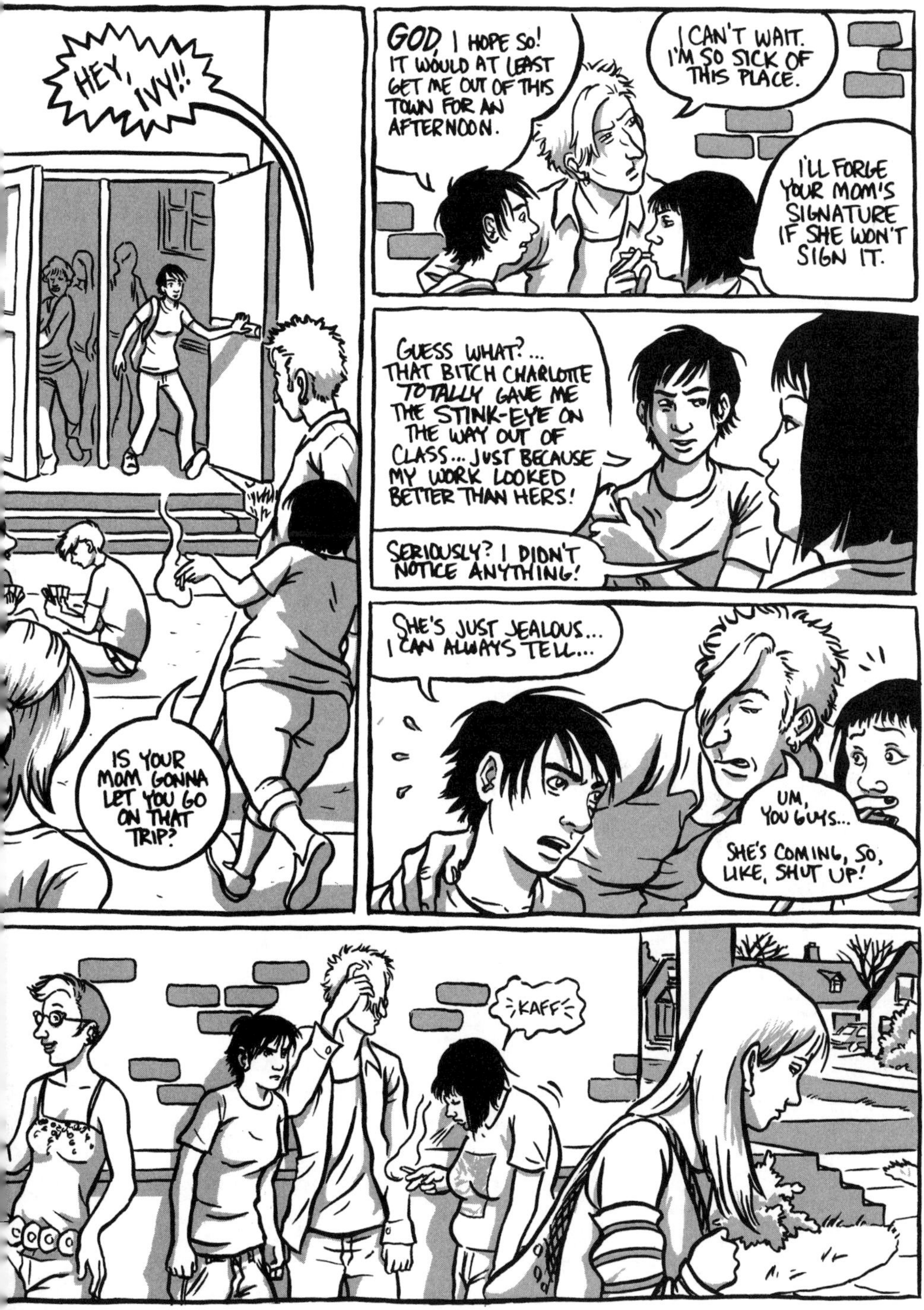

HEY, IVY!!
IS YOUR MOM GONNA LET YOU GO ON THAT TRIP?
GOD, I HOPE SO! IT WOULD AT LEAST GET ME OUT OF THIS TOWN FOR AN AFTERNOON.
I CAN'T WAIT. I'M SO SICK OF THIS PLACE.
I'LL FORGE YOUR MOM'S SIGNATURE IF SHE WON'T SIGN IT.
GUESS WHAT?... THAT BITCH CHARLOTTE TOTALLY GAVE ME THE STINK-EYE ON THE WAY OUT OF CLASS... JUST BECAUSE MY WORK LOOKED BETTER THAN HERS!
SERIOUSLY? I DIDN'T NOTICE ANYTHING!
SHE'S JUST JEALOUS... I CAN ALWAYS TELL...
UM, YOU GUYS...
SHE'S COMING, SO, LIKE, SHUT UP!
KAFF

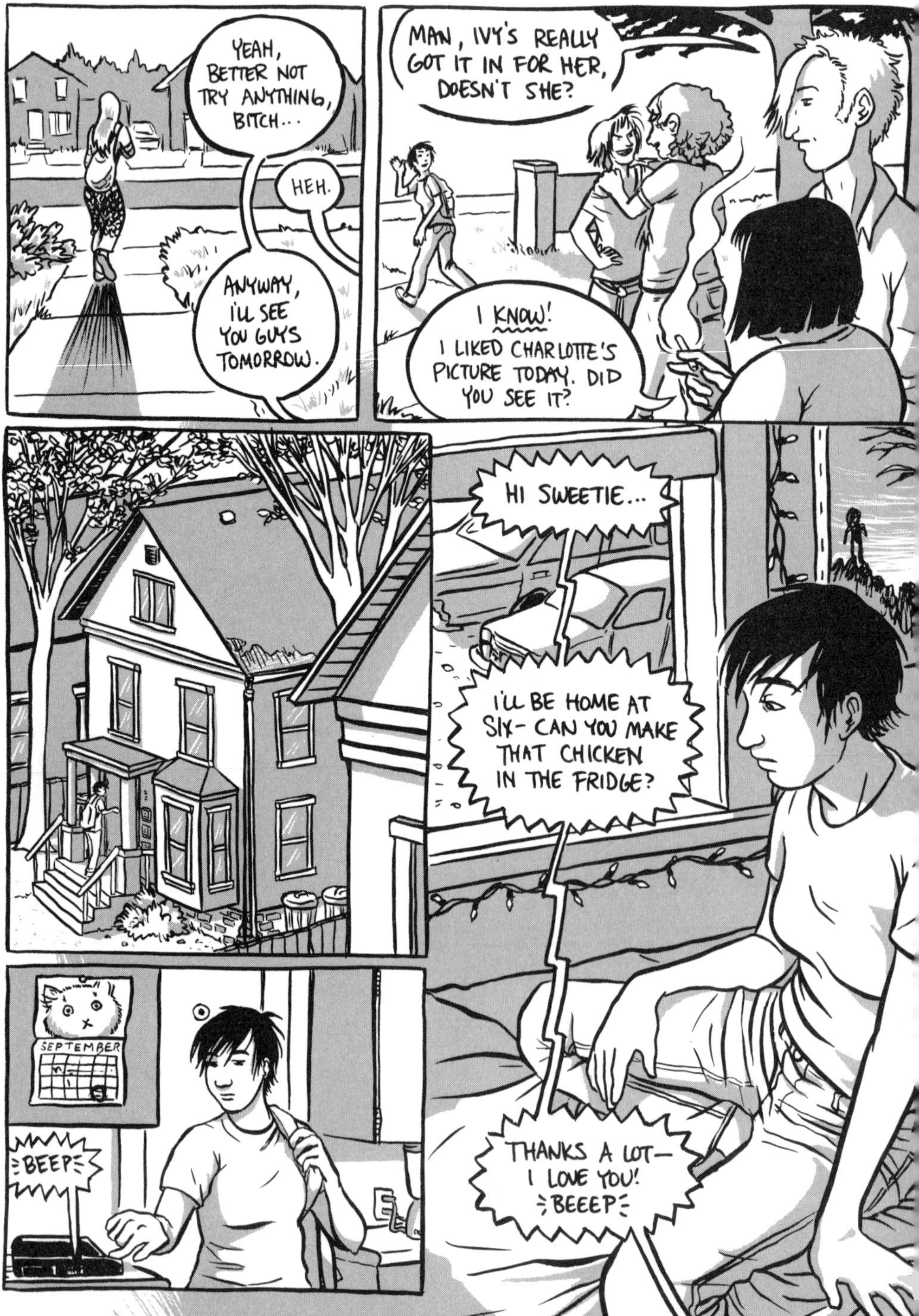

YEAH, BETTER NOT TRY ANYTHING, BITCH...
HEH.
ANYWAY, I'LL SEE YOU GUYS TOMORROW.
MAN, IVY'S REALLY GOT IT IN FOR HER, DOESN'T SHE?
I KNOW! I LIKED CHARLOTTE'S PICTURE TODAY. DID YOU SEE IT?
SEPTEMBER
BEEP
HI SWEETIE...
I'LL BE HOME AT SIX- CAN YOU MAKE THAT CHICKEN IN THE FRIDGE?
THANKS A LOT- I LOVE YOU! BEEEP

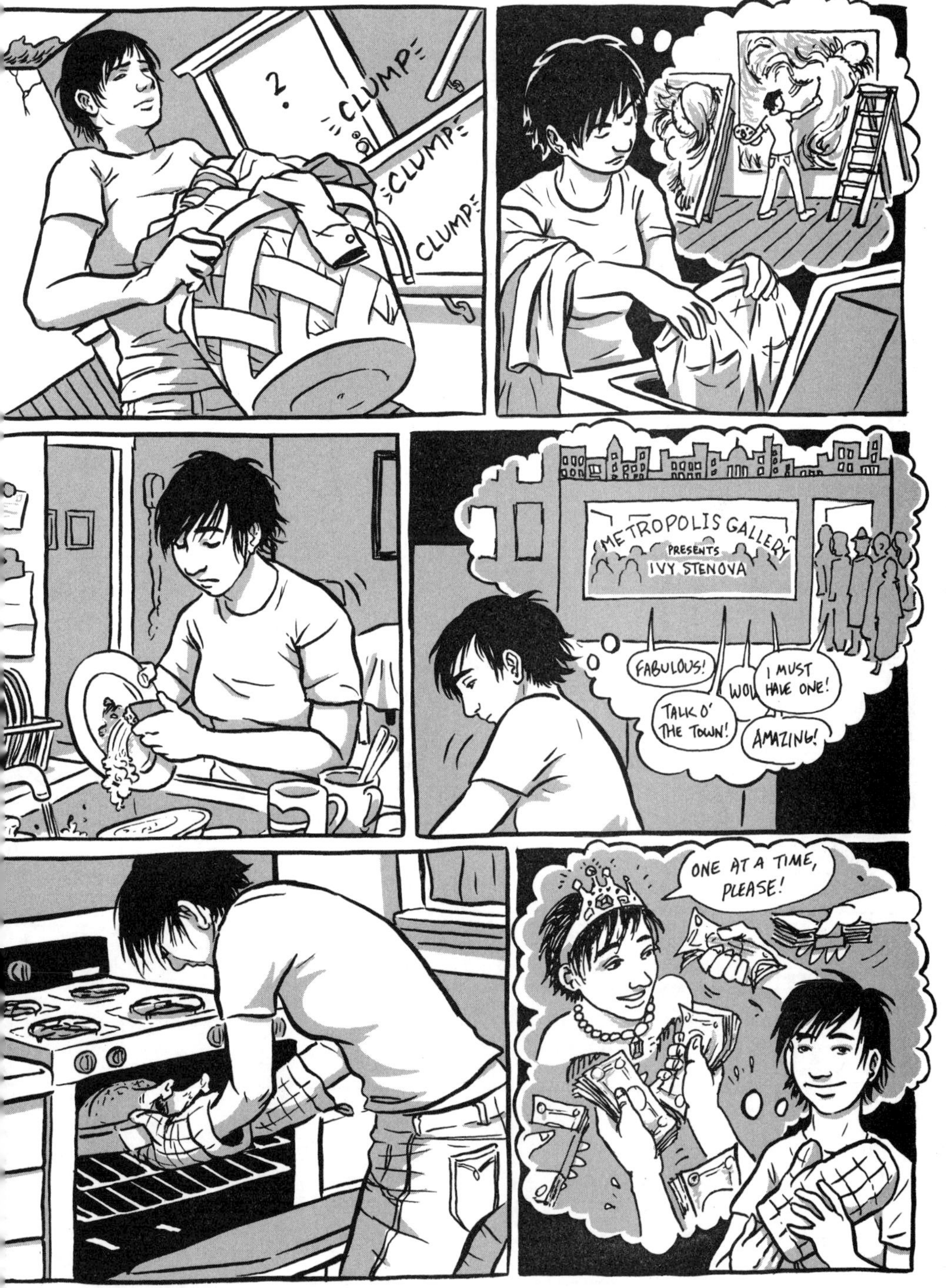
2
CLUMP
CLUMP
CLUMP
CLUMP
METROPOLIS GALLERY
PRESENTS
IVY STENOVA
FABULOUS!
TALK O' THE TOWN!
WO
I MUST HAVE ONE!
AMAZING!
ONE AT A TIME, PLEASE!

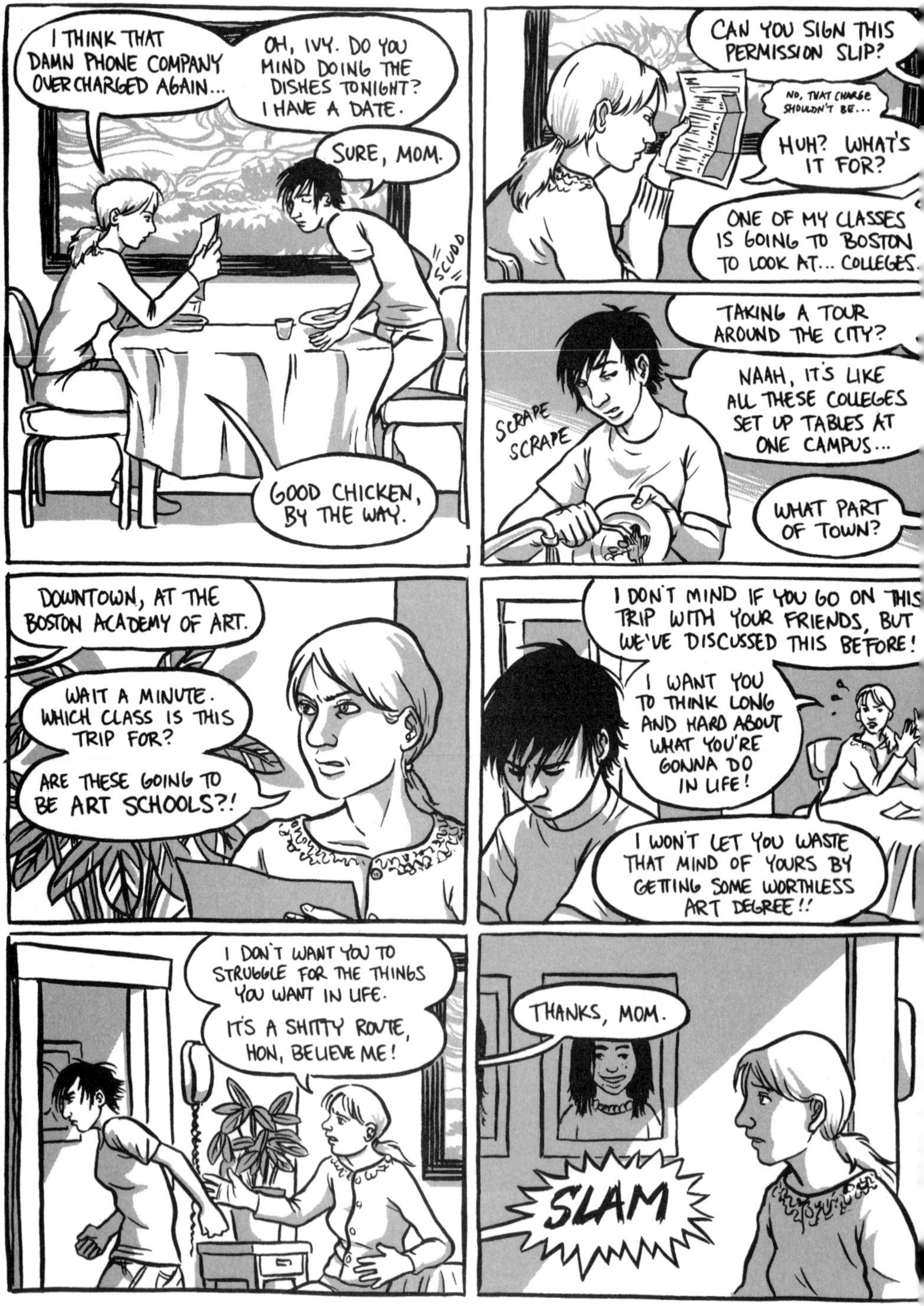
I THINK THAT DAMN PHONE COMPANY OVERCHARGED AGAIN...
OH, IVY. DO YOU MIND DOING THE DISHES TONIGHT? I HAVE A DATE.
SURE, MOM.
SCUDD
GOOD CHICKEN, BY THE WAY.
CAN YOU SIGN THIS PERMISSION SLIP?
NO, THAT CHARGE SHOULDN'T BE...
HUH? WHAT'S IT FOR?
ONE OF MY CLASSES IS GOING TO BOSTON TO LOOK AT... COLLEGES.
TAKING A TOUR AROUND THE CITY?
NAAH, IT'S LIKE ALL THESE COLLEGES SET UP TABLES AT ONE CAMPUS...
SCRAPE SCRAPE
WHAT PART OF TOWN?
DOWNTOWN, AT THE BOSTON ACADEMY OF ART.
WAIT A MINUTE. WHICH CLASS IS THIS TRIP FOR?
ARE THESE GOING TO BE ART SCHOOLS?!
I DON'T MIND IF YOU GO ON THIS TRIP WITH YOUR FRIENDS, BUT WE'VE DISCUSSED THIS BEFORE!
I WANT YOU TO THINK LONG AND HARD ABOUT WHAT YOU'RE GONNA DO IN LIFE!
I WON'T LET YOU WASTE THAT MIND OF YOURS BY GETTING SOME WORTHLESS ART DEGREE!!
I DON'T WANT YOU TO STRUGGLE FOR THE THINGS YOU WANT IN LIFE.
IT'S A SHITTY ROUTE, HON, BELIEVE ME!
THANKS, MOM.
SLAM

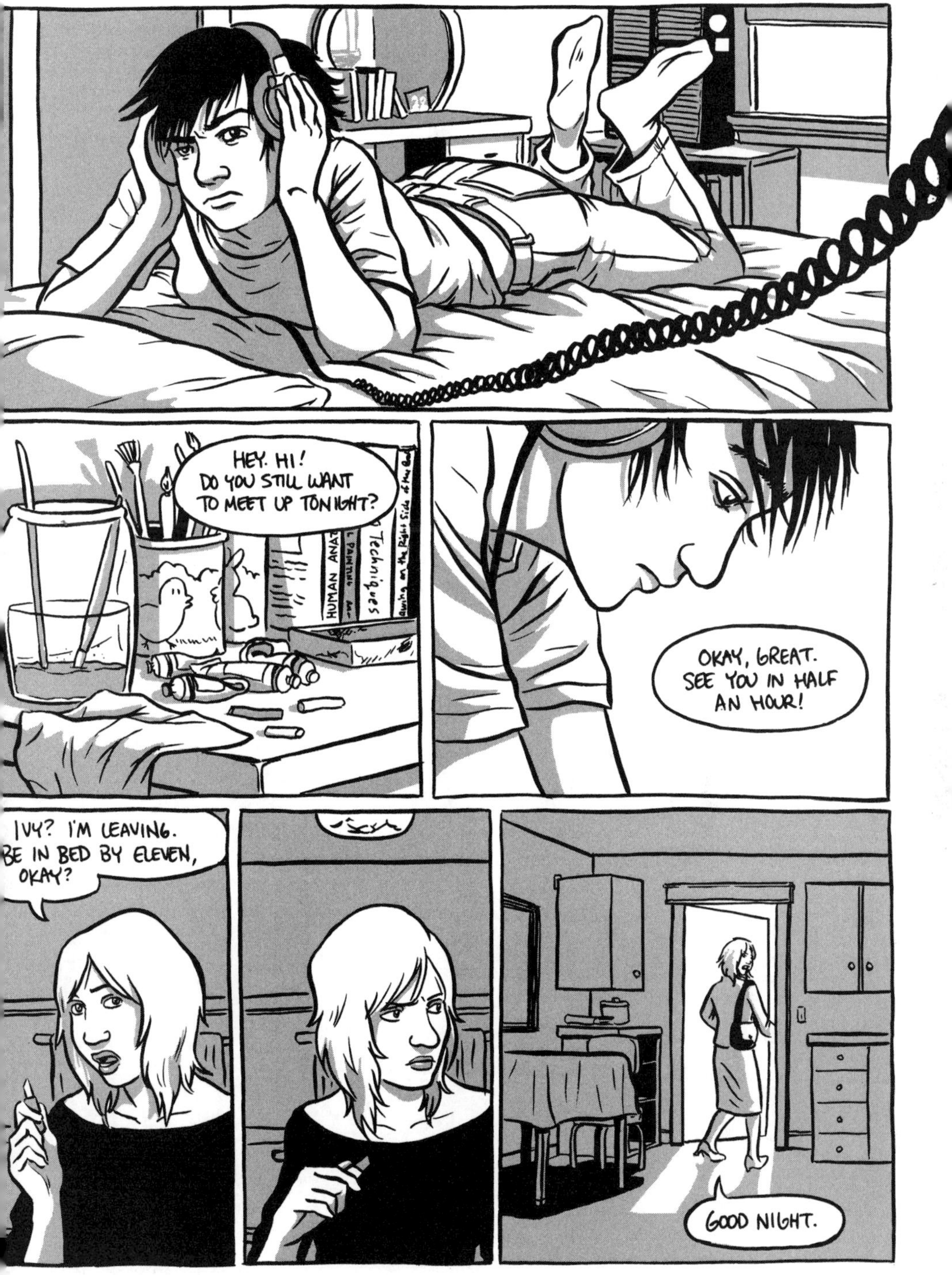
HEY. HI!
DO YOU STILL WANT TO MEET UP TONIGHT?
OKAY, GREAT. SEE YOU IN HALF AN HOUR!
IVY? I'M LEAVING. BE IN BED BY ELEVEN, OKAY?
GOOD NIGHT.

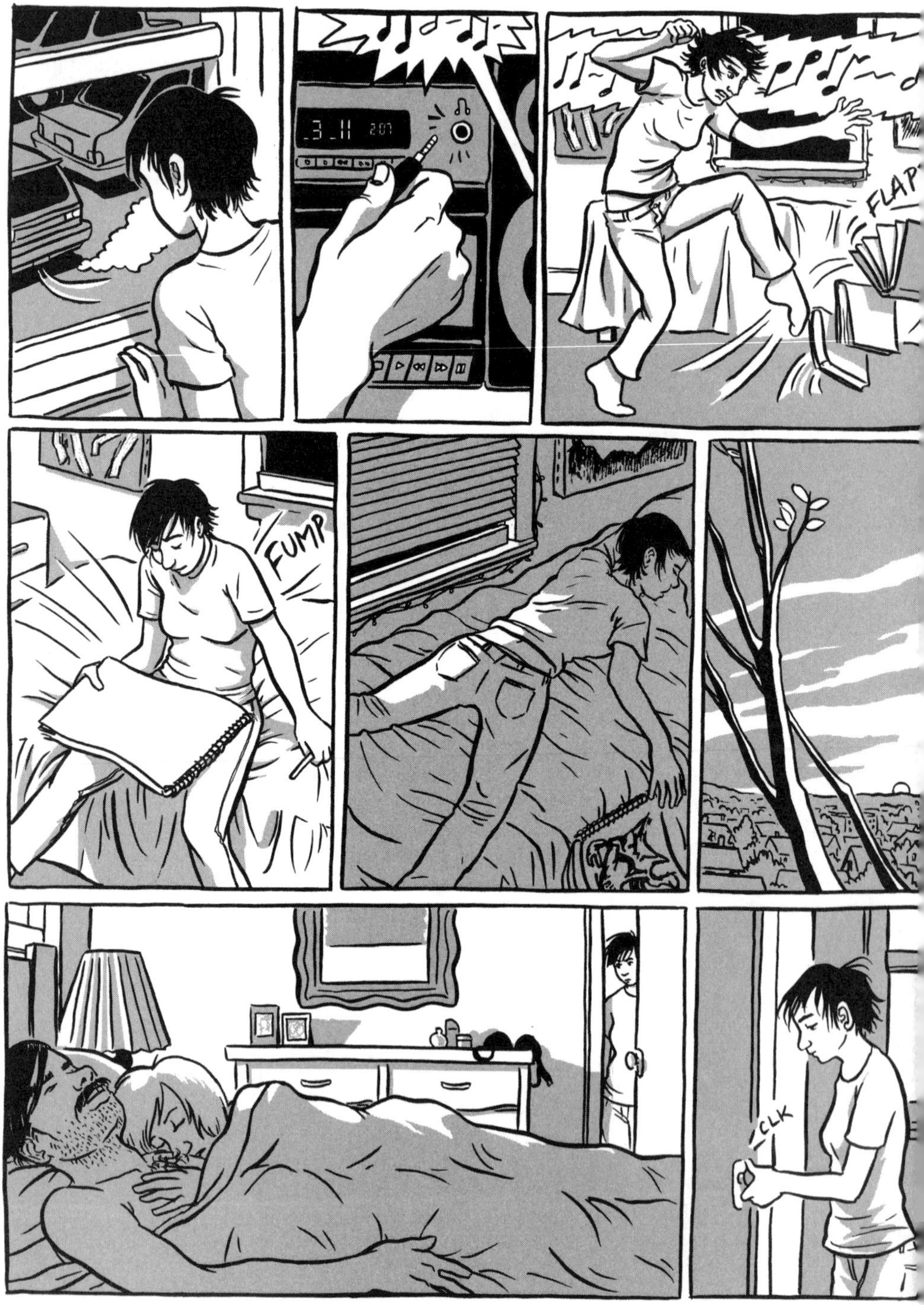
FLAP
FUMP
CLK

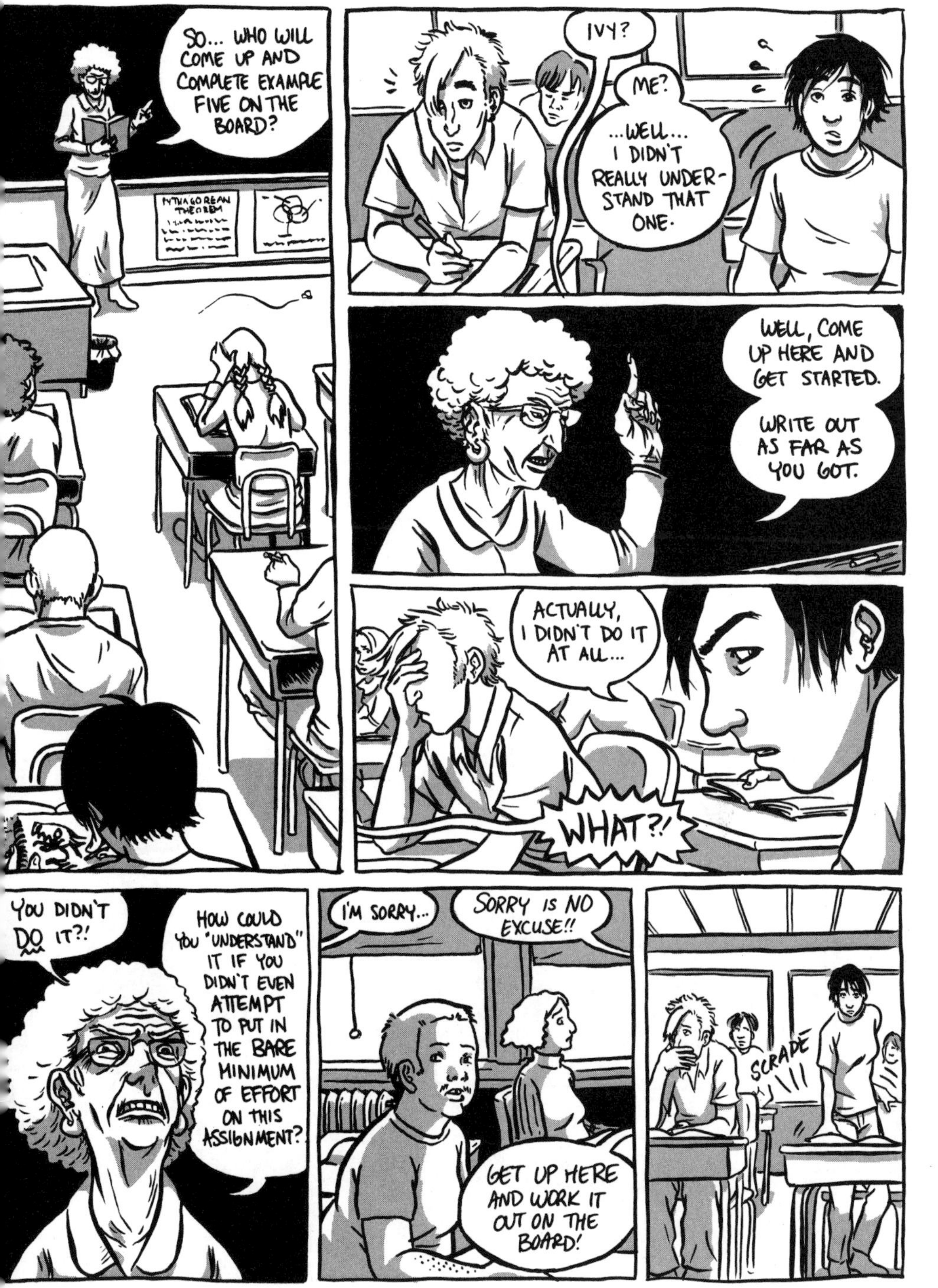
SO... WHO WILL COME UP AND COMPLETE EXAMPLE FIVE ON THE BOARD?
PYTHAGOREAN THEOREM
IVY?
ME?
...WELL... I DIDN'T REALLY UNDERSTAND THAT ONE.
WELL, COME UP HERE AND GET STARTED.
WRITE OUT AS FAR AS YOU GOT.
ACTUALLY, I DIDN'T DO IT AT ALL...
WHAT?!
YOU DIDN'T DO IT?!
HOW COULD YOU "UNDERSTAND" IT IF YOU DIDN'T EVEN ATTEMPT TO PUT IN THE BARE MINIMUM OF EFFORT ON THIS ASSIGNMENT?
I'M SORRY...
SORRY IS NO EXCUSE!!
GET UP HERE AND WORK IT OUT ON THE BOARD!
SCRAPE

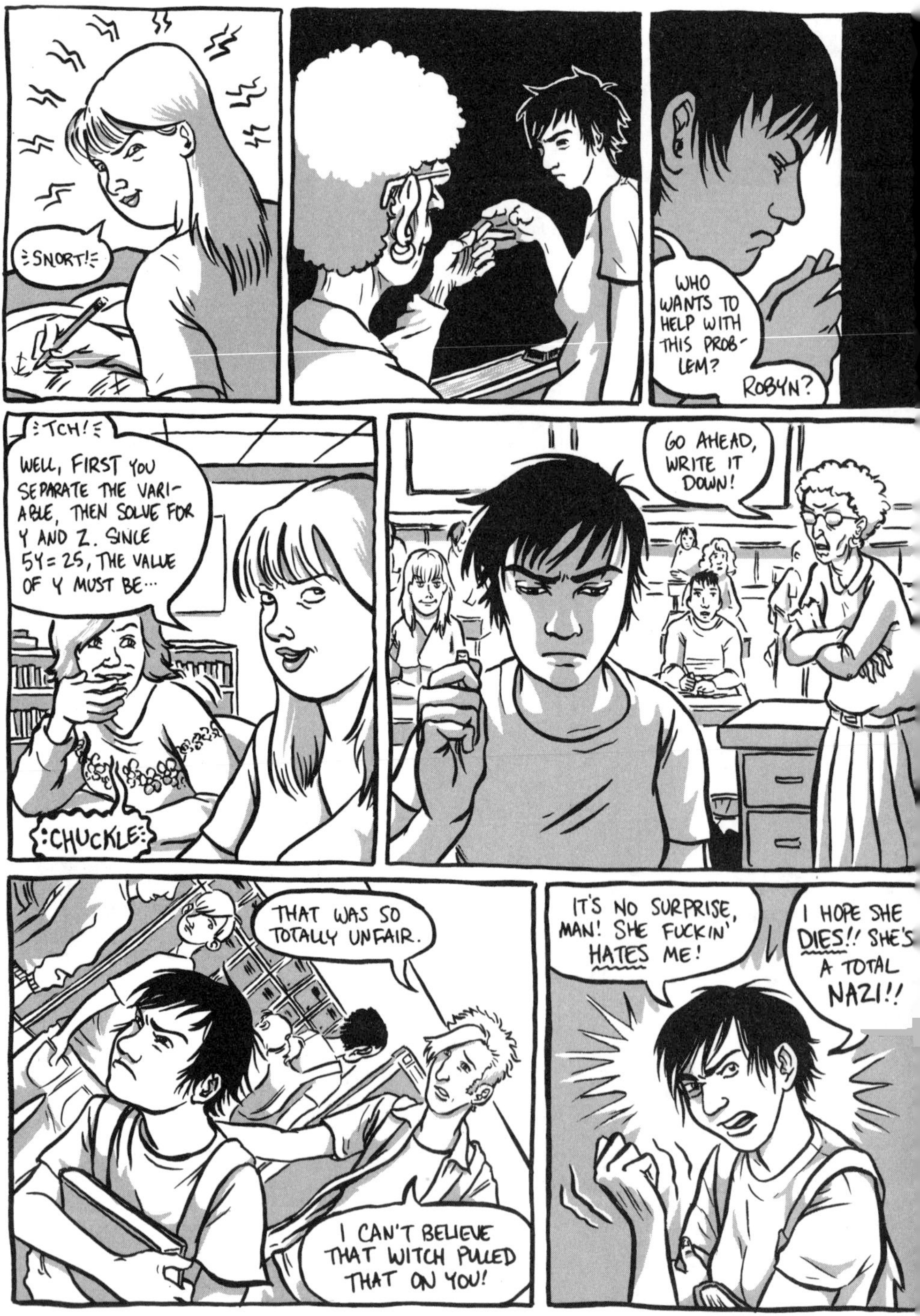
SNORT!
WHO WANTS TO HELP WITH THIS PROB-LEM?
ROBYN?
TCH!
WELL, FIRST YOU SEPARATE THE VARI-ABLE, THEN SOLVE FOR Y AND Z. SINCE 5Y=25, THE VALUE OF Y MUST BE...
CHUCKLE
GO AHEAD, WRITE IT DOWN!
THAT WAS SO TOTALLY UNFAIR.
I CAN'T BELIEVE THAT WITCH PULLED THAT ON YOU!
IT'S NO SURPRISE, MAN! SHE FUCKIN' HATES ME!
I HOPE SHE DIES!! SHE'S A TOTAL NAZI!!

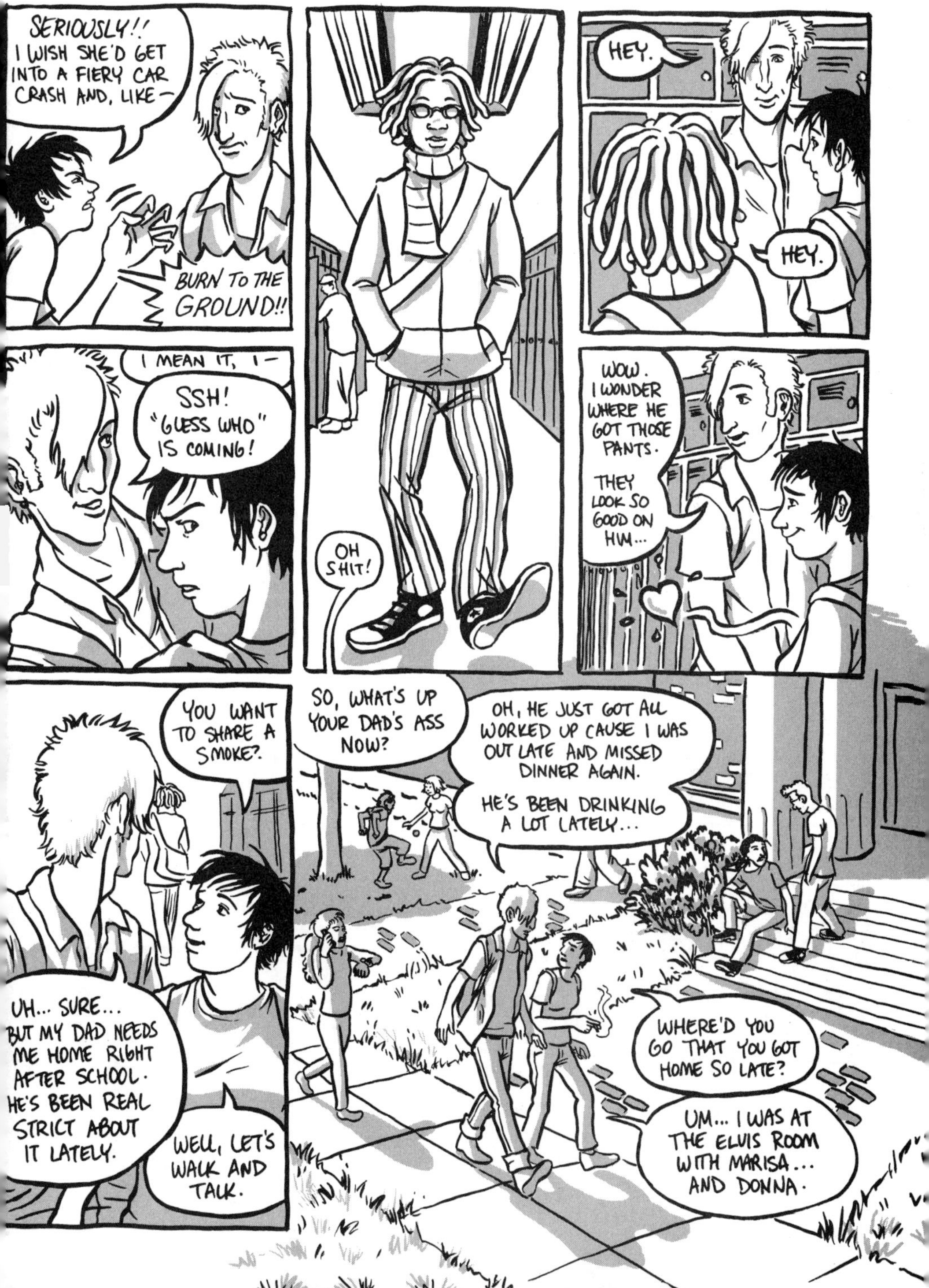
SERIOUSLY!! I WISH SHE'D GET INTO A FIERY CAR CRASH AND, LIKE—
BURN TO THE GROUND!!
HEY.
HEY.
I MEAN IT, I—
SSH! "GUESS WHO" IS COMING!
OH SHIT!
WOW. I WONDER WHERE HE GOT THOSE PANTS.
THEY LOOK SO GOOD ON HIM...
YOU WANT TO SHARE A SMOKE?
UH... SURE... BUT MY DAD NEEDS ME HOME RIGHT AFTER SCHOOL. HE'S BEEN REAL STRICT ABOUT IT LATELY.
WELL, LET'S WALK AND TALK.
SO, WHAT'S UP YOUR DAD'S ASS NOW?
OH, HE JUST GOT ALL WORKED UP CAUSE I WAS OUT LATE AND MISSED DINNER AGAIN.
HE'S BEEN DRINKING A LOT LATELY...
WHERE'D YOU GO THAT YOU GOT HOME SO LATE?
UM... I WAS AT THE ELVIS ROOM WITH MARISA... AND DONNA.

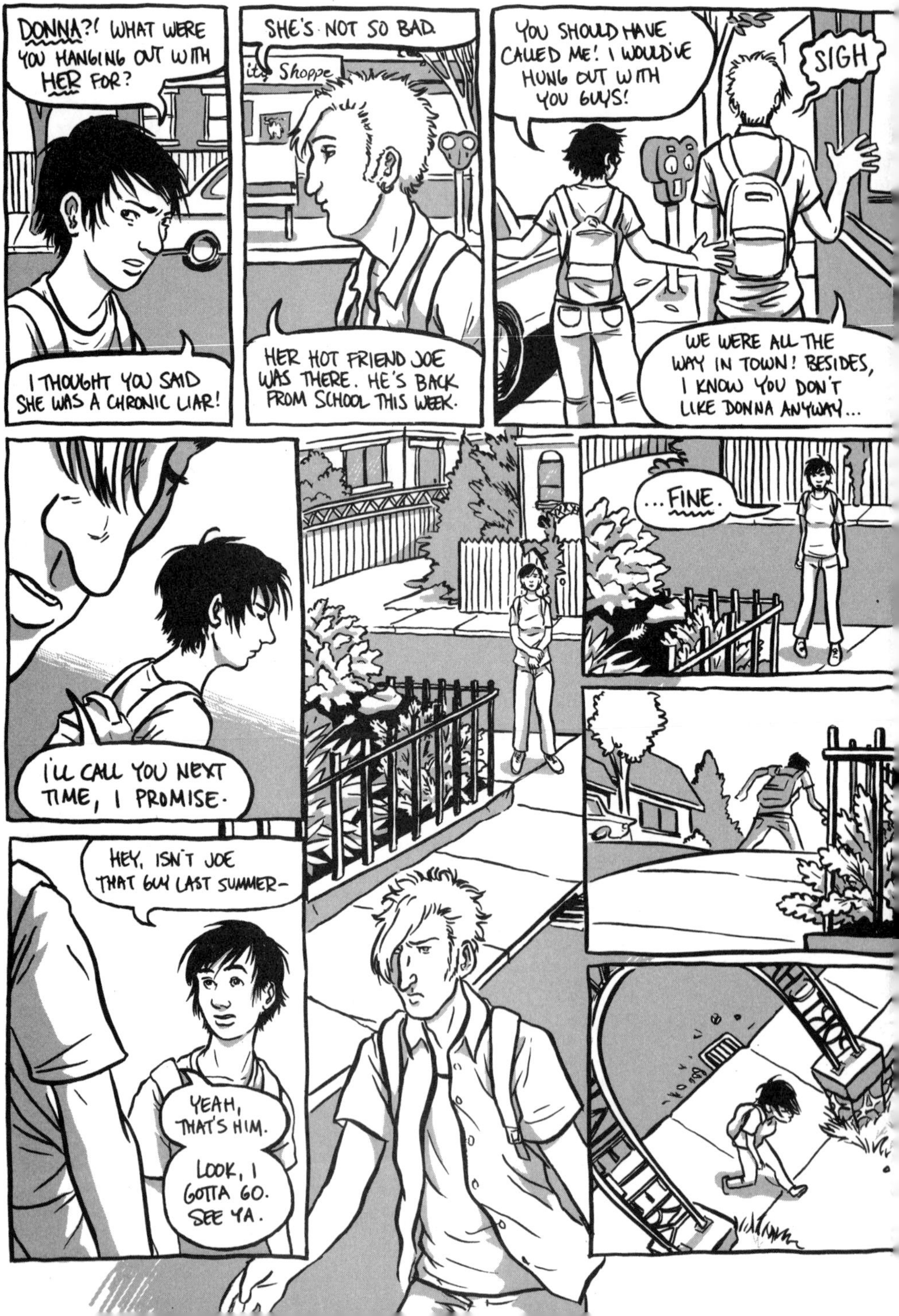
DONNA?! WHAT WERE YOU HANGING OUT WITH HER FOR?
I THOUGHT YOU SAID SHE WAS A CHRONIC LIAR!
SHE'S NOT SO BAD.
Shoppe
HER HOT FRIEND JOE WAS THERE. HE'S BACK FROM SCHOOL THIS WEEK.
YOU SHOULD HAVE CALLED ME! I WOULD'VE HUNG OUT WITH YOU GUYS!
SIGH
WE WERE ALL THE WAY IN TOWN! BESIDES, I KNOW YOU DON'T LIKE DONNA ANYWAY...
I'LL CALL YOU NEXT TIME, I PROMISE.
...FINE.
HEY, ISN'T JOE THAT GUY LAST SUMMER-
YEAH, THAT'S HIM.
LOOK, I GOTTA GO. SEE YA.

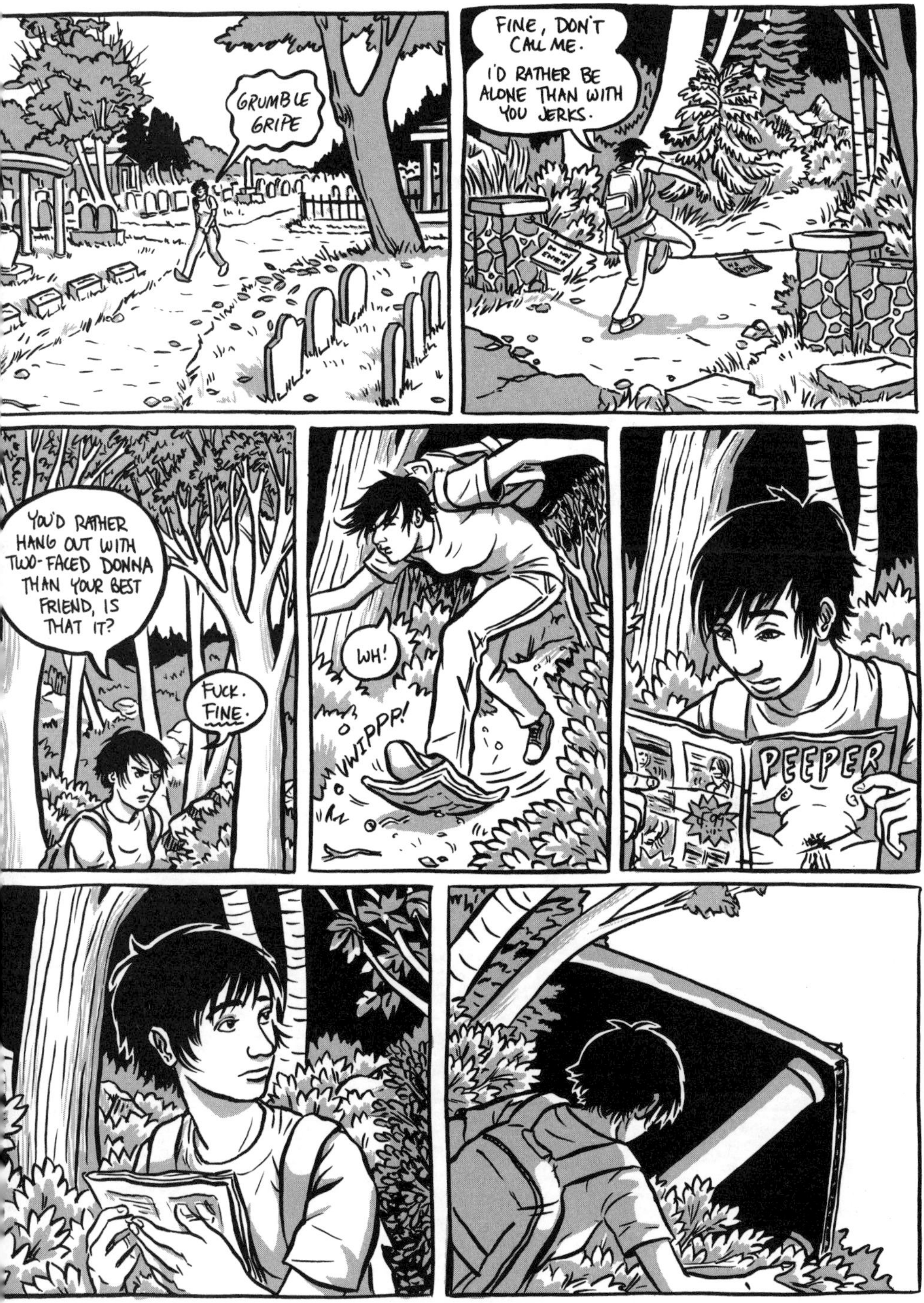
GRUMBLE GRIPE
FINE, DON'T CALL ME.
I'D RATHER BE ALONE THAN WITH YOU JERKS.
YOU'D RATHER HANG OUT WITH TWO-FACED DONNA THAN YOUR BEST FRIEND, IS THAT IT?
FUCK. FINE.
WH!
WIPPP!
PEEPER

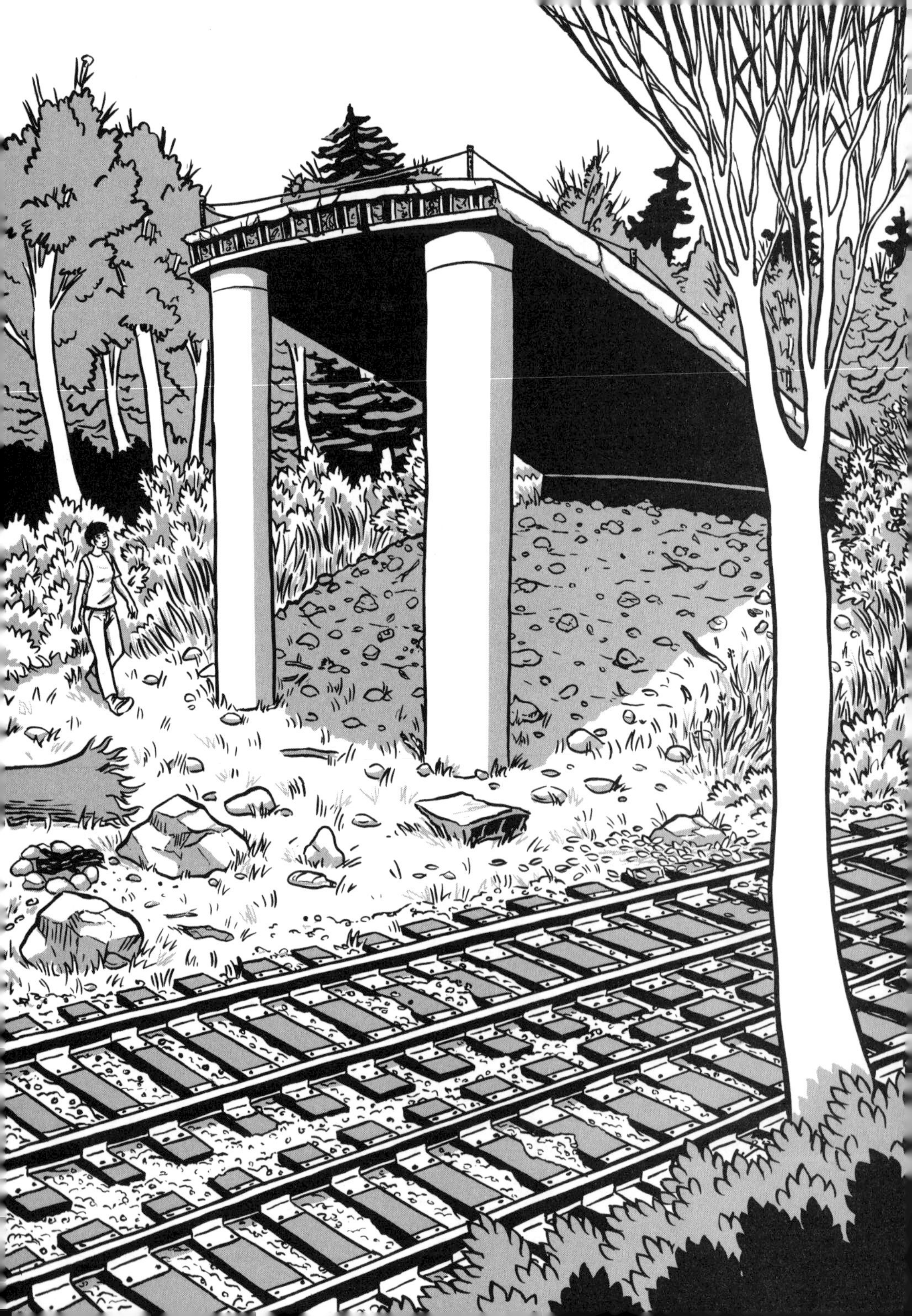

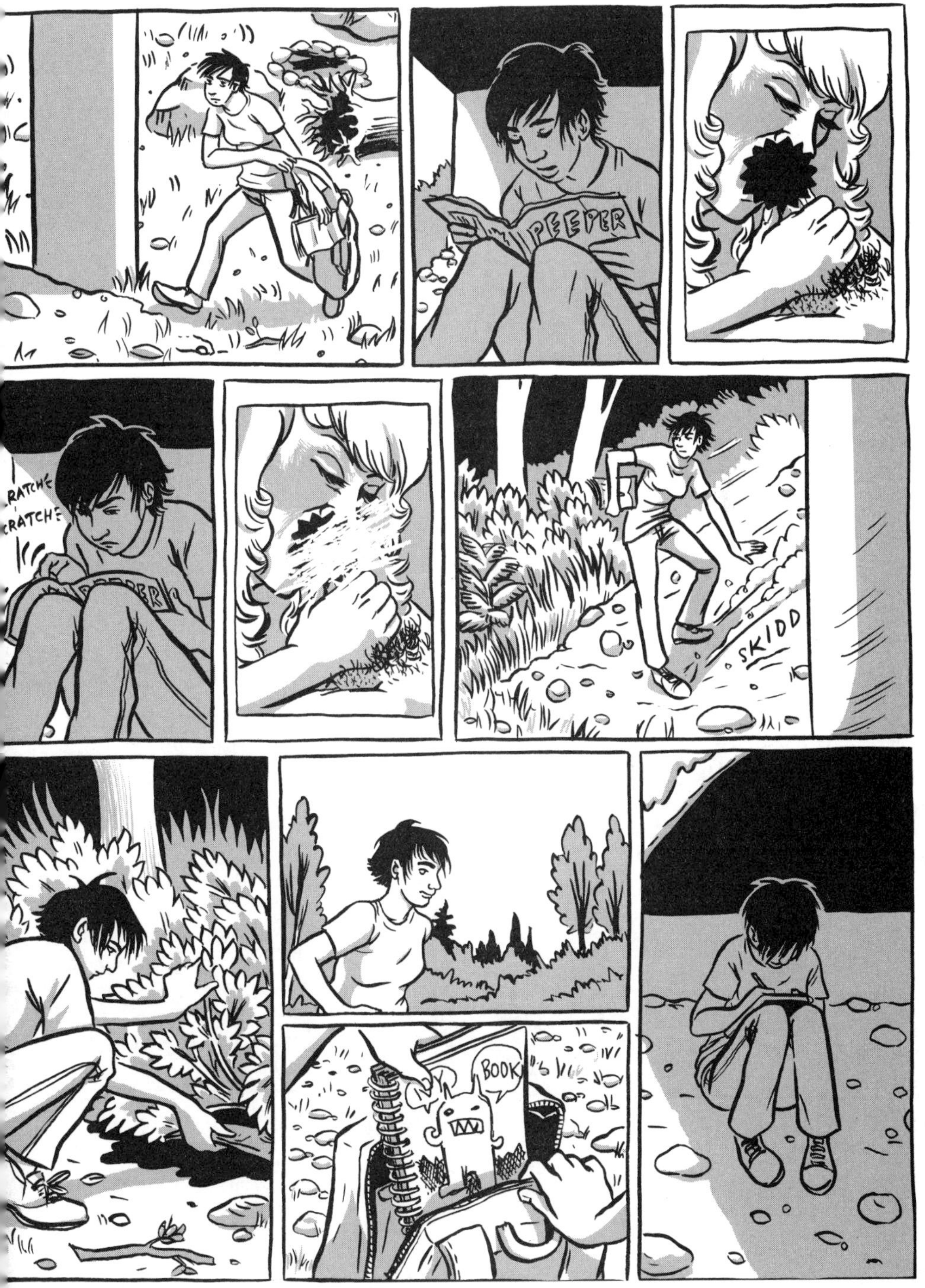
PEEPER
RATCHE
RATCHE
SKIDD
BOOK

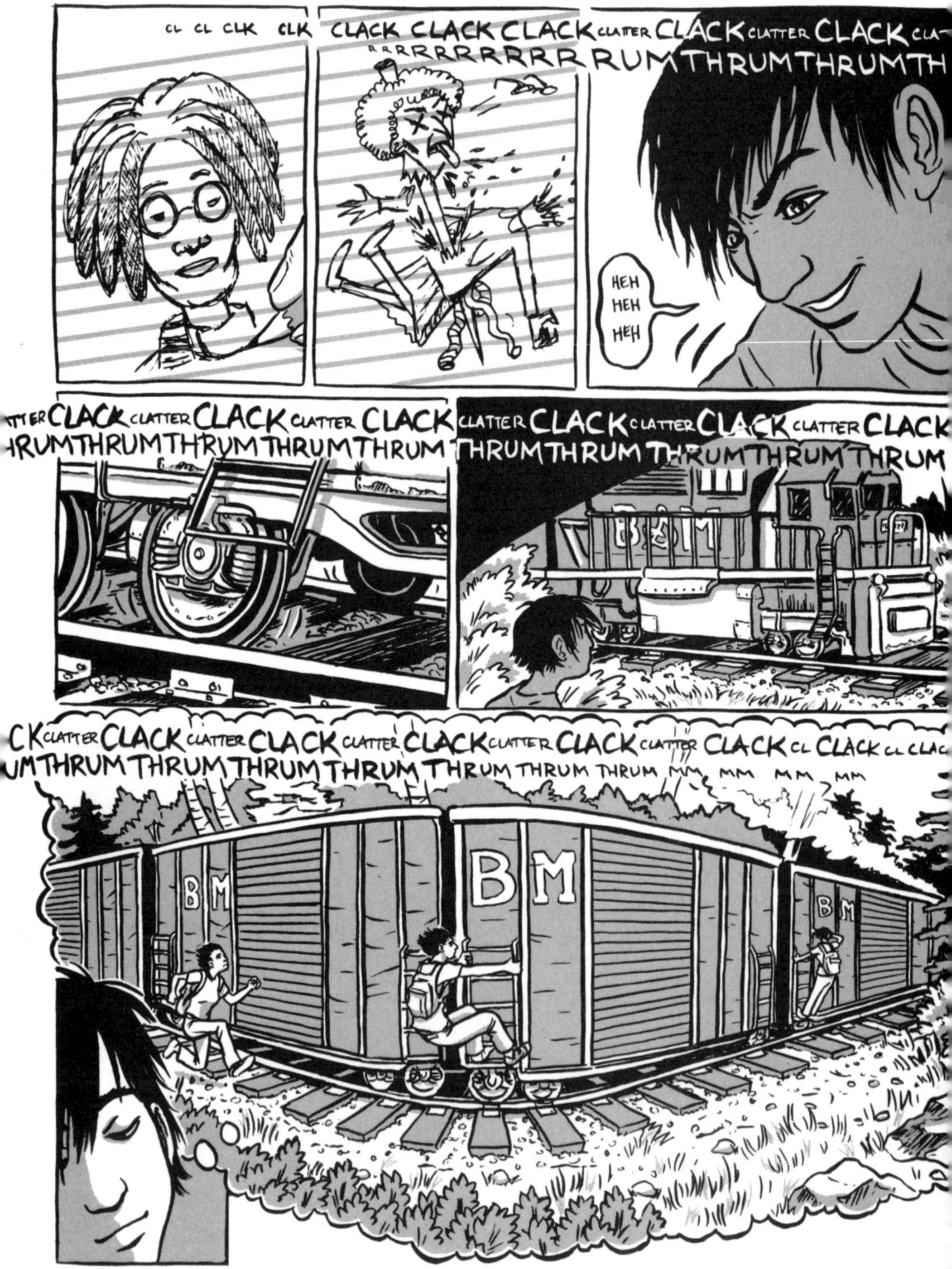
CL CL CLK CLK
CLACK CLACK CLACK CLATTER CLACK CLATTER CLACK
RRRRRRRRRRRRRRUM THRUM THRUM
HEH HEH HEH
CLACK CLATTER CLACK CLATTER CLACK
THRUM THRUM THRUM THRUM
CLATTER CLACK CLATTER CLACK CLATTER CLACK
THRUM THRUM THRUM THRUM THRUM
CLATTER CLACK CLATTER CLACK CLATTER CLACK CLATTER CLACK CLATTER CLACK CLATTER CLACK CL CLACK CL
THRUM THRUM THRUM THRUM THRUM THRUM THRUM MM MM MM MM

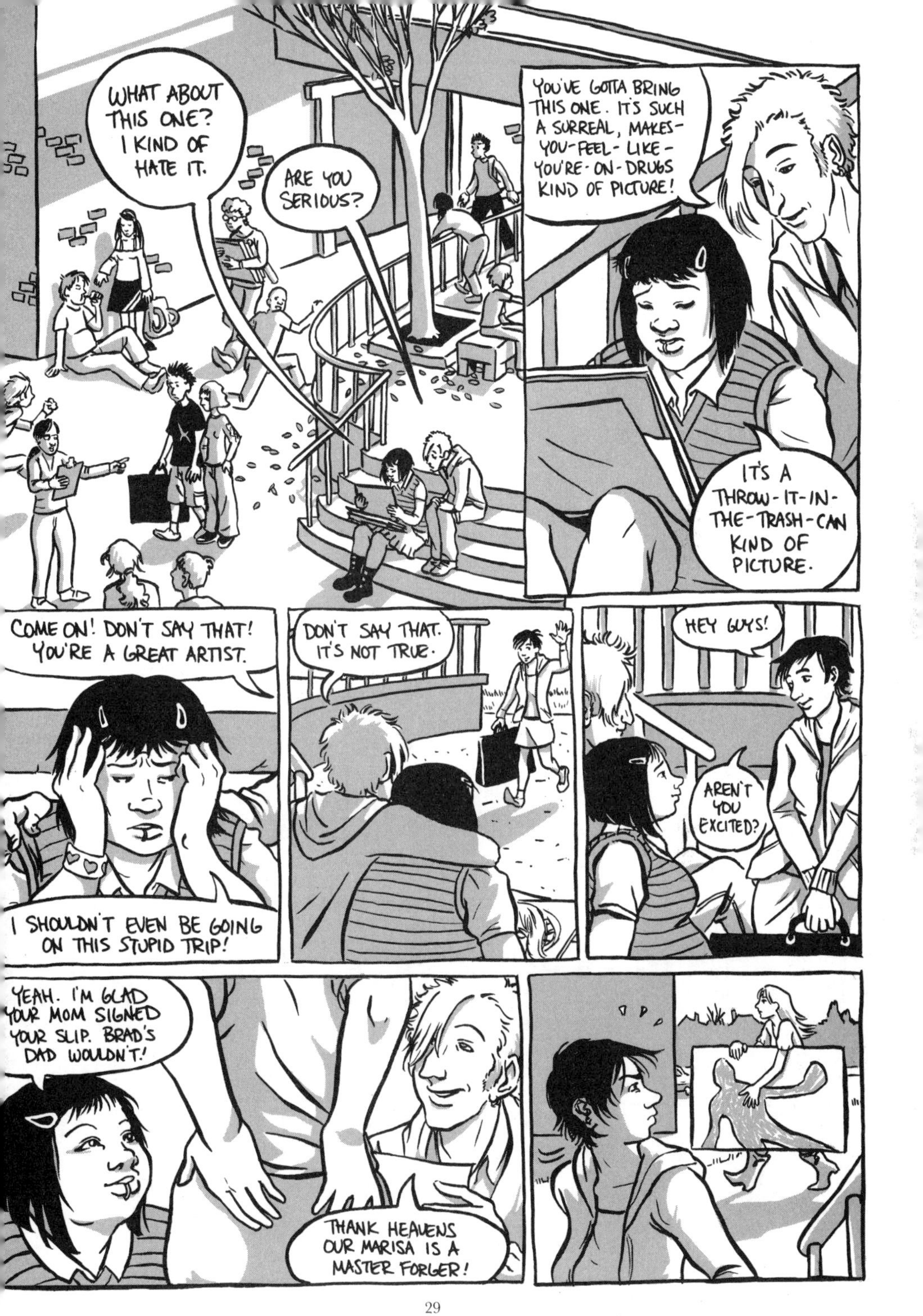
WHAT ABOUT THIS ONE? I KIND OF HATE IT.
ARE YOU SERIOUS?
YOU'VE GOTTA BRING THIS ONE. IT'S SUCH A SURREAL, MAKES-YOU-FEEL-LIKE-YOU'RE-ON-DRUGS KIND OF PICTURE!
IT'S A THROW-IT-IN-THE-TRASH-CAN KIND OF PICTURE.
COME ON! DON'T SAY THAT! YOU'RE A GREAT ARTIST.
I SHOULDN'T EVEN BE GOING ON THIS STUPID TRIP!
DON'T SAY THAT. IT'S NOT TRUE.
HEY GUYS!
AREN'T YOU EXCITED?
YEAH. I'M GLAD YOUR MOM SIGNED YOUR SLIP. BRAD'S DAD WOULDN'T!
THANK HEAVENS OUR MARISA IS A MASTER FORGER!

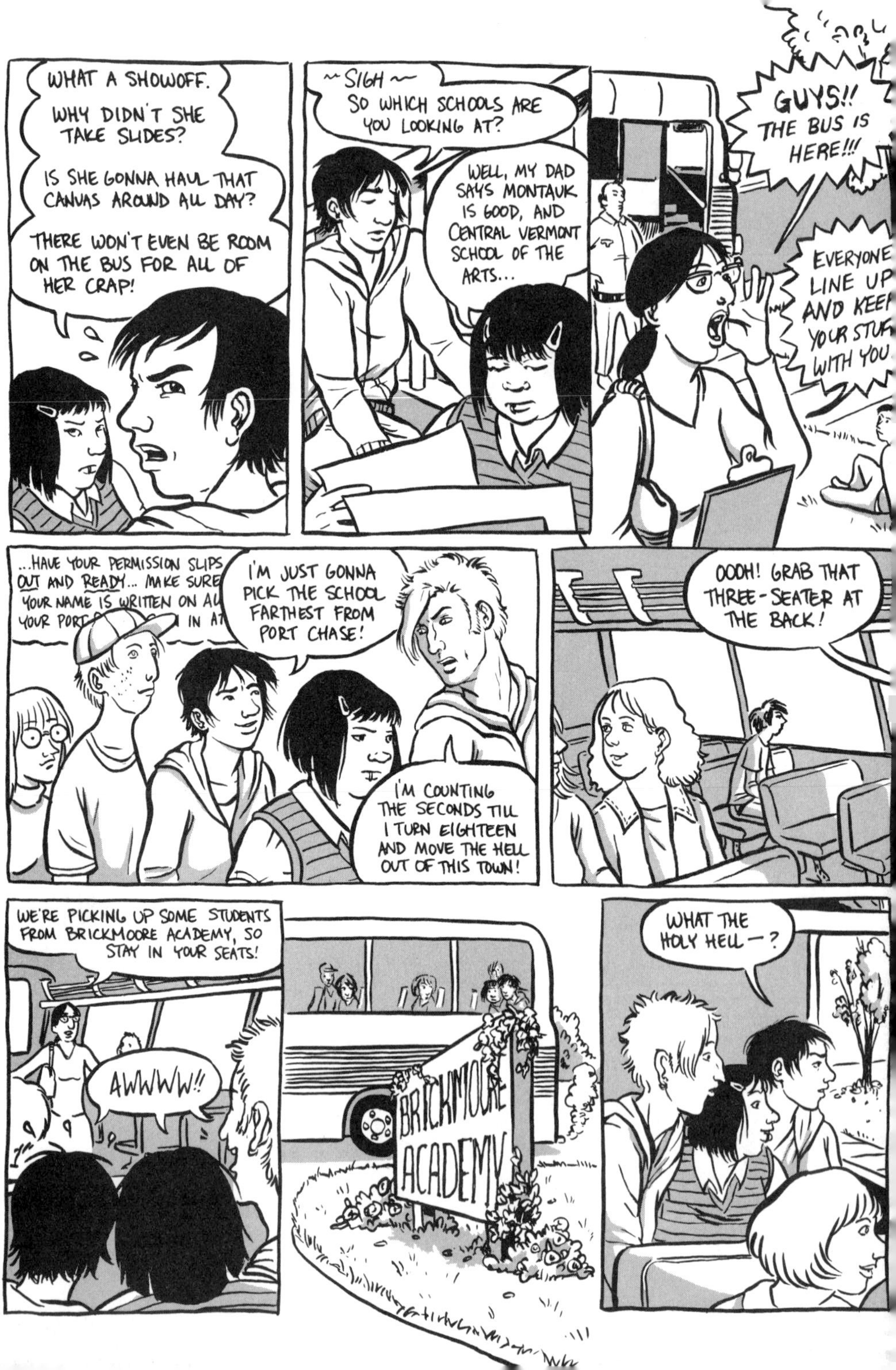
WHAT A SHOWOFF.
WHY DIDN'T SHE TAKE SLIDES?
IS SHE GONNA HAUL THAT CANVAS AROUND ALL DAY?
THERE WON'T EVEN BE ROOM ON THE BUS FOR ALL OF HER CRAP!
~SIGH~
SO WHICH SCHOOLS ARE YOU LOOKING AT?
WELL, MY DAD SAYS MONTAUK IS GOOD, AND CENTRAL VERMONT SCHOOL OF THE ARTS...
GUYS!! THE BUS IS HERE!!!
EVERYONE LINE UP AND KEEP YOUR STUF WITH YOU
...HAVE YOUR PERMISSION SLIPS OUT AND READY... MAKE SURE YOUR NAME IS WRITTEN ON AL
YOUR PORT
IN AT
I'M JUST GONNA PICK THE SCHOOL FARTHEST FROM PORT CHASE!
I'M COUNTING THE SECONDS TILL I TURN EIGHTEEN AND MOVE THE HELL OUT OF THIS TOWN!
OOOH! GRAB THAT THREE-SEATER AT THE BACK!
WE'RE PICKING UP SOME STUDENTS FROM BRICKMOORE ACADEMY, SO STAY IN YOUR SEATS!
AWWWW!!
BRICKMOORE ACADEMY
WHAT THE HOLY HELL—?

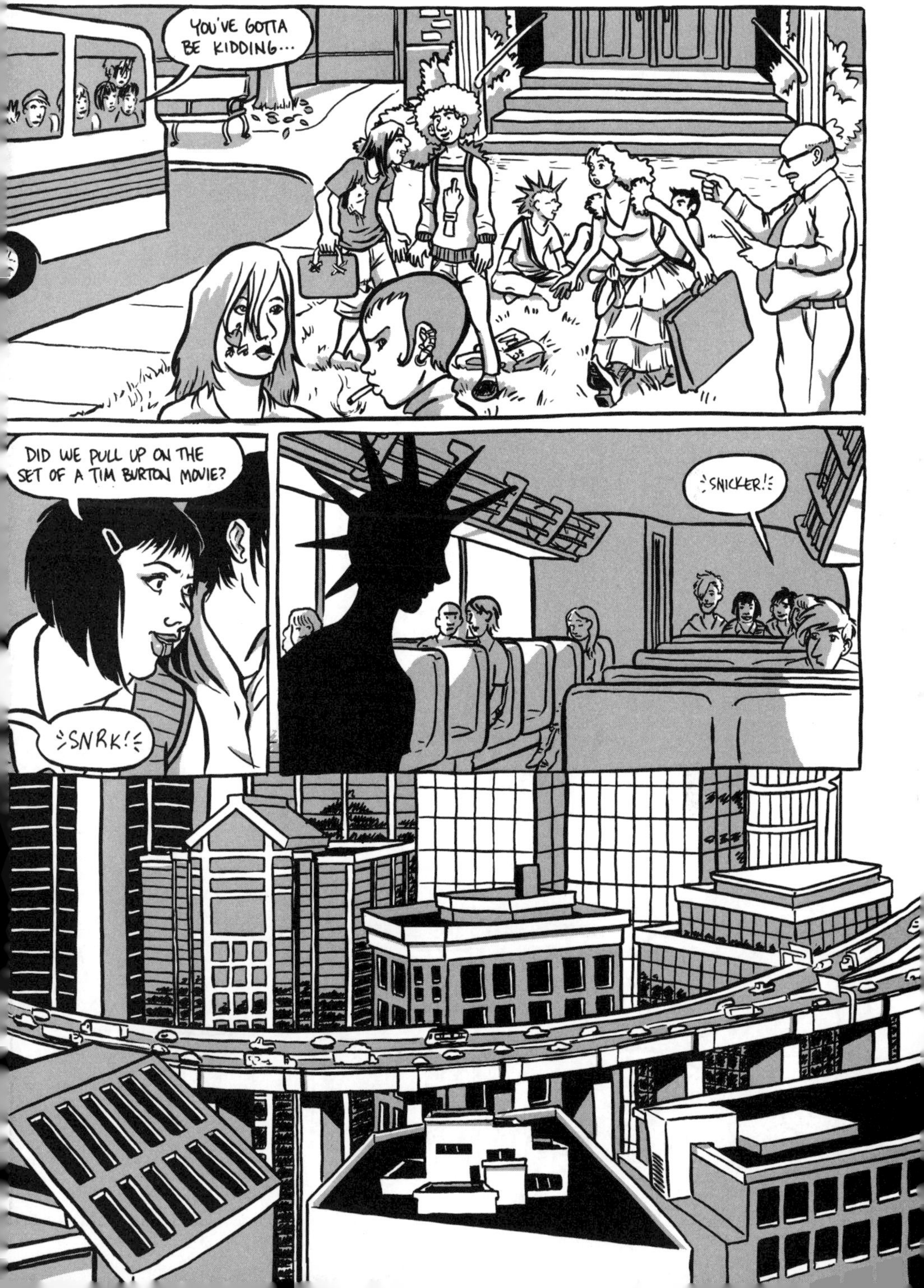
YOU'VE GOTTA BE KIDDING...
DID WE PULL UP ON THE SET OF A TIM BURTON MOVIE?
SNRK!
SNICKER!

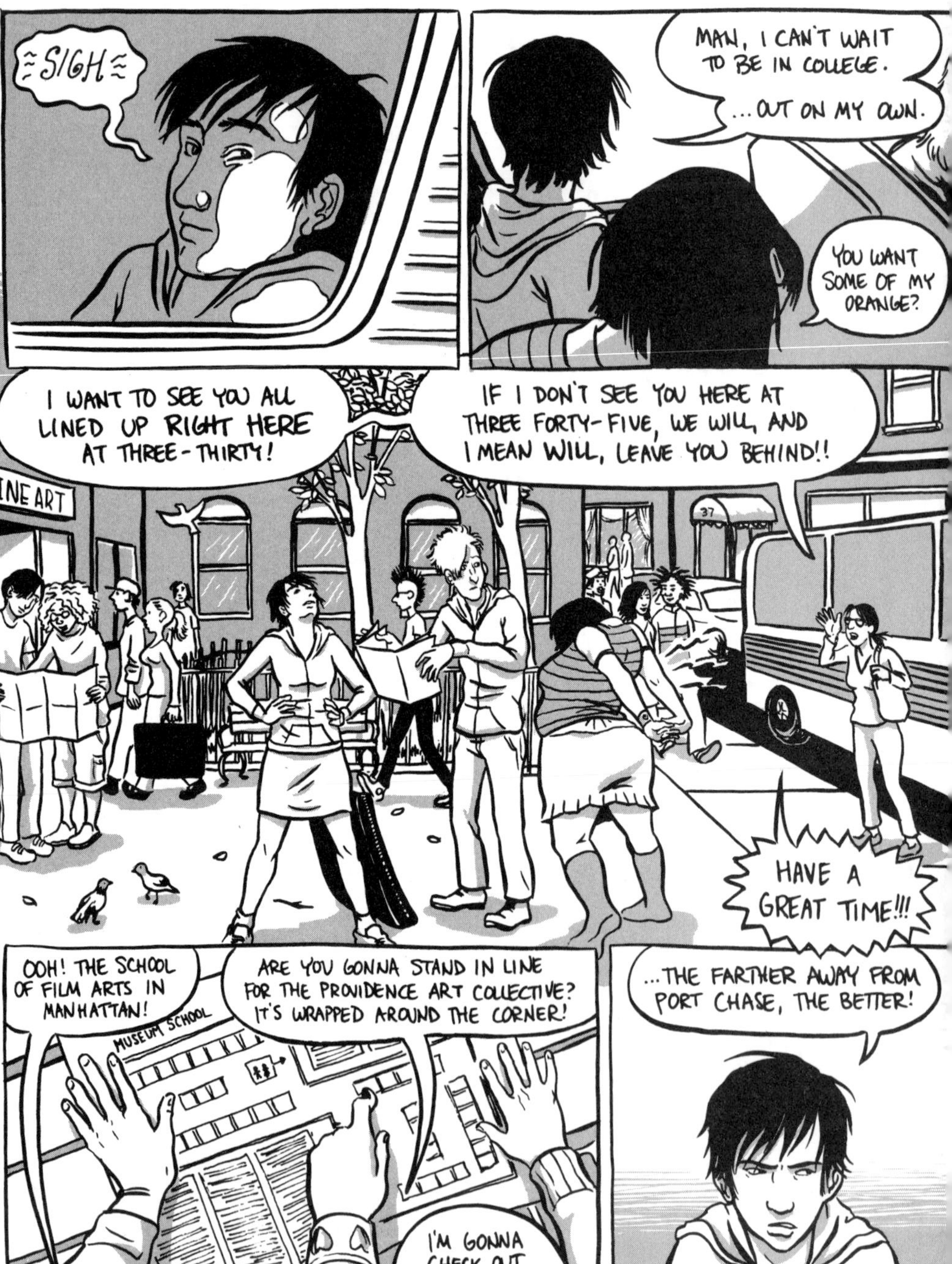
SIGH
MAN, I CAN'T WAIT TO BE IN COLLEGE.
... OUT ON MY OWN.
YOU WANT SOME OF MY ORANGE?
I WANT TO SEE YOU ALL LINED UP RIGHT HERE AT THREE-THIRTY!
IF I DON'T SEE YOU HERE AT THREE FORTY-FIVE, WE WILL, AND I MEAN WILL, LEAVE YOU BEHIND!!
...OF FINE ART
37
HAVE A GREAT TIME!!!
OOH! THE SCHOOL OF FILM ARTS IN MANHATTAN!
ARE YOU GONNA STAND IN LINE FOR THE PROVIDENCE ART COLLECTIVE? IT'S WRAPPED AROUND THE CORNER!
MUSEUM SCHOOL
I'M GONNA CHECK OUT SO-CAL DESIGN'S TABLE FIRST.
...THE FARTHER AWAY FROM PORT CHASE, THE BETTER!

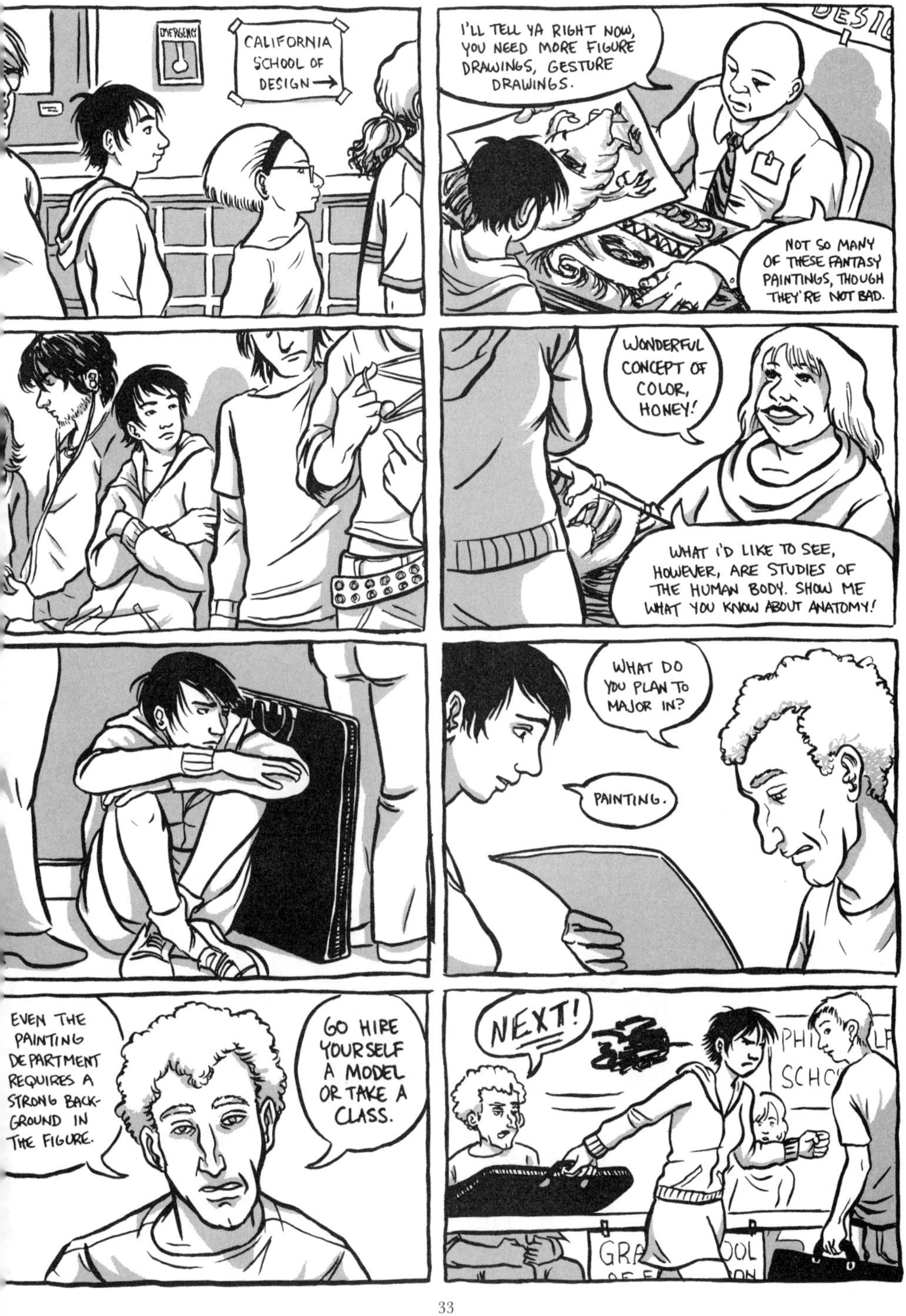
EMERGENCY
CALIFORNIA SCHOOL OF DESIGN →
I'LL TELL YA RIGHT NOW, YOU NEED MORE FIGURE DRAWINGS, GESTURE DRAWINGS.
NOT SO MANY OF THESE FANTASY PAINTINGS, THOUGH THEY'RE NOT BAD.
WONDERFUL CONCEPT OF COLOR, HONEY!
WHAT I'D LIKE TO SEE, HOWEVER, ARE STUDIES OF THE HUMAN BODY. SHOW ME WHAT YOU KNOW ABOUT ANATOMY!
WHAT DO YOU PLAN TO MAJOR IN?
PAINTING.
EVEN THE PAINTING DEPARTMENT REQUIRES A STRONG BACKGROUND IN THE FIGURE.
GO HIRE YOURSELF A MODEL OR TAKE A CLASS.
NEXT!

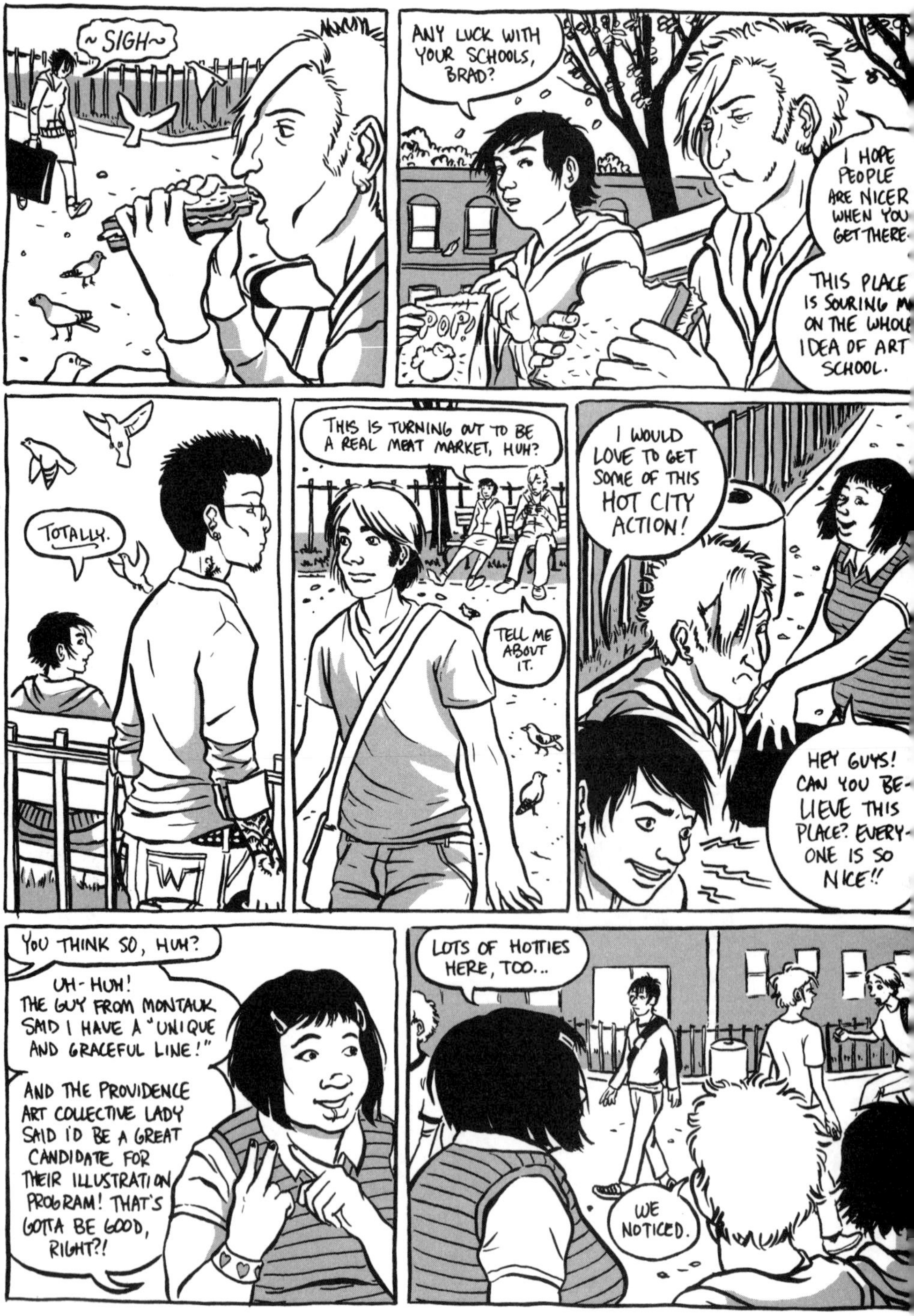
~SIGH~
ANY LUCK WITH YOUR SCHOOLS, BRAD?
I HOPE PEOPLE ARE NICER WHEN YOU GET THERE.
THIS PLACE IS SOURING ME ON THE WHOLE IDEA OF ART SCHOOL.
TOTALLY.
THIS IS TURNING OUT TO BE A REAL MEAT MARKET, HUH?
TELL ME ABOUT IT.
I WOULD LOVE TO GET SOME OF THIS HOT CITY ACTION!
HEY GUYS! CAN YOU BE-LIEVE THIS PLACE? EVERY-ONE IS SO NICE!!
YOU THINK SO, HUH?
UH-HUH! THE GUY FROM MONTAUK SAID I HAVE A "UNIQUE AND GRACEFUL LINE!"
AND THE PROVIDENCE ART COLLECTIVE LADY SAID I'D BE A GREAT CANDIDATE FOR THEIR ILLUSTRATION PROGRAM! THAT'S GOTTA BE GOOD, RIGHT?!
LOTS OF HOTTIES HERE, TOO...
WE NOTICED.

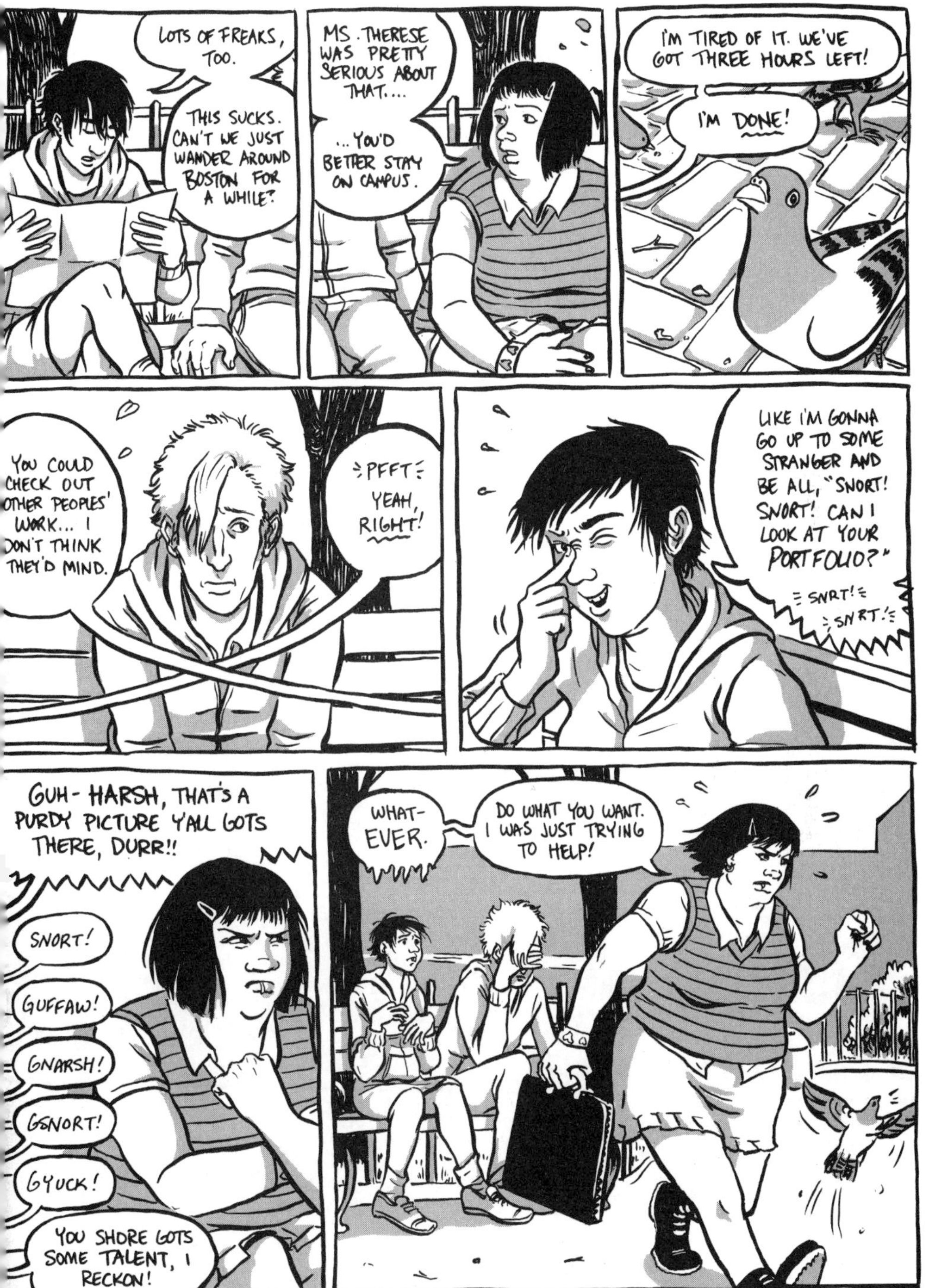
LOTS OF FREAKS, TOO.
THIS SUCKS. CAN'T WE JUST WANDER AROUND BOSTON FOR A WHILE?
MS. THERESE WAS PRETTY SERIOUS ABOUT THAT....
...YOU'D BETTER STAY ON CAMPUS.
I'M TIRED OF IT. WE'VE GOT THREE HOURS LEFT!
I'M DONE!
YOU COULD CHECK OUT OTHER PEOPLES' WORK... I DON'T THINK THEY'D MIND.
PFFT YEAH, RIGHT!
LIKE I'M GONNA GO UP TO SOME STRANGER AND BE ALL, "SNORT! SNORT! CAN I LOOK AT YOUR PORTFOLIO?"
SNRT!
SNRT!
GUH-HARSH, THAT'S A PURDY PICTURE Y'ALL GOTS THERE, DURR!!
SNORT!
GUFFAW!
GNARSH!
GSNORT!
GYUCK!
YOU SHORE GOTS SOME TALENT, I RECKON!
WHAT-EVER.
DO WHAT YOU WANT. I WAS JUST TRYING TO HELP!

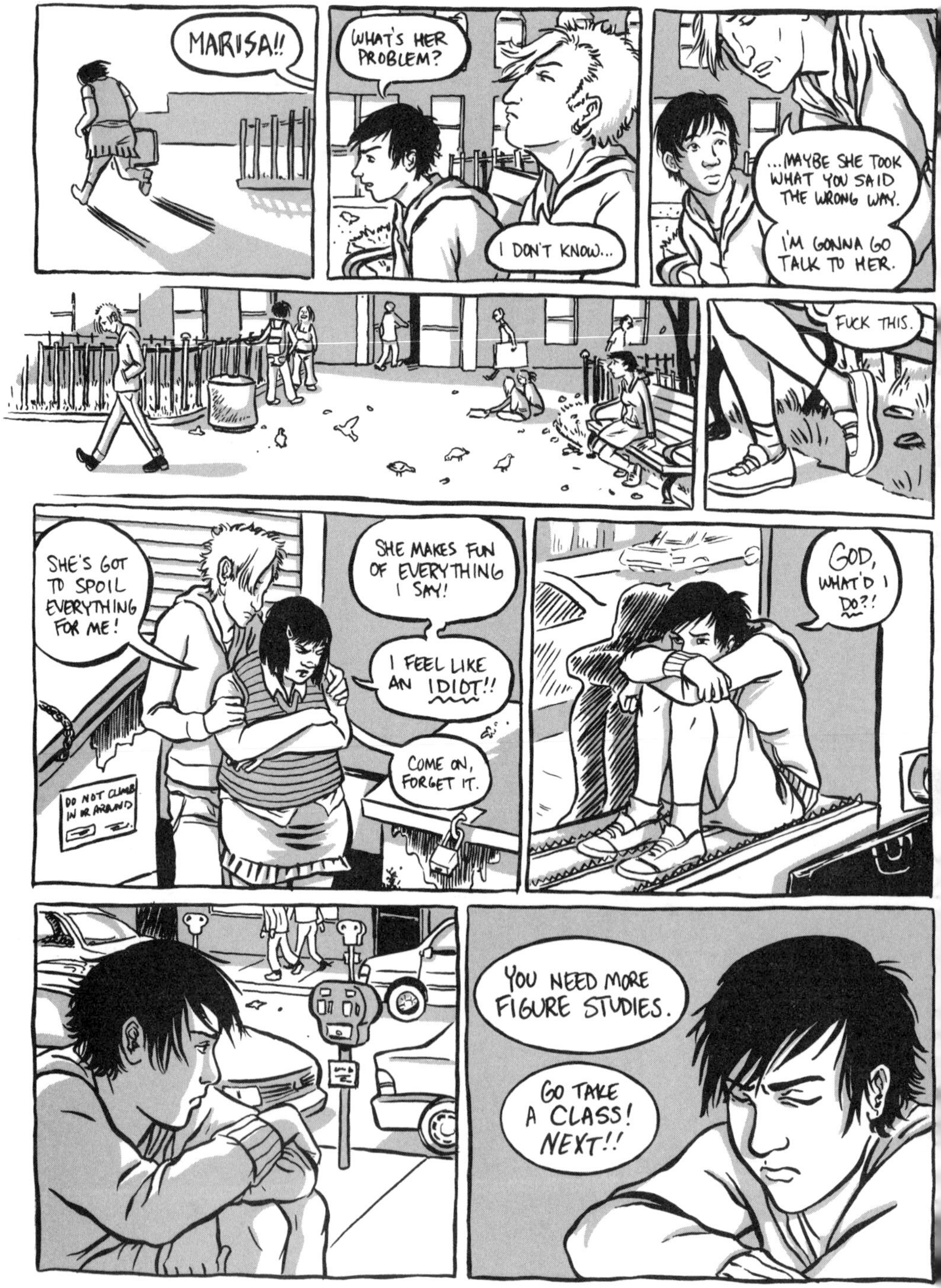
MARISA!!
WHAT'S HER PROBLEM?
I DON'T KNOW...
...MAYBE SHE TOOK WHAT YOU SAID THE WRONG WAY.
I'M GONNA GO TALK TO HER.
FUCK THIS.
SHE'S GOT TO SPOIL EVERYTHING FOR ME!
SHE MAKES FUN OF EVERYTHING I SAY!
I FEEL LIKE AN IDIOT!!
COME ON, FORGET IT.
DO NOT CLIMB IN OR AROUND
GOD, WHAT'D I DO?!
YOU NEED MORE FIGURE STUDIES.
GO TAKE A CLASS! NEXT!!

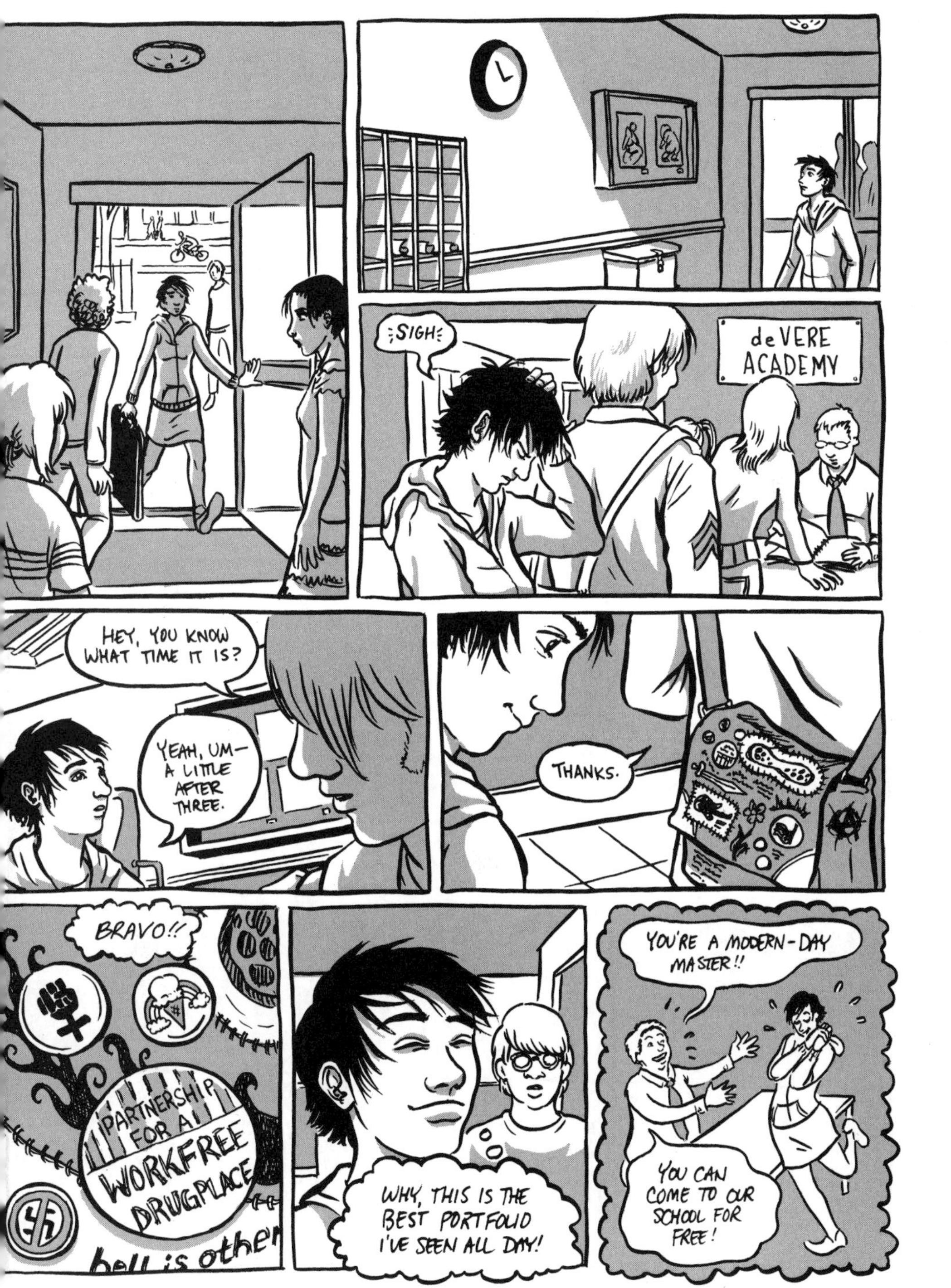
SIGH
deVERE ACADEMY
HEY, YOU KNOW WHAT TIME IT IS?
YEAH, UM— A LITTLE AFTER THREE.
THANKS.
BRAVO!!
PARTNERSHIP FOR A WORKFREE DRUGPLACE
hell is othe
WHY, THIS IS THE BEST PORTFOLIO I'VE SEEN ALL DAY!
YOU'RE A MODERN-DAY MASTER!!
YOU CAN COME TO OUR SCHOOL FOR FREE!

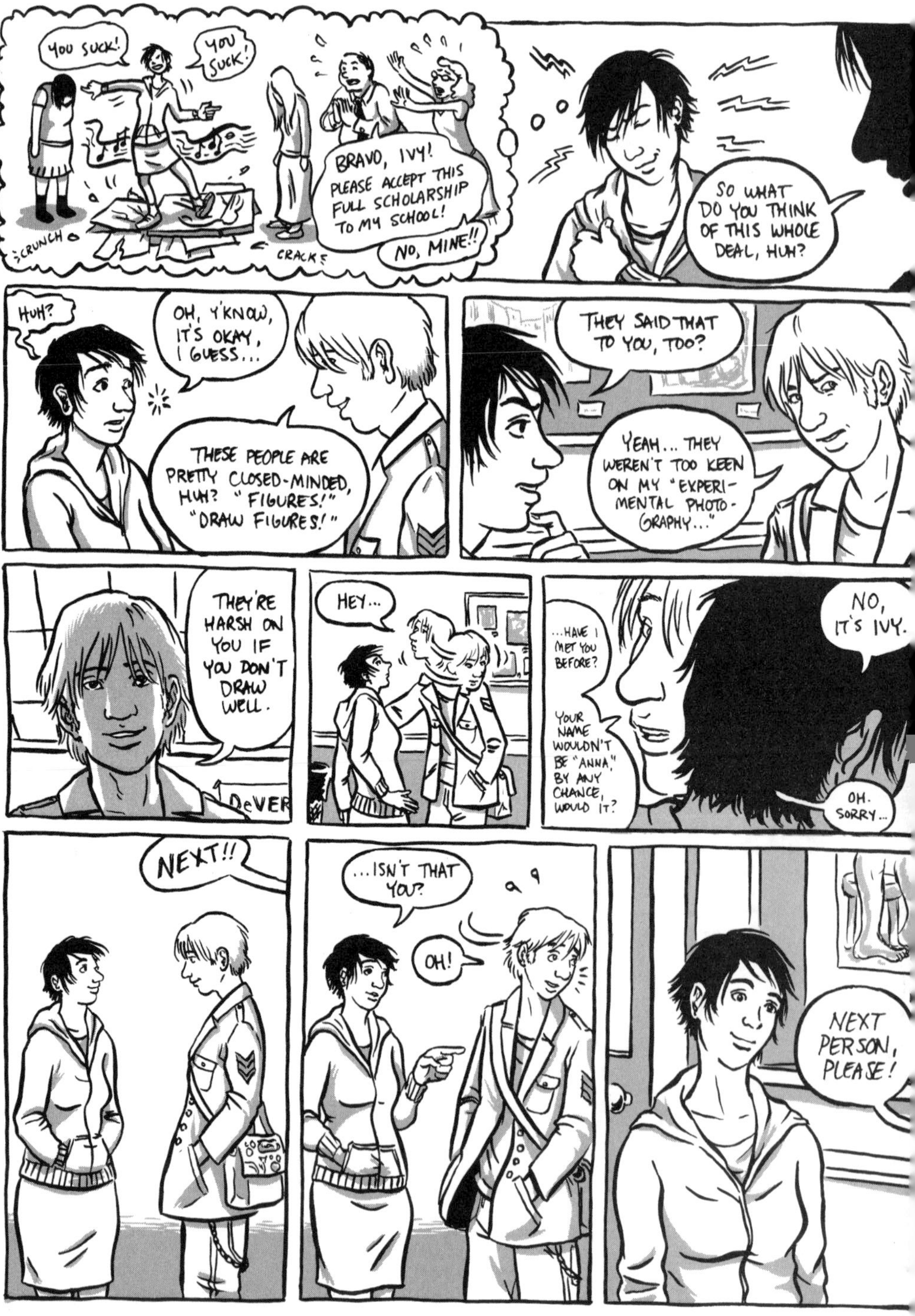
YOU SUCK!
YOU SUCK!
BRAVO, IVY! PLEASE ACCEPT THIS FULL SCHOLARSHIP TO MY SCHOOL!
NO, MINE!!
CRUNCH
CRACK
SO WHAT DO YOU THINK OF THIS WHOLE DEAL, HUH?
HUH?
OH, Y'KNOW, IT'S OKAY, I GUESS...
THESE PEOPLE ARE PRETTY CLOSED-MINDED, HUH? "FIGURES!" "DRAW FIGURES!"
THEY SAID THAT TO YOU, TOO?
YEAH... THEY WEREN'T TOO KEEN ON MY "EXPERIMENTAL PHOTOGRAPHY..."
THEY'RE HARSH ON YOU IF YOU DON'T DRAW WELL.
DeVER
HEY...
...HAVE I MET YOU BEFORE?
YOUR NAME WOULDN'T BE "ANNA," BY ANY CHANCE, WOULD IT?
NO, IT'S IVY.
OH. SORRY...
NEXT!!
...ISN'T THAT YOU?
OH!
NEXT PERSON, PLEASE!

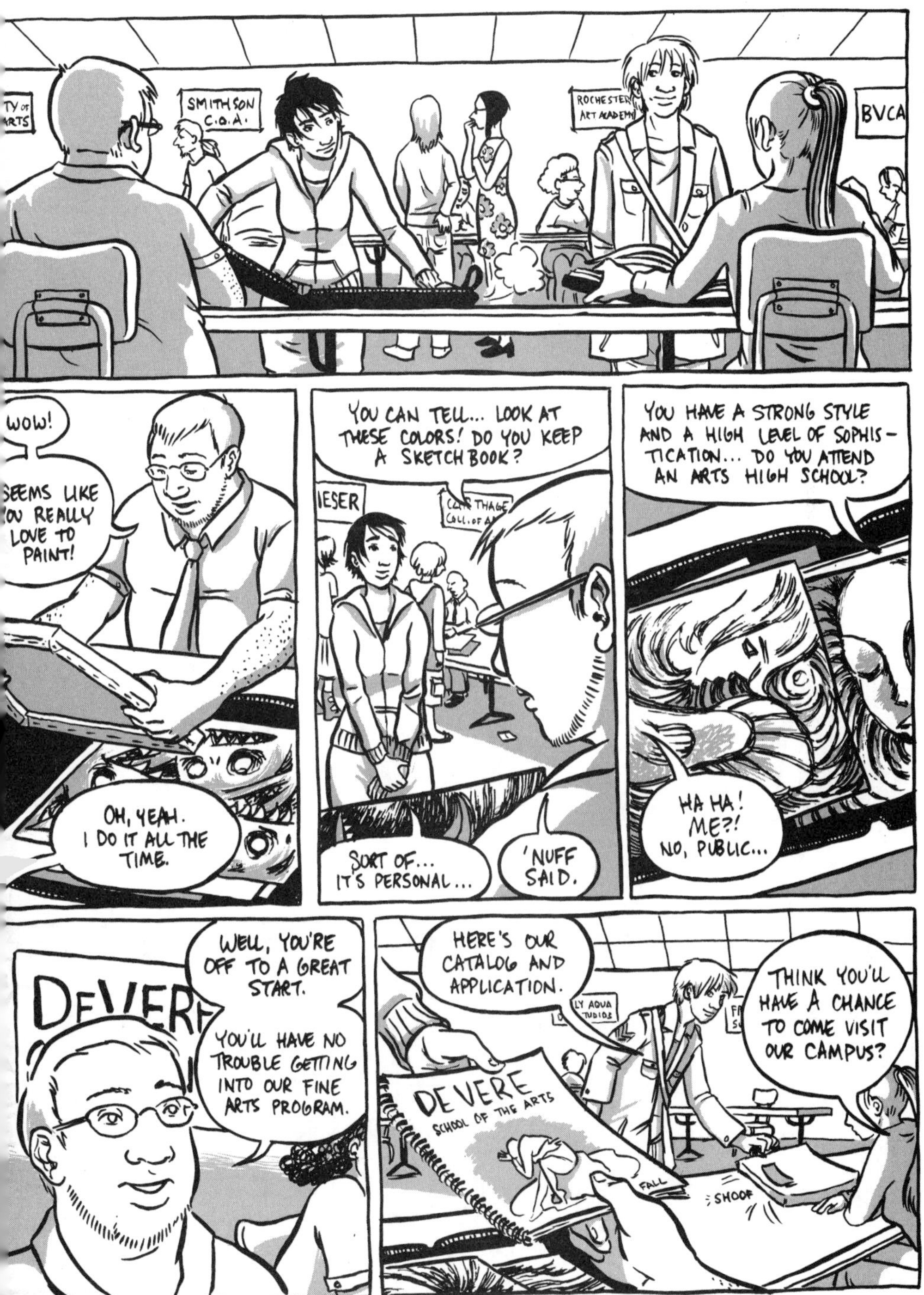
SMITHSON C.O.A.
ROCHESTER ART ACADEMY
BVCA
WOW!
SEEMS LIKE YOU REALLY LOVE TO PAINT!
OH, YEAH. I DO IT ALL THE TIME.
YOU CAN TELL... LOOK AT THESE COLORS! DO YOU KEEP A SKETCHBOOK?
SORT OF... IT'S PERSONAL...
'NUFF SAID.
YOU HAVE A STRONG STYLE AND A HIGH LEVEL OF SOPHISTICATION... DO YOU ATTEND AN ARTS HIGH SCHOOL?
HA HA! ME?! NO, PUBLIC...
WELL, YOU'RE OFF TO A GREAT START.
YOU'LL HAVE NO TROUBLE GETTING INTO OUR FINE ARTS PROGRAM.
HERE'S OUR CATALOG AND APPLICATION.
THINK YOU'LL HAVE A CHANCE TO COME VISIT OUR CAMPUS?
DE VERE SCHOOL OF THE ARTS
FALL
SHOOF

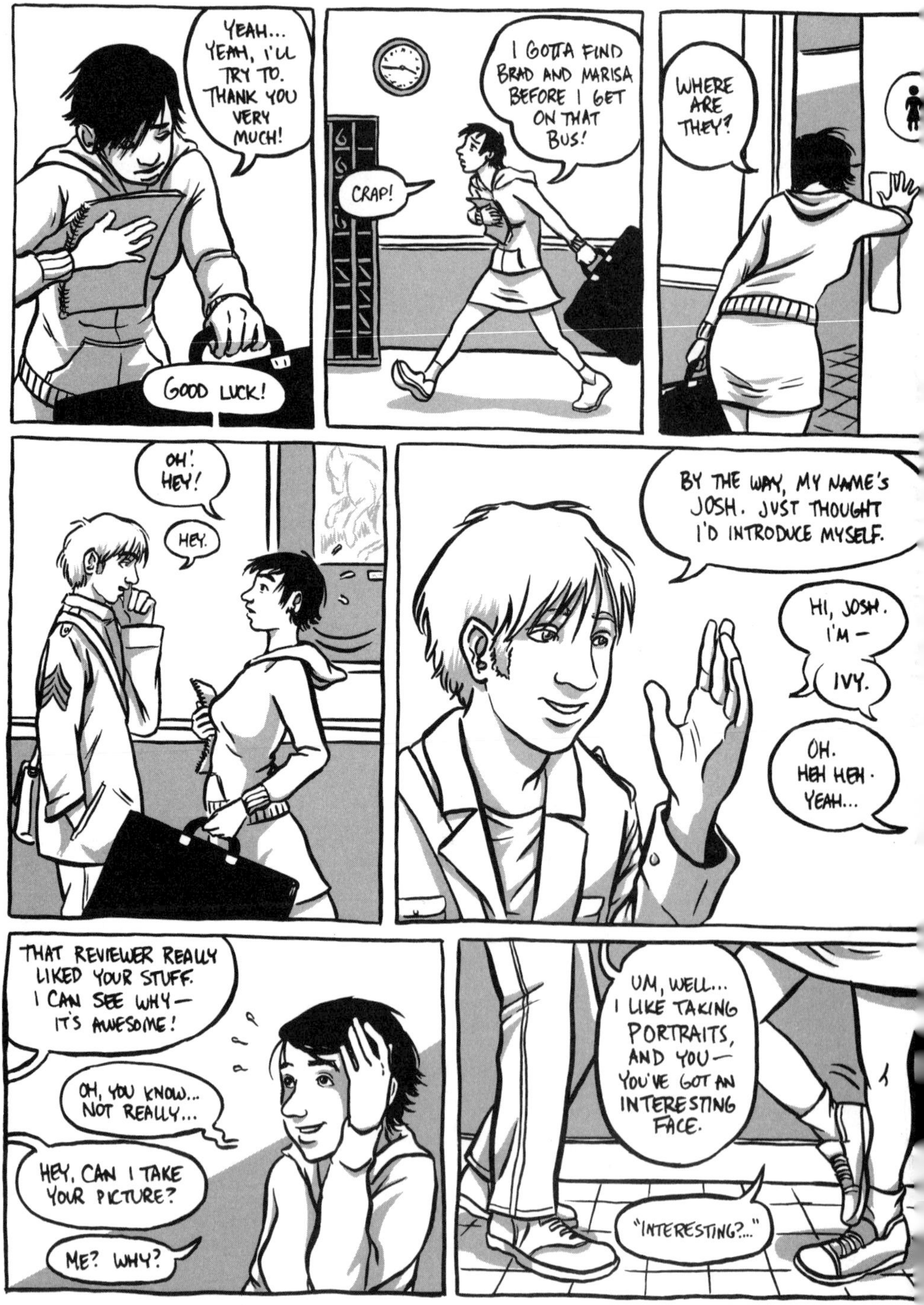
YEAH... YEAH, I'LL TRY TO. THANK YOU VERY MUCH!
GOOD LUCK!
I GOTTA FIND BRAD AND MARISA BEFORE I GET ON THAT BUS!
CRAP!
WHERE ARE THEY?
OH! HEY!
HEY.
BY THE WAY, MY NAME'S JOSH. JUST THOUGHT I'D INTRODUCE MYSELF.
HI, JOSH. I'M —
IVY.
OH. HEH HEH. YEAH...
THAT REVIEWER REALLY LIKED YOUR STUFF. I CAN SEE WHY— IT'S AWESOME!
OH, YOU KNOW... NOT REALLY...
HEY, CAN I TAKE YOUR PICTURE?
ME? WHY?
UM, WELL... I LIKE TAKING PORTRAITS, AND YOU— YOU'VE GOT AN INTERESTING FACE.
"INTERESTING?..."

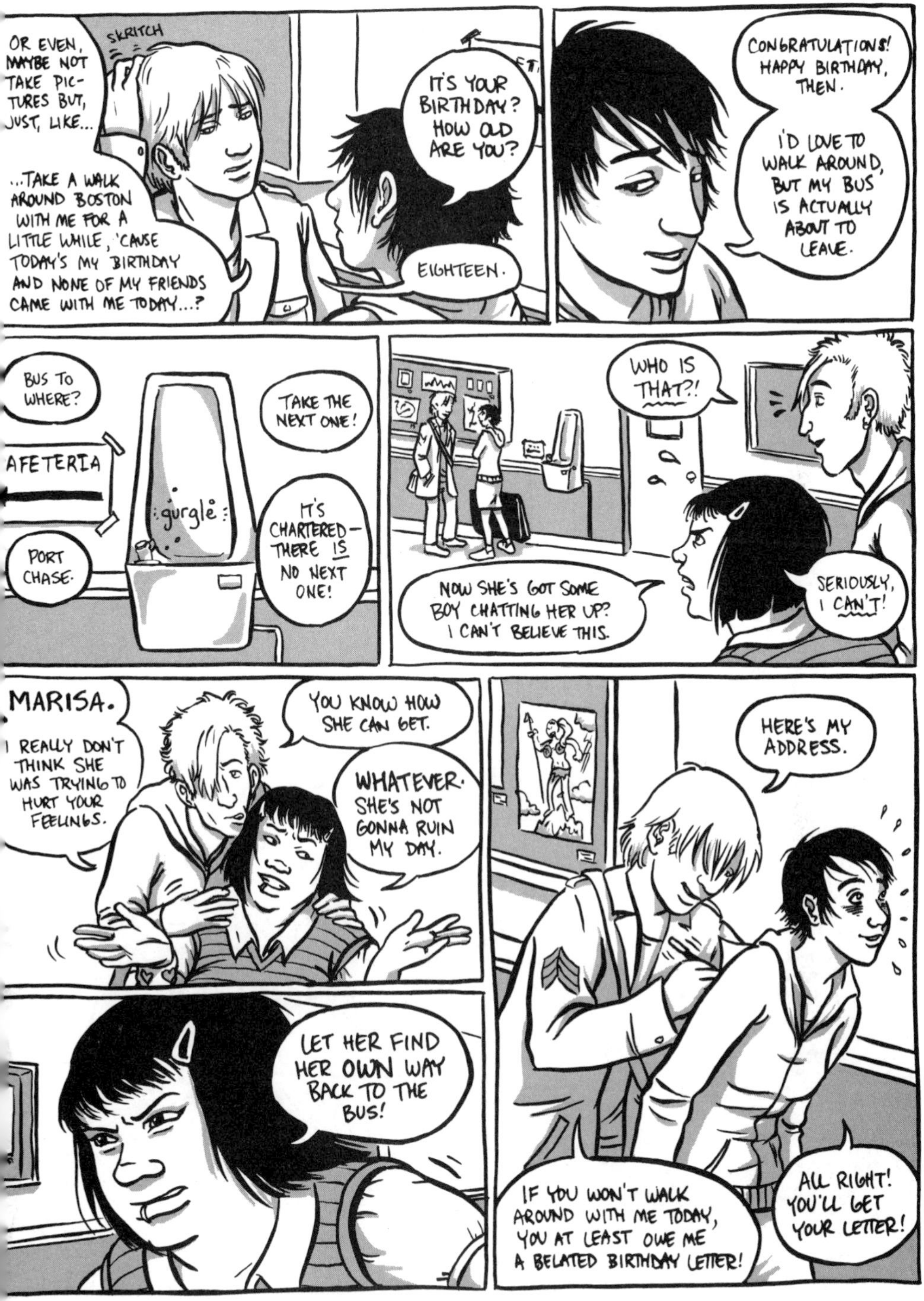
OR EVEN, MAYBE NOT TAKE PICTURES BUT, JUST, LIKE...
SKRITCH
...TAKE A WALK AROUND BOSTON WITH ME FOR A LITTLE WHILE, 'CAUSE TODAY'S MY BIRTHDAY AND NONE OF MY FRIENDS CAME WITH ME TODAY...?
IT'S YOUR BIRTHDAY? HOW OLD ARE YOU?
EIGHTEEN.
CONGRATULATIONS! HAPPY BIRTHDAY, THEN.
I'D LOVE TO WALK AROUND, BUT MY BUS IS ACTUALLY ABOUT TO LEAVE.
BUS TO WHERE?
AFETERIA
PORT CHASE.
gurgle
TAKE THE NEXT ONE!
IT'S CHARTERED— THERE IS NO NEXT ONE!
WHO IS THAT?!
NOW SHE'S GOT SOME BOY CHATTING HER UP? I CAN'T BELIEVE THIS.
SERIOUSLY, I CAN'T!
MARISA.
I REALLY DON'T THINK SHE WAS TRYING TO HURT YOUR FEELINGS.
YOU KNOW HOW SHE CAN GET.
WHATEVER. SHE'S NOT GONNA RUIN MY DAY.
LET HER FIND HER OWN WAY BACK TO THE BUS!
HERE'S MY ADDRESS.
IF YOU WON'T WALK AROUND WITH ME TODAY, YOU AT LEAST OWE ME A BELATED BIRTHDAY LETTER!
ALL RIGHT! YOU'LL GET YOUR LETTER!

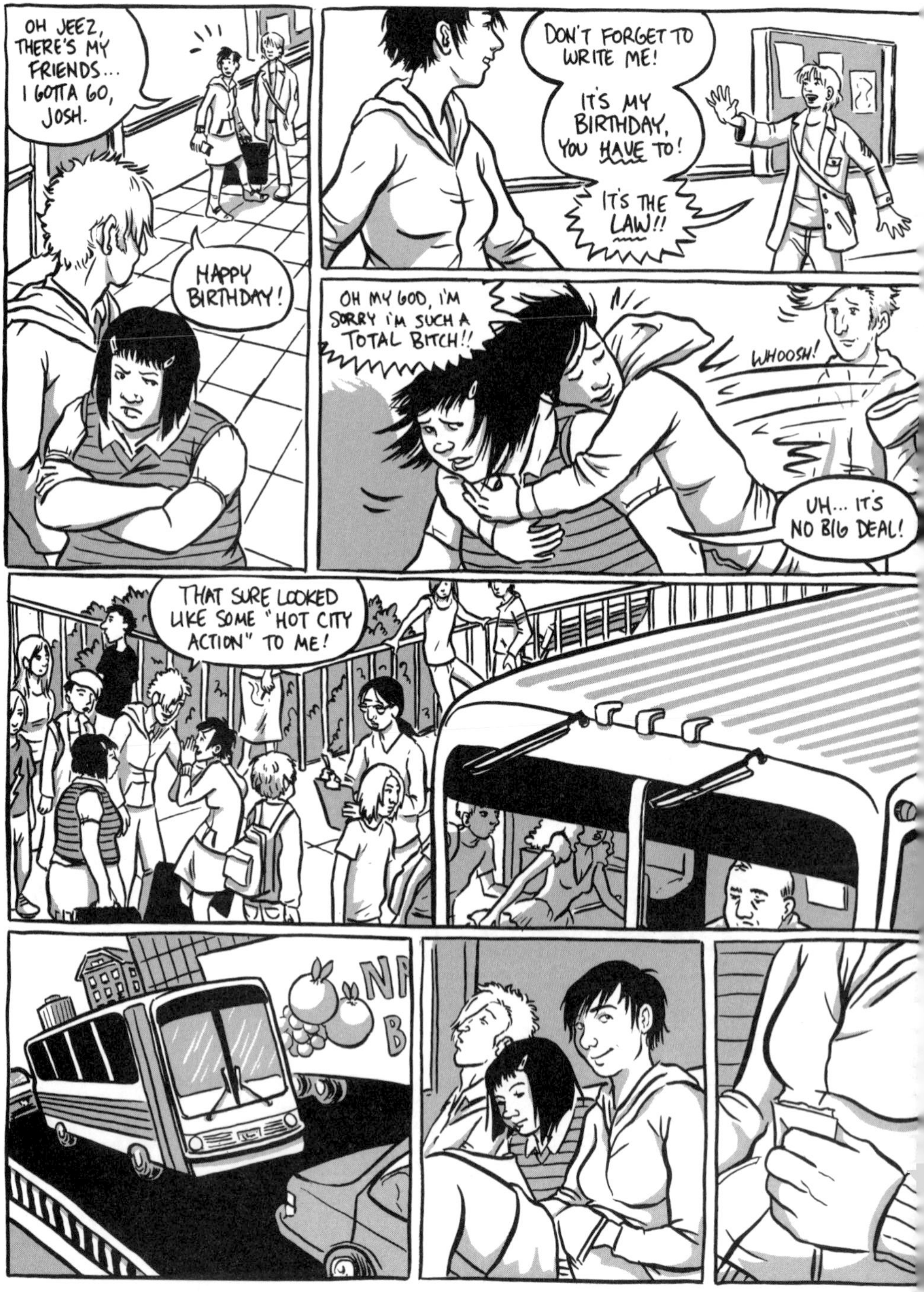
OH JEEZ, THERE'S MY FRIENDS... I GOTTA GO, JOSH.
HAPPY BIRTHDAY!
DON'T FORGET TO WRITE ME!
IT'S MY BIRTHDAY, YOU HAVE TO!
IT'S THE LAW!!
OH MY GOD, I'M SORRY I'M SUCH A TOTAL BITCH!!
WHOOSH!
UH... IT'S NO BIG DEAL!
THAT SURE LOOKED LIKE SOME "HOT CITY ACTION" TO ME!

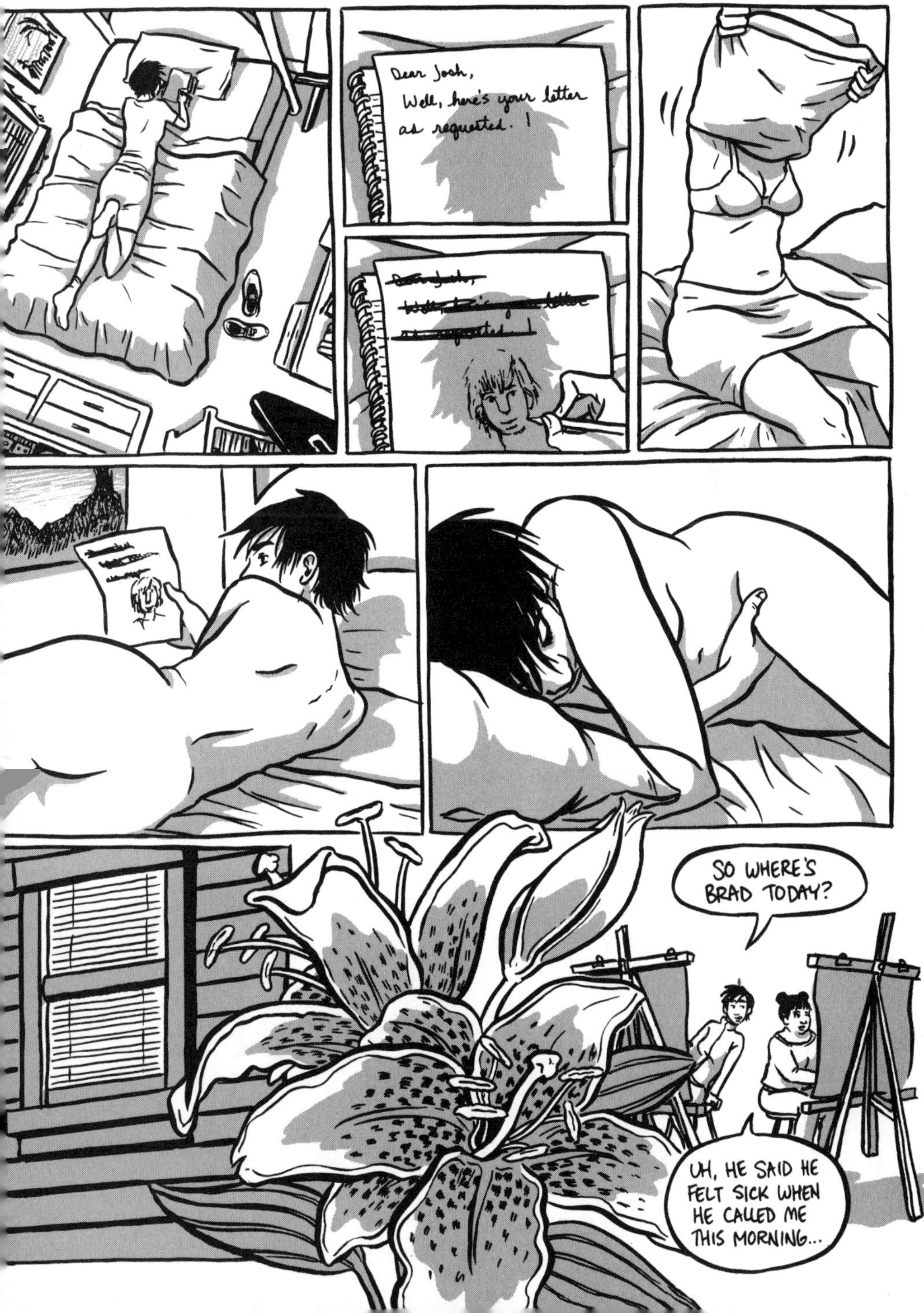
Dear Josh,
Well, here's your letter
as requested.
SO WHERE'S BRAD TODAY?
UH, HE SAID HE FELT SICK WHEN HE CALLED ME THIS MORNING...

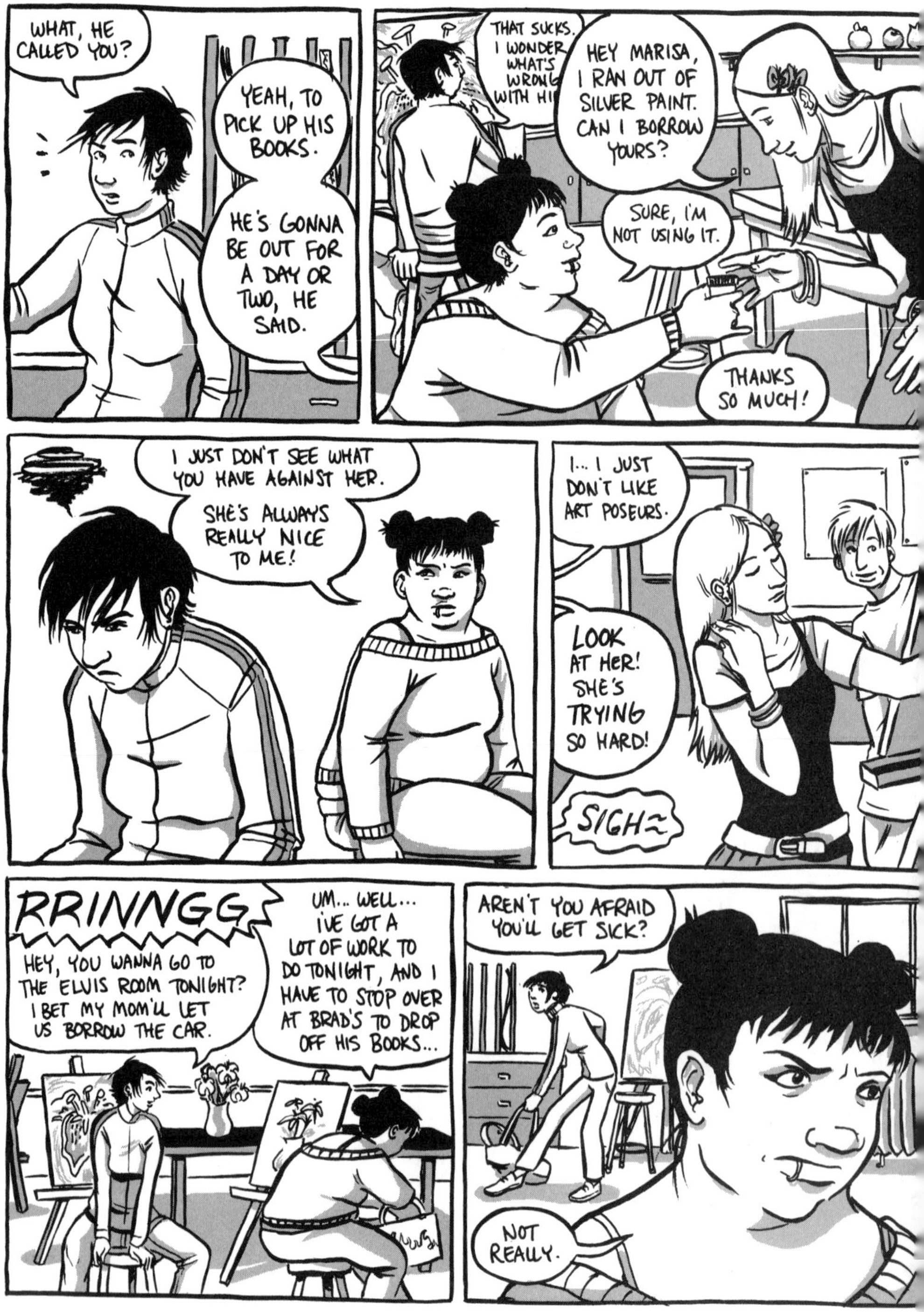
WHAT, HE CALLED YOU?
YEAH, TO PICK UP HIS BOOKS.
HE'S GONNA BE OUT FOR A DAY OR TWO, HE SAID.
THAT SUCKS. I WONDER WHAT'S WRONG WITH HI
HEY MARISA, I RAN OUT OF SILVER PAINT. CAN I BORROW YOURS?
SURE, I'M NOT USING IT.
THANKS SO MUCH!
I JUST DON'T SEE WHAT YOU HAVE AGAINST HER.
SHE'S ALWAYS REALLY NICE TO ME!
I... I JUST DON'T LIKE ART POSEURS.
LOOK AT HER! SHE'S TRYING SO HARD!
SIGH
RRINNGG
HEY, YOU WANNA GO TO THE ELVIS ROOM TONIGHT? I BET MY MOM'LL LET US BORROW THE CAR.
UM... WELL... I'VE GOT A LOT OF WORK TO DO TONIGHT, AND I HAVE TO STOP OVER AT BRAD'S TO DROP OFF HIS BOOKS...
AREN'T YOU AFRAID YOU'LL GET SICK?
NOT REALLY.

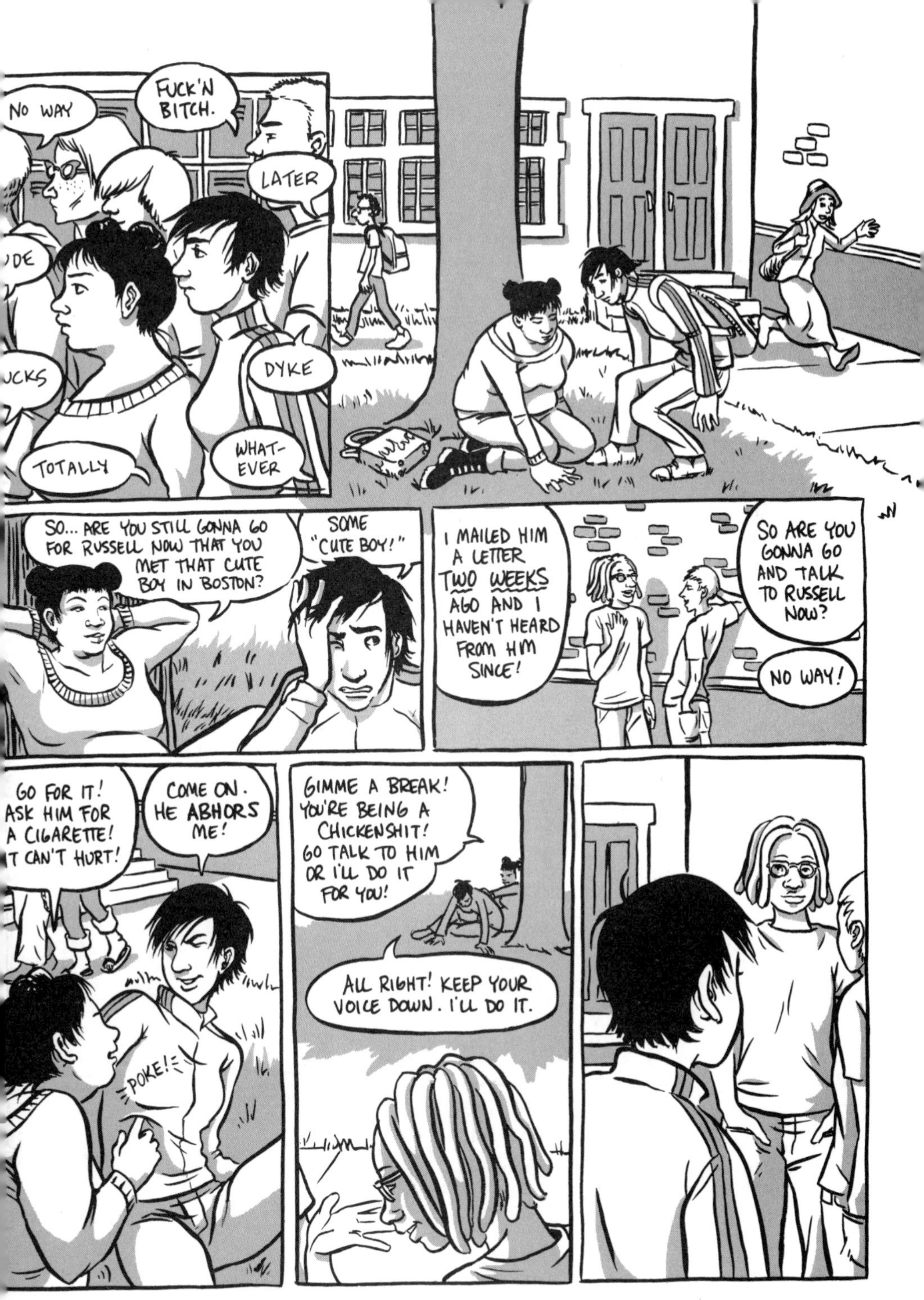

NO WAY
FUCK'N BITCH.
LATER
DE
UCKS
DYKE
TOTALLY
WHAT-EVER
SO... ARE YOU STILL GONNA GO FOR RUSSELL NOW THAT YOU MET THAT CUTE BOY IN BOSTON?
SOME "CUTE BOY!"
I MAILED HIM A LETTER TWO WEEKS AGO AND I HAVEN'T HEARD FROM HIM SINCE!
SO ARE YOU GONNA GO AND TALK TO RUSSELL NOW?
NO WAY!
GO FOR IT! ASK HIM FOR A CIGARETTE! T CAN'T HURT!
COME ON. HE ABHORS ME!
POKE!
GIMME A BREAK! YOU'RE BEING A CHICKENSHIT! GO TALK TO HIM OR I'LL DO IT FOR YOU!
ALL RIGHT! KEEP YOUR VOICE DOWN. I'LL DO IT.

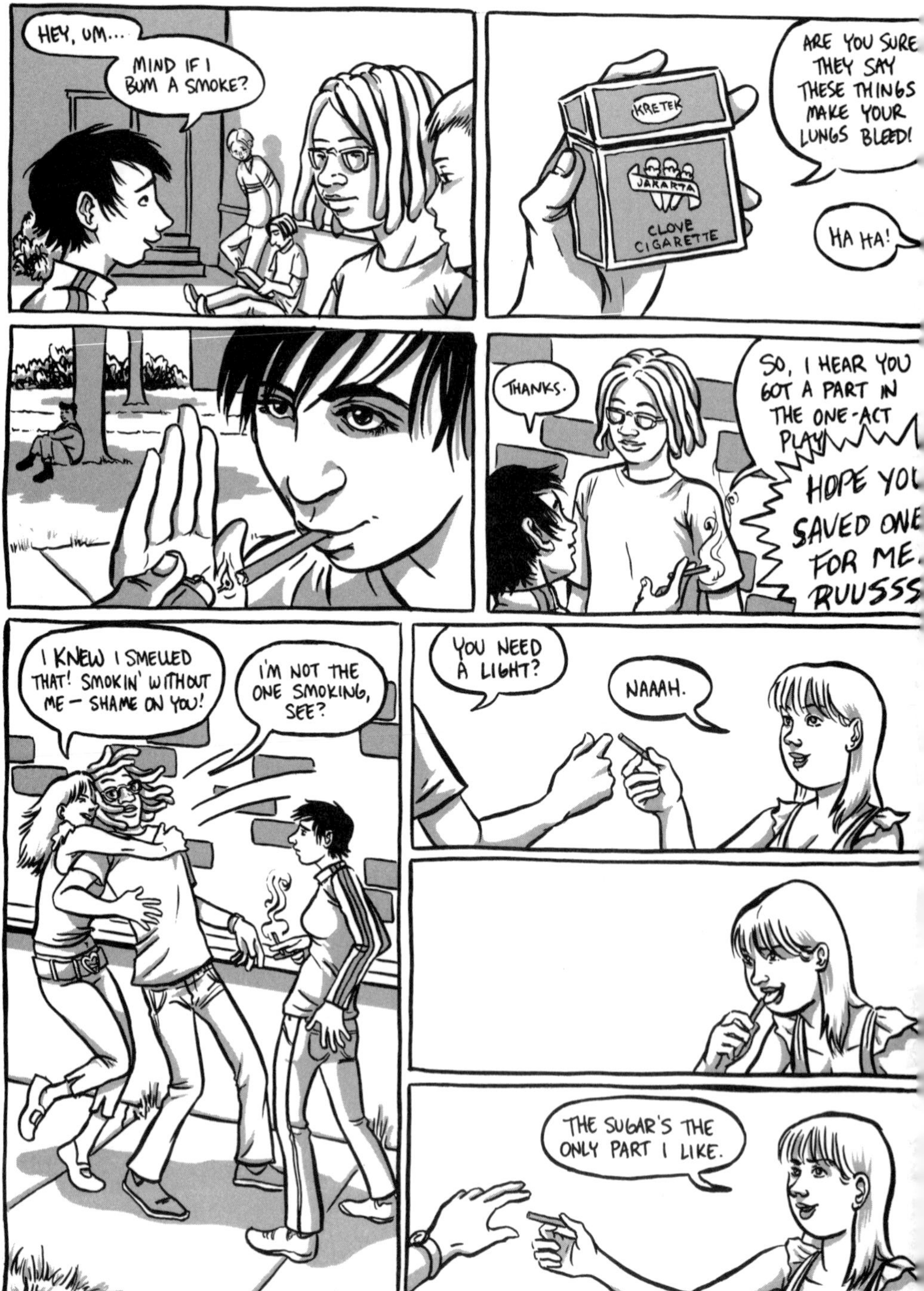
HEY, UM...
MIND IF I BUM A SMOKE?
KRETEK
JAKARTA
CLOVE CIGARETTE
ARE YOU SURE THEY SAY THESE THINGS MAKE YOUR LUNGS BLEED!
HA HA!
THANKS.
SO, I HEAR YOU GOT A PART IN THE ONE-ACT PLAY
HOPE YOU SAVED ONE FOR ME, RUUSSS
I KNEW I SMELLED THAT! SMOKIN' WITHOUT ME— SHAME ON YOU!
I'M NOT THE ONE SMOKING, SEE?
YOU NEED A LIGHT?
NAAAH.
THE SUGAR'S THE ONLY PART I LIKE.

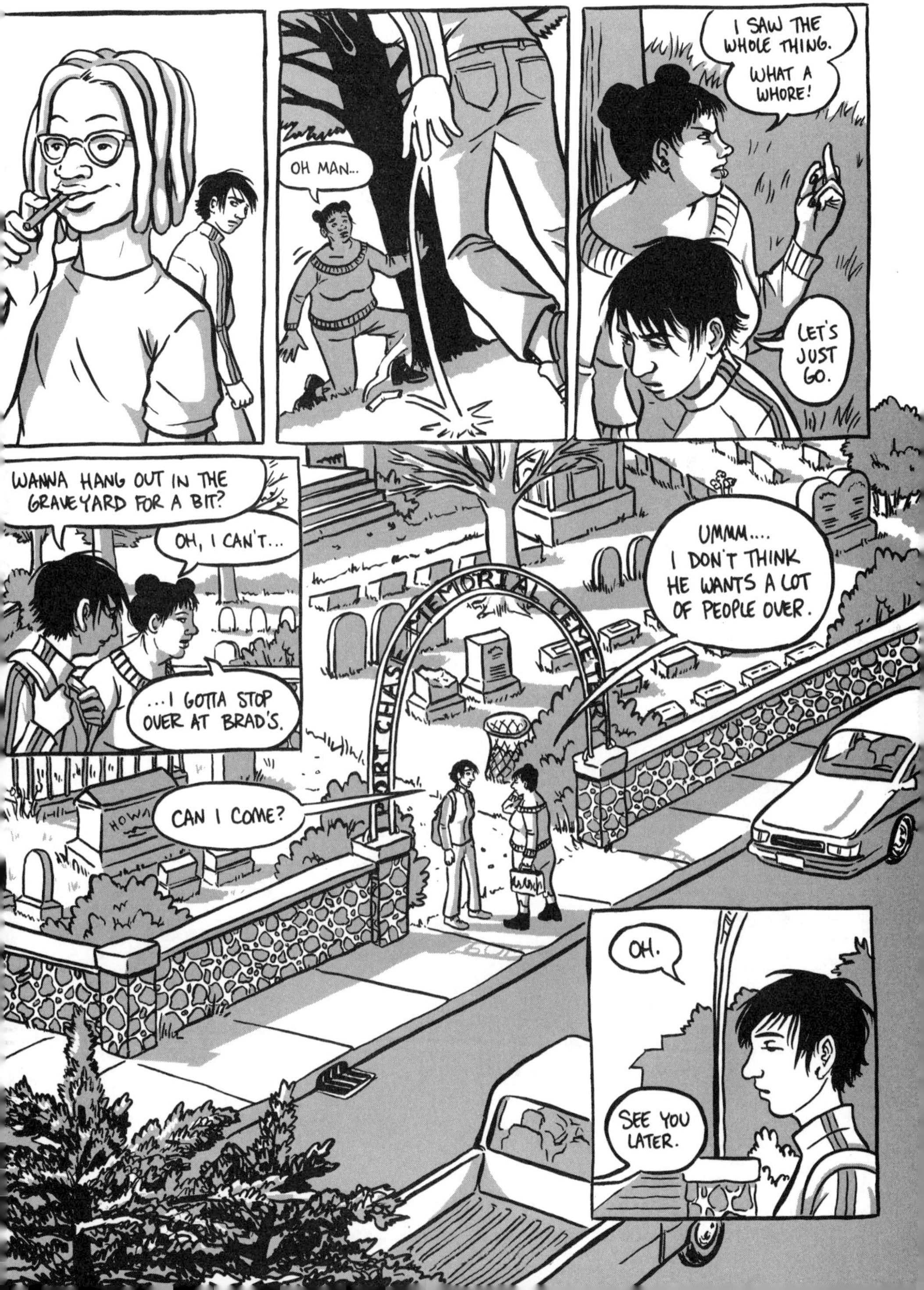
OH MAN...
I SAW THE WHOLE THING.
WHAT A WHORE!
LET'S JUST GO.
WANNA HANG OUT IN THE GRAVEYARD FOR A BIT?
OH, I CAN'T...
...I GOTTA STOP OVER AT BRAD'S.
CAN I COME?
UMMM.... I DON'T THINK HE WANTS A LOT OF PEOPLE OVER.
OH.
SEE YOU LATER.

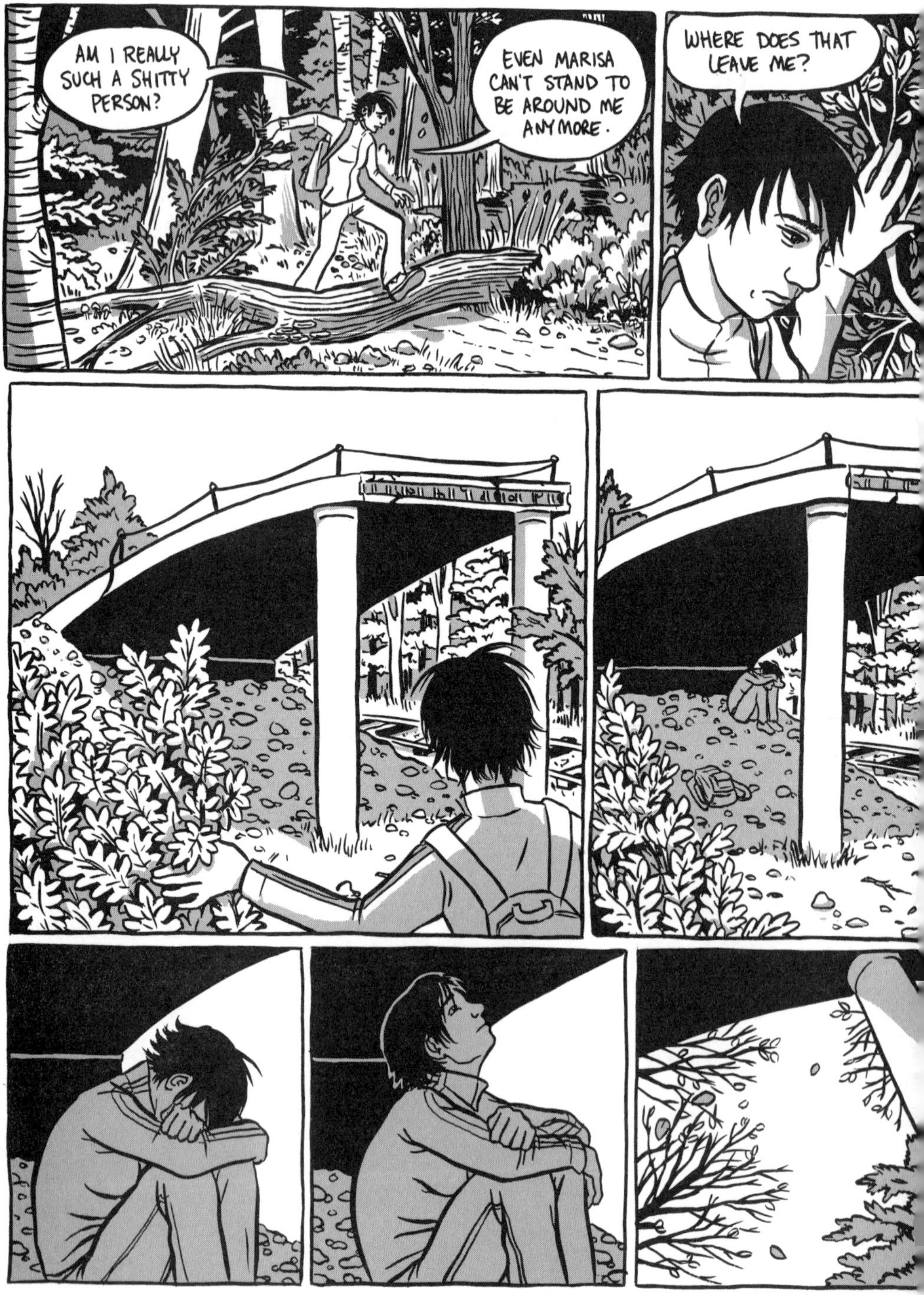
AM I REALLY SUCH A SHITTY PERSON?
EVEN MARISA CAN'T STAND TO BE AROUND ME ANYMORE.
WHERE DOES THAT LEAVE ME?

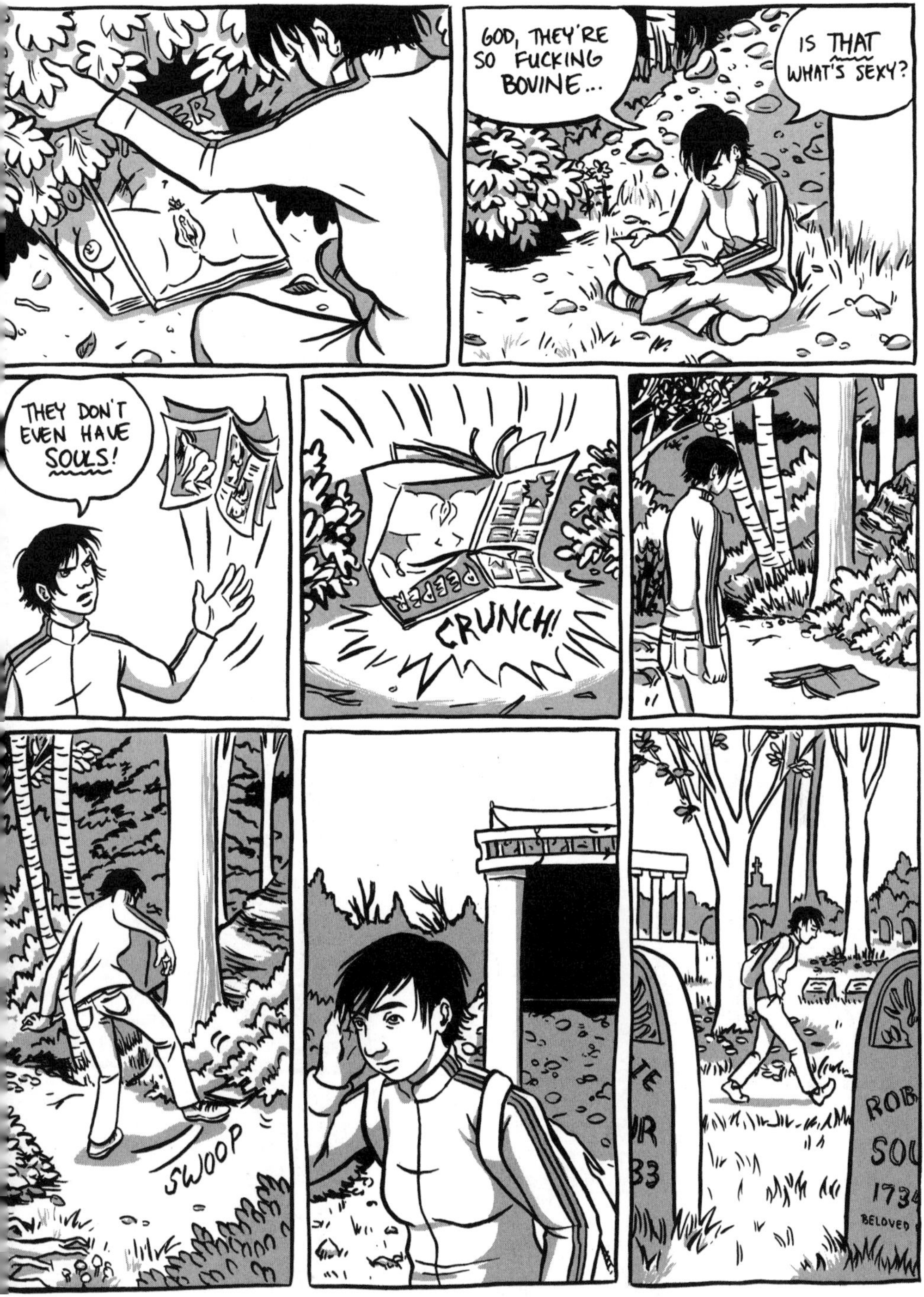
GOD, THEY'RE SO FUCKING BOVINE...
IS THAT WHAT'S SEXY?
THEY DON'T EVEN HAVE SOULS!
PEEPER
CRUNCH!
SWOOP
ROB
SOU
1734
BELOVED

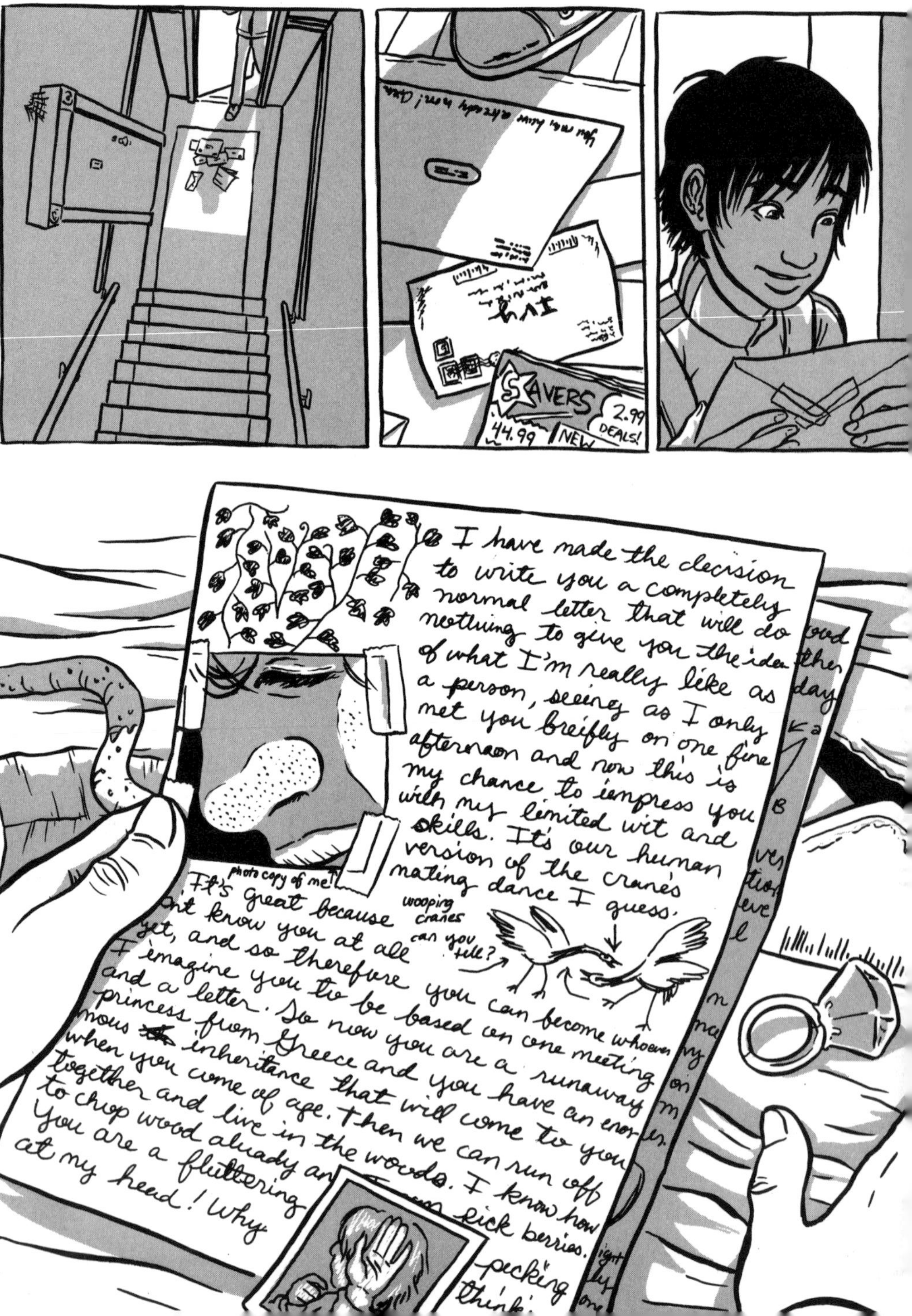
SAVERS
2.99
DEALS!
44.99
NEW
I have made the decision to write you a completely normal letter that will do nothing to give you the idea of what I'm really like as a person, seeing as I only met you breifly on one fine afternoon and now this is my chance to impress you with my limited wit and skills. It's our human version of the crane's mating dance I guess.
photo copy of me!
wooping cranes can you tell?
It's Great because
nt know you at all
yet, and so therefore you can become whoever
I imagine you to be based on one meeting
and a letter. So now you are a runaway
princess from Greece and you have an enormous inheritance that will come to you
when you come of age. Then we can run off
together and live in the woods. I know how
to chop wood and live in the woods.
pick berries.
You are already an
You are a fluttering
at my head! Why
pecking
think

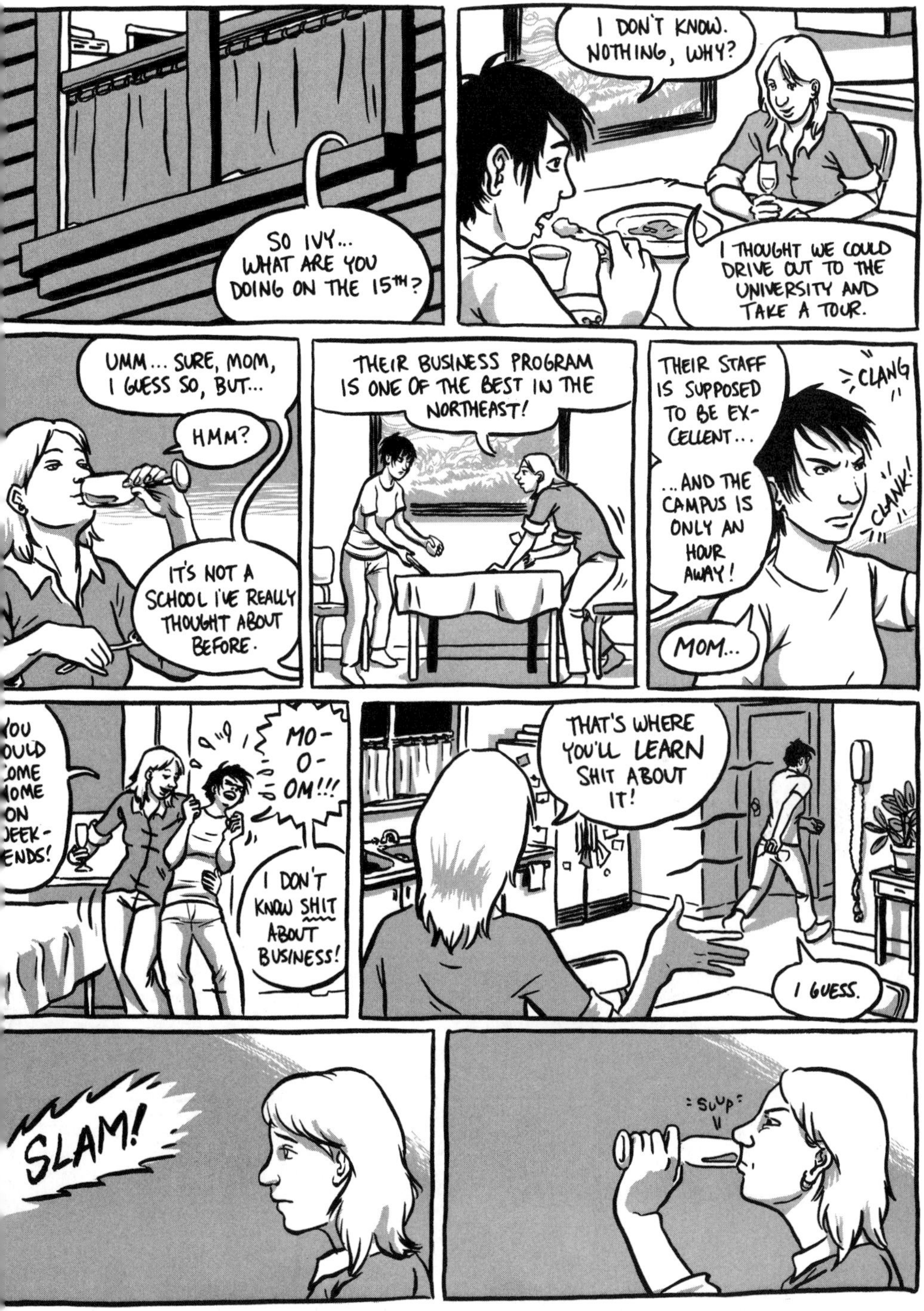

SO IVY... WHAT ARE YOU DOING ON THE 15TH?
I DON'T KNOW. NOTHING, WHY?
I THOUGHT WE COULD DRIVE OUT TO THE UNIVERSITY AND TAKE A TOUR.
UMM... SURE, MOM, I GUESS SO, BUT...
HMM?
IT'S NOT A SCHOOL I'VE REALLY THOUGHT ABOUT BEFORE.
THEIR BUSINESS PROGRAM IS ONE OF THE BEST IN THE NORTHEAST!
THEIR STAFF IS SUPPOSED TO BE EX-CELLENT...
CLANG
CLANK!
...AND THE CAMPUS IS ONLY AN HOUR AWAY!
MOM...
YOU COULD COME HOME ON WEEK-ENDS!
MO-O-OM!!!
I DON'T KNOW SHIT ABOUT BUSINESS!
THAT'S WHERE YOU'LL LEARN SHIT ABOUT IT!
I GUESS.
SLAM!
SUUP

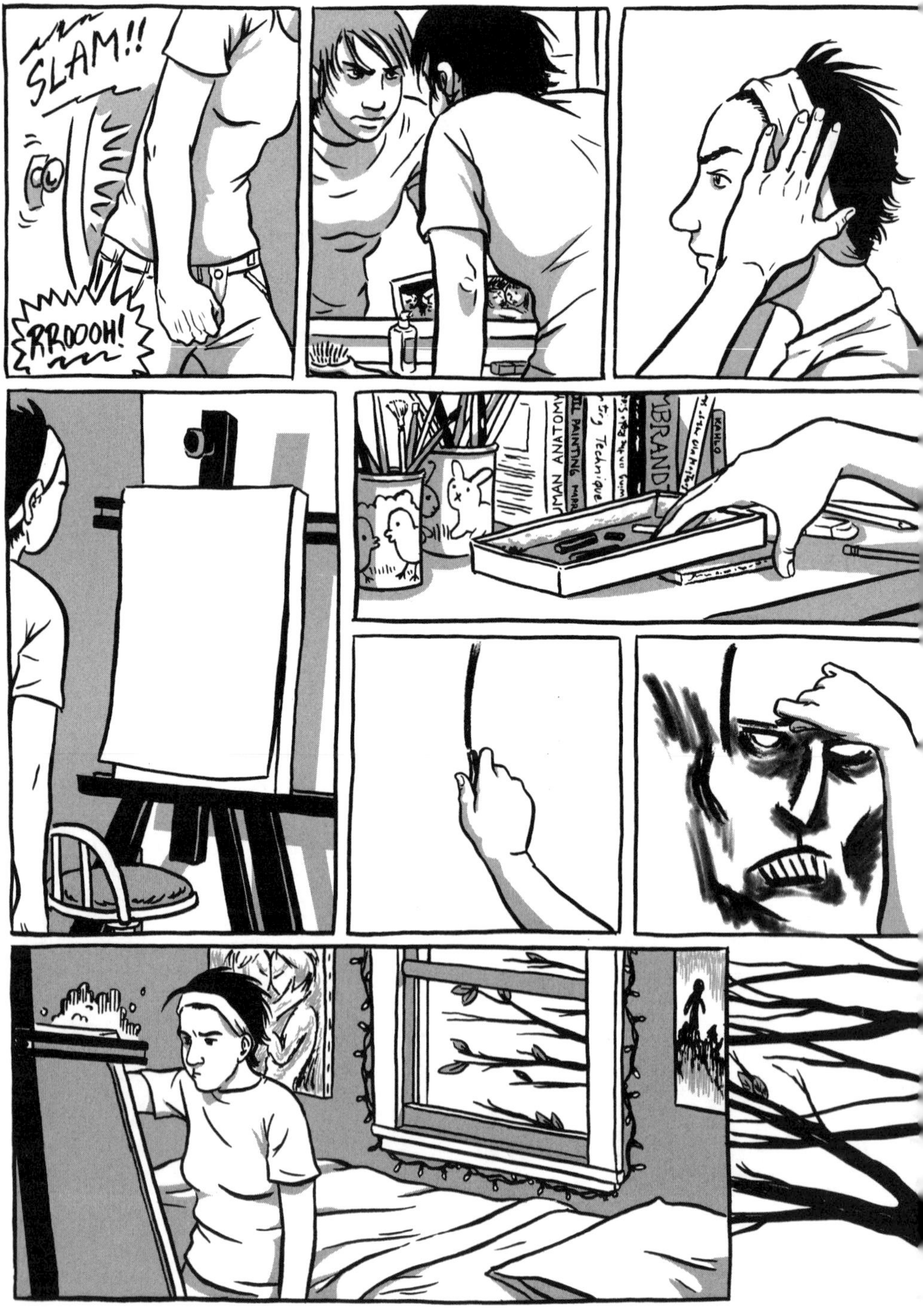
SLAM!!
RROOOH!
UMAN ANATOMY
MBRANDT
KAHLO

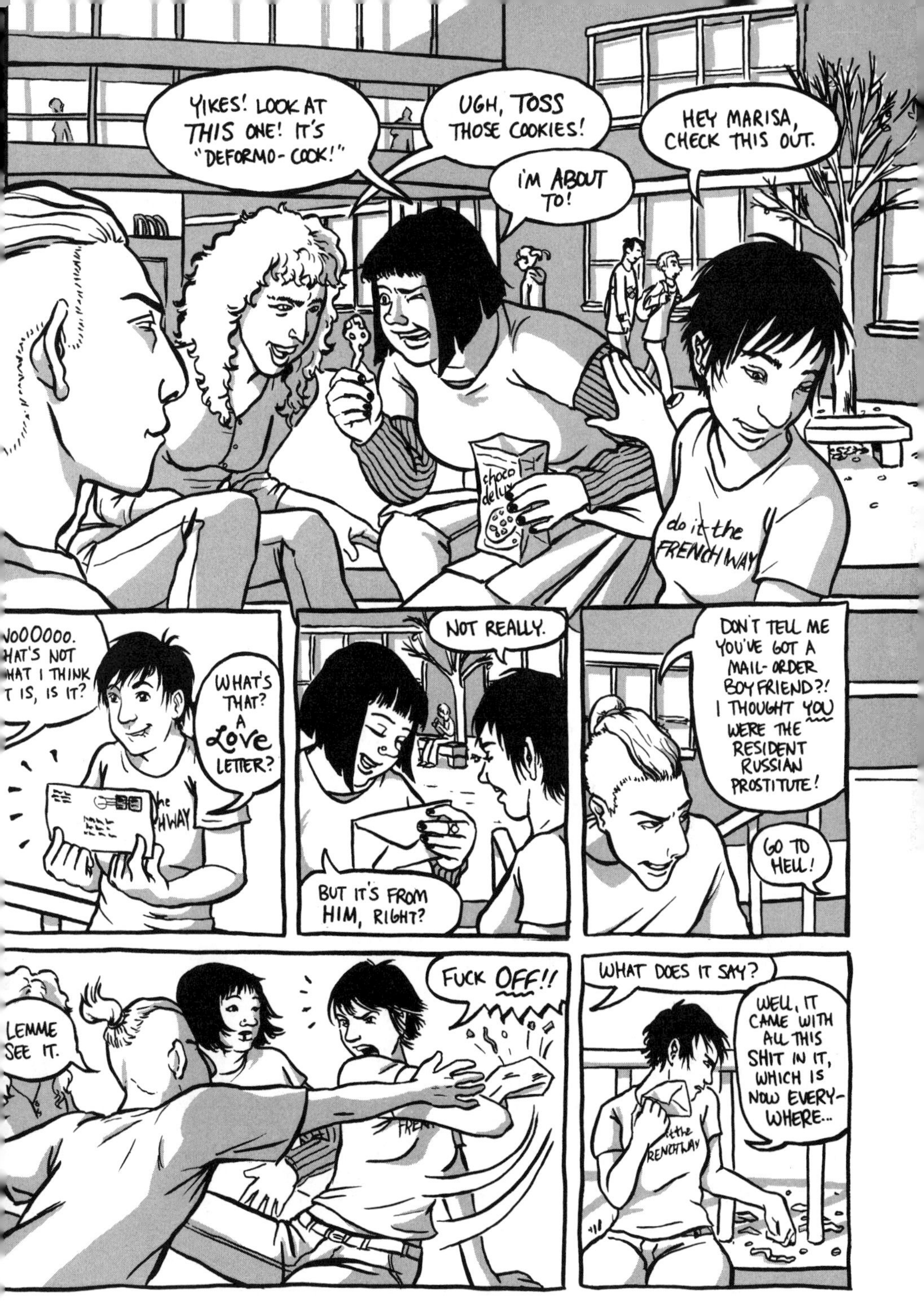
YIKES! LOOK AT THIS ONE! IT'S "DEFORMO-COOK!"
UGH, TOSS THOSE COOKIES!
I'M ABOUT TO!
HEY MARISA, CHECK THIS OUT.
choco delux
do it the FRENCH WAY
NOOOOOO. THAT'S NOT WHAT I THINK IT IS, IS IT?
WHAT'S THAT? A Love LETTER?
NOT REALLY.
BUT IT'S FROM HIM, RIGHT?
DON'T TELL ME YOU'VE GOT A MAIL-ORDER BOYFRIEND?! I THOUGHT YOU WERE THE RESIDENT RUSSIAN PROSTITUTE!
GO TO HELL!
LEMME SEE IT.
FUCK OFF!!
WHAT DOES IT SAY?
WELL, IT CAME WITH ALL THIS SHIT IN IT, WHICH IS NOW EVERY-WHERE...

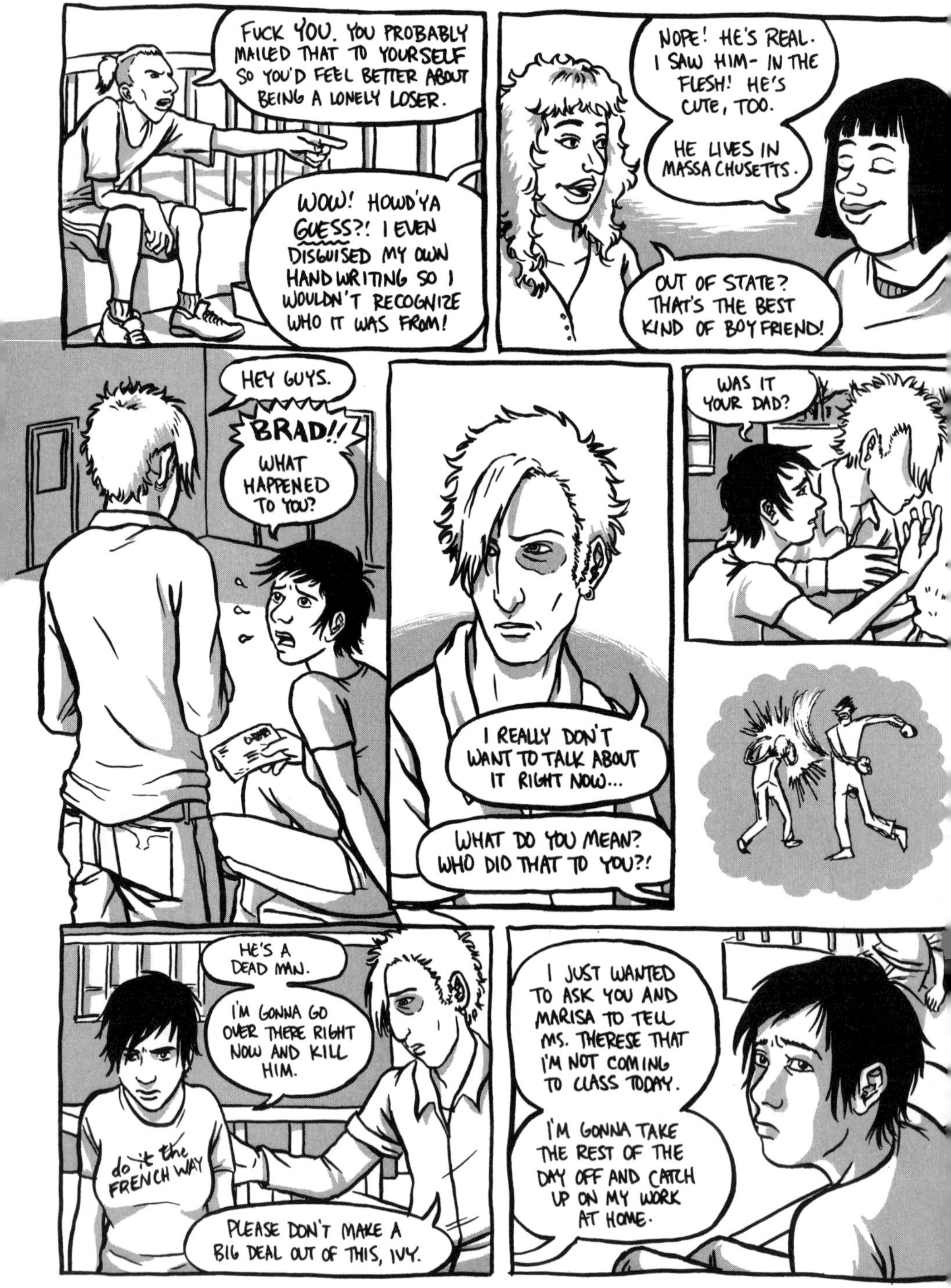
FUCK YOU. YOU PROBABLY MAILED THAT TO YOURSELF SO YOU'D FEEL BETTER ABOUT BEING A LONELY LOSER.
WOW! HOWD'YA GUESS?! I EVEN DISGUISED MY OWN HANDWRITING SO I WOULDN'T RECOGNIZE WHO IT WAS FROM!
NOPE! HE'S REAL. I SAW HIM- IN THE FLESH! HE'S CUTE, TOO.
HE LIVES IN MASSACHUSETTS.
OUT OF STATE? THAT'S THE BEST KIND OF BOYFRIEND!
HEY GUYS.
BRAD!!
WHAT HAPPENED TO YOU?
I REALLY DON'T WANT TO TALK ABOUT IT RIGHT NOW...
WHAT DO YOU MEAN? WHO DID THAT TO YOU?!
WAS IT YOUR DAD?
HE'S A DEAD MAN.
I'M GONNA GO OVER THERE RIGHT NOW AND KILL HIM.
do it the FRENCH WAY
PLEASE DON'T MAKE A BIG DEAL OUT OF THIS, IVY.
I JUST WANTED TO ASK YOU AND MARISA TO TELL MS. THERESE THAT I'M NOT COMING TO CLASS TODAY.
I'M GONNA TAKE THE REST OF THE DAY OFF AND CATCH UP ON MY WORK AT HOME.

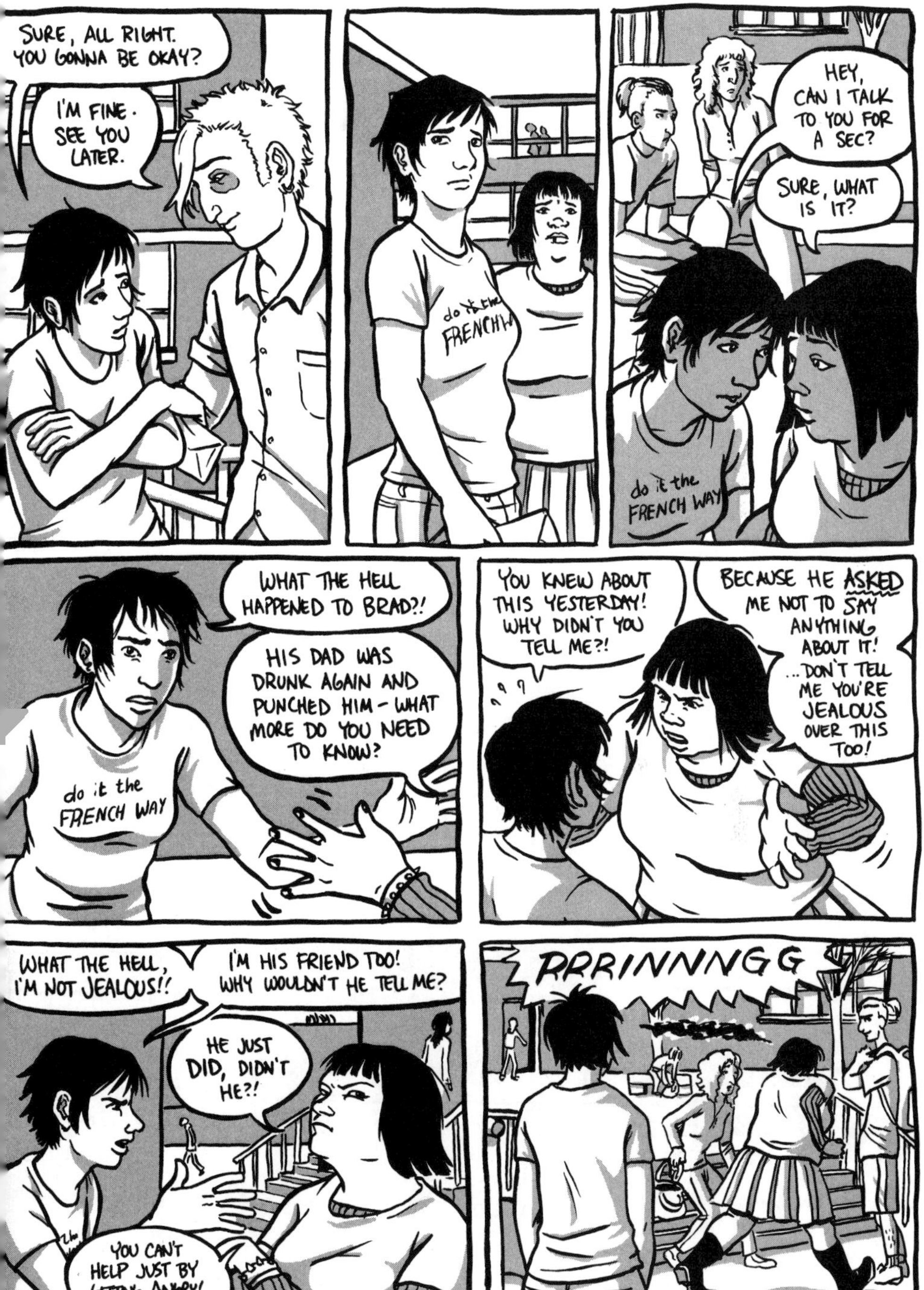
SURE, ALL RIGHT. YOU GONNA BE OKAY?
I'M FINE. SEE YOU LATER.
do it the FRENCH W
HEY, CAN I TALK TO YOU FOR A SEC?
SURE, WHAT IS IT?
do it the FRENCH WAY
WHAT THE HELL HAPPENED TO BRAD?!
HIS DAD WAS DRUNK AGAIN AND PUNCHED HIM - WHAT MORE DO YOU NEED TO KNOW?
do it the FRENCH WAY
YOU KNEW ABOUT THIS YESTERDAY! WHY DIDN'T YOU TELL ME?!
BECAUSE HE ASKED ME NOT TO SAY ANYTHING ABOUT IT! ...DON'T TELL ME YOU'RE JEALOUS OVER THIS TOO!
WHAT THE HELL, I'M NOT JEALOUS!!
I'M HIS FRIEND TOO! WHY WOULDN'T HE TELL ME?
HE JUST DID, DIDN'T HE?!
YOU CAN'T HELP JUST BY GETTING ANGRY!
RRRINNNNGG

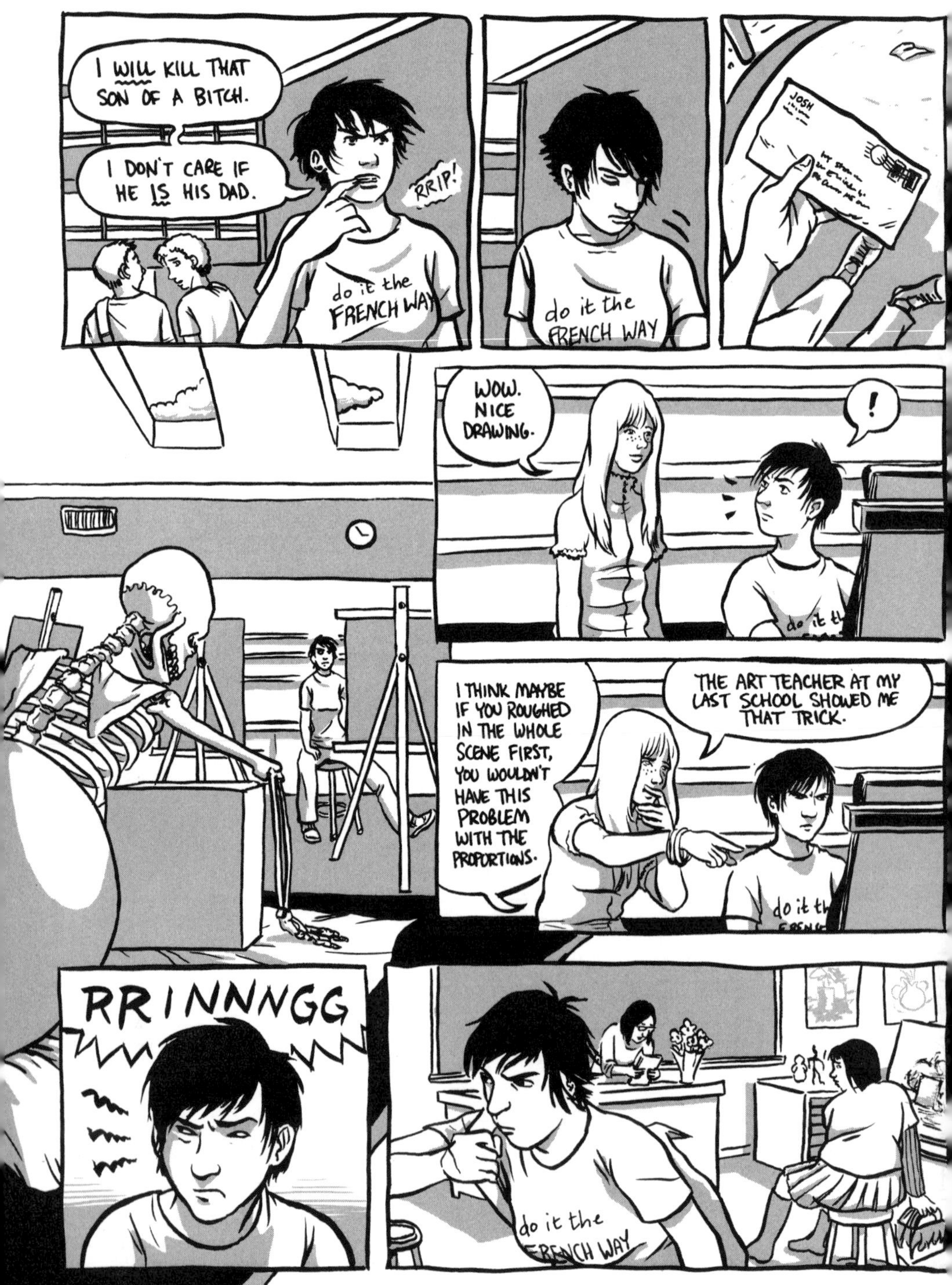
I WILL KILL THAT SON OF A BITCH.
I DON'T CARE IF HE IS HIS DAD.
RRIP!
do it the FRENCH WAY
do it the FRENCH WAY
JOSH
WOW. NICE DRAWING.
!
I THINK MAYBE IF YOU ROUGHED IN THE WHOLE SCENE FIRST, YOU WOULDN'T HAVE THIS PROBLEM WITH THE PROPORTIONS.
THE ART TEACHER AT MY LAST SCHOOL SHOWED ME THAT TRICK.
RRINNNGG
do it the FRENCH WAY

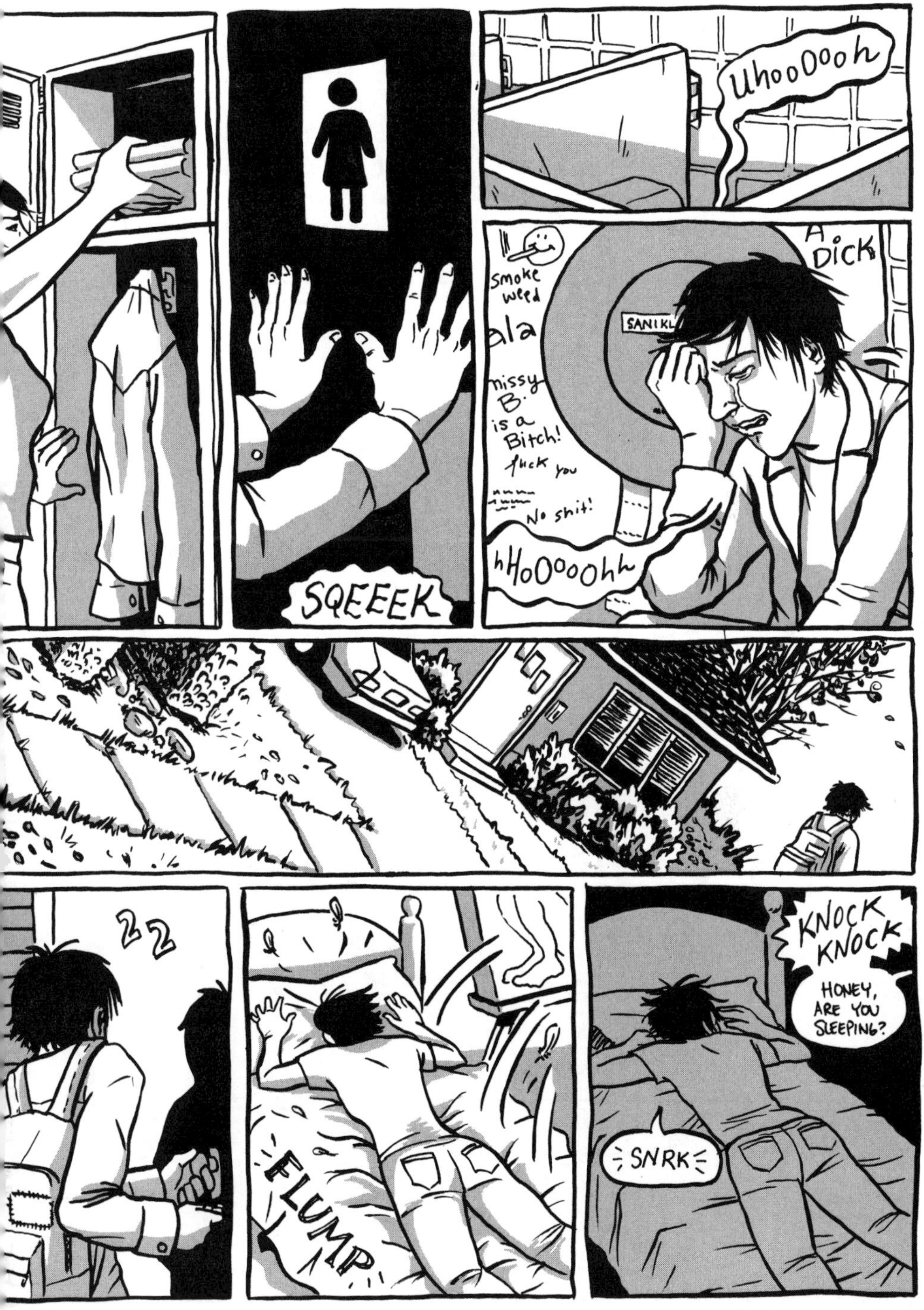
SQEEEK
UhooOooh
A DICK
smoke weed
ala
missy B. is a Bitch!
fuck you
No shit!
hHoOoooOhh
22
FLUMP
KNOCK KNOCK
HONEY, ARE YOU SLEEPING?
SNRK

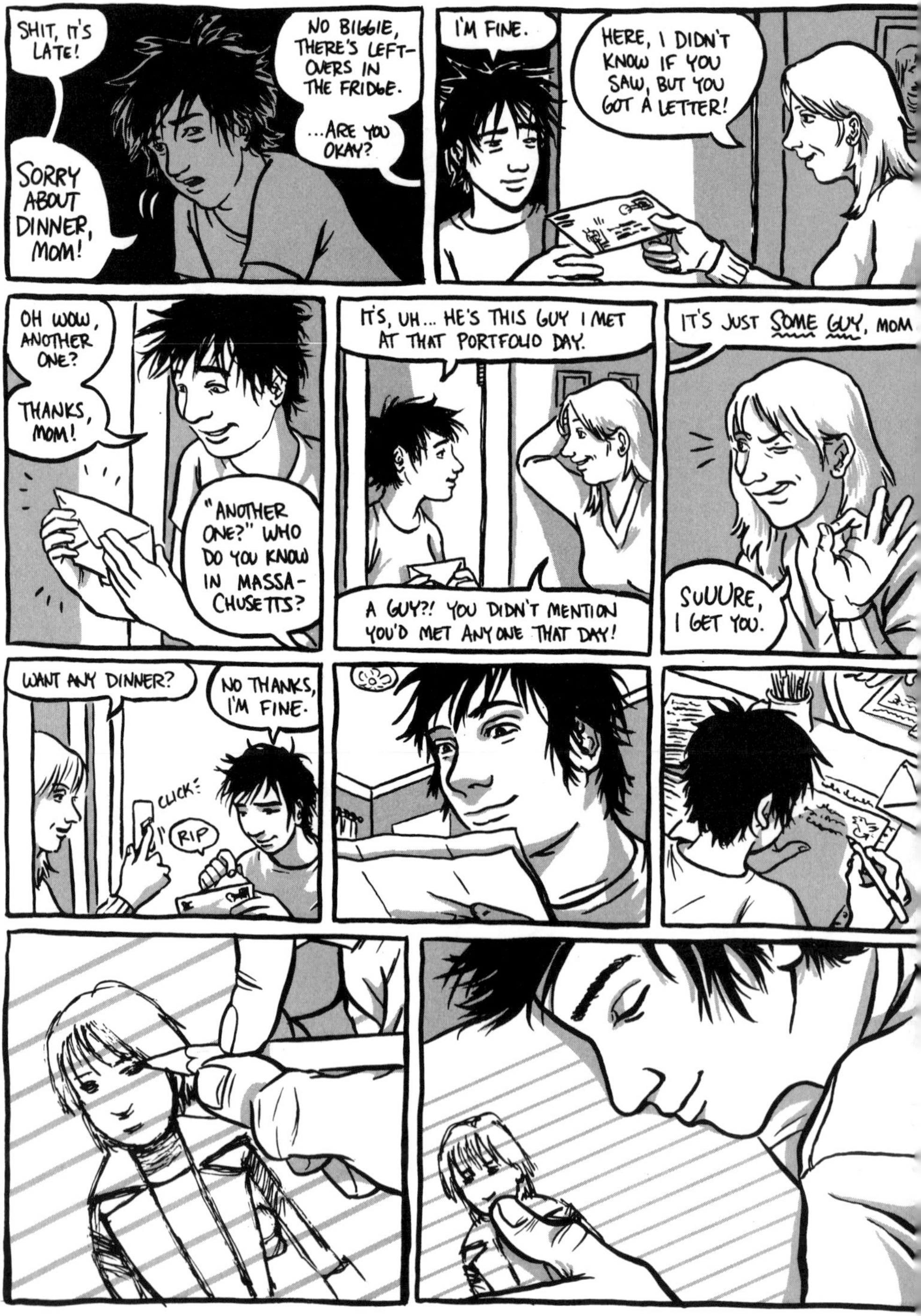
SHIT, IT'S LATE!
SORRY ABOUT DINNER, MOM!
NO BIGGIE, THERE'S LEFT-OVERS IN THE FRIDGE.
...ARE YOU OKAY?
I'M FINE.
HERE, I DIDN'T KNOW IF YOU SAW, BUT YOU GOT A LETTER!
OH WOW, ANOTHER ONE?
THANKS, MOM!
"ANOTHER ONE?" WHO DO YOU KNOW IN MASSA-CHUSETTS?
IT'S, UH... HE'S THIS GUY I MET AT THAT PORTFOLIO DAY.
A GUY?! YOU DIDN'T MENTION YOU'D MET ANYONE THAT DAY!
IT'S JUST SOME GUY, MOM
SUUURE, I GET YOU.
WANT ANY DINNER?
NO THANKS, I'M FINE.
CLICK
RIP

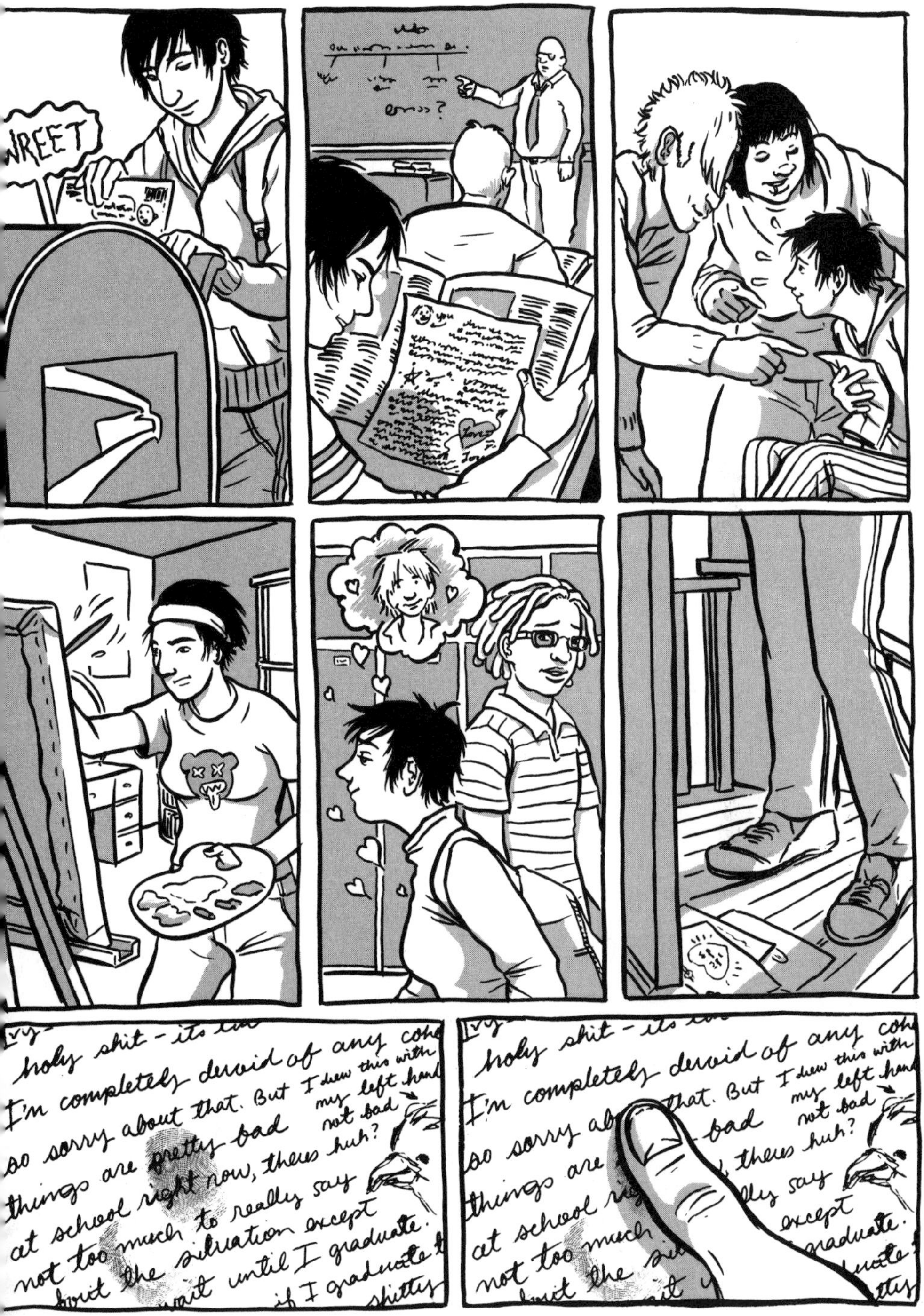
WREET
holy shit - its
I'm completely devoid of any
so sorry about that.
things are pretty bad
at school right now, theres
not too much to really say
the situation except
until I graduate
if I graduate
But I drew this with
my left hand
not bad
huh?

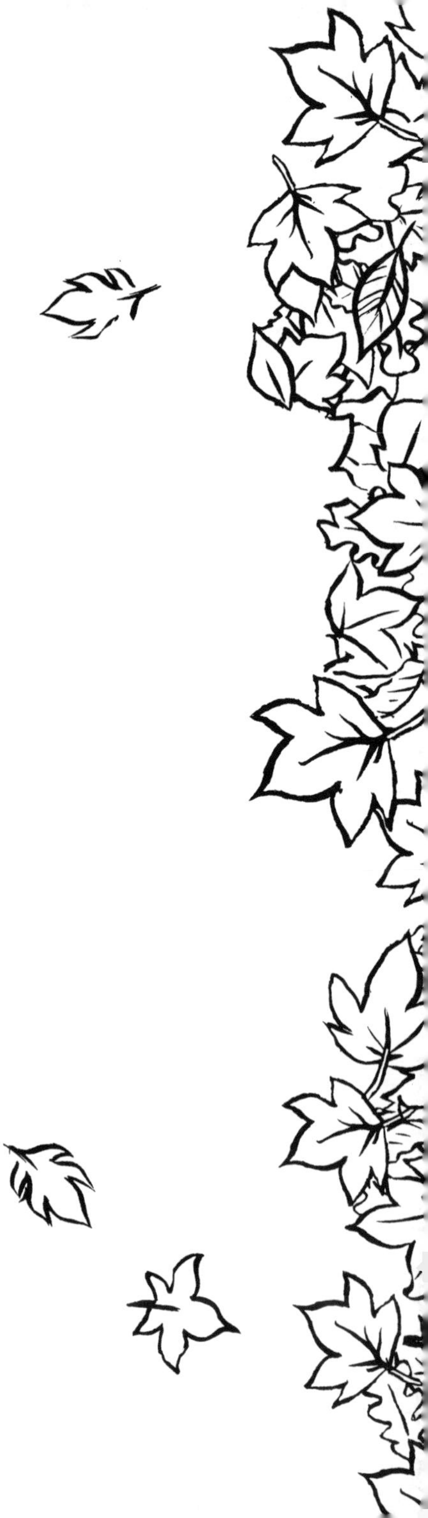

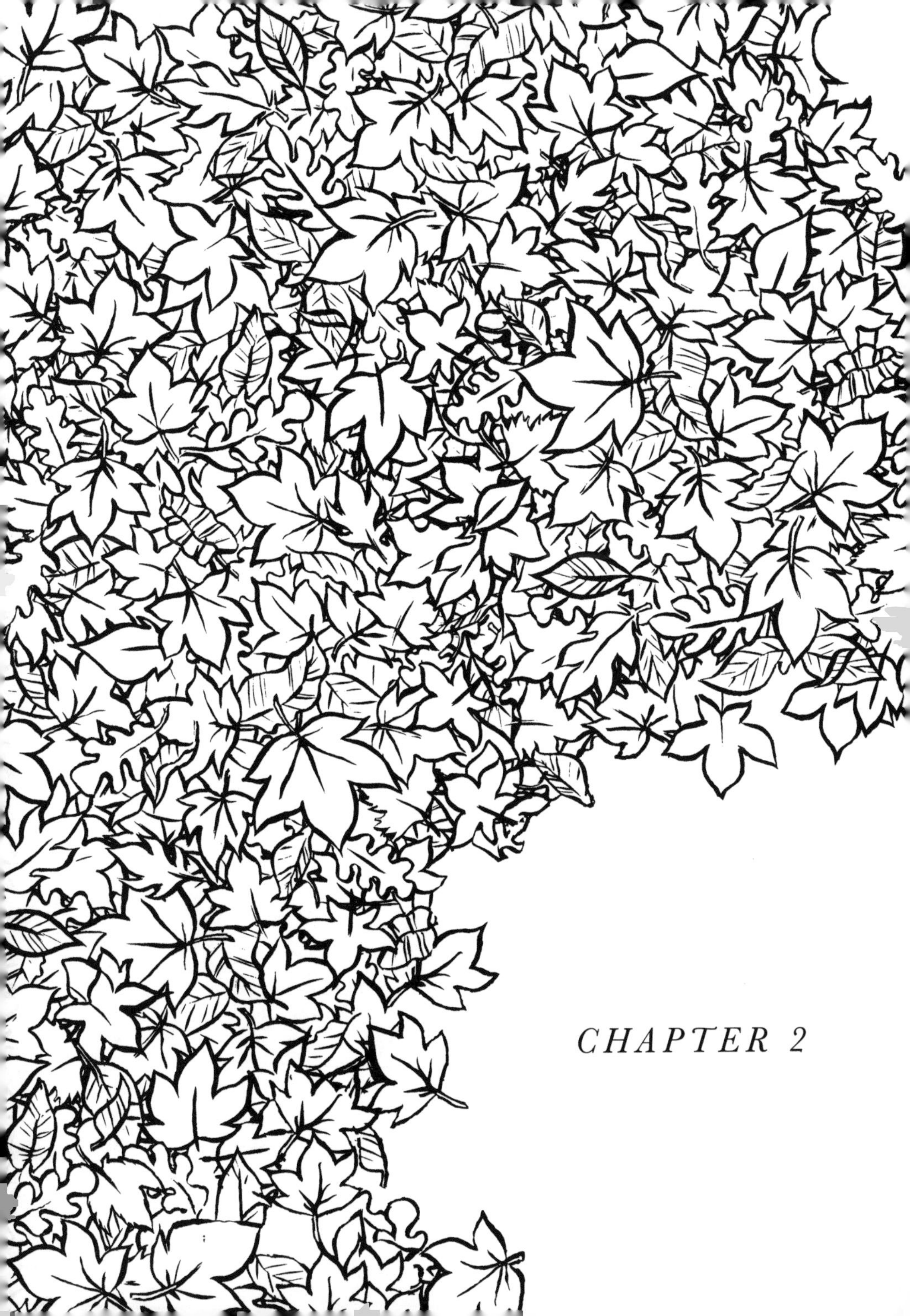

CHAPTER 2

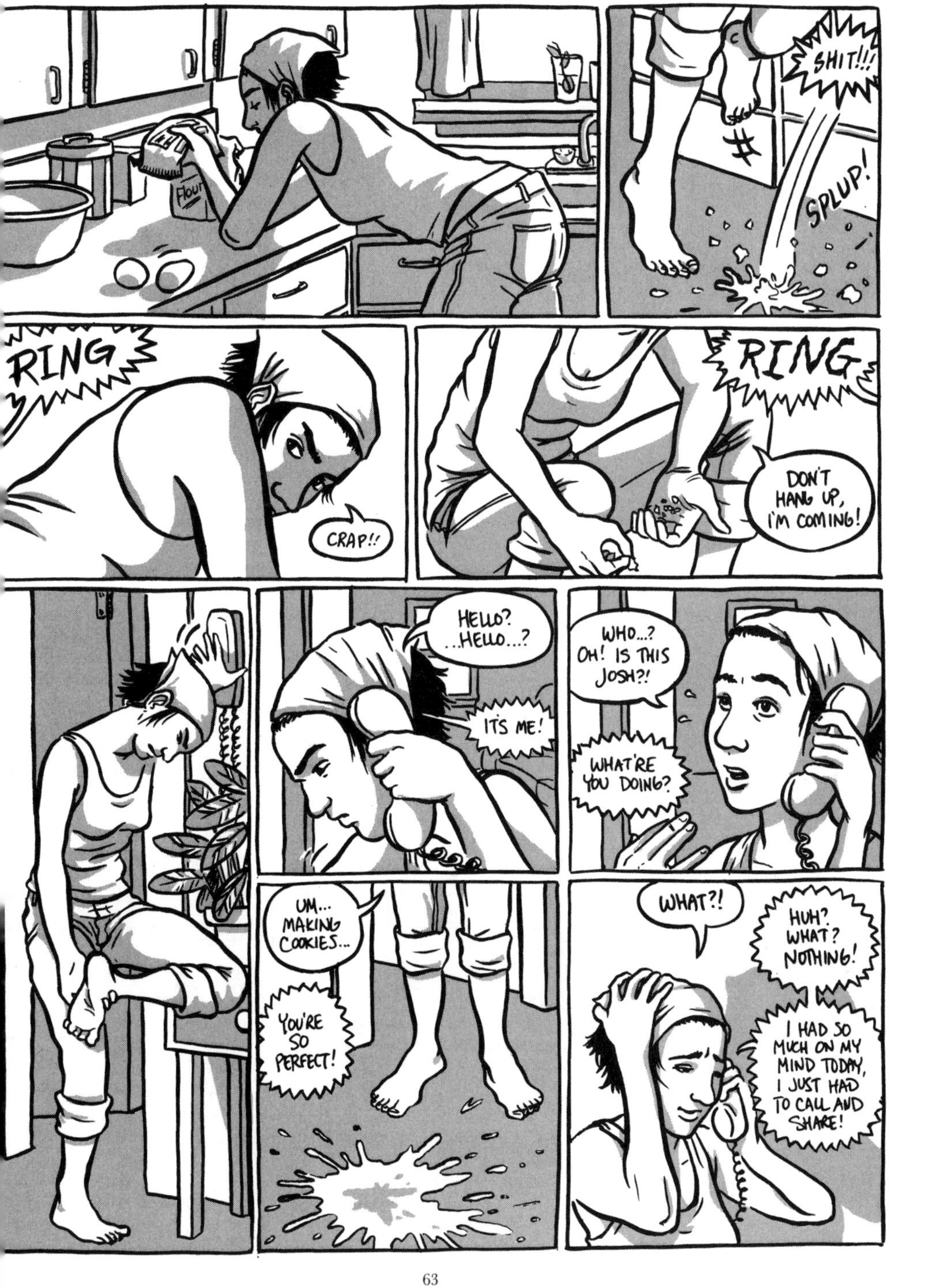
FLOUR
SHIT!!!
SPLUP!
RING
CRAP!!
RING
DON'T HANG UP, I'M COMING!
HELLO? ...HELLO...?
ITS ME!
WHO...? OH! IS THIS JOSH?!
WHAT'RE YOU DOING?
UM... MAKING COOKIES...
YOU'RE SO PERFECT!
WHAT?!
HUH? WHAT? NOTHING!
I HAD SO MUCH ON MY MIND TODAY, I JUST HAD TO CALL AND SHARE!

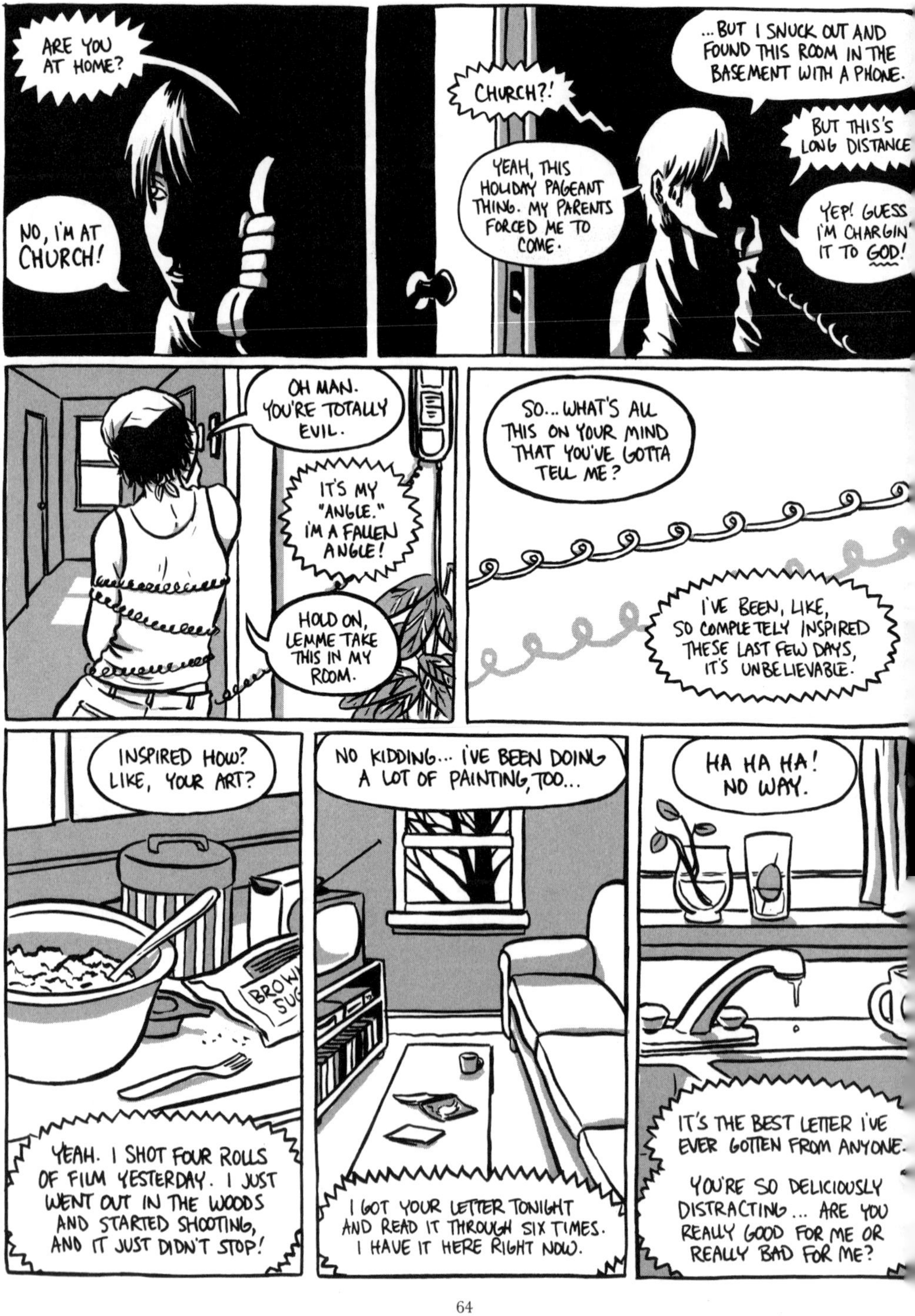
ARE YOU AT HOME?
NO, I'M AT CHURCH!
CHURCH?!
YEAH, THIS HOLIDAY PAGEANT THING. MY PARENTS FORCED ME TO COME.
...BUT I SNUCK OUT AND FOUND THIS ROOM IN THE BASEMENT WITH A PHONE.
BUT THIS'S LONG DISTANCE
YEP! GUESS I'M CHARGIN' IT TO GOD!
OH MAN. YOU'RE TOTALLY EVIL.
IT'S MY "ANGLE." I'M A FALLEN ANGLE!
HOLD ON, LEMME TAKE THIS IN MY ROOM.
SO... WHAT'S ALL THIS ON YOUR MIND THAT YOU'VE GOTTA TELL ME?
I'VE BEEN, LIKE, SO COMPLETELY INSPIRED THESE LAST FEW DAYS, IT'S UNBELIEVABLE.
INSPIRED HOW? LIKE, YOUR ART?
YEAH. I SHOT FOUR ROLLS OF FILM YESTERDAY. I JUST WENT OUT IN THE WOODS AND STARTED SHOOTING, AND IT JUST DIDN'T STOP!
NO KIDDING... I'VE BEEN DOING A LOT OF PAINTING, TOO...
I GOT YOUR LETTER TONIGHT AND READ IT THROUGH SIX TIMES. I HAVE IT HERE RIGHT NOW.
HA HA HA! NO WAY.
IT'S THE BEST LETTER I'VE EVER GOTTEN FROM ANYONE.
YOU'RE SO DELICIOUSLY DISTRACTING... ARE YOU REALLY GOOD FOR ME OR REALLY BAD FOR ME?

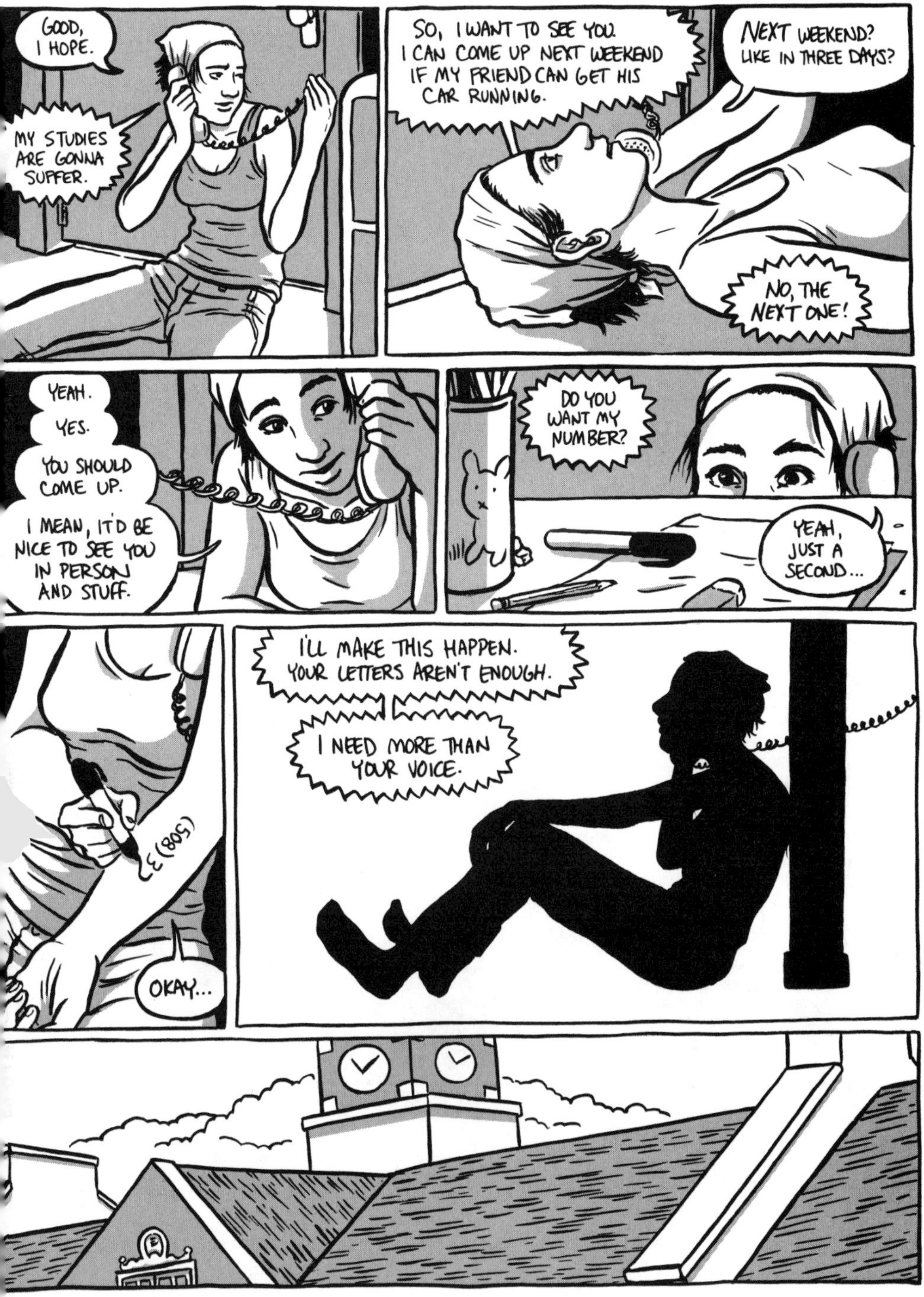
GOOD, I HOPE.
MY STUDIES ARE GONNA SUFFER.
SO, I WANT TO SEE YOU. I CAN COME UP NEXT WEEKEND IF MY FRIEND CAN GET HIS CAR RUNNING.
NEXT WEEKEND? LIKE IN THREE DAYS?
NO, THE NEXT ONE!
YEAH.
YES.
YOU SHOULD COME UP.
I MEAN, IT'D BE NICE TO SEE YOU IN PERSON AND STUFF.
DO YOU WANT MY NUMBER?
YEAH, JUST A SECOND...
(508) 3
OKAY...
I'LL MAKE THIS HAPPEN. YOUR LETTERS AREN'T ENOUGH.
I NEED MORE THAN YOUR VOICE.

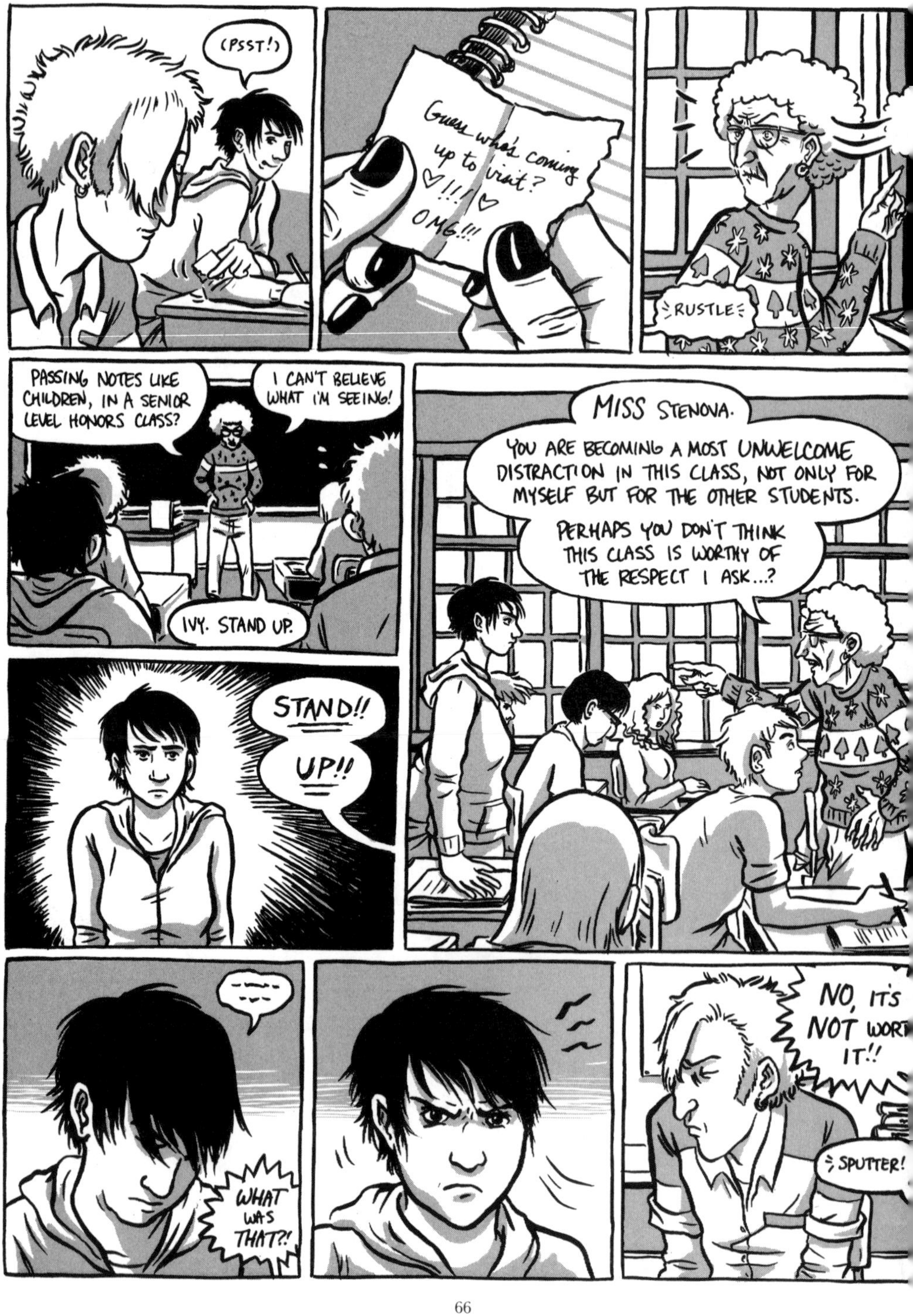
(PSST!)
Guess who's coming up to visit? ♡!!! ♡ OMG!!!
RUSTLE
PASSING NOTES LIKE CHILDREN, IN A SENIOR LEVEL HONORS CLASS?
I CAN'T BELIEVE WHAT I'M SEEING!
IVY. STAND UP.
STAND!!
UP!!
MISS STENOVA.
YOU ARE BECOMING A MOST UNWELCOME DISTRACTION IN THIS CLASS, NOT ONLY FOR MYSELF BUT FOR THE OTHER STUDENTS.
PERHAPS YOU DON'T THINK THIS CLASS IS WORTHY OF THE RESPECT I ASK...?
WHAT WAS THAT?!
NO, IT'S NOT WORT
IT!!
SPUTTER!

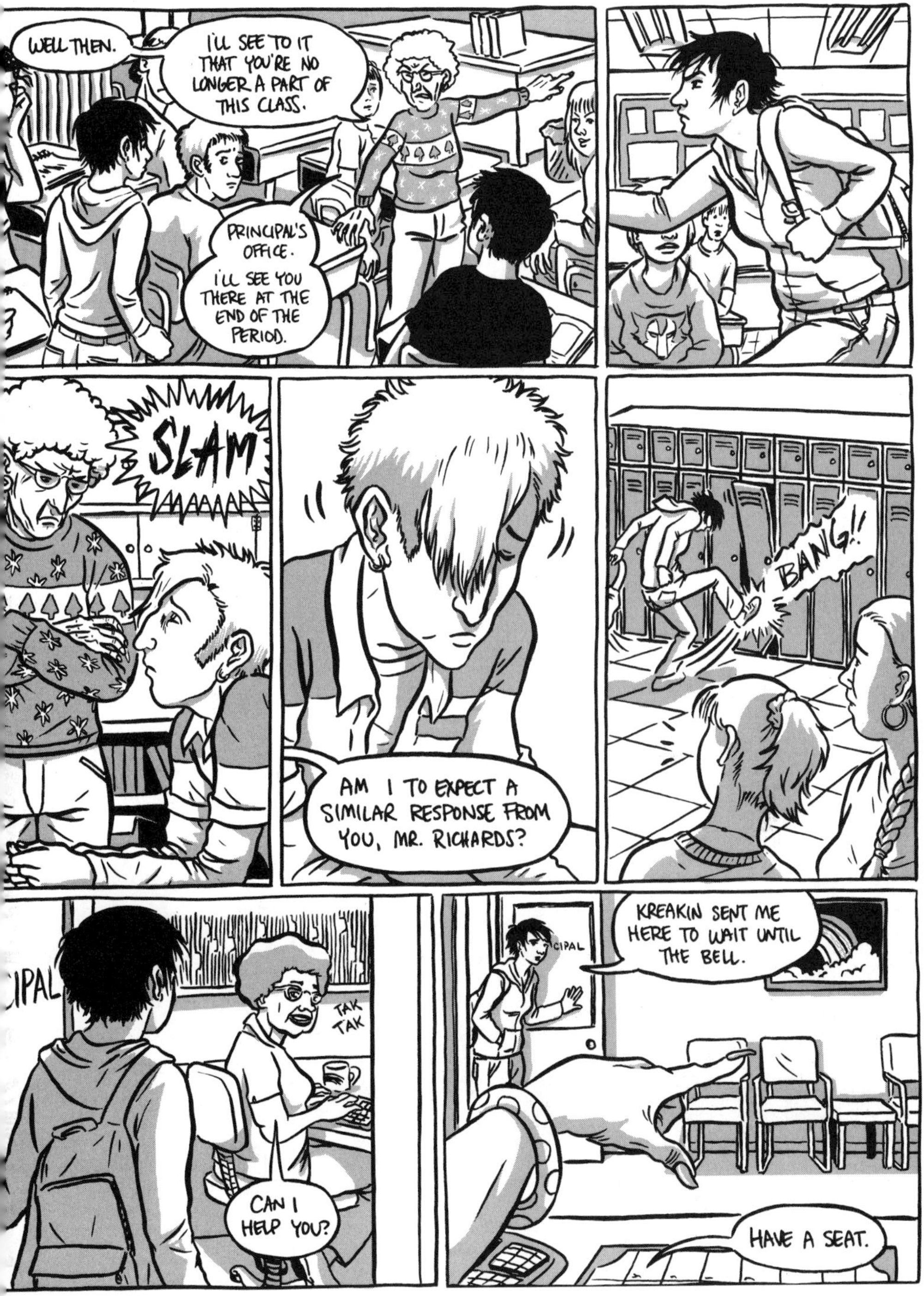
WELL THEN.
I'LL SEE TO IT THAT YOU'RE NO LONGER A PART OF THIS CLASS.
PRINCIPAL'S OFFICE.
I'LL SEE YOU THERE AT THE END OF THE PERIOD.
SLAM
AM I TO EXPECT A SIMILAR RESPONSE FROM YOU, MR. RICHARDS?
BANG!!
CIPAL
TAK TAK
CAN I HELP YOU?
CIPAL
KREAKIN SENT ME HERE TO WAIT UNTIL THE BELL.
HAVE A SEAT.

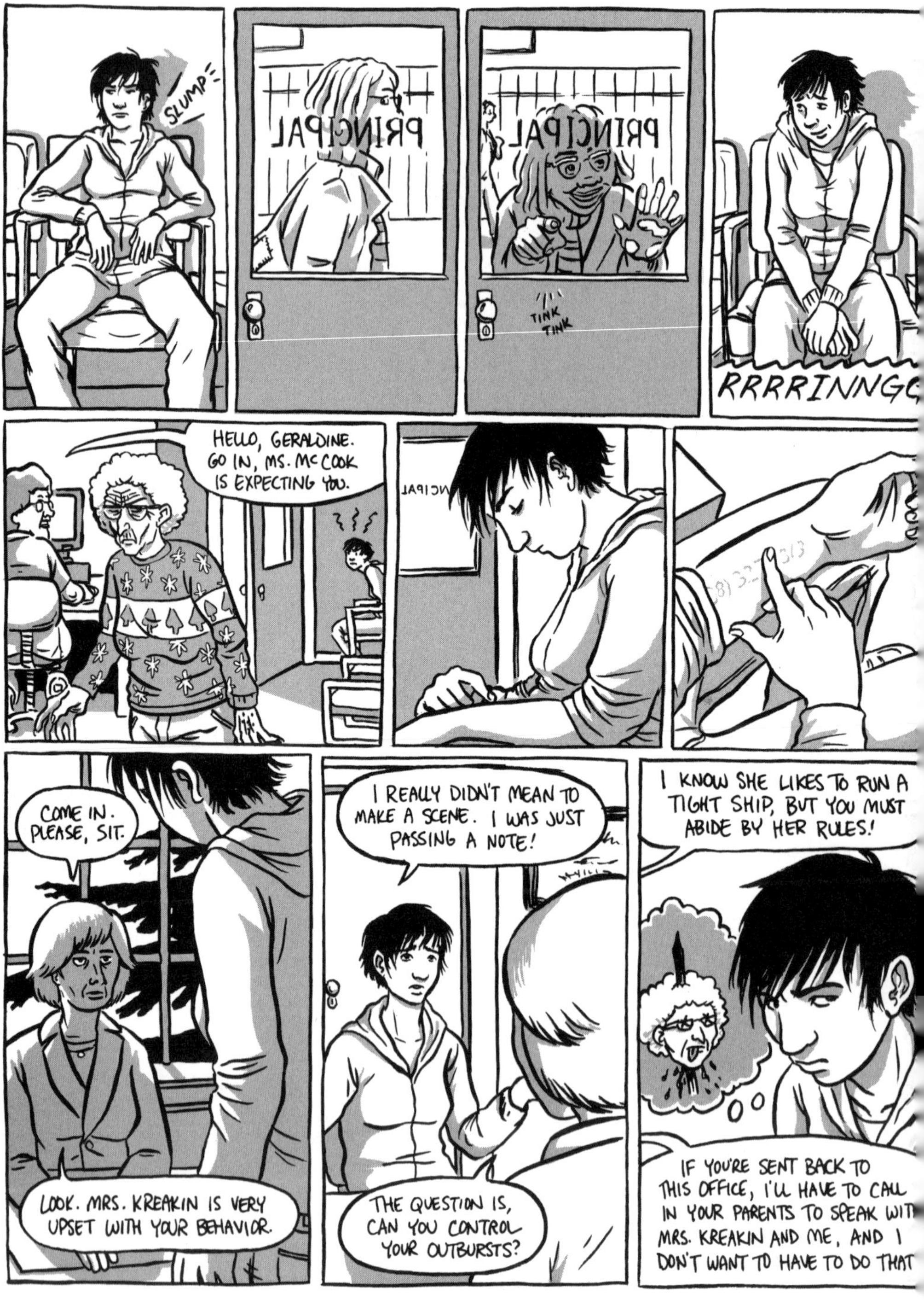
SLUMP
PRINCIPAL
PRINCIPAL
TINK TINK
RRRRINNGG
HELLO, GERALDINE. GO IN, MS. McCOOK IS EXPECTING YOU.
COME IN. PLEASE, SIT.
LOOK. MRS. KREAKIN IS VERY UPSET WITH YOUR BEHAVIOR.
I REALLY DIDN'T MEAN TO MAKE A SCENE. I WAS JUST PASSING A NOTE!
THE QUESTION IS, CAN YOU CONTROL YOUR OUTBURSTS?
I KNOW SHE LIKES TO RUN A TIGHT SHIP, BUT YOU MUST ABIDE BY HER RULES!
IF YOU'RE SENT BACK TO THIS OFFICE, I'LL HAVE TO CALL IN YOUR PARENTS TO SPEAK WIT MRS. KREAKIN AND ME, AND I DON'T WANT TO HAVE TO DO THAT

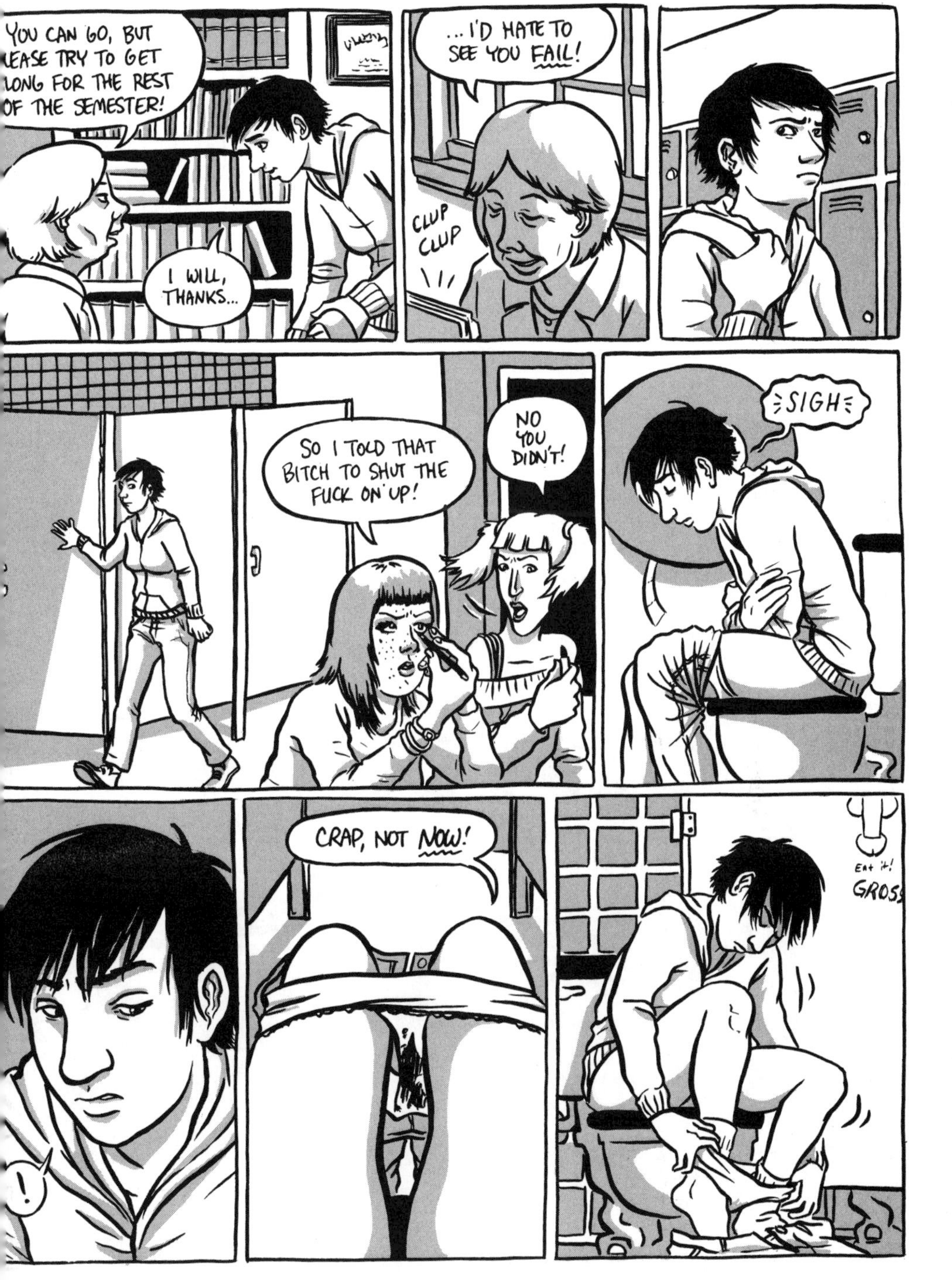
YOU CAN GO, BUT LEASE TRY TO GET LONG FOR THE REST OF THE SEMESTER!
I WILL, THANKS...
...I'D HATE TO SEE YOU FAIL!
CLUP CLUP
SO I TOLD THAT BITCH TO SHUT THE FUCK ON' UP!
NO YOU DIDN'T!
SIGH
!
CRAP, NOT NOW!
Eat it!
GROS

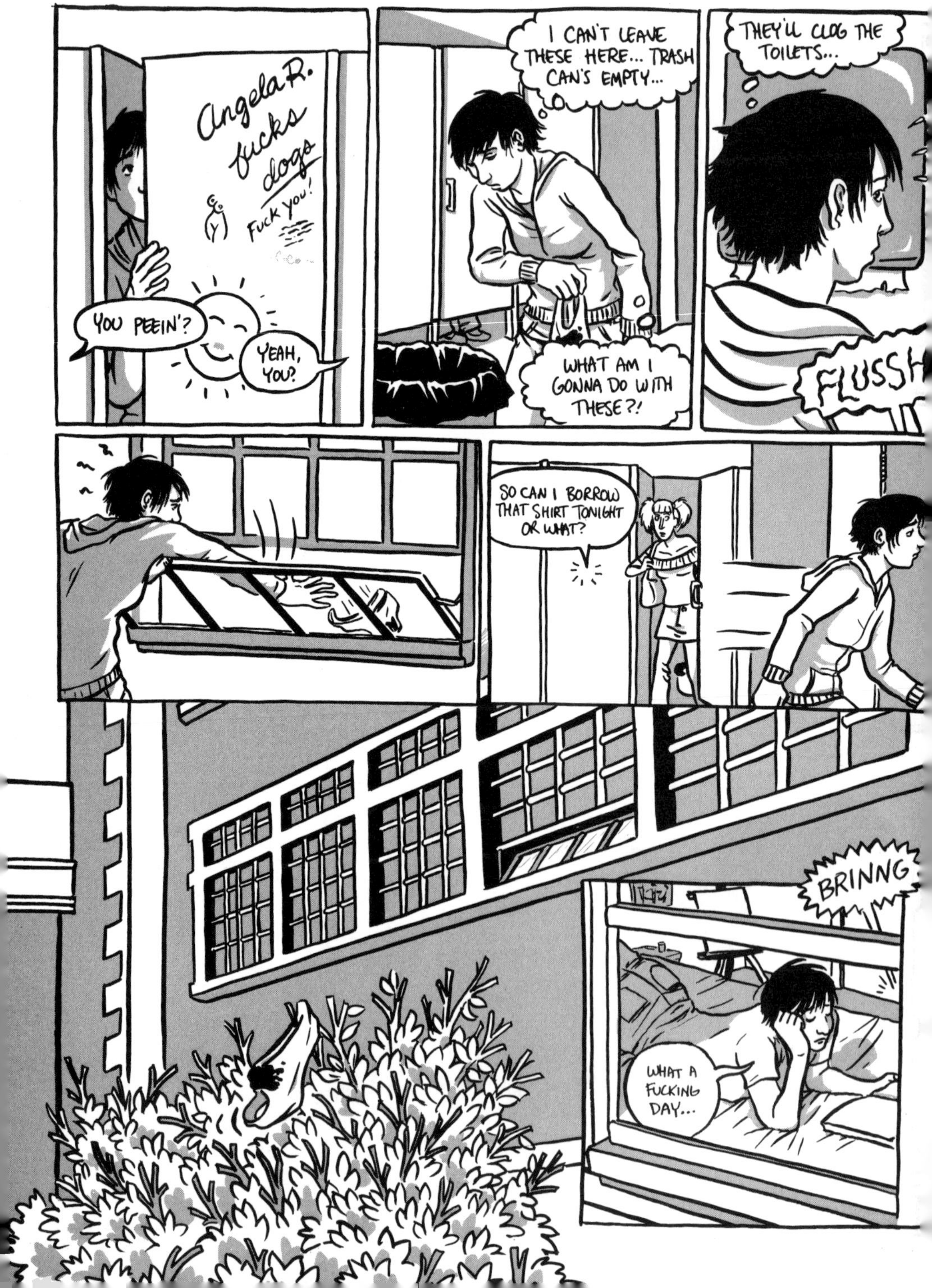
Angela R. fucks dogs
Fuck you!
YOU PEEIN'?
YEAH, YOU?
I CAN'T LEAVE THESE HERE... TRASH CAN'S EMPTY...
WHAT AM I GONNA DO WITH THESE?!
THEY'LL CLOG THE TOILETS...
FLUSSH
SO CAN I BORROW THAT SHIRT TONIGHT OR WHAT?
BRINNG
WHAT A FUCKING DAY...

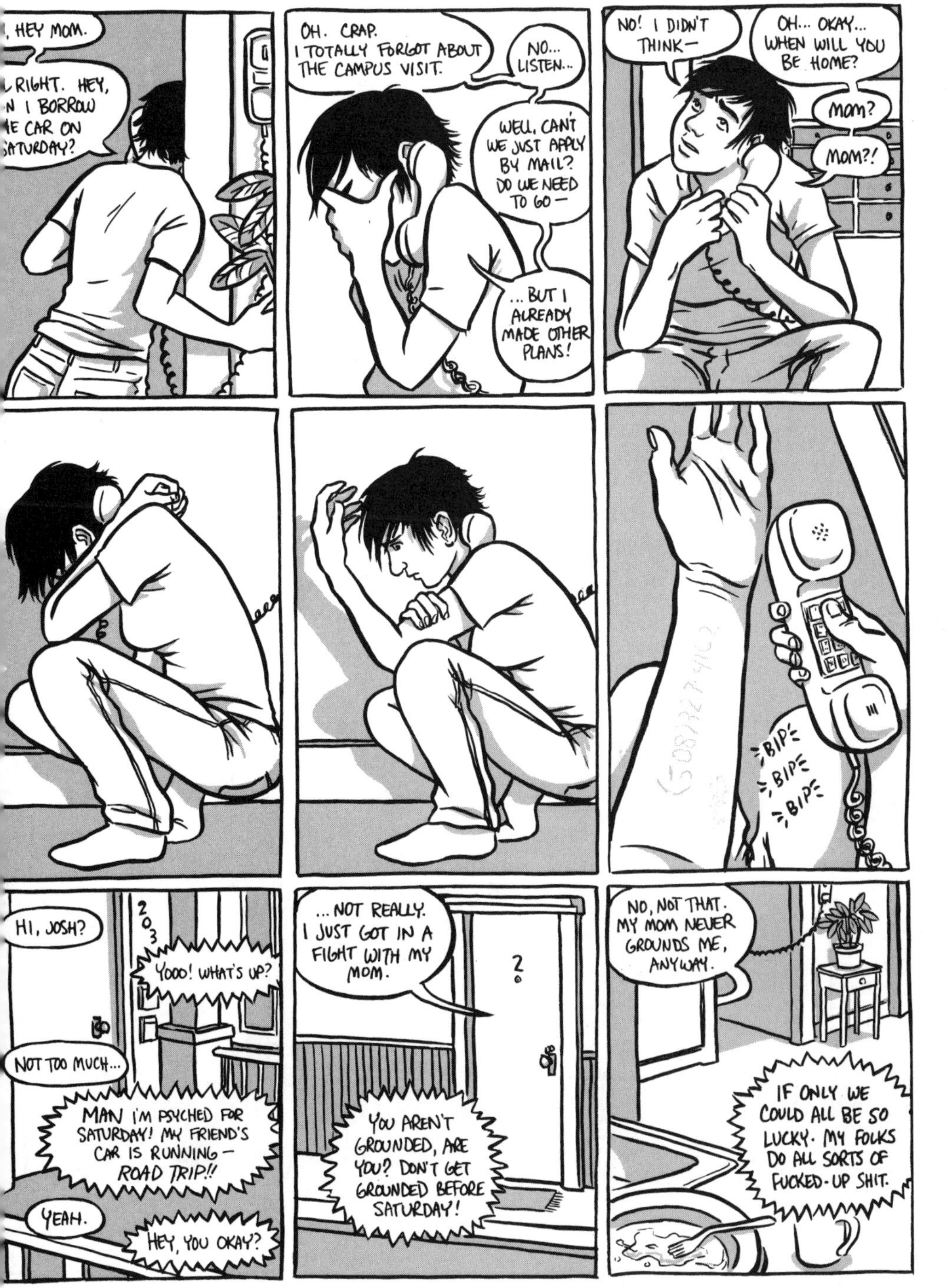
, HEY MOM.
L RIGHT. HEY, N I BORROW HE CAR ON SATURDAY?
OH. CRAP. I TOTALLY FORGOT ABOUT THE CAMPUS VISIT.
NO... LISTEN...
WELL, CAN'T WE JUST APPLY BY MAIL? DO WE NEED TO GO—
...BUT I ALREADY MADE OTHER PLANS!
NO! I DIDN'T THINK—
OH... OKAY... WHEN WILL YOU BE HOME?
MOM?
MOM?!
BIP
BIP
BIP
HI, JOSH?
YOOO! WHAT'S UP?
NOT TOO MUCH...
MAN I'M PSYCHED FOR SATURDAY! MY FRIEND'S CAR IS RUNNING— ROAD TRIP!!
YEAH.
HEY, YOU OKAY?
...NOT REALLY. I JUST GOT IN A FIGHT WITH MY MOM.
YOU AREN'T GROUNDED, ARE YOU? DON'T GET GROUNDED BEFORE SATURDAY!
NO, NOT THAT. MY MOM NEVER GROUNDS ME, ANYWAY.
IF ONLY WE COULD ALL BE SO LUCKY. MY FOLKS DO ALL SORTS OF FUCKED-UP SHIT.

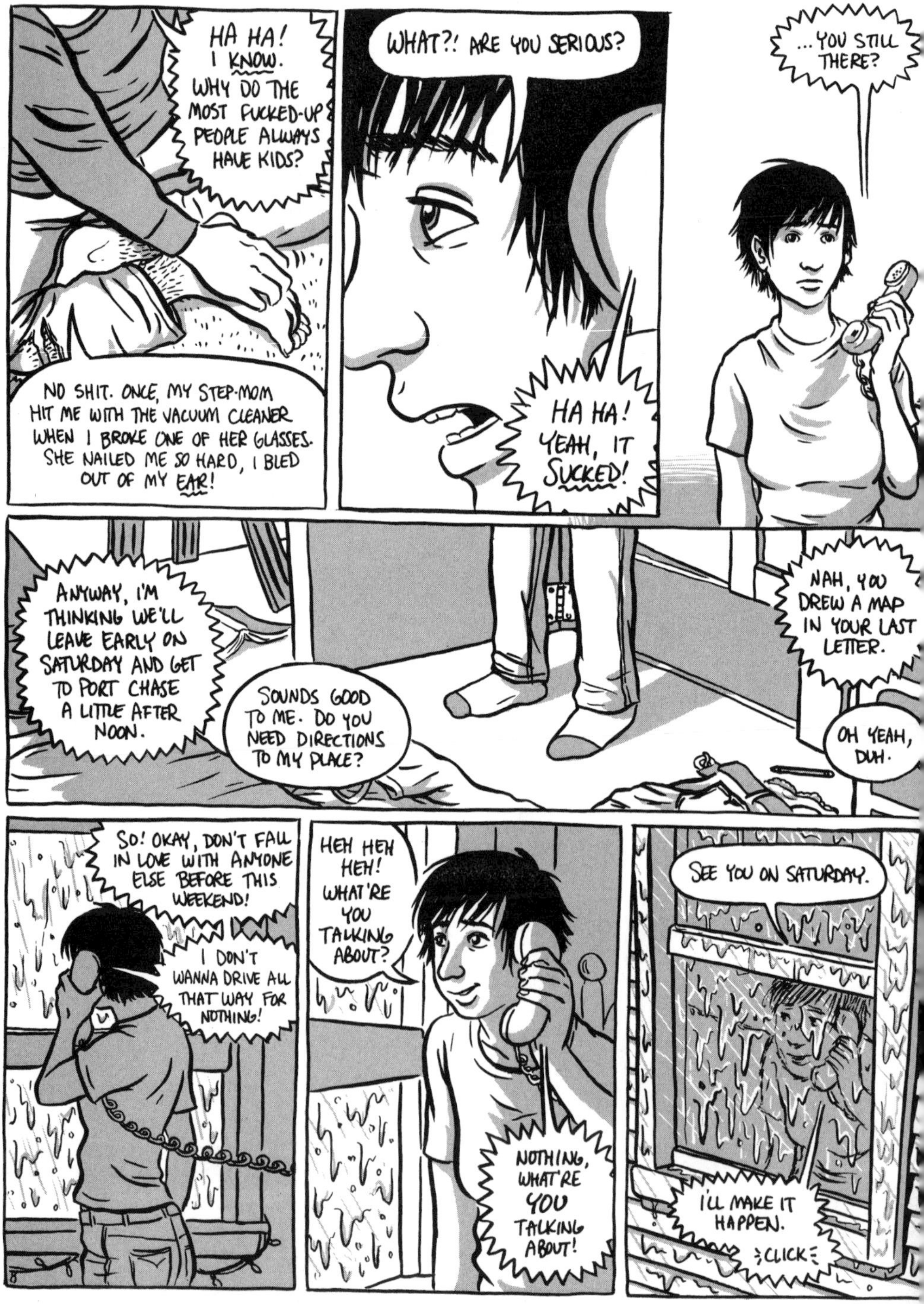
HA HA! I KNOW. WHY DO THE MOST FUCKED-UP PEOPLE ALWAYS HAVE KIDS?
NO SHIT. ONCE, MY STEP-MOM HIT ME WITH THE VACUUM CLEANER WHEN I BROKE ONE OF HER GLASSES. SHE NAILED ME SO HARD, I BLED OUT OF MY EAR!
WHAT?! ARE YOU SERIOUS?
HA HA! YEAH, IT SUCKED!
...YOU STILL THERE?
ANYWAY, I'M THINKING WE'LL LEAVE EARLY ON SATURDAY AND GET TO PORT CHASE A LITTLE AFTER NOON.
SOUNDS GOOD TO ME. DO YOU NEED DIRECTIONS TO MY PLACE?
NAH, YOU DREW A MAP IN YOUR LAST LETTER.
OH YEAH, DUH.
SO! OKAY, DON'T FALL IN LOVE WITH ANYONE ELSE BEFORE THIS WEEKEND!
I DON'T WANNA DRIVE ALL THAT WAY FOR NOTHING!
HEH HEH HEH! WHAT'RE YOU TALKING ABOUT?
NOTHING, WHAT'RE YOU TALKING ABOUT!
SEE YOU ON SATURDAY.
I'LL MAKE IT HAPPEN.
CLICK

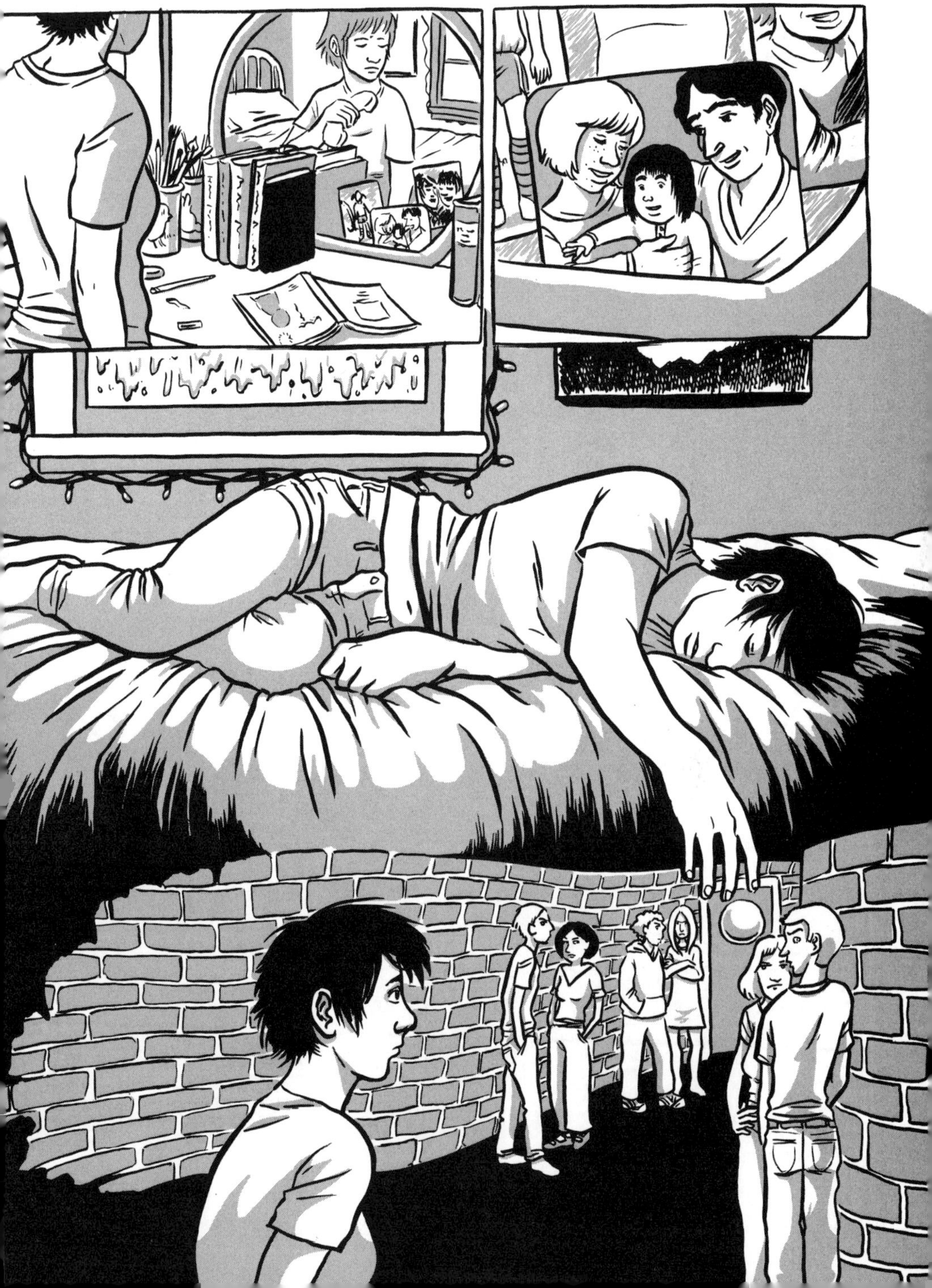

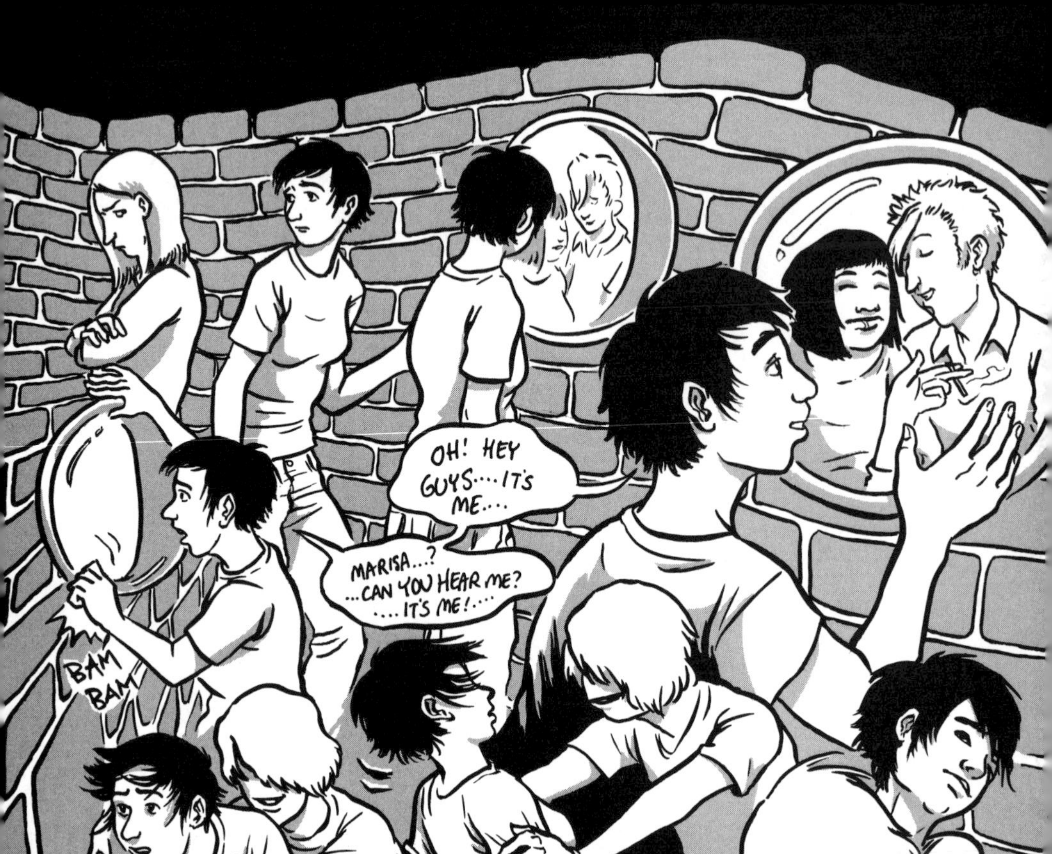
OH! HEY GUYS.... IT'S ME....
MARISA...? ...CAN YOU HEAR ME? .... IT'S ME!....
BAM BAM

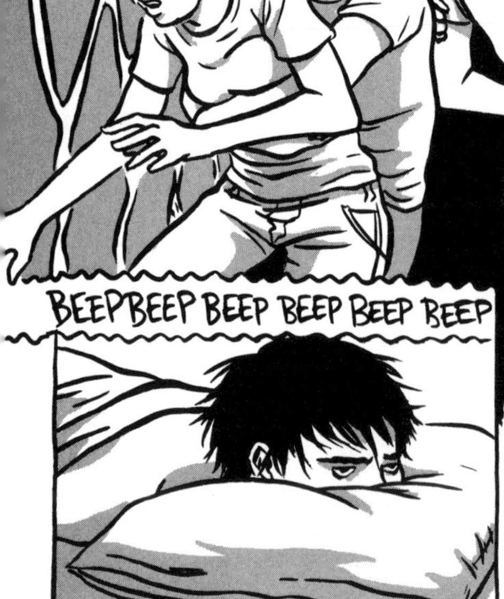
BEEPBEEP BEEP BEEP BEEP BEEP

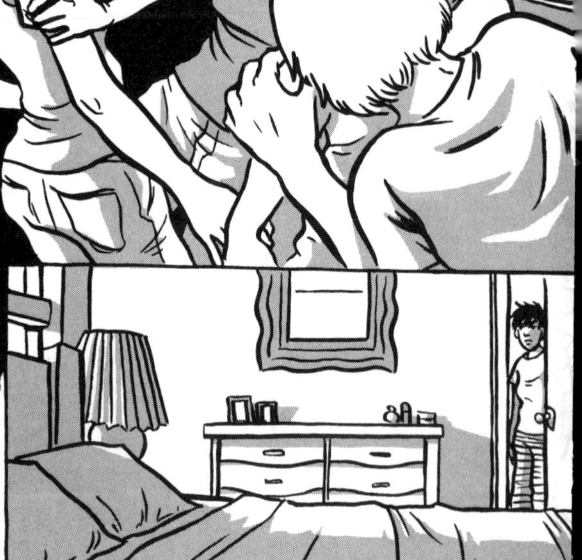

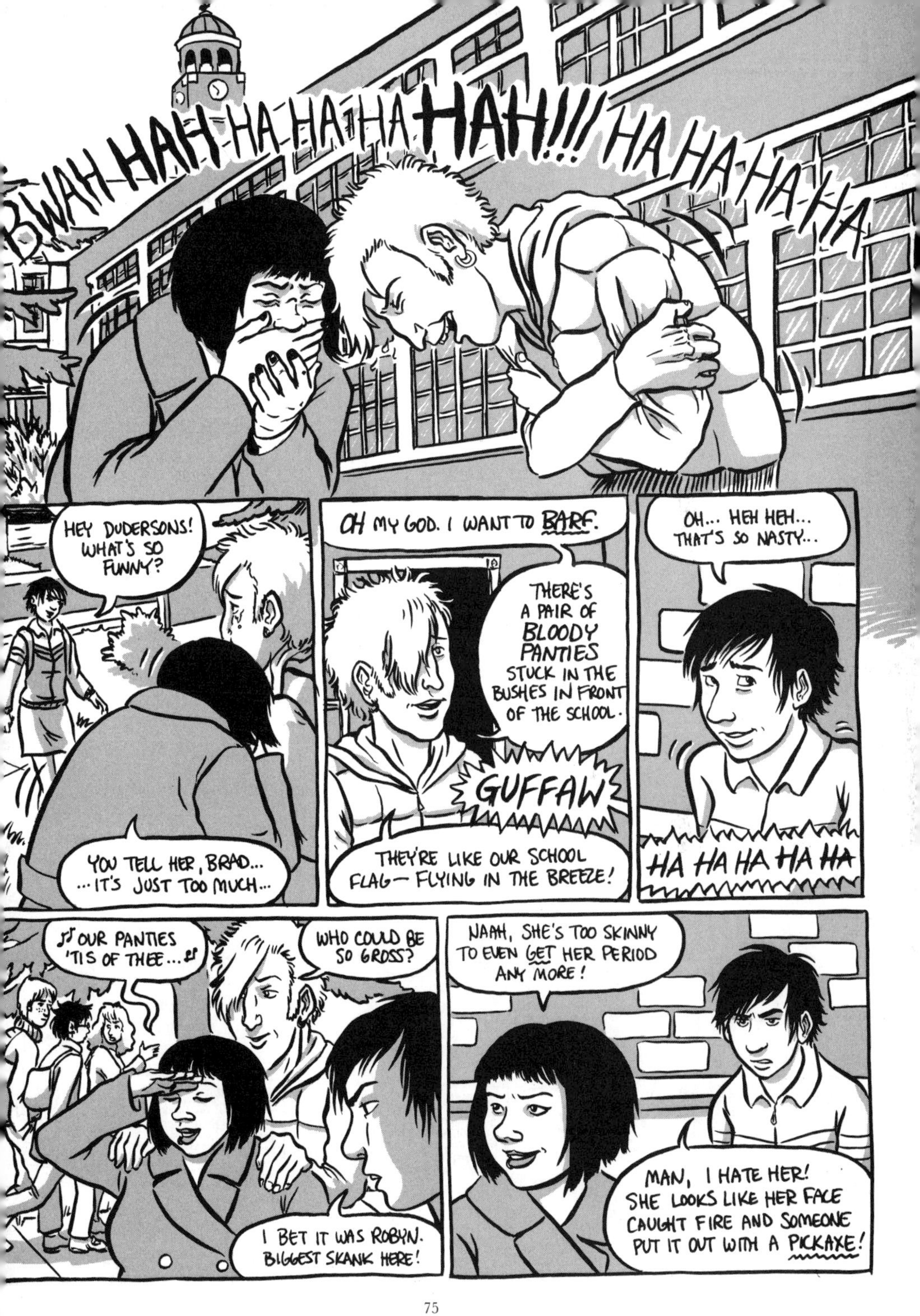
BWAH HAH HA HA HA HA HAH!!! HA HA HA HA HA
HEY DUDERSONS! WHAT'S SO FUNNY?
YOU TELL HER, BRAD... ...IT'S JUST TOO MUCH...
OH MY GOD. I WANT TO BARF.
THERE'S A PAIR OF BLOODY PANTIES STUCK IN THE BUSHES IN FRONT OF THE SCHOOL.
GUFFAW
THEY'RE LIKE OUR SCHOOL FLAG— FLYING IN THE BREEZE!
OH... HEH HEH... THAT'S SO NASTY...
HA HA HA HA HA
♪ OUR PANTIES 'TIS OF THEE... ♪
WHO COULD BE SO GROSS?
I BET IT WAS ROBYN. BIGGEST SKANK HERE!
NAAH, SHE'S TOO SKINNY TO EVEN GET HER PERIOD ANY MORE!
MAN, I HATE HER! SHE LOOKS LIKE HER FACE CAUGHT FIRE AND SOMEONE PUT IT OUT WITH A PICKAXE!

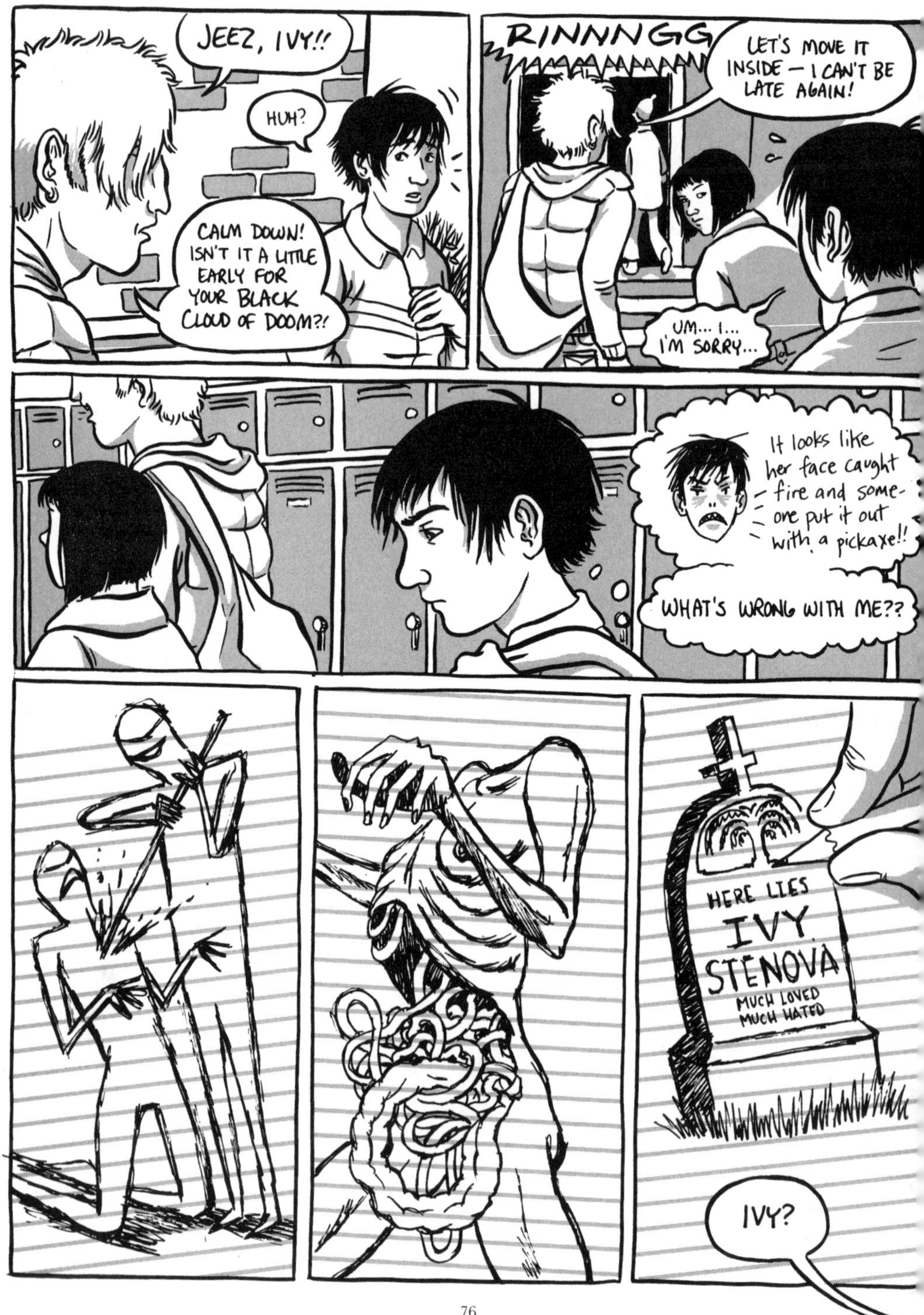
JEEZ, IVY!!
HUH?
CALM DOWN! ISN'T IT A LITTLE EARLY FOR YOUR BLACK CLOUD OF DOOM?!
RINNNGG
LET'S MOVE IT INSIDE — I CAN'T BE LATE AGAIN!
UM... I... I'M SORRY...
It looks like her face caught fire and someone put it out with a pickaxe!!
WHAT'S WRONG WITH ME??
HERE LIES IVY STENOVA
MUCH LOVED MUCH HATED
IVY?

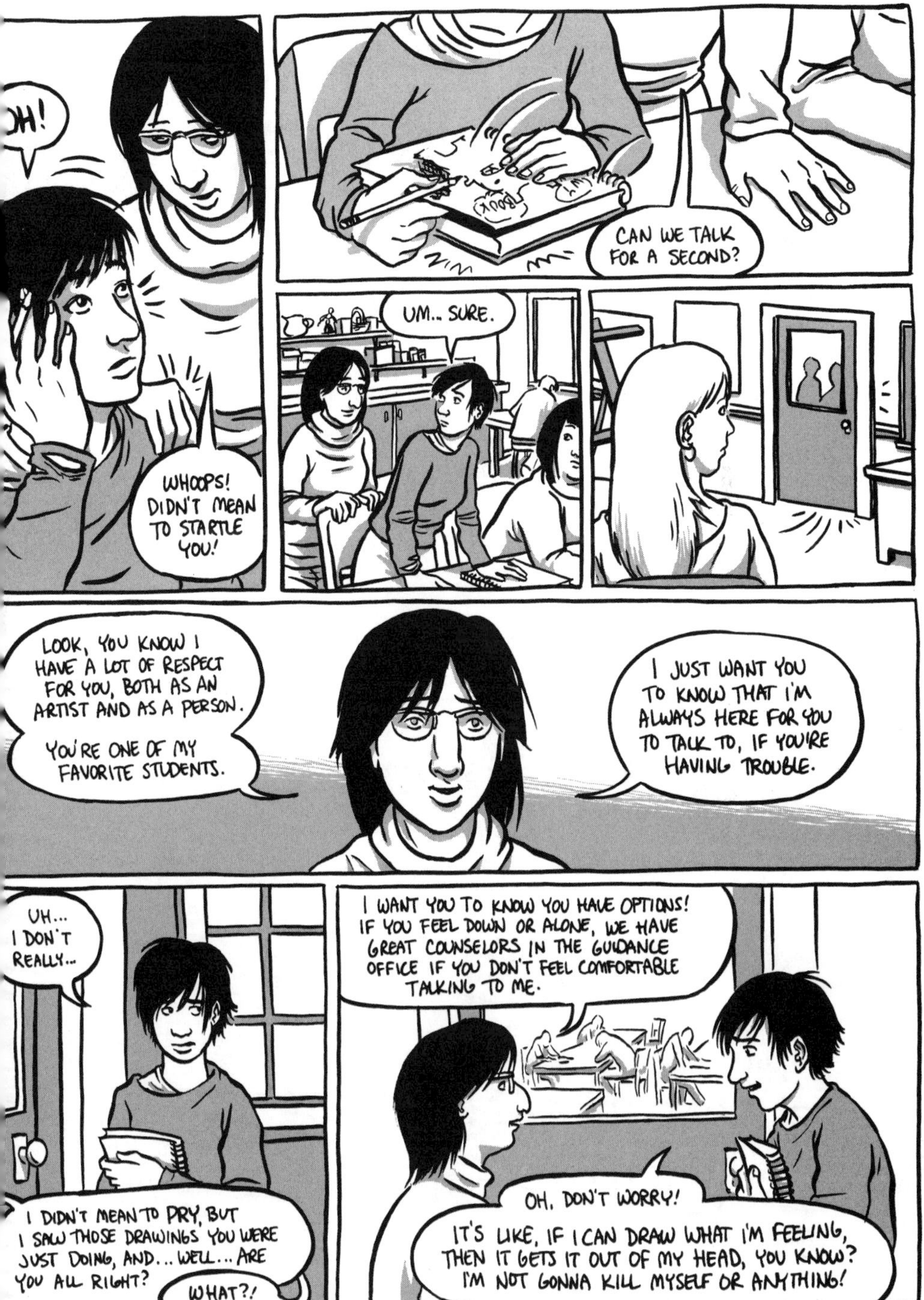
OH!
WHOOPS! DIDN'T MEAN TO STARTLE YOU!
CAN WE TALK FOR A SECOND?
UM.. SURE.
LOOK, YOU KNOW I HAVE A LOT OF RESPECT FOR YOU, BOTH AS AN ARTIST AND AS A PERSON.
YOU'RE ONE OF MY FAVORITE STUDENTS.
I JUST WANT YOU TO KNOW THAT I'M ALWAYS HERE FOR YOU TO TALK TO, IF YOU'RE HAVING TROUBLE.
UH... I DON'T REALLY...
I DIDN'T MEAN TO PRY, BUT I SAW THOSE DRAWINGS YOU WERE JUST DOING, AND... WELL... ARE YOU ALL RIGHT?
WHAT?!
I WANT YOU TO KNOW YOU HAVE OPTIONS! IF YOU FEEL DOWN OR ALONE, WE HAVE GREAT COUNSELORS IN THE GUIDANCE OFFICE IF YOU DON'T FEEL COMFORTABLE TALKING TO ME.
OH, DON'T WORRY!
IT'S LIKE, IF I CAN DRAW WHAT I'M FEELING, THEN IT GETS IT OUT OF MY HEAD, YOU KNOW? I'M NOT GONNA KILL MYSELF OR ANYTHING!

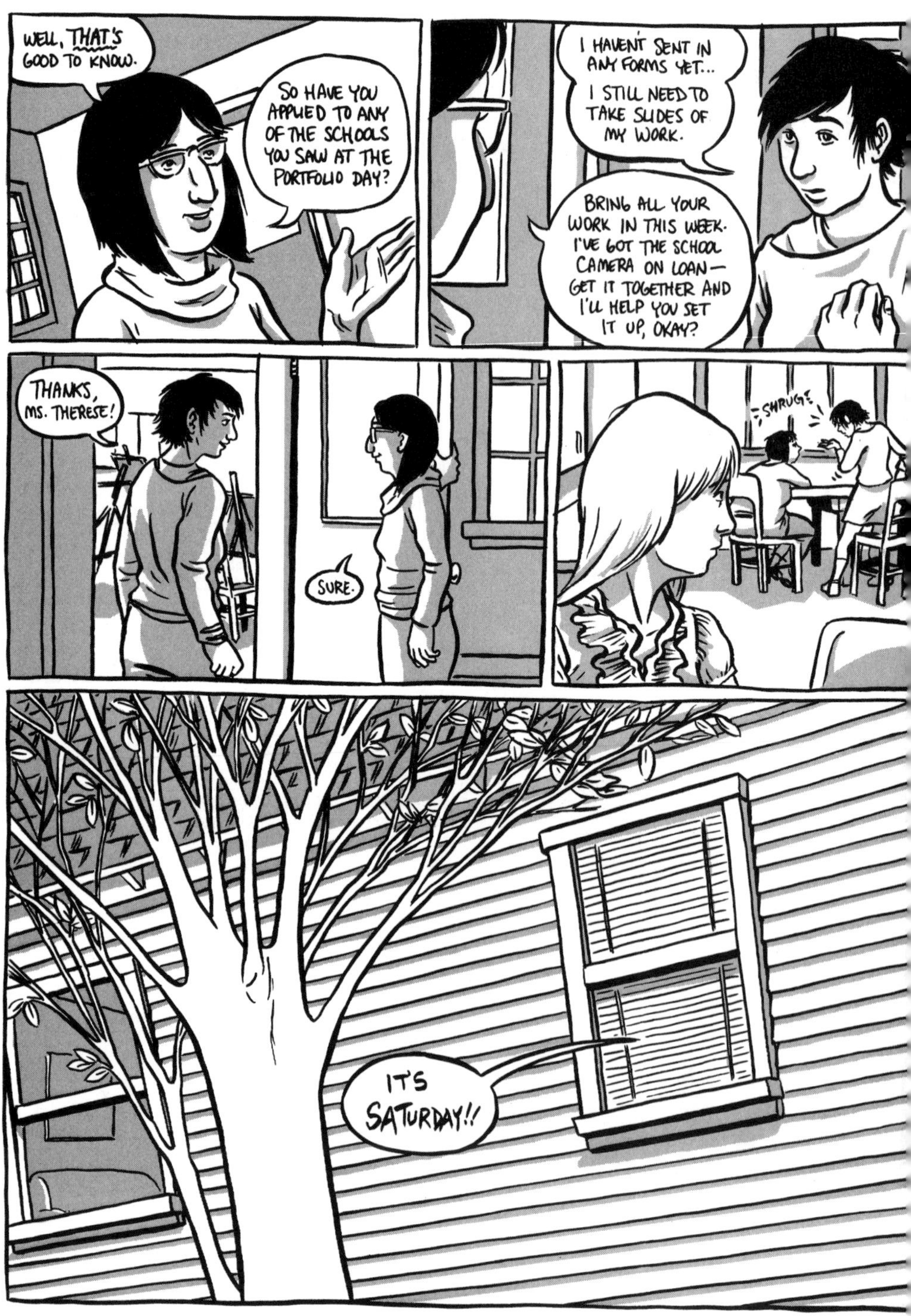
WELL, THAT'S GOOD TO KNOW.
SO HAVE YOU APPLIED TO ANY OF THE SCHOOLS YOU SAW AT THE PORTFOLIO DAY?
I HAVEN'T SENT IN ANY FORMS YET... I STILL NEED TO TAKE SLIDES OF MY WORK.
BRING ALL YOUR WORK IN THIS WEEK. I'VE GOT THE SCHOOL CAMERA ON LOAN— GET IT TOGETHER AND I'LL HELP YOU SET IT UP, OKAY?
THANKS, MS. THERESE!
SURE.
SHRUG
IT'S SATURDAY!!

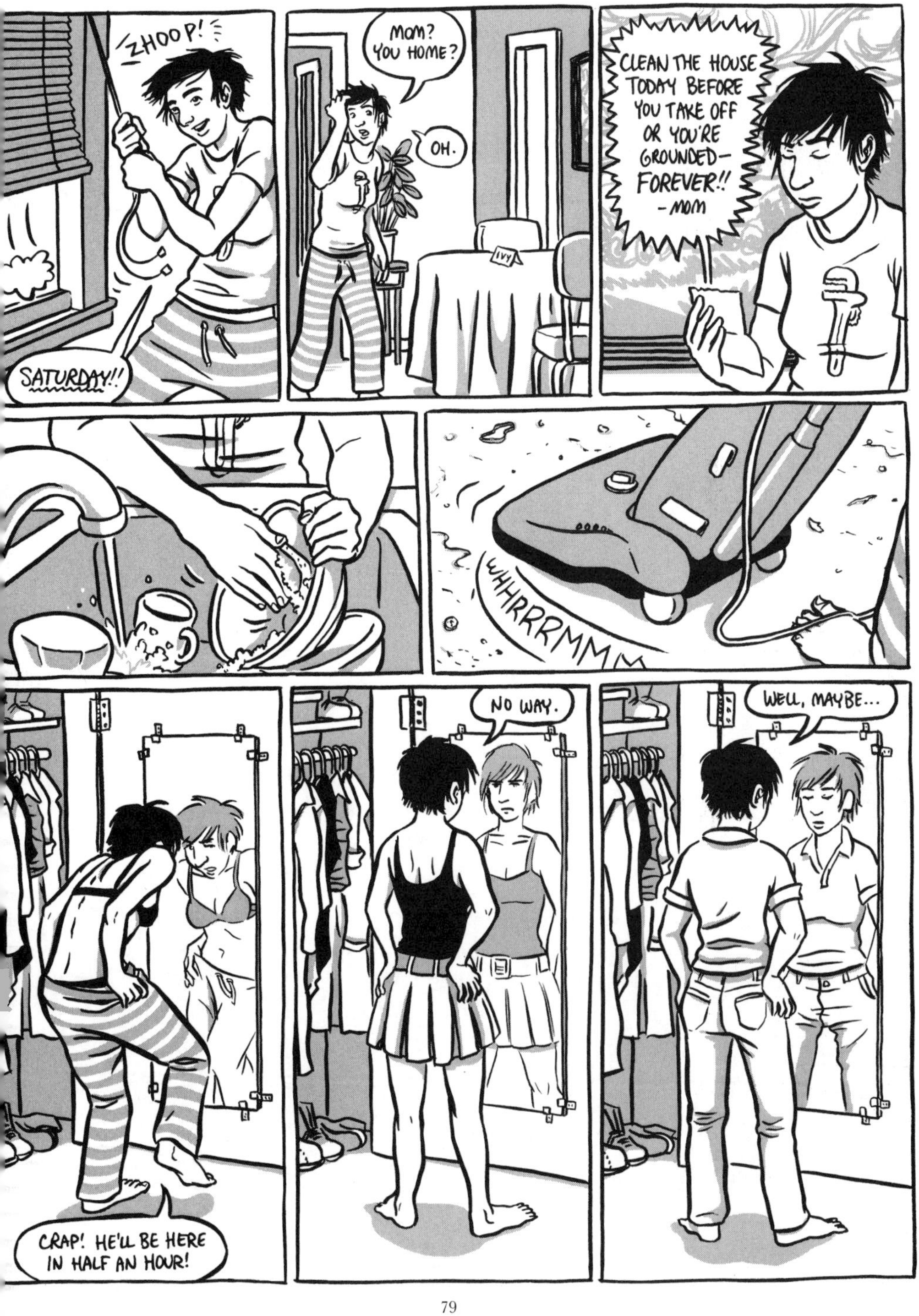
ZHOOP!
SATURDAY!!
MOM? YOU HOME?
OH.
CLEAN THE HOUSE TODAY BEFORE YOU TAKE OFF OR YOU'RE GROUNDED— FOREVER!! -MOM
IVY
WHHRRRRMMM
CRAP! HE'LL BE HERE IN HALF AN HOUR!
NO WAY.
WELL, MAYBE...

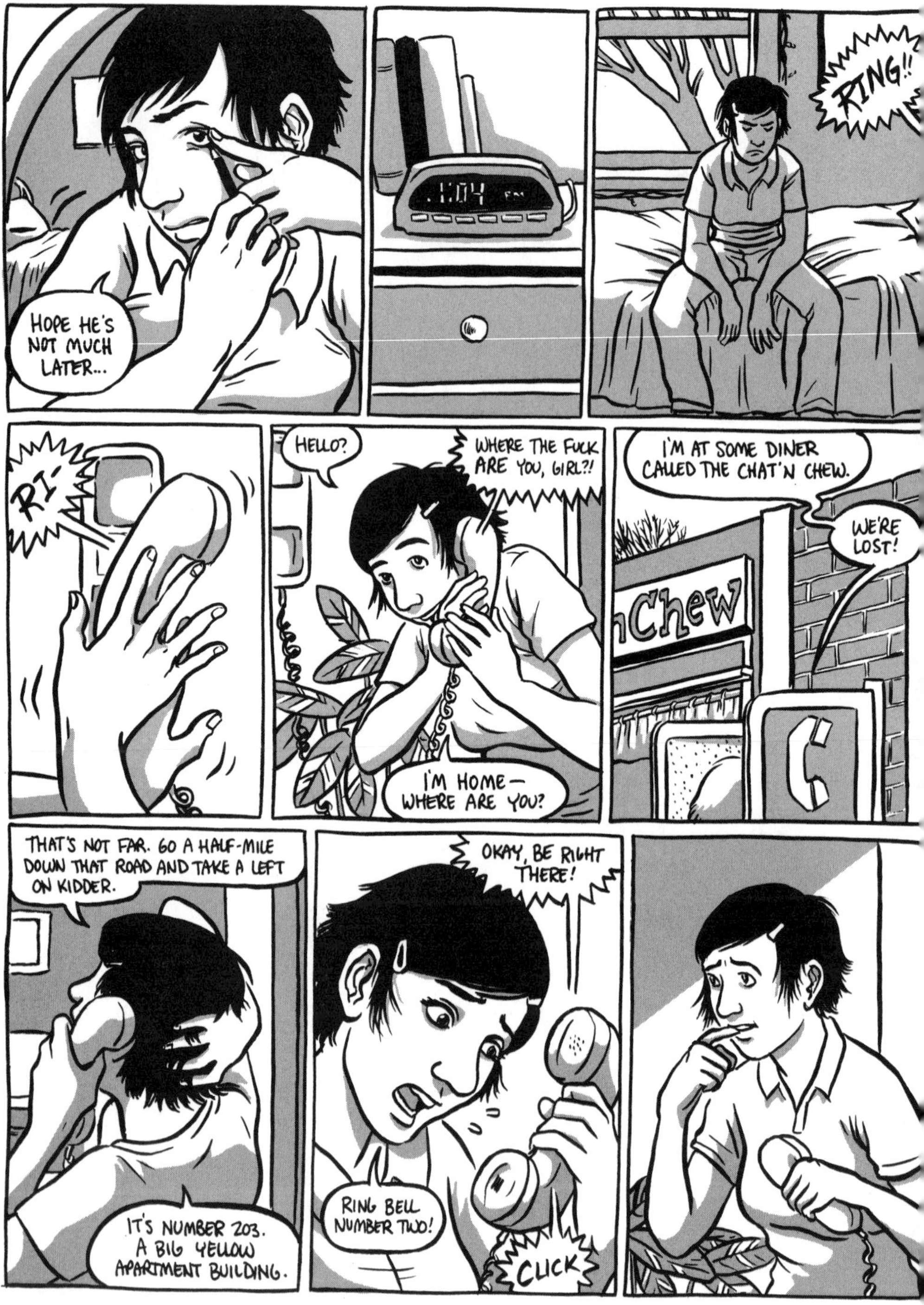
HOPE HE'S NOT MUCH LATER...
1:04 PM
RING!!
RI-
HELLO?
WHERE THE FUCK ARE YOU, GIRL?!
I'M HOME— WHERE ARE YOU?
I'M AT SOME DINER CALLED THE CHAT'N CHEW.
WE'RE LOST!
nChew
THAT'S NOT FAR. GO A HALF-MILE DOWN THAT ROAD AND TAKE A LEFT ON KIDDER.
IT'S NUMBER 203. A BIG YELLOW APARTMENT BUILDING.
OKAY, BE RIGHT THERE!
RING BELL NUMBER TWO!
CLICK

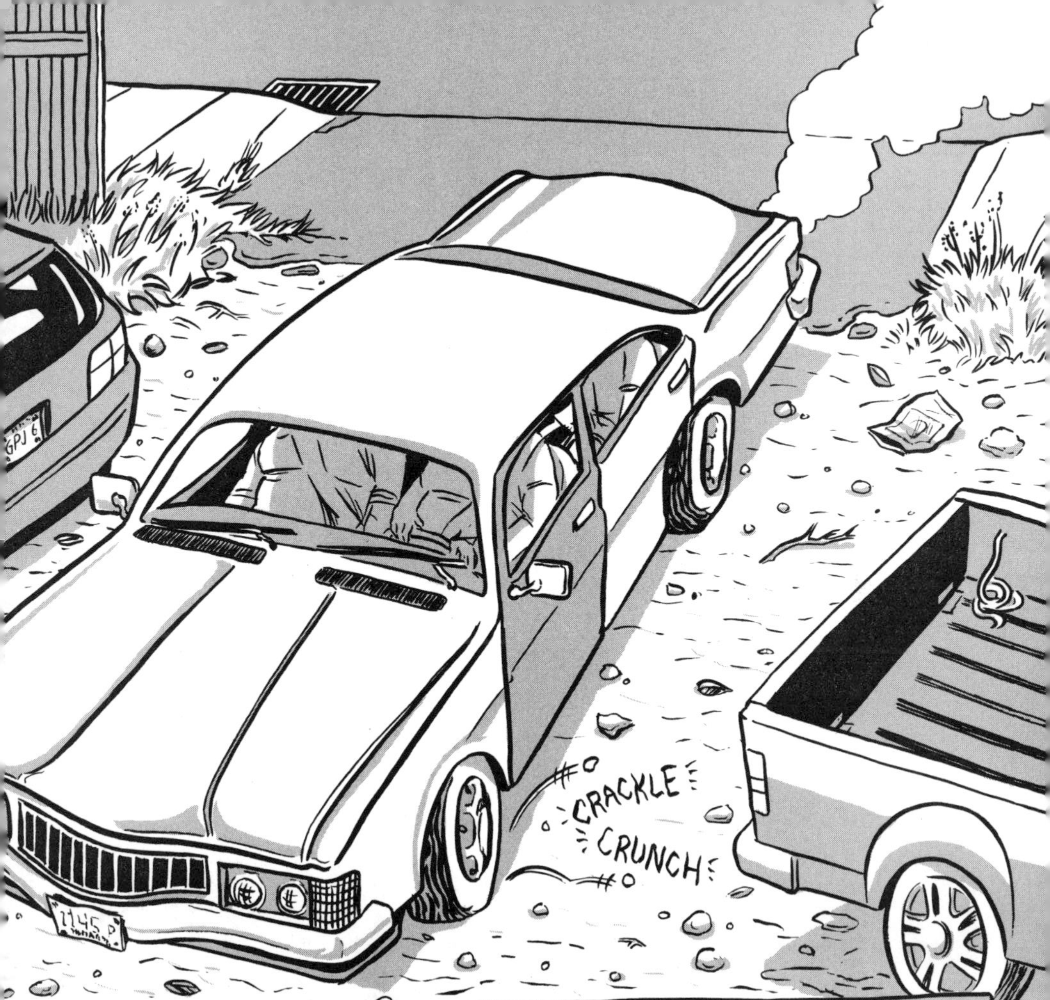
CRACKLE
CRUNCH

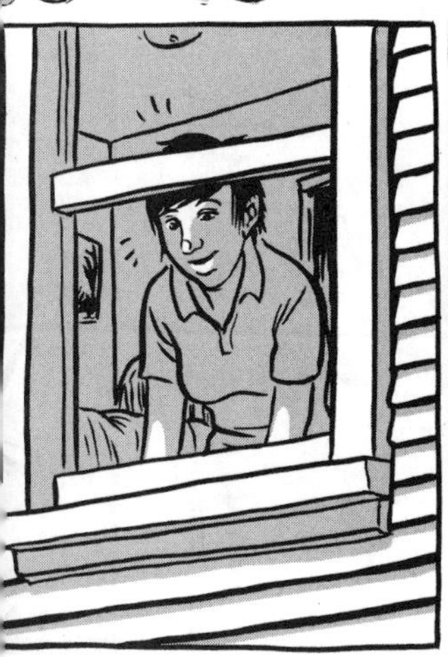

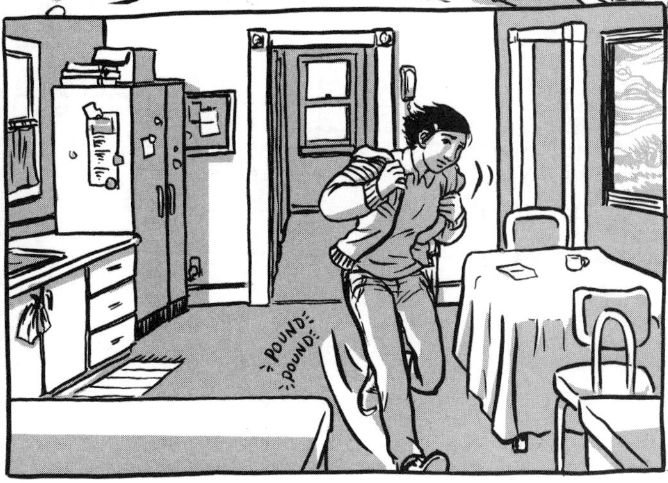
POUND
POUND

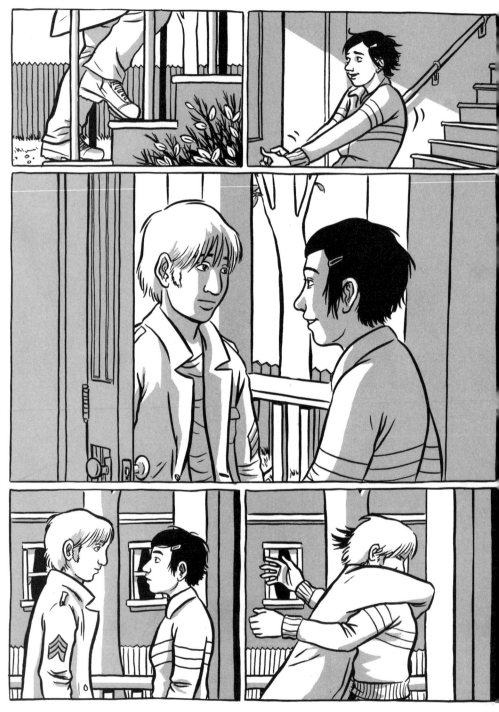

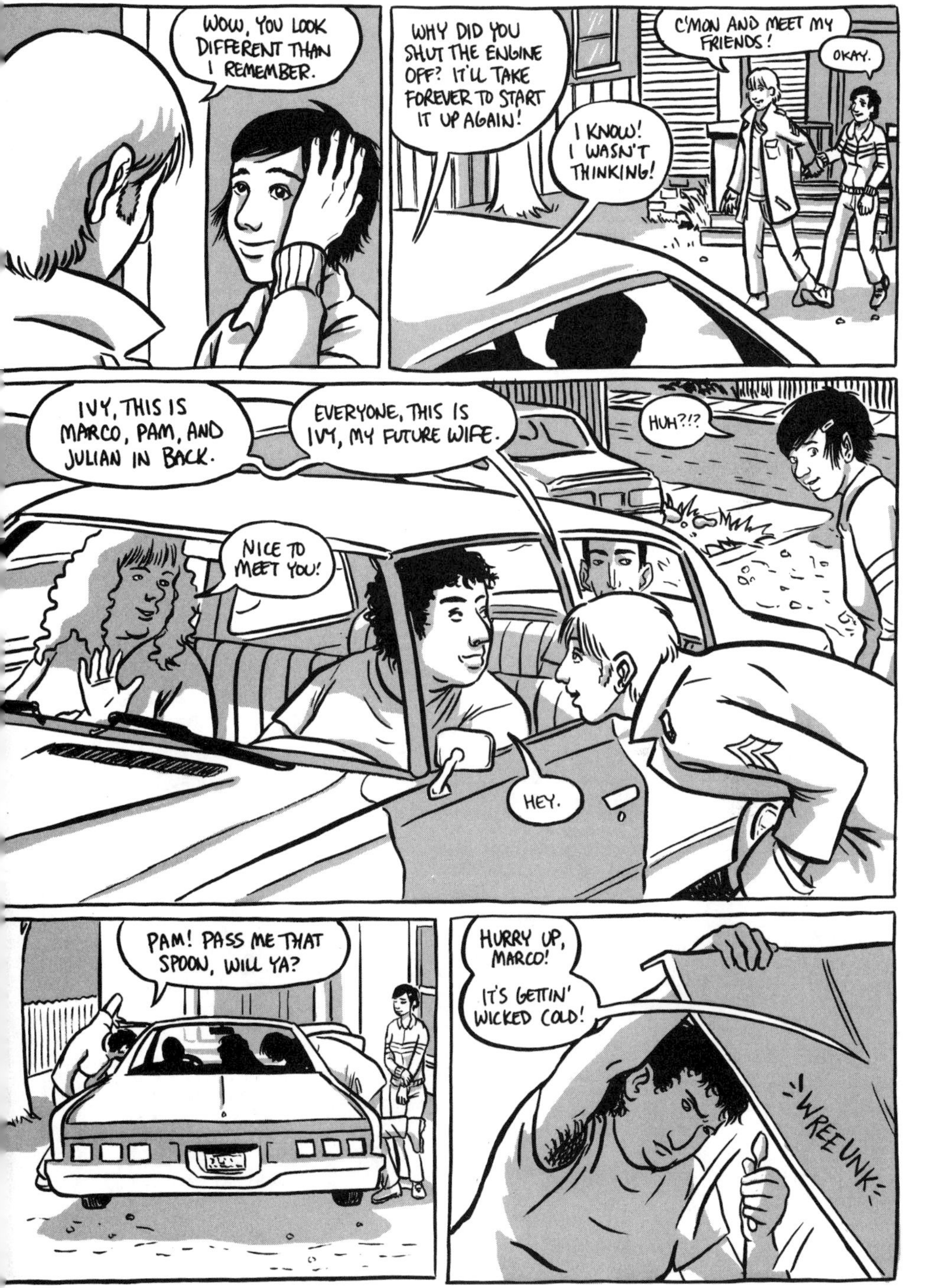
WOW, YOU LOOK DIFFERENT THAN I REMEMBER.
WHY DID YOU SHUT THE ENGINE OFF? IT'LL TAKE FOREVER TO START IT UP AGAIN!
I KNOW! I WASN'T THINKING!
C'MON AND MEET MY FRIENDS!
OKAY.
IVY, THIS IS MARCO, PAM, AND JULIAN IN BACK.
EVERYONE, THIS IS IVY, MY FUTURE WIFE.
HUH?!?
NICE TO MEET YOU!
HEY.
PAM! PASS ME THAT SPOON, WILL YA?
HURRY UP, MARCO!
IT'S GETTIN' WICKED COLD!
WREEUNK

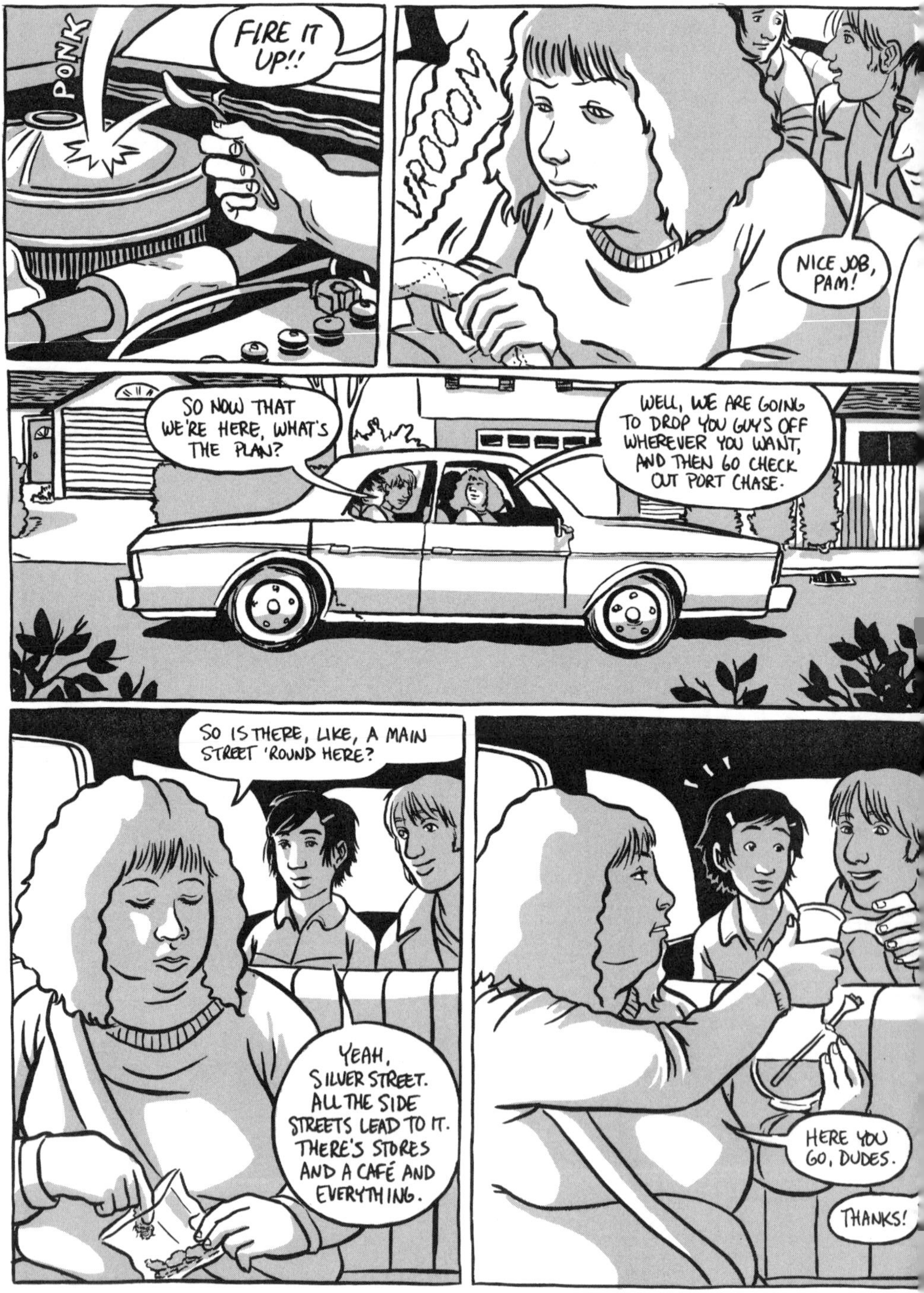

PONK
FIRE IT UP!!
VROOOM
NICE JOB, PAM!
SO NOW THAT WE'RE HERE, WHAT'S THE PLAN?
WELL, WE ARE GOING TO DROP YOU GUYS OFF WHEREVER YOU WANT, AND THEN GO CHECK OUT PORT CHASE.
SO IS THERE, LIKE, A MAIN STREET 'ROUND HERE?
YEAH, SILVER STREET. ALL THE SIDE STREETS LEAD TO IT. THERE'S STORES AND A CAFÉ AND EVERYTHING.
HERE YOU GO, DUDES.
THANKS!

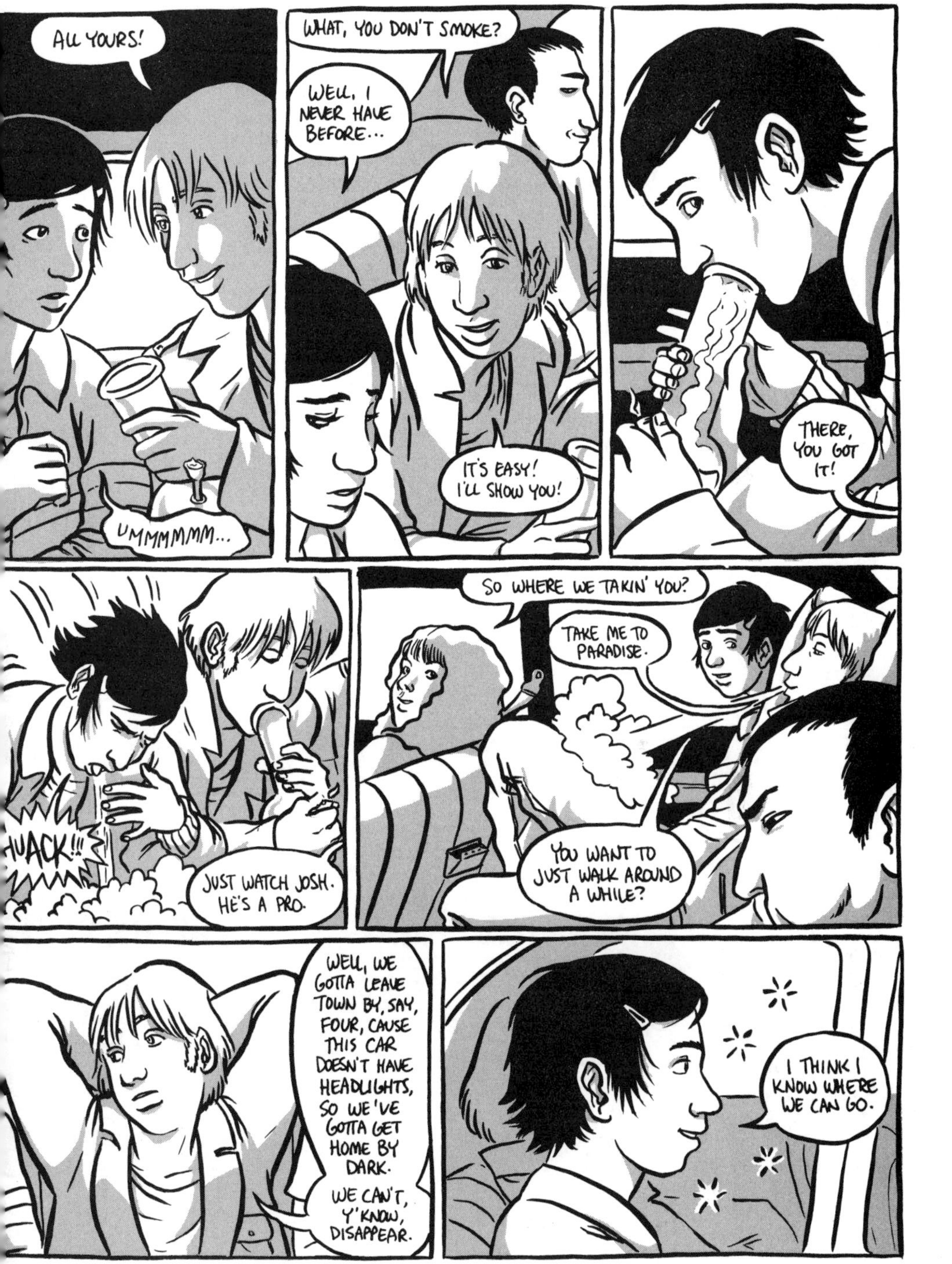
ALL YOURS!
UMMMMMM...
WHAT, YOU DON'T SMOKE?
WELL, I NEVER HAVE BEFORE...
IT'S EASY! I'LL SHOW YOU!
THERE, YOU GOT IT!
HUACK!!!
JUST WATCH JOSH. HE'S A PRO.
SO WHERE WE TAKIN' YOU?
TAKE ME TO PARADISE.
YOU WANT TO JUST WALK AROUND A WHILE?
WELL, WE GOTTA LEAVE TOWN BY, SAY, FOUR, CAUSE THIS CAR DOESN'T HAVE HEADLIGHTS, SO WE'VE GOTTA GET HOME BY DARK.
WE CAN'T, Y'KNOW, DISAPPEAR.
I THINK I KNOW WHERE WE CAN GO.

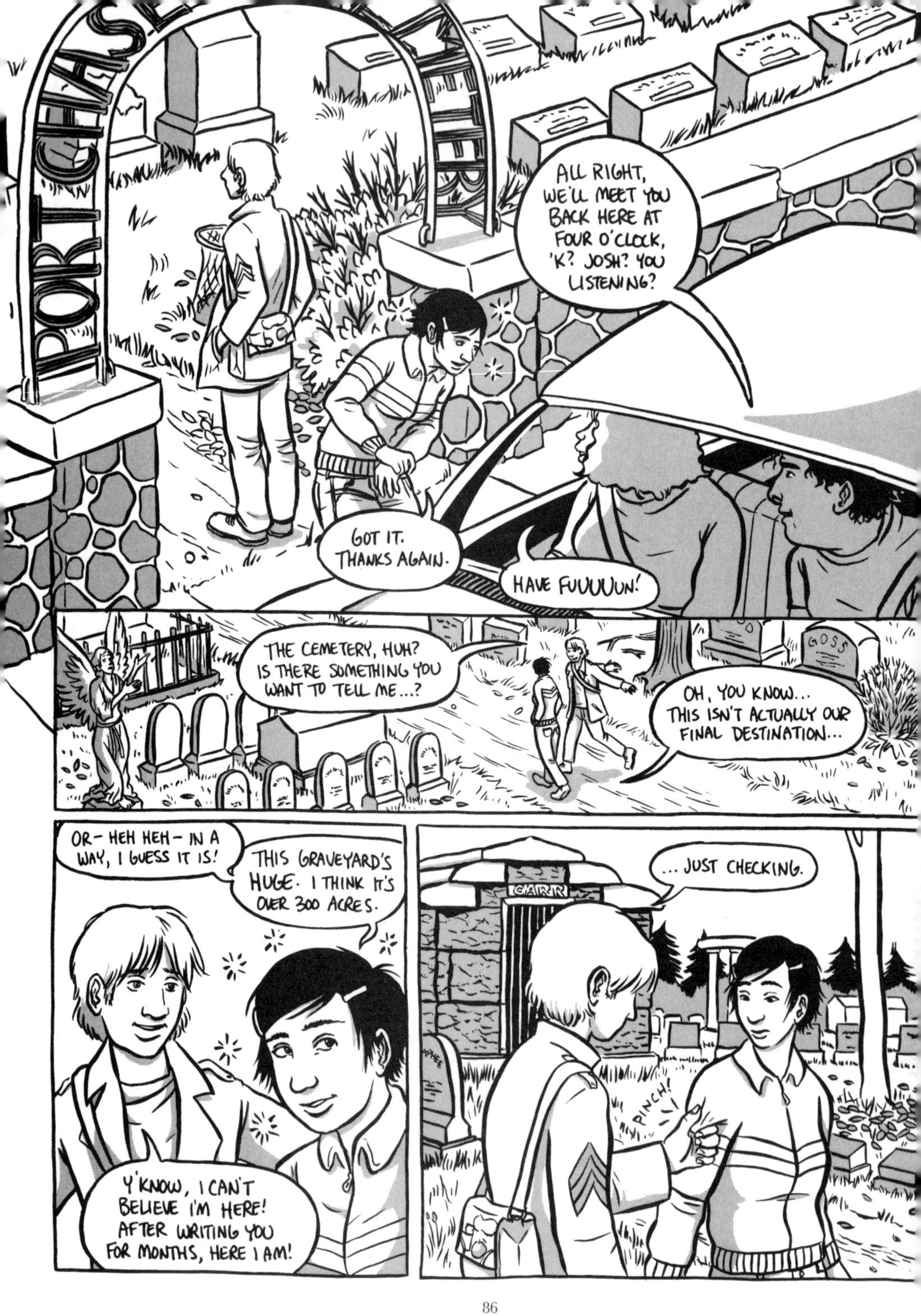
PORTCHASE
ALL RIGHT, WE'LL MEET YOU BACK HERE AT FOUR O'CLOCK, 'K? JOSH? YOU LISTENING?
GOT IT. THANKS AGAIN.
HAVE FUUUUUN!
THE CEMETERY, HUH? IS THERE SOMETHING YOU WANT TO TELL ME...?
GOSS
OH, YOU KNOW... THIS ISN'T ACTUALLY OUR FINAL DESTINATION...
OR– HEH HEH– IN A WAY, I GUESS IT IS!
THIS GRAVEYARD'S HUGE. I THINK IT'S OVER 300 ACRES.
Y'KNOW, I CAN'T BELIEVE I'M HERE! AFTER WRITING YOU FOR MONTHS, HERE I AM!
GARR
... JUST CHECKING.
PINCH!

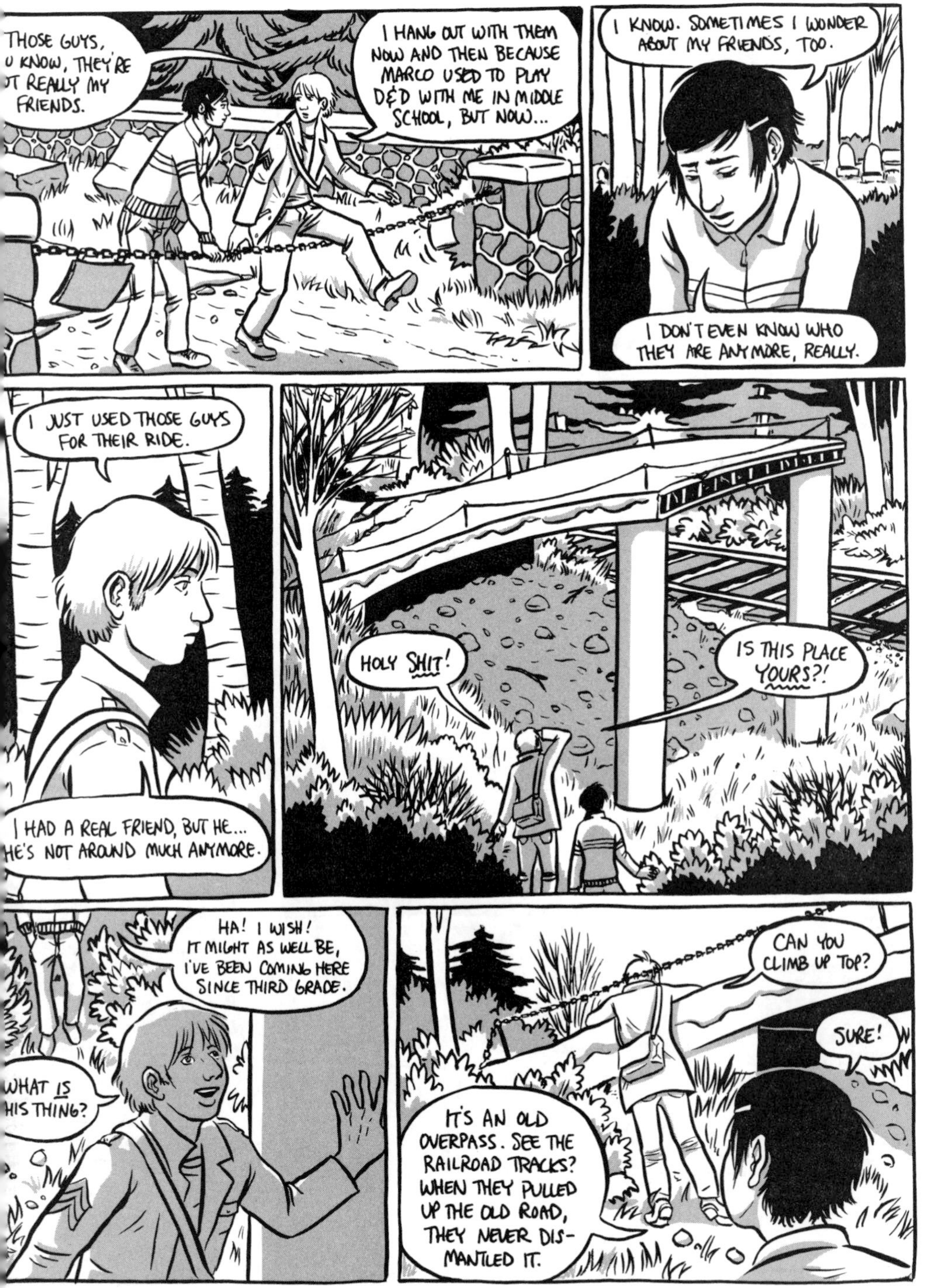
THOSE GUYS, U KNOW, THEY'RE T REALLY MY FRIENDS.
I HANG OUT WITH THEM NOW AND THEN BECAUSE MARCO USED TO PLAY D&D WITH ME IN MIDDLE SCHOOL, BUT NOW...
I KNOW. SOMETIMES I WONDER ABOUT MY FRIENDS, TOO.
I DON'T EVEN KNOW WHO THEY ARE ANYMORE, REALLY.
I JUST USED THOSE GUYS FOR THEIR RIDE.
I HAD A REAL FRIEND, BUT HE... HE'S NOT AROUND MUCH ANYMORE.
HOLY SHIT!
IS THIS PLACE YOURS?!
HA! I WISH! IT MIGHT AS WELL BE, I'VE BEEN COMING HERE SINCE THIRD GRADE.
WHAT IS HIS THING?
CAN YOU CLIMB UP TOP?
SURE!
IT'S AN OLD OVERPASS. SEE THE RAILROAD TRACKS? WHEN THEY PULLED UP THE OLD ROAD, THEY NEVER DIS-MANTLED IT.

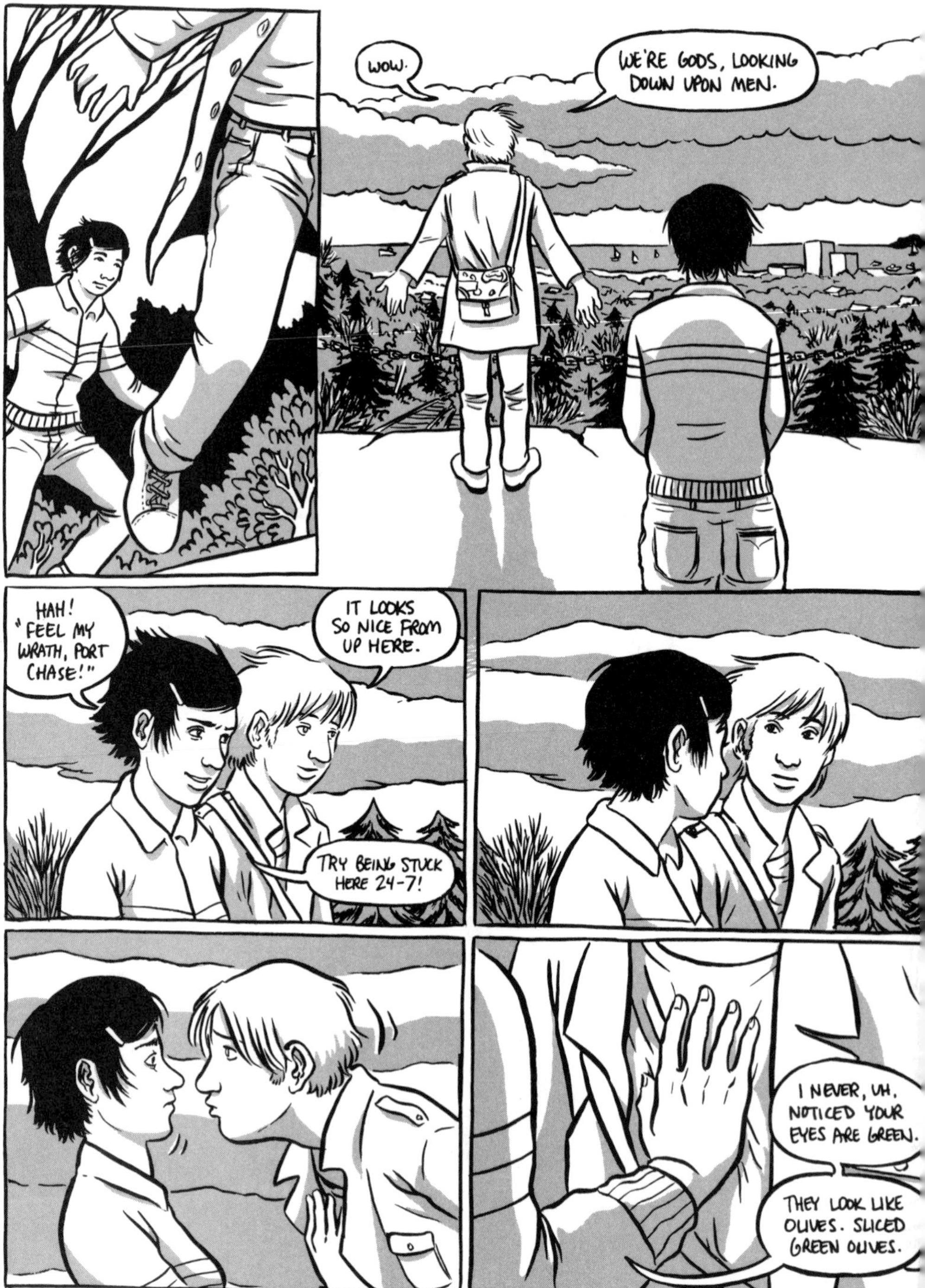
WOW.
WE'RE GODS, LOOKING DOWN UPON MEN.
HAH! "FEEL MY WRATH, PORT CHASE!"
IT LOOKS SO NICE FROM UP HERE.
TRY BEING STUCK HERE 24-7!
I NEVER, UH, NOTICED YOUR EYES ARE GREEN.
THEY LOOK LIKE OLIVES. SLICED GREEN OLIVES.

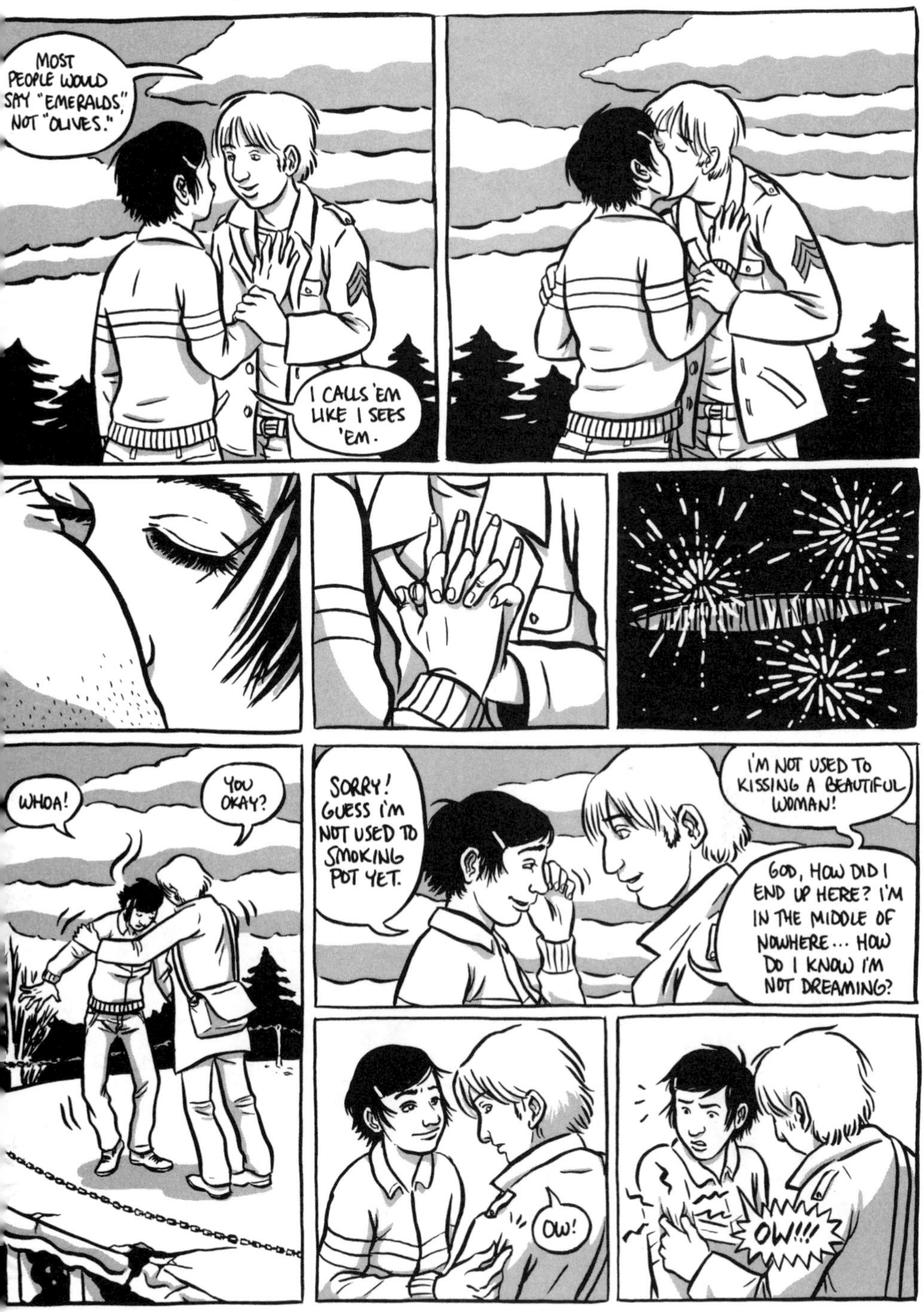
MOST PEOPLE WOULD SAY "EMERALDS," NOT "OLIVES."
I CALLS 'EM LIKE I SEES 'EM.
WHOA!
YOU OKAY?
SORRY! GUESS I'M NOT USED TO SMOKING POT YET.
I'M NOT USED TO KISSING A BEAUTIFUL WOMAN!
GOD, HOW DID I END UP HERE? I'M IN THE MIDDLE OF NOWHERE... HOW DO I KNOW I'M NOT DREAMING?
OW!
OW!!!

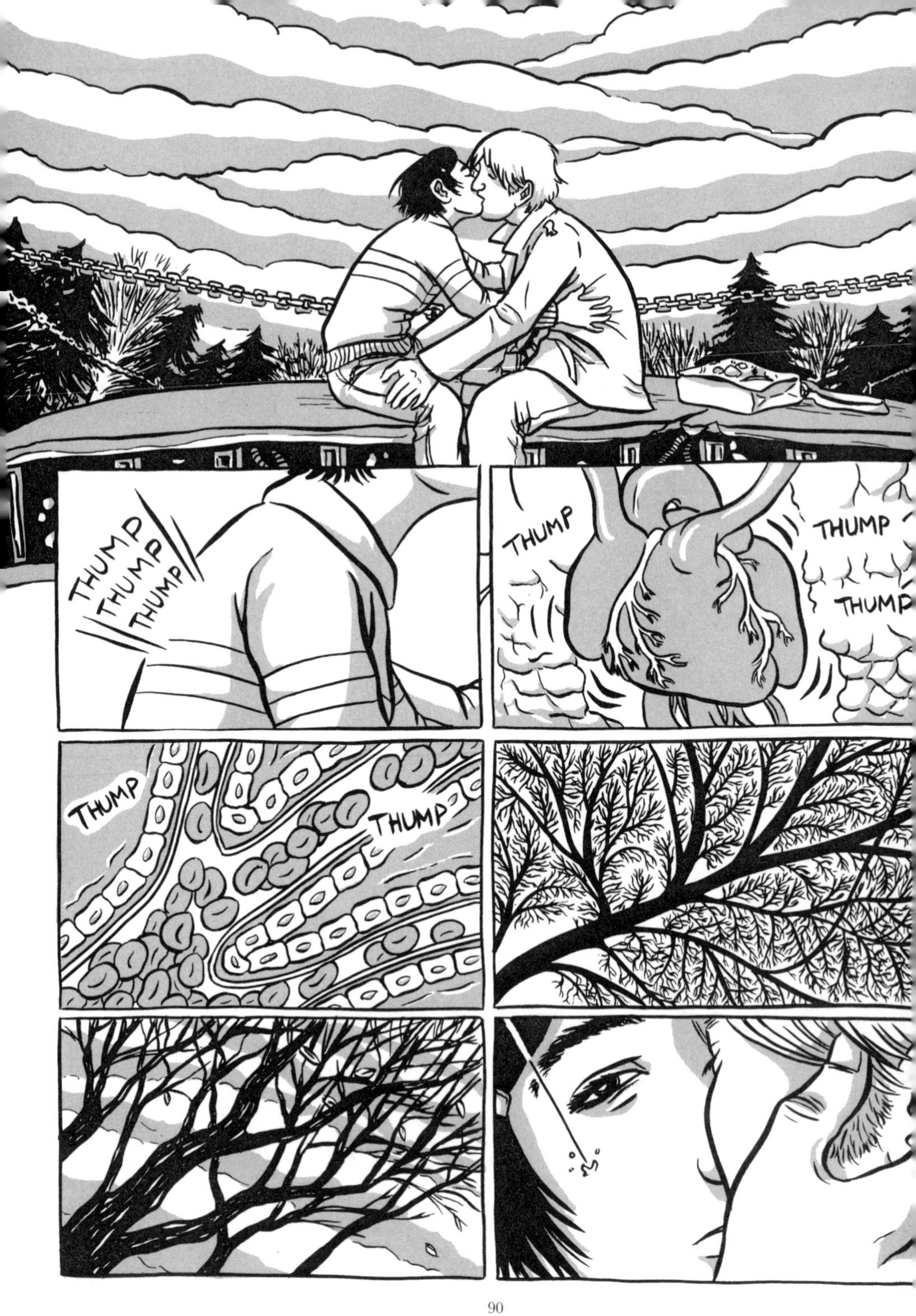
THUMP
THUMP
THUMP
THUMP
THUMP
THUMP
THUMP
THUMP

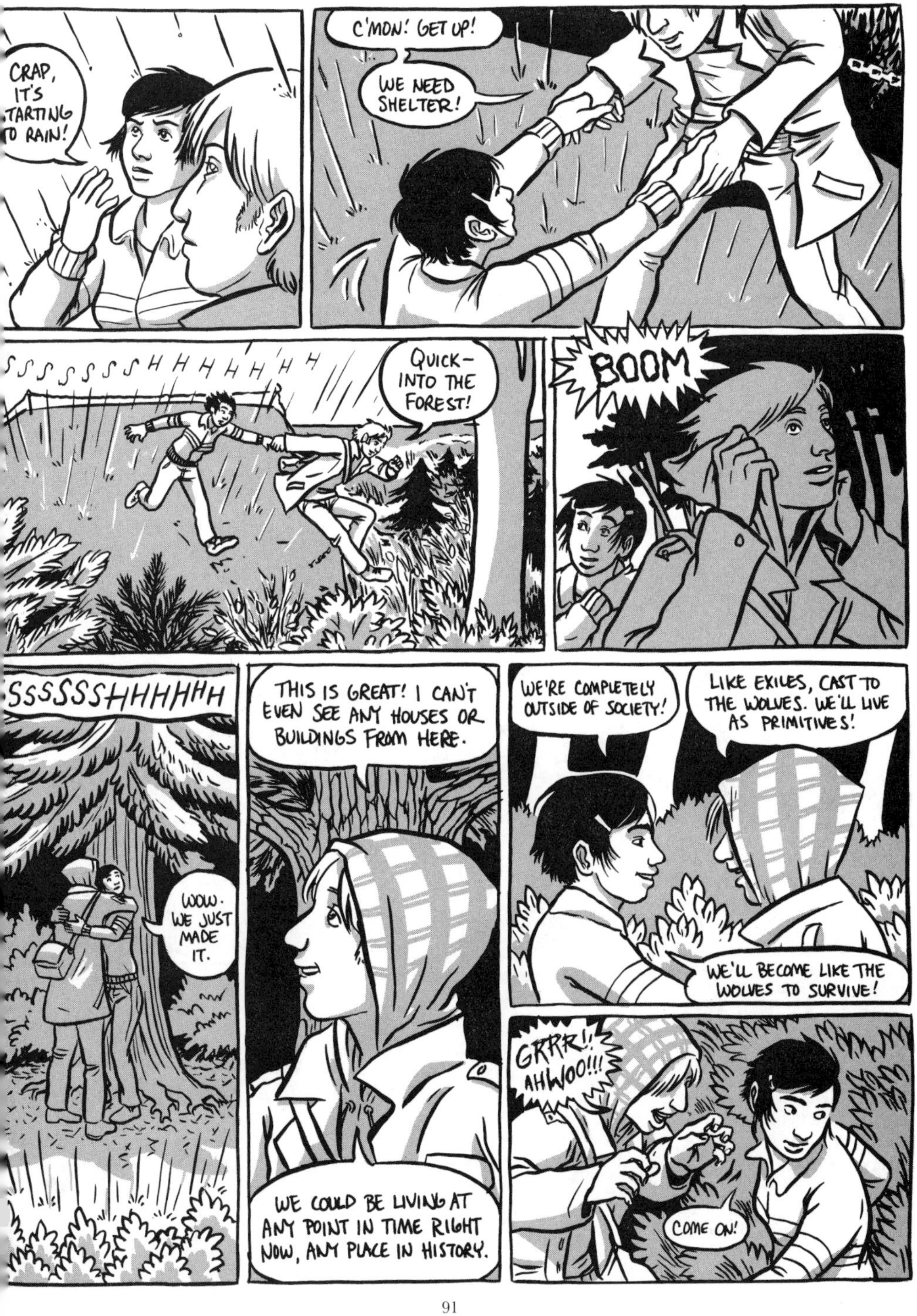
CRAP, IT'S STARTING TO RAIN!
C'MON! GET UP!
WE NEED SHELTER!
SSSSSSSHHHHHHHH
QUICK- INTO THE FOREST!
BOOM
SSSSSSHHHHHH
WOW. WE JUST MADE IT.
THIS IS GREAT! I CAN'T EVEN SEE ANY HOUSES OR BUILDINGS FROM HERE.
WE COULD BE LIVING AT ANY POINT IN TIME RIGHT NOW, ANY PLACE IN HISTORY.
WE'RE COMPLETELY OUTSIDE OF SOCIETY!
LIKE EXILES, CAST TO THE WOLVES. WE'LL LIVE AS PRIMITIVES!
WE'LL BECOME LIKE THE WOLVES TO SURVIVE!
GRRR! AHWOO!!!
COME ON!

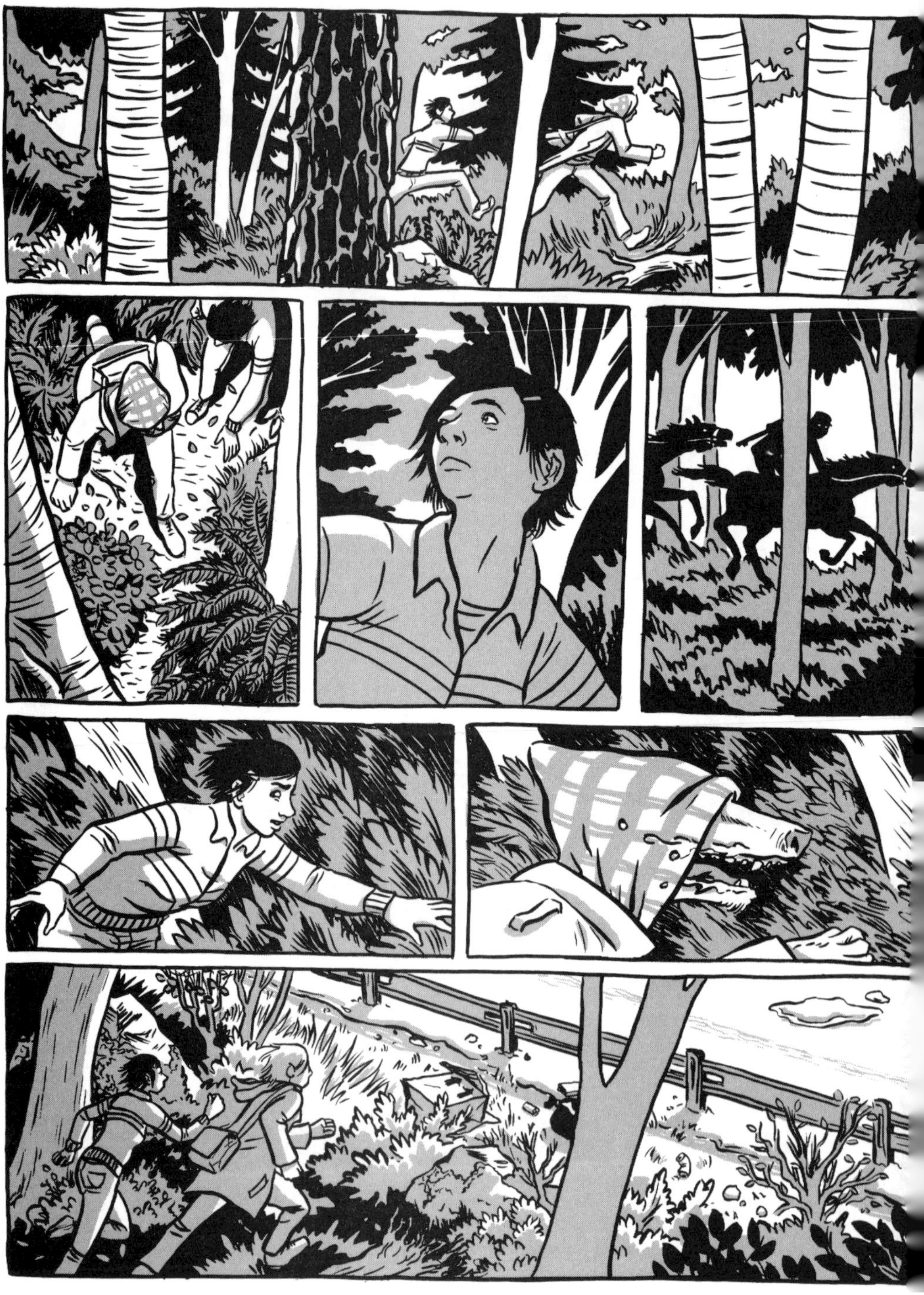

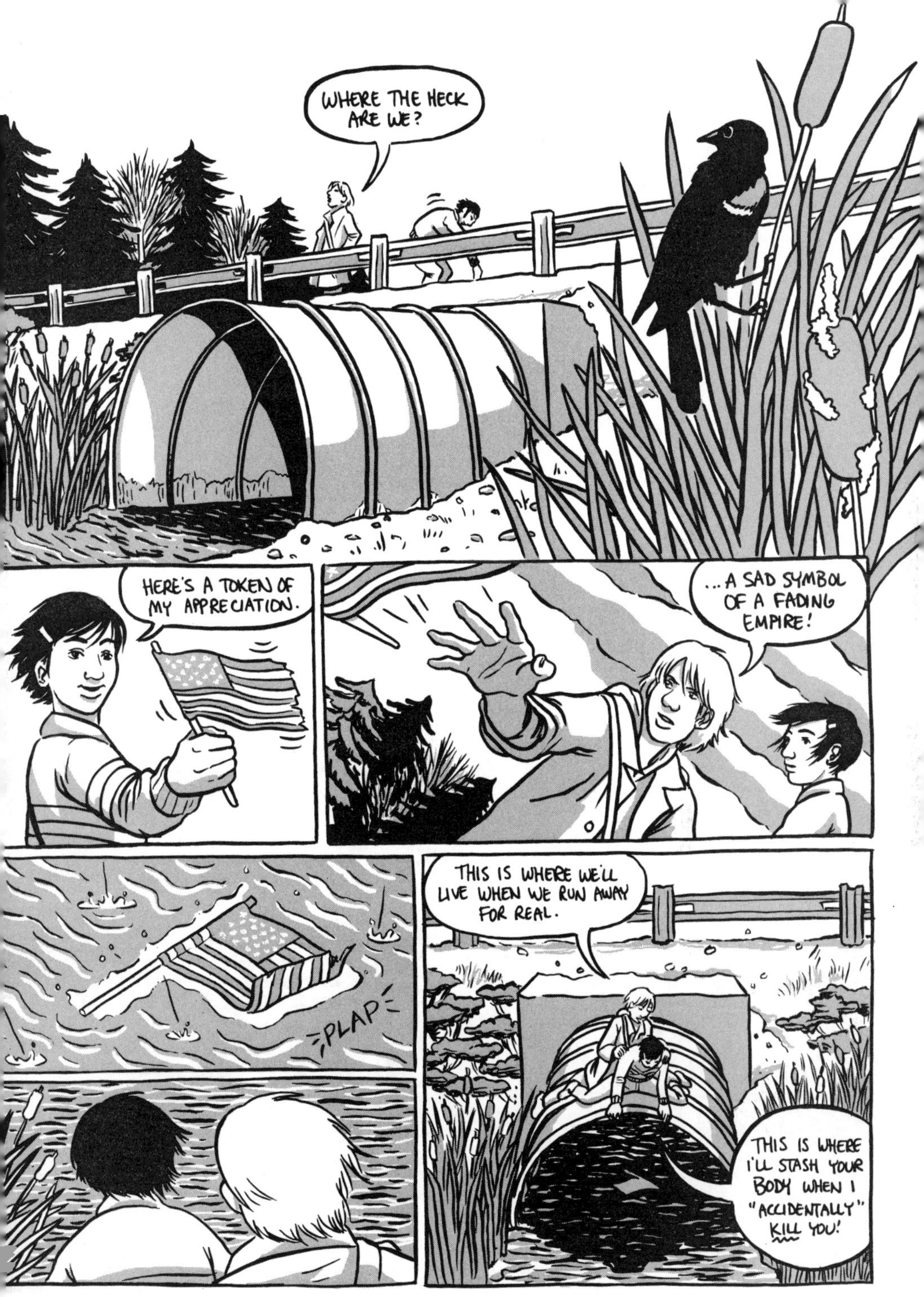
WHERE THE HECK ARE WE?
HERE'S A TOKEN OF MY APPRECIATION.
...A SAD SYMBOL OF A FADING EMPIRE!
PLAP
THIS IS WHERE WE'LL LIVE WHEN WE RUN AWAY FOR REAL.
THIS IS WHERE I'LL STASH YOUR BODY WHEN I "ACCIDENTALLY" KILL YOU!

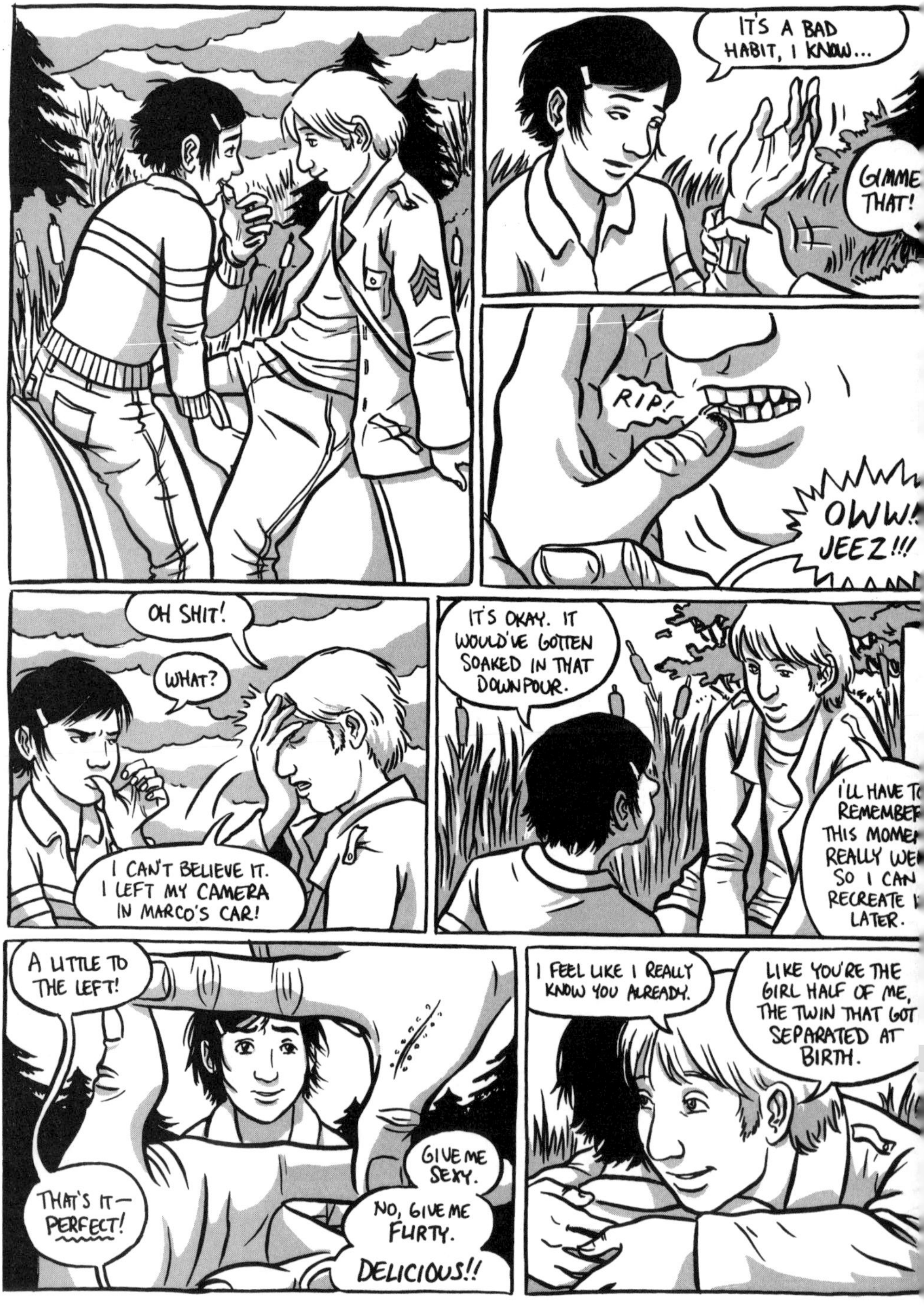
IT'S A BAD HABIT, I KNOW...
GIMME THAT!
RIP!
OWW! JEEZ!!!
OH SHIT!
WHAT?
I CAN'T BELIEVE IT. I LEFT MY CAMERA IN MARCO'S CAR!
IT'S OKAY. IT WOULD'VE GOTTEN SOAKED IN THAT DOWNPOUR.
A LITTLE TO THE LEFT!
THAT'S IT— PERFECT!
GIVE ME SEXY.
NO, GIVE ME FLIRTY.
DELICIOUS!!
I FEEL LIKE I REALLY KNOW YOU ALREADY.
LIKE YOU'RE THE GIRL HALF OF ME, THE TWIN THAT GOT SEPARATED AT BIRTH.

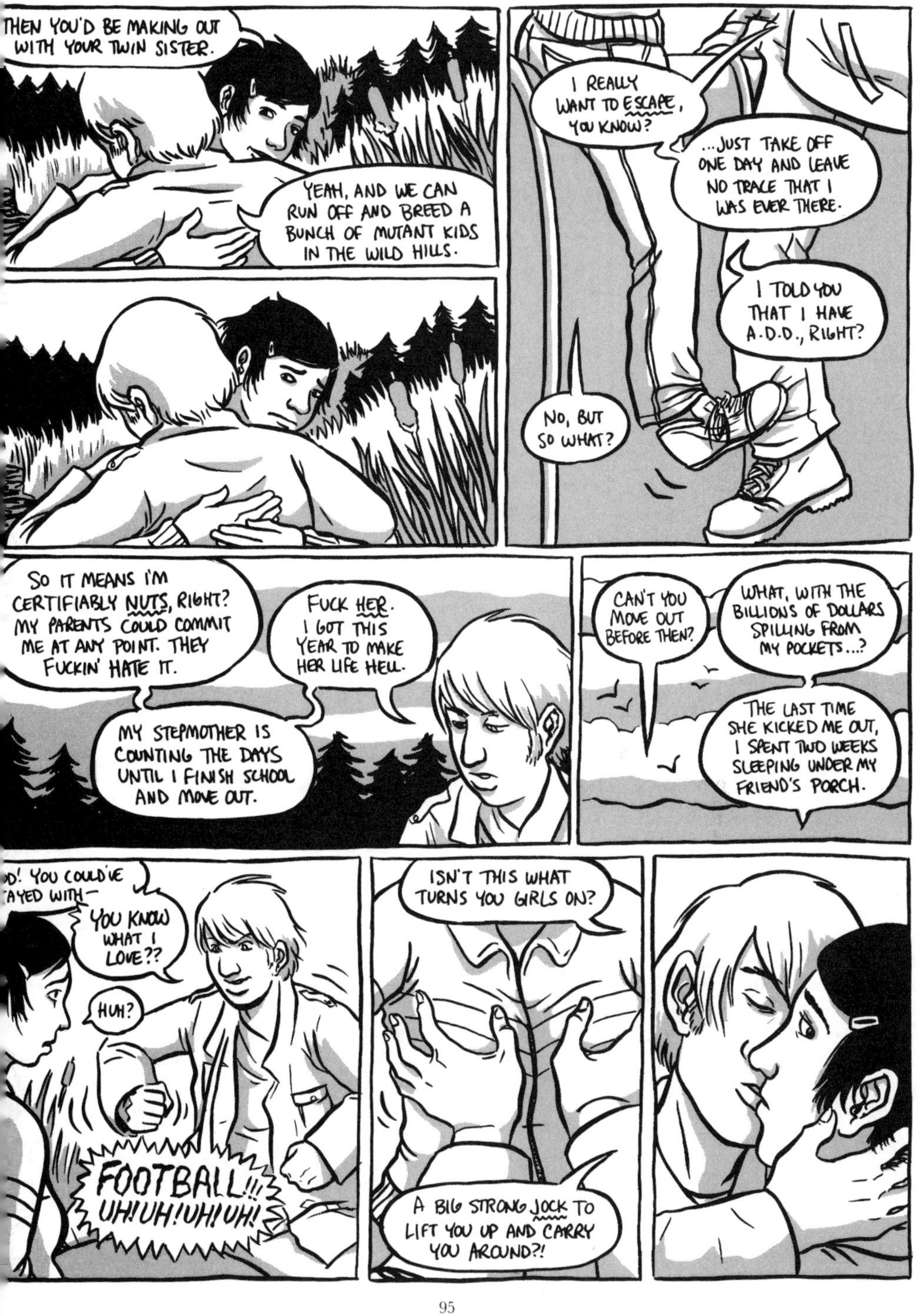
THEN YOU'D BE MAKING OUT WITH YOUR TWIN SISTER.
YEAH, AND WE CAN RUN OFF AND BREED A BUNCH OF MUTANT KIDS IN THE WILD HILLS.
I REALLY WANT TO ESCAPE, YOU KNOW?
...JUST TAKE OFF ONE DAY AND LEAVE NO TRACE THAT I WAS EVER THERE.
I TOLD YOU THAT I HAVE A.D.D., RIGHT?
NO, BUT SO WHAT?
SO IT MEANS I'M CERTIFIABLY NUTS, RIGHT? MY PARENTS COULD COMMIT ME AT ANY POINT. THEY FUCKIN' HATE IT.
MY STEPMOTHER IS COUNTING THE DAYS UNTIL I FINISH SCHOOL AND MOVE OUT.
FUCK HER. I GOT THIS YEAR TO MAKE HER LIFE HELL.
CAN'T YOU MOVE OUT BEFORE THEN?
WHAT, WITH THE BILLIONS OF DOLLARS SPILLING FROM MY POCKETS...?
THE LAST TIME SHE KICKED ME OUT, I SPENT TWO WEEKS SLEEPING UNDER MY FRIEND'S PORCH.
YOU COULD'VE
YOU KNOW WHAT I LOVE??
HUH?
FOOTBALL!!! UH! UH! UH! UH!
ISN'T THIS WHAT TURNS YOU GIRLS ON?
A BIG STRONG JOCK TO LIFT YOU UP AND CARRY YOU AROUND?!

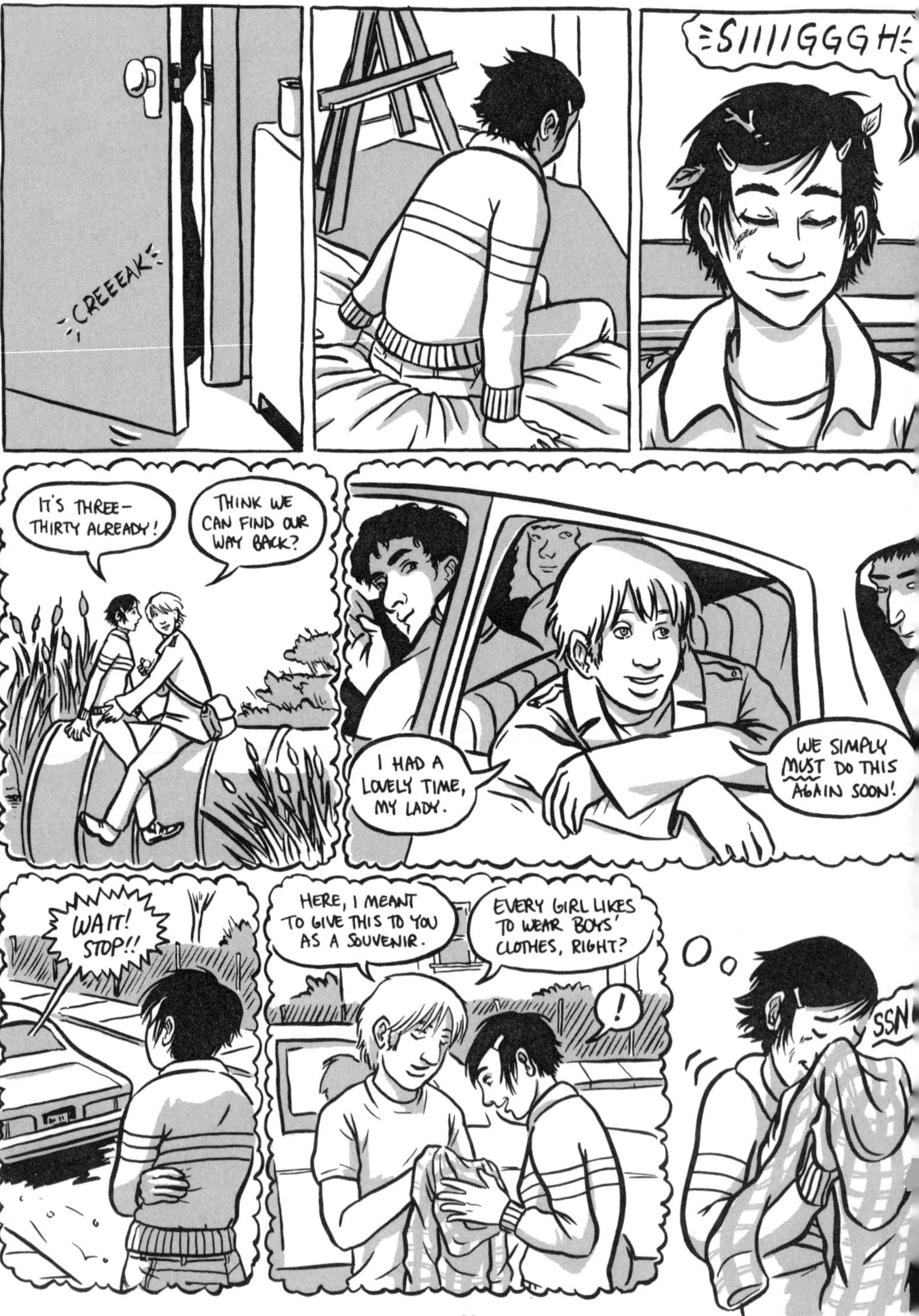

CREEEAK
SIIIGGGH
IT'S THREE-THIRTY ALREADY!
THINK WE CAN FIND OUR WAY BACK?
I HAD A LOVELY TIME, MY LADY.
WE SIMPLY MUST DO THIS AGAIN SOON!
WAIT! STOP!!
HERE, I MEANT TO GIVE THIS TO YOU AS A SOUVENIR.
EVERY GIRL LIKES TO WEAR BOYS' CLOTHES, RIGHT?
!
SSN

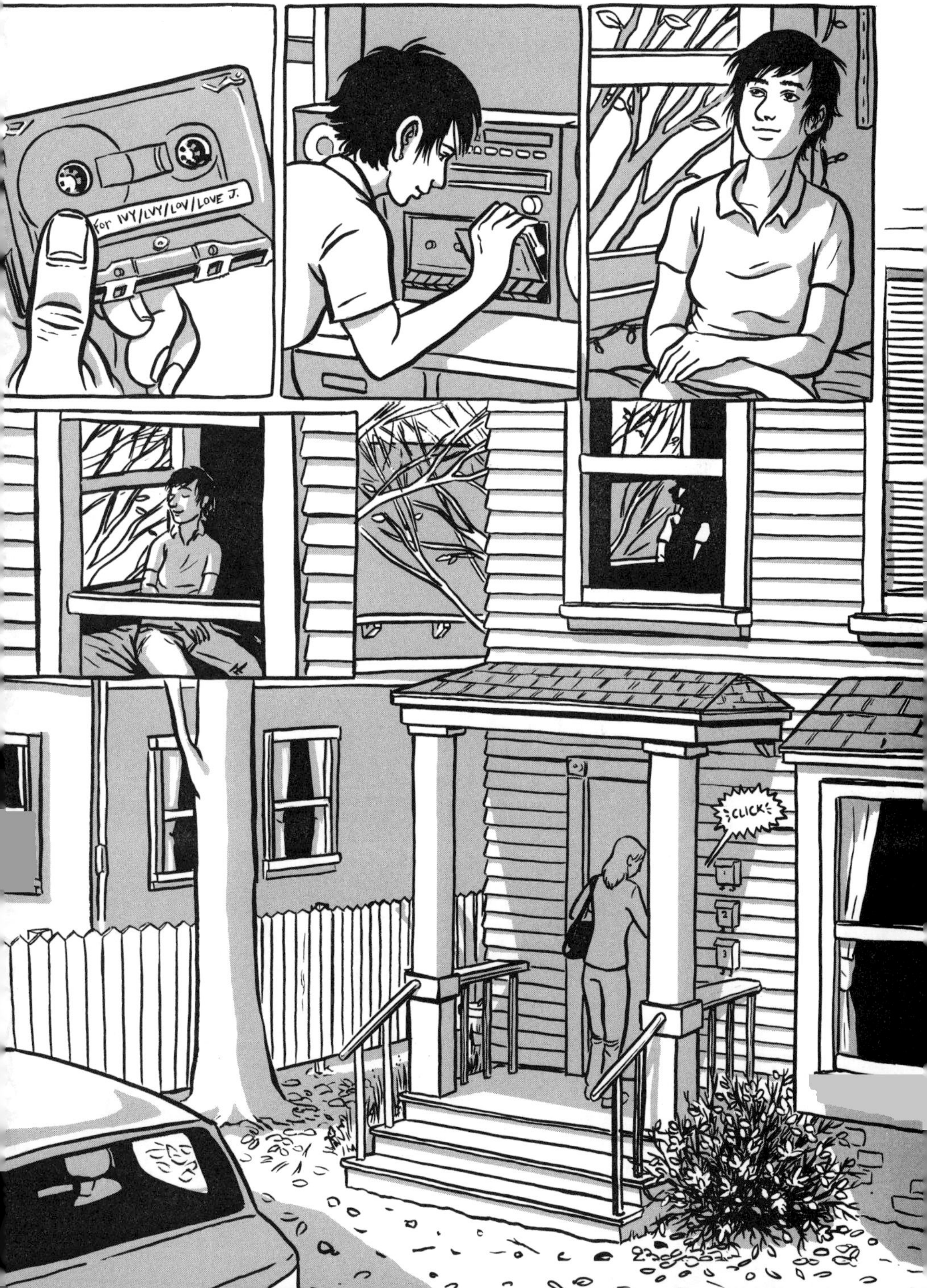
For IVY/LVY/LOV/LOVE J.
CLICK

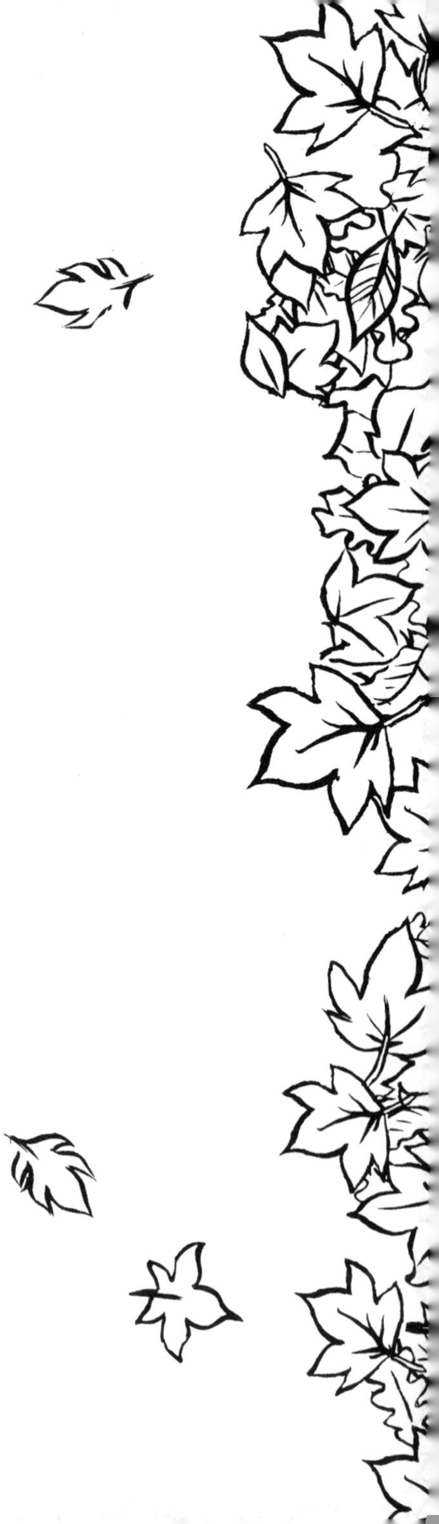

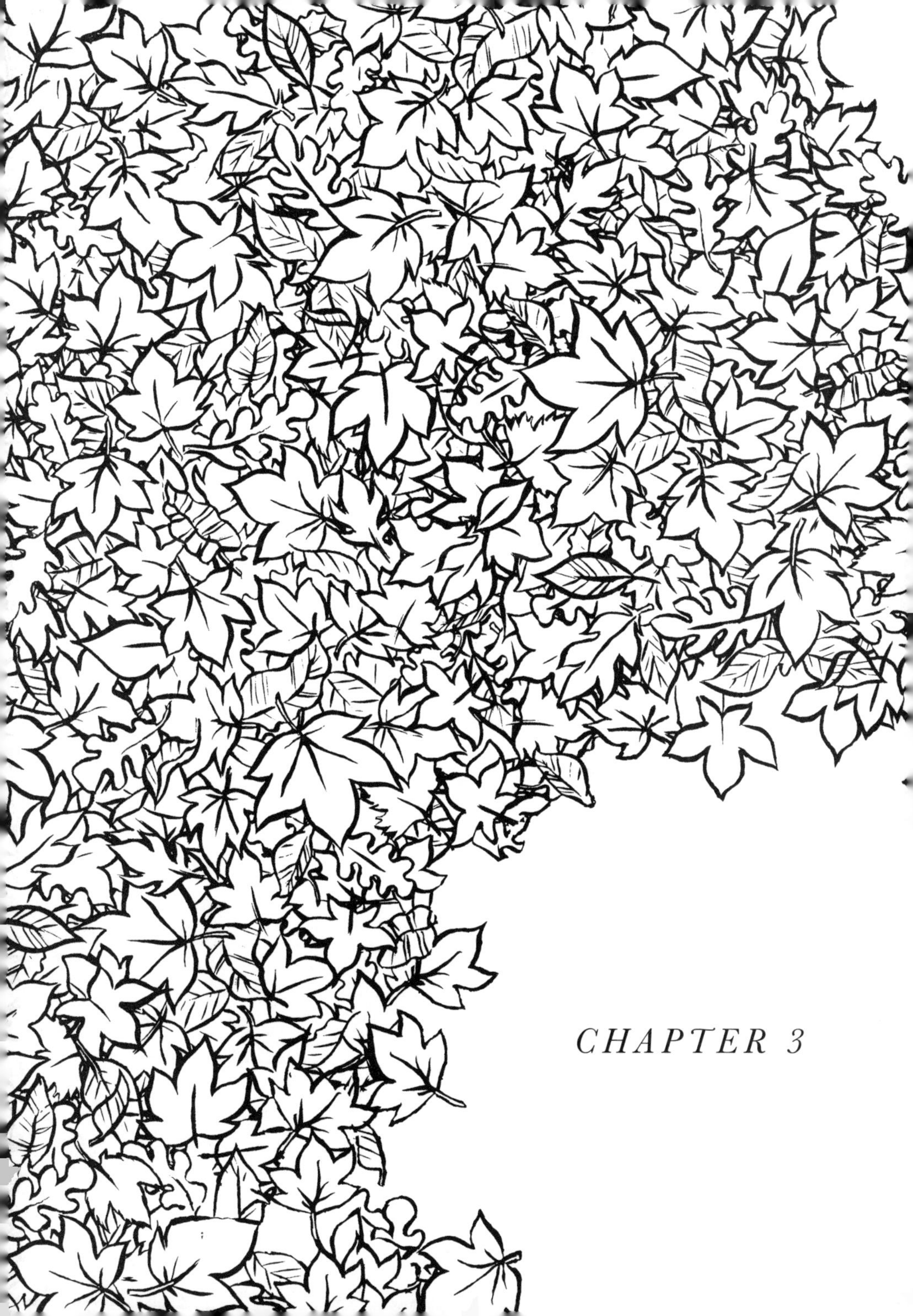

CHAPTER 3

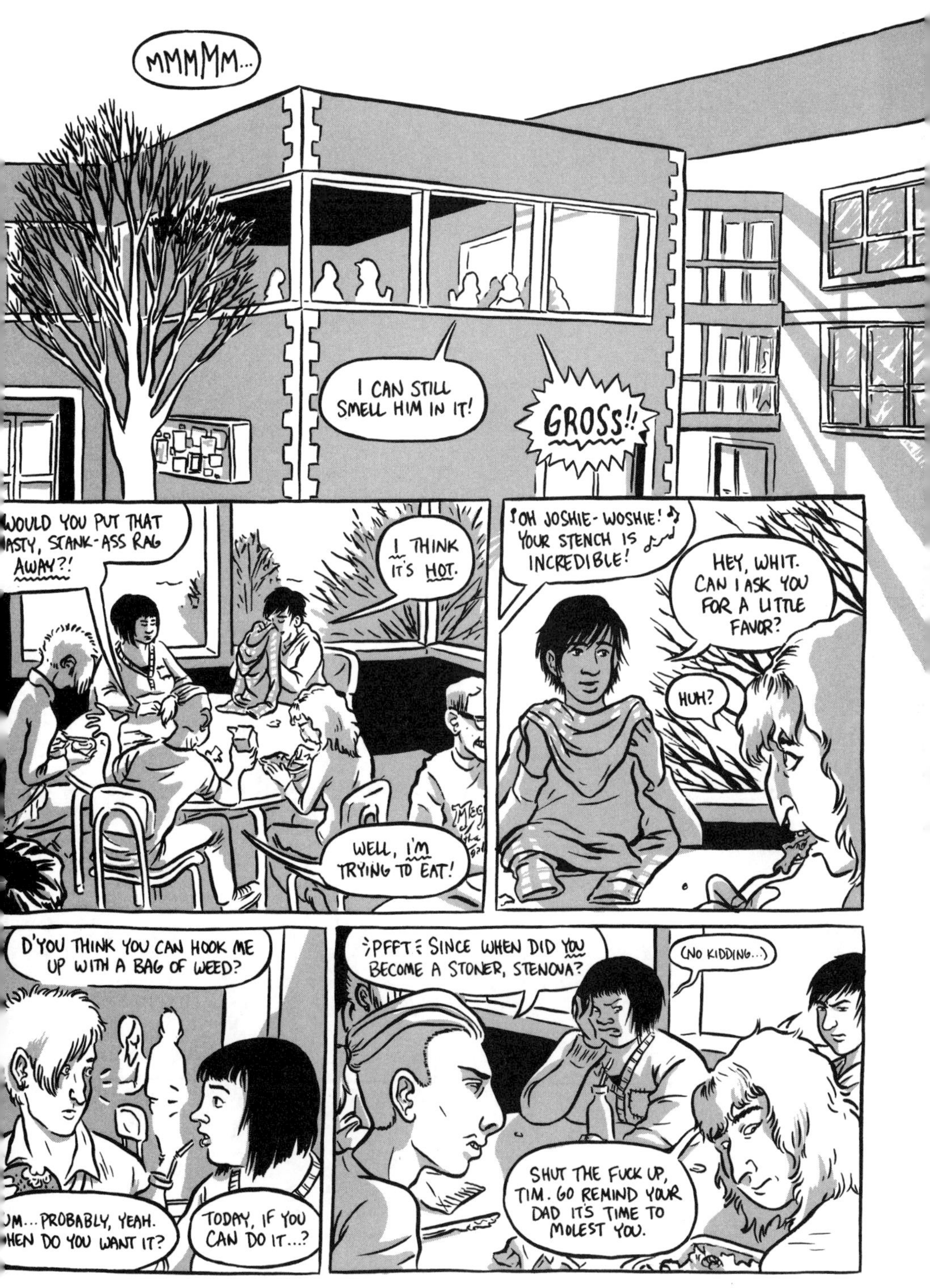
MMMMM...
I CAN STILL SMELL HIM IN IT!
GROSS!!
WOULD YOU PUT THAT NASTY, STANK-ASS RAG AWAY?!
I THINK IT'S HOT.
WELL, I'M TRYING TO EAT!
♪OH JOSHIE-WOSHIE! YOUR STENCH IS INCREDIBLE!♪
HEY, WHIT. CAN I ASK YOU FOR A LITTLE FAVOR?
HUH?
D'YOU THINK YOU CAN HOOK ME UP WITH A BAG OF WEED?
UM... PROBABLY, YEAH. WHEN DO YOU WANT IT?
TODAY, IF YOU CAN DO IT...?
PFFT SINCE WHEN DID YOU BECOME A STONER, STENOVA?
(NO KIDDING...)
SHUT THE FUCK UP, TIM. GO REMIND YOUR DAD IT'S TIME TO MOLEST YOU.

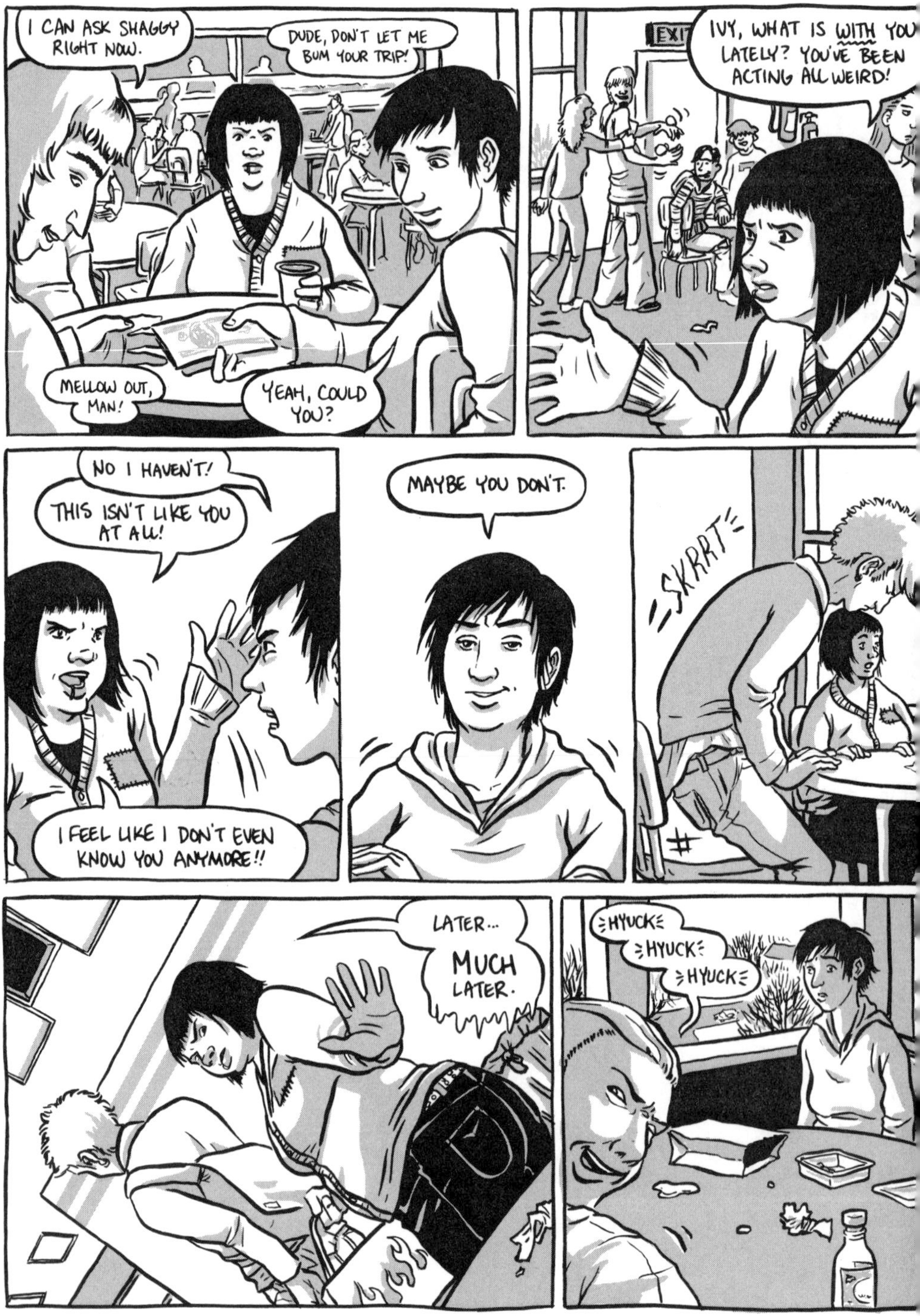
I CAN ASK SHAGGY RIGHT NOW.
DUDE, DON'T LET ME BUM YOUR TRIP!
MELLOW OUT, MAN!
YEAH, COULD YOU?
EXIT
IVY, WHAT IS WITH YOU LATELY? YOU'VE BEEN ACTING ALL WEIRD!
NO I HAVEN'T!
THIS ISN'T LIKE YOU AT ALL!
I FEEL LIKE I DON'T EVEN KNOW YOU ANYMORE!!
MAYBE YOU DON'T.
SKRRT
LATER...
MUCH LATER.
HYUCK
HYUCK
HYUCK

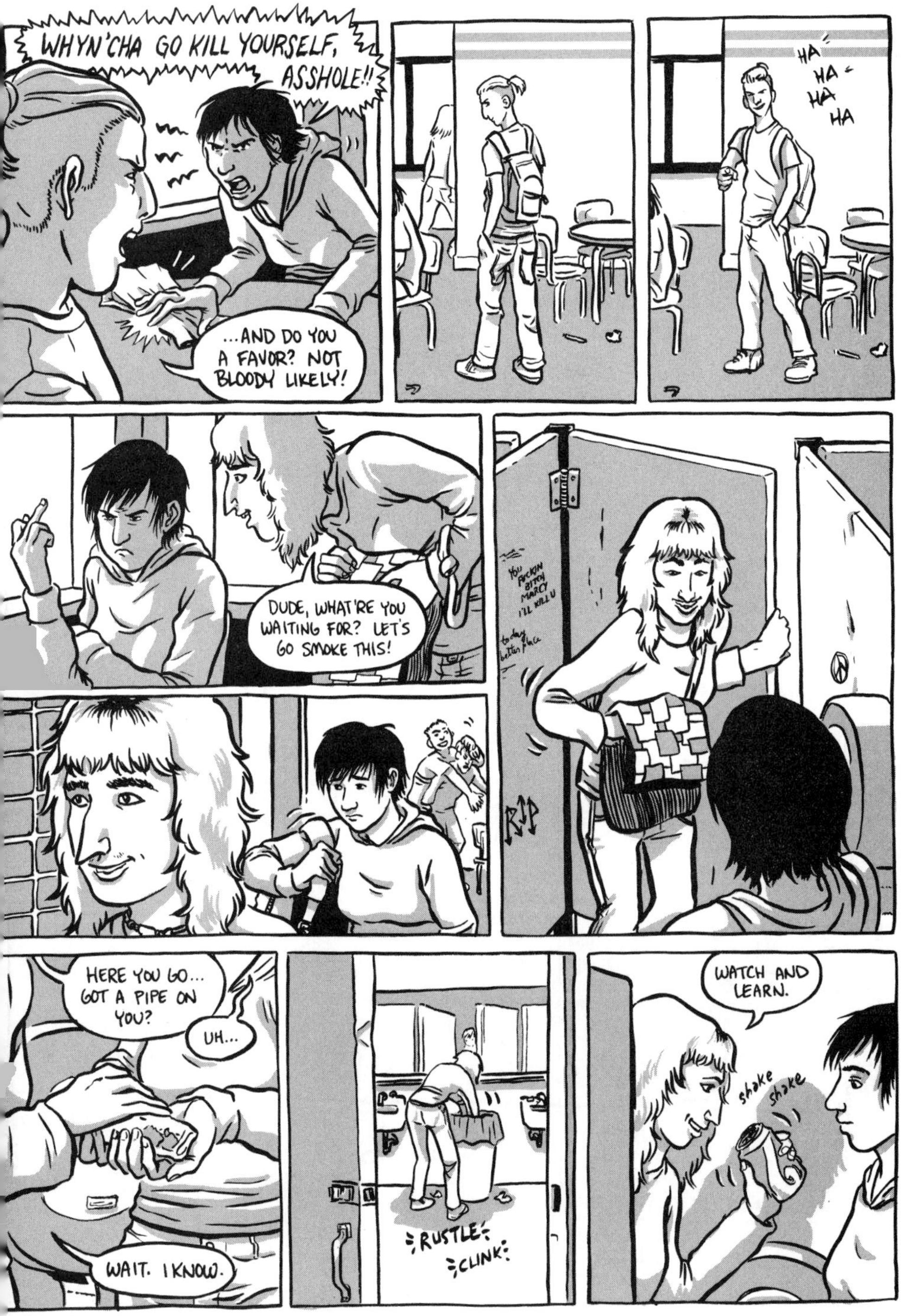
WHYN'CHA GO KILL YOURSELF, ASSHOLE!!
...AND DO YOU A FAVOR? NOT BLOODY LIKELY!
HA HA HA HA
DUDE, WHAT'RE YOU WAITING FOR? LET'S GO SMOKE THIS!
YOU FUCKIN BITCH MARCY I'LL KILL U
today better place
RIP
HERE YOU GO... GOT A PIPE ON YOU?
UH...
WAIT. I KNOW.
RUSTLE
CLINK
WATCH AND LEARN.
shake shake

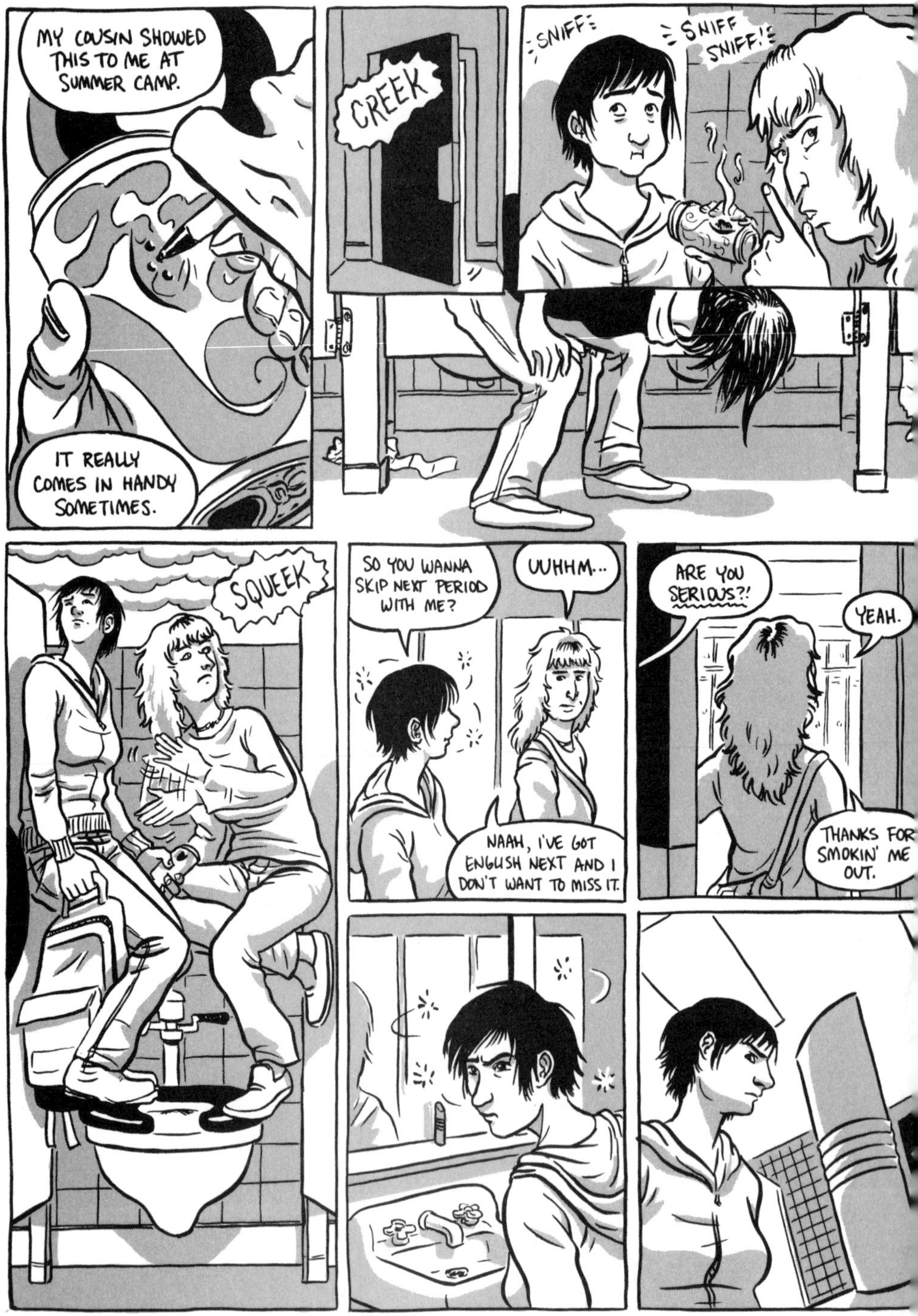
MY COUSIN SHOWED THIS TO ME AT SUMMER CAMP.
IT REALLY COMES IN HANDY SOMETIMES.
CREEK
SNIFF
SNIFF SNIFF!
SQUEEK
SO YOU WANNA SKIP NEXT PERIOD WITH ME?
UUHHM...
NAAH, I'VE GOT ENGLISH NEXT AND I DON'T WANT TO MISS IT.
ARE YOU SERIOUS?!
YEAH.
THANKS FOR SMOKIN' ME OUT.

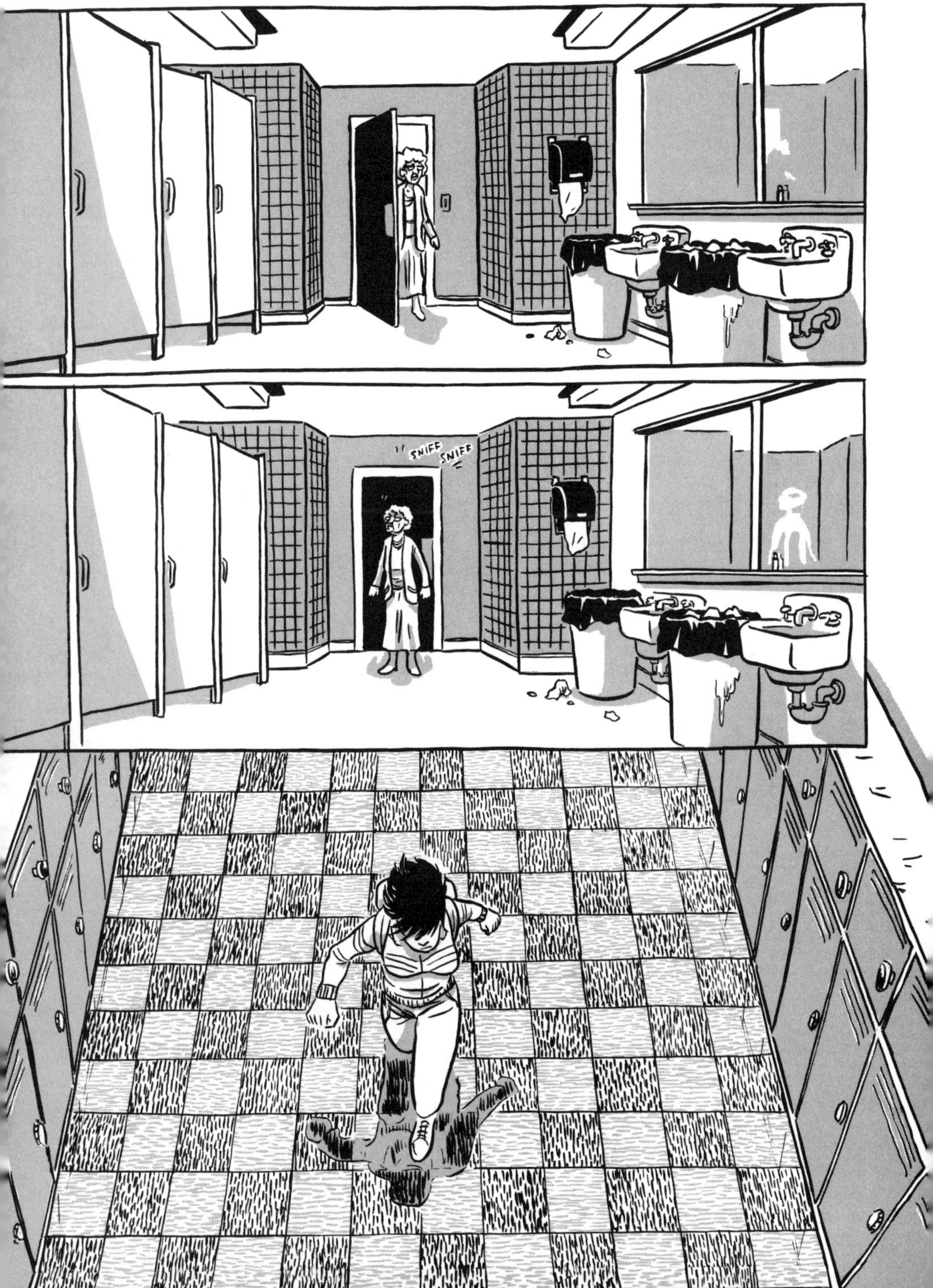
SNIFF
SNIFF

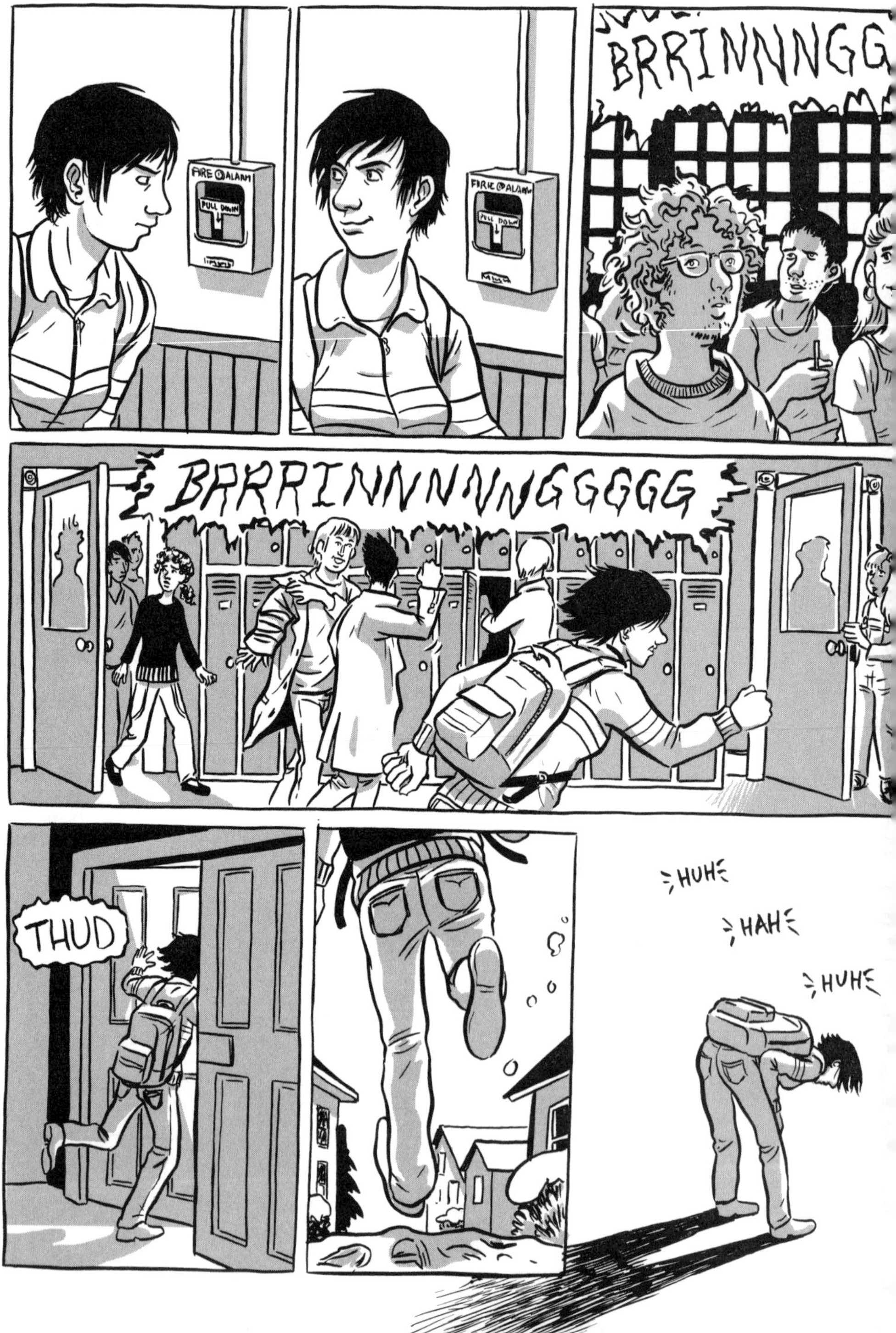
FIRE ALARM
PULL DOWN
FIRE ALARM
PULL DOWN
BRRINNNGG
BRRRINNNNNGGGGG
THUD
HUH
HAH
HUH

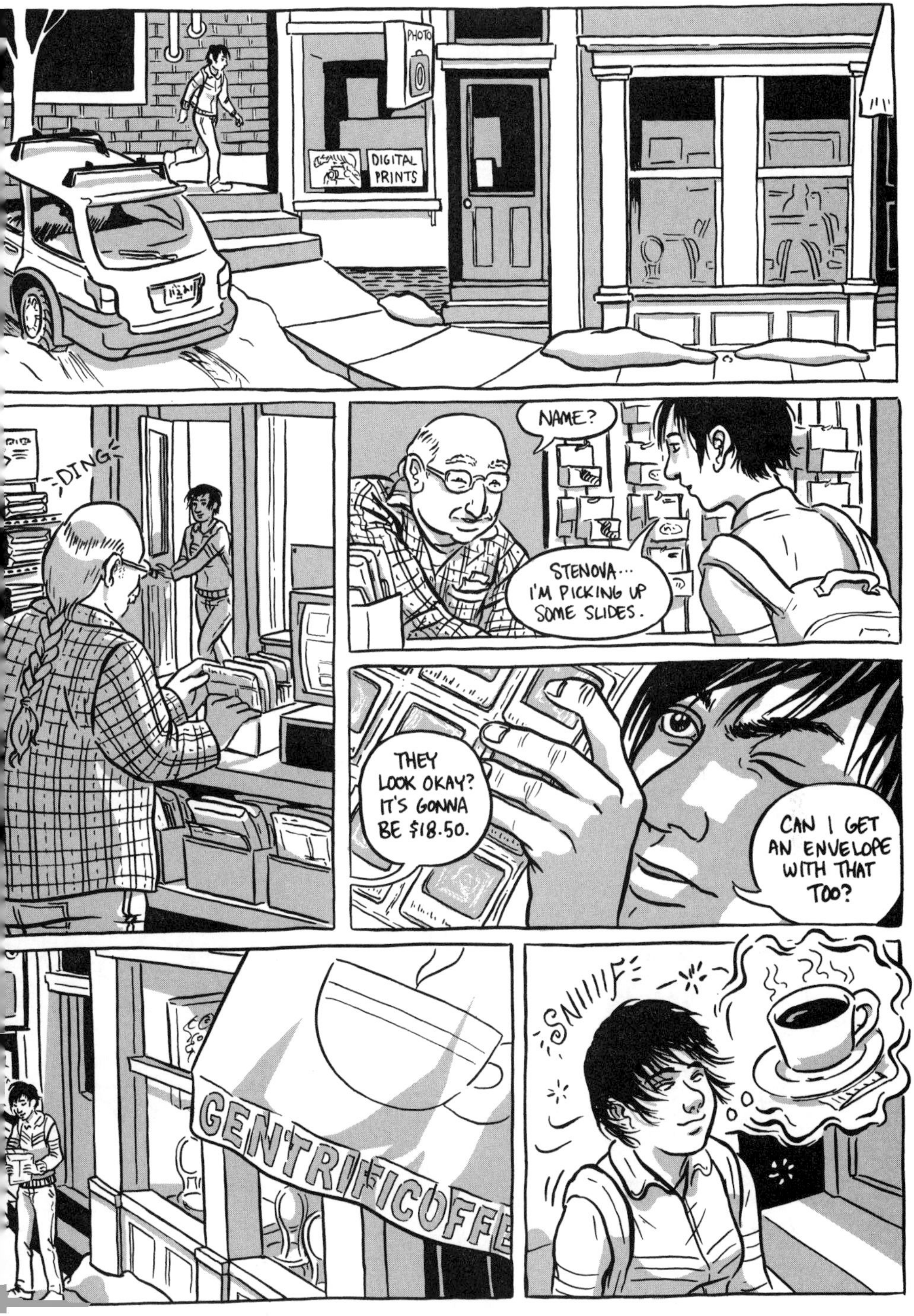
PHOTO
DIGITAL PRINTS
DING
NAME?
STENOVA... I'M PICKING UP SOME SLIDES.
THEY LOOK OKAY? IT'S GONNA BE $18.50.
CAN I GET AN ENVELOPE WITH THAT TOO?
GENTRIFICOFFE
SNIIIIF

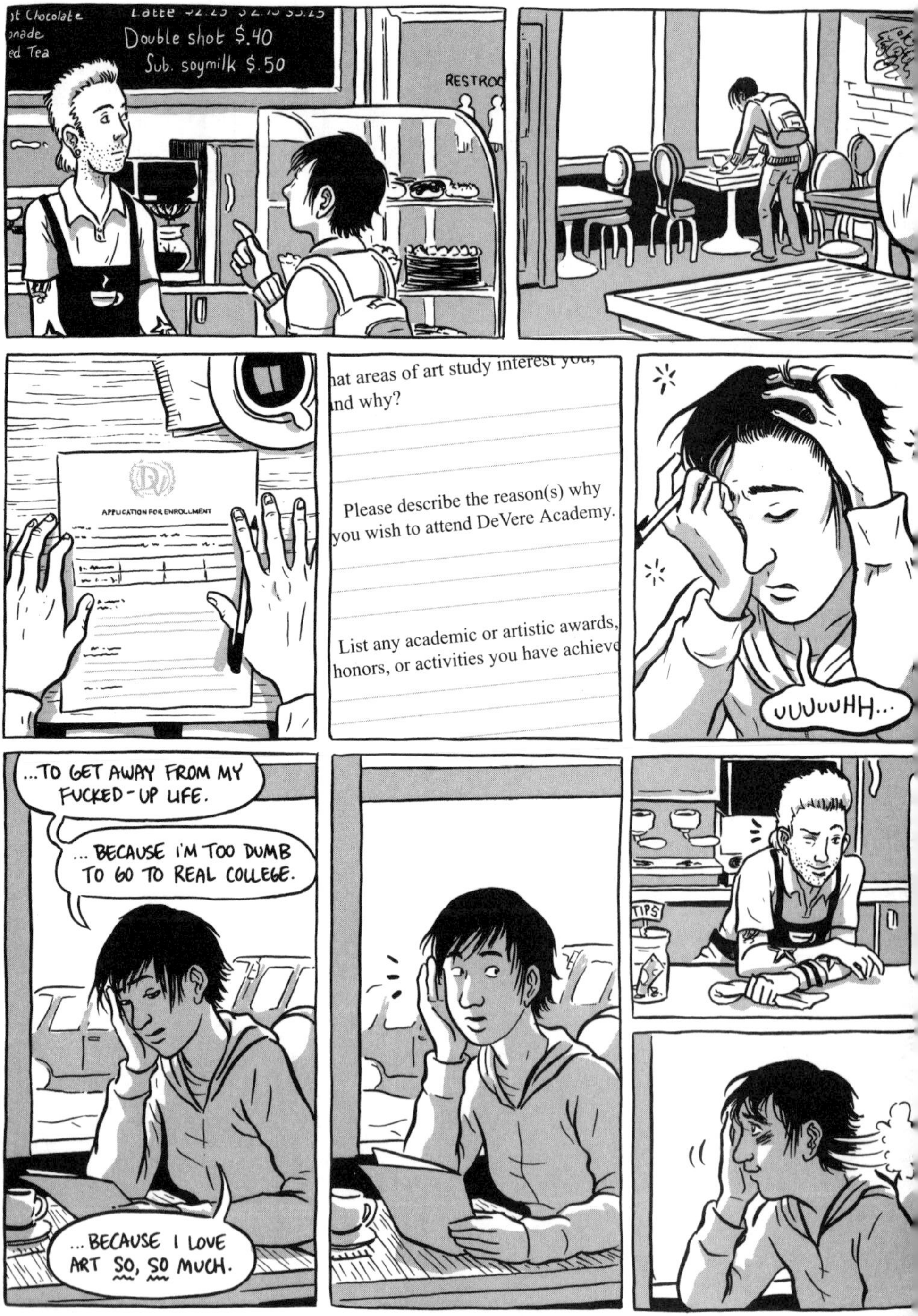

Latte
Double shot $.40
Sub. soymilk $.50
APPLICATION FOR ENROLLMENT
Please describe the reason(s) why you wish to attend DeVere Academy.
List any academic or artistic awards, honors, or activities you have achieve
UUUUUHH...
...TO GET AWAY FROM MY FUCKED-UP LIFE.
...BECAUSE I'M TOO DUMB TO GO TO REAL COLLEGE.
...BECAUSE I LOVE ART SO, SO MUCH.
TIPS

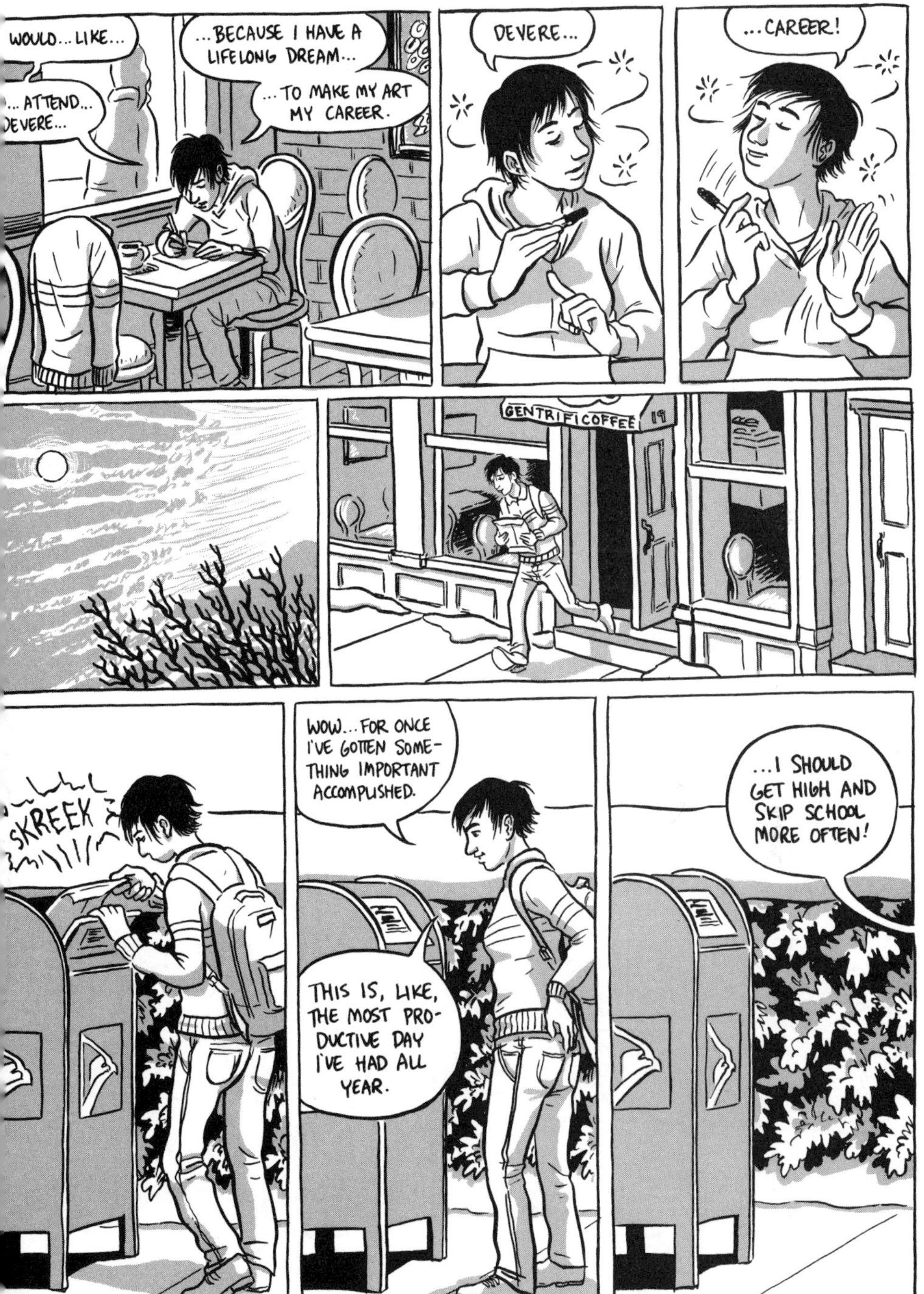
WOULD... LIKE...
...ATTEND... DEVERE...
...BECAUSE I HAVE A LIFELONG DREAM...
...TO MAKE MY ART MY CAREER.
DEVERE...
...CAREER!
GENTRIFICOFFEE 19
SKREEK
WOW... FOR ONCE I'VE GOTTEN SOME-THING IMPORTANT ACCOMPLISHED.
THIS IS, LIKE, THE MOST PRO-DUCTIVE DAY I'VE HAD ALL YEAR.
...I SHOULD GET HIGH AND SKIP SCHOOL MORE OFTEN!

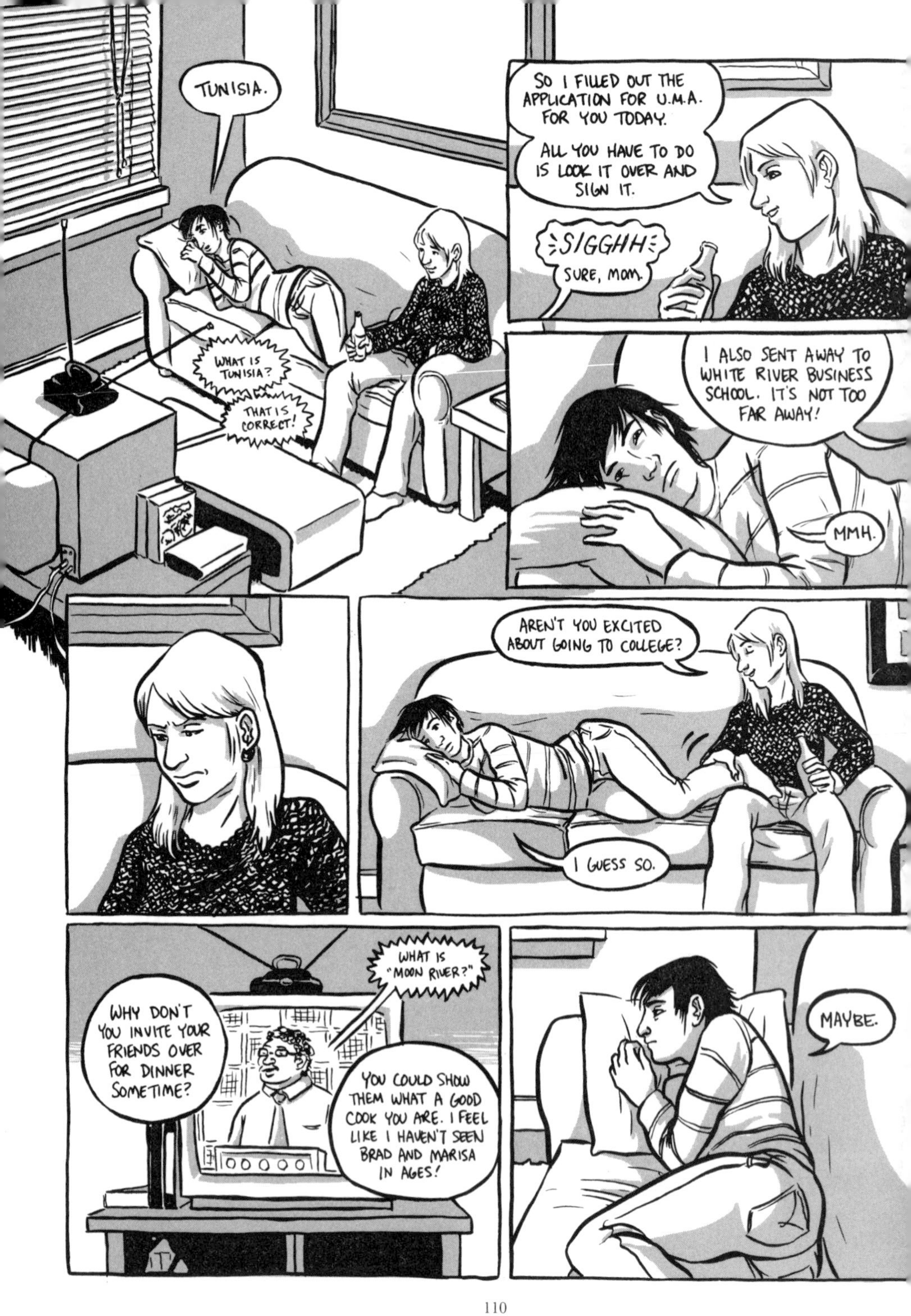
TUNISIA.
WHAT IS TUNISIA?
THAT IS CORRECT!
SO I FILLED OUT THE APPLICATION FOR U.M.A. FOR YOU TODAY.
ALL YOU HAVE TO DO IS LOOK IT OVER AND SIGN IT.
SIGGHH
SURE, MOM.
I ALSO SENT AWAY TO WHITE RIVER BUSINESS SCHOOL. IT'S NOT TOO FAR AWAY!
MMH.
AREN'T YOU EXCITED ABOUT GOING TO COLLEGE?
I GUESS SO.
WHY DON'T YOU INVITE YOUR FRIENDS OVER FOR DINNER SOMETIME?
WHAT IS "MOON RIVER?"
YOU COULD SHOW THEM WHAT A GOOD COOK YOU ARE. I FEEL LIKE I HAVEN'T SEEN BRAD AND MARISA IN AGES!
MAYBE.

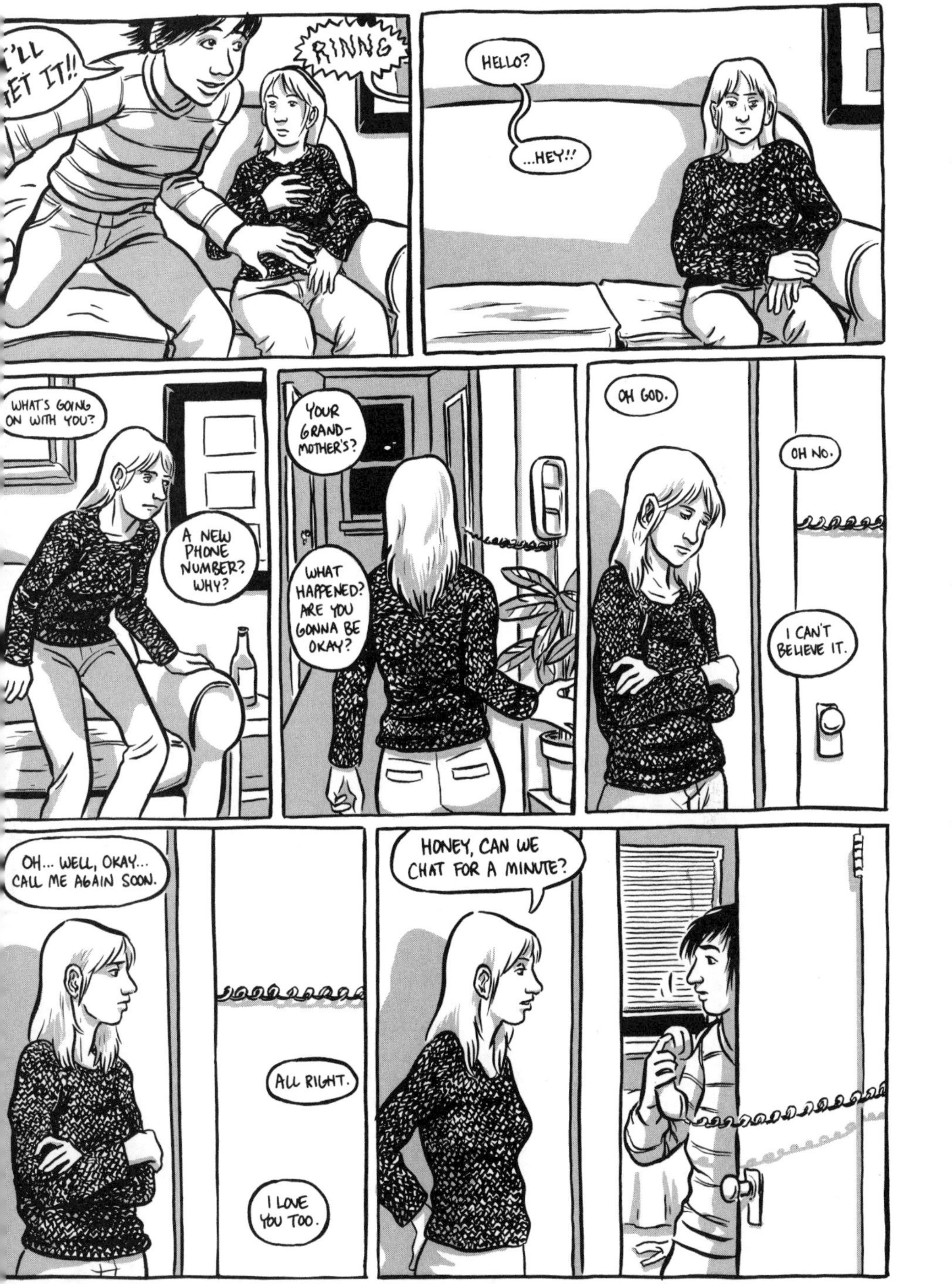
I'LL GET IT!!
RINNG
HELLO?
...HEY!!
WHAT'S GOING ON WITH YOU?
A NEW PHONE NUMBER? WHY?
YOUR GRAND-MOTHER'S?
WHAT HAPPENED? ARE YOU GONNA BE OKAY?
OH GOD.
OH NO.
I CAN'T BELIEVE IT.
OH... WELL, OKAY... CALL ME AGAIN SOON.
ALL RIGHT.
I LOVE YOU TOO.
HONEY, CAN WE CHAT FOR A MINUTE?

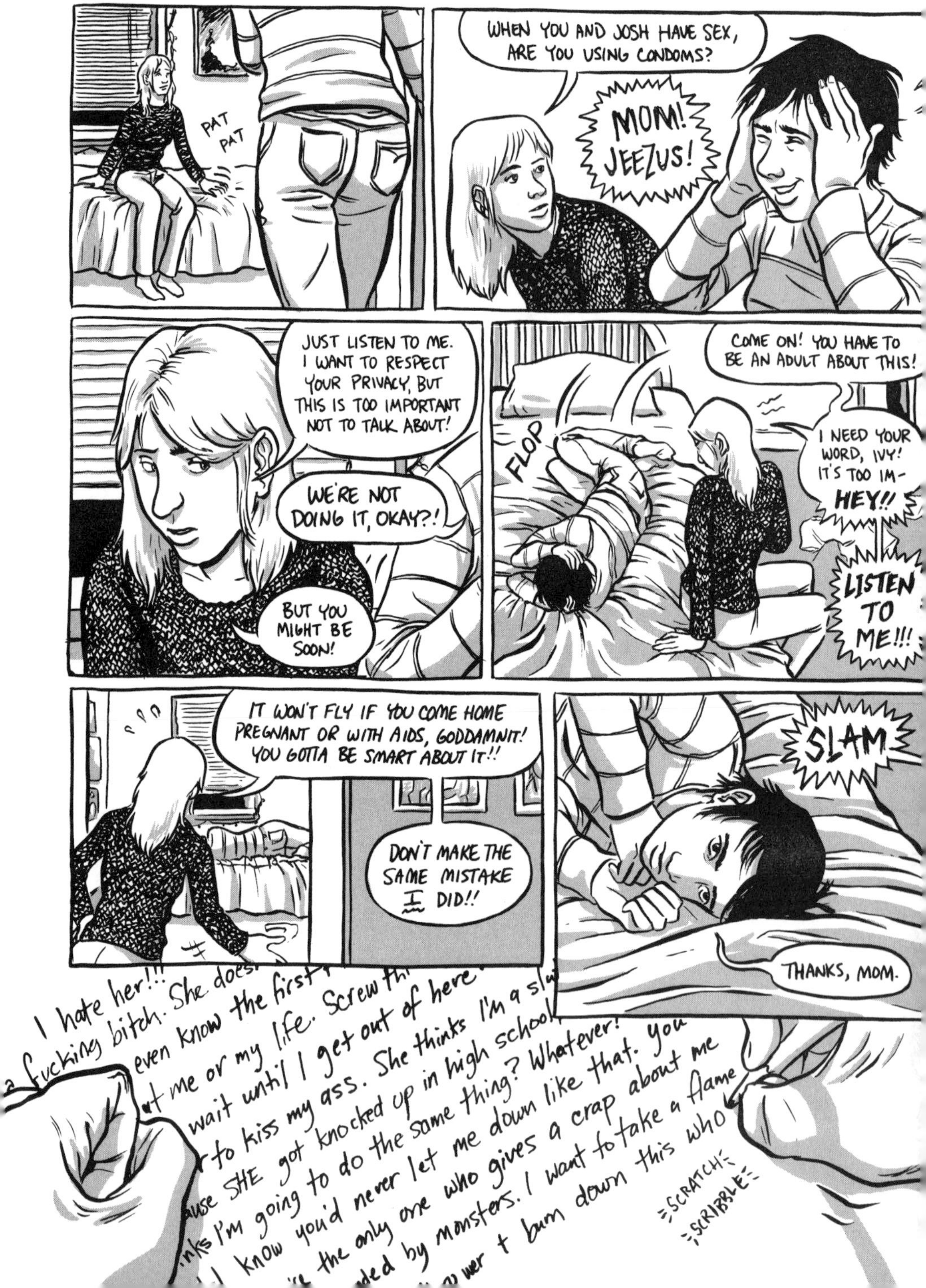
PAT PAT
WHEN YOU AND JOSH HAVE SEX, ARE YOU USING CONDOMS?
MOM! JEEZUS!
JUST LISTEN TO ME. I WANT TO RESPECT YOUR PRIVACY, BUT THIS IS TOO IMPORTANT NOT TO TALK ABOUT!
WE'RE NOT DOING IT, OKAY?!
BUT YOU MIGHT BE SOON!
FLOP
COME ON! YOU HAVE TO BE AN ADULT ABOUT THIS!
I NEED YOUR WORD, IVY! IT'S TOO IM-
HEY!!
LISTEN TO ME!!!
IT WON'T FLY IF YOU COME HOME PREGNANT OR WITH AIDS, GODDAMNIT! YOU GOTTA BE SMART ABOUT IT!!
DON'T MAKE THE SAME MISTAKE I DID!!
SLAM
THANKS, MOM.
I hate her!!! She
a fucking bitch.
even know the first
me or my life. Screw
wait until I get out of here
to kiss my ass. She thinks I'm a
SHE got knocked up in high school
I'm going to do the same thing? Whatever!
know you'd never let me down like that. You
the only one who gives a crap about me
by monsters. I want to take a flame
burn down this who
SCRATCH
SCRIBBLE

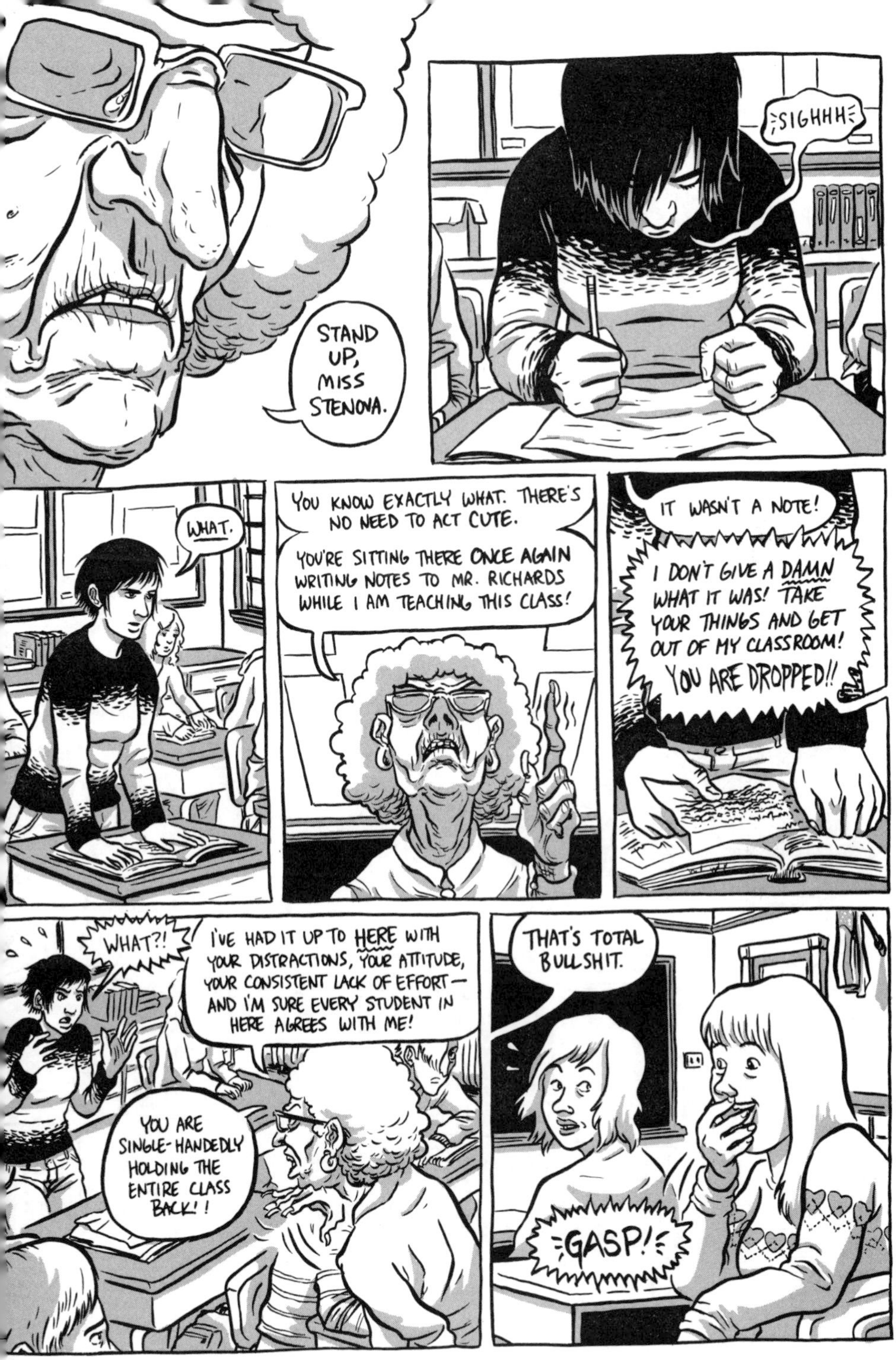
STAND UP, MISS STENOVA.
SIGHHH
WHAT.
YOU KNOW EXACTLY WHAT. THERE'S NO NEED TO ACT CUTE.
YOU'RE SITTING THERE ONCE AGAIN WRITING NOTES TO MR. RICHARDS WHILE I AM TEACHING THIS CLASS!
IT WASN'T A NOTE!
I DON'T GIVE A DAMN WHAT IT WAS! TAKE YOUR THINGS AND GET OUT OF MY CLASSROOM! YOU ARE DROPPED!!
WHAT?!
I'VE HAD IT UP TO HERE WITH YOUR DISTRACTIONS, YOUR ATTITUDE, YOUR CONSISTENT LACK OF EFFORT— AND I'M SURE EVERY STUDENT IN HERE AGREES WITH ME!
YOU ARE SINGLE-HANDEDLY HOLDING THE ENTIRE CLASS BACK!!
THAT'S TOTAL BULLSHIT.
GASP!

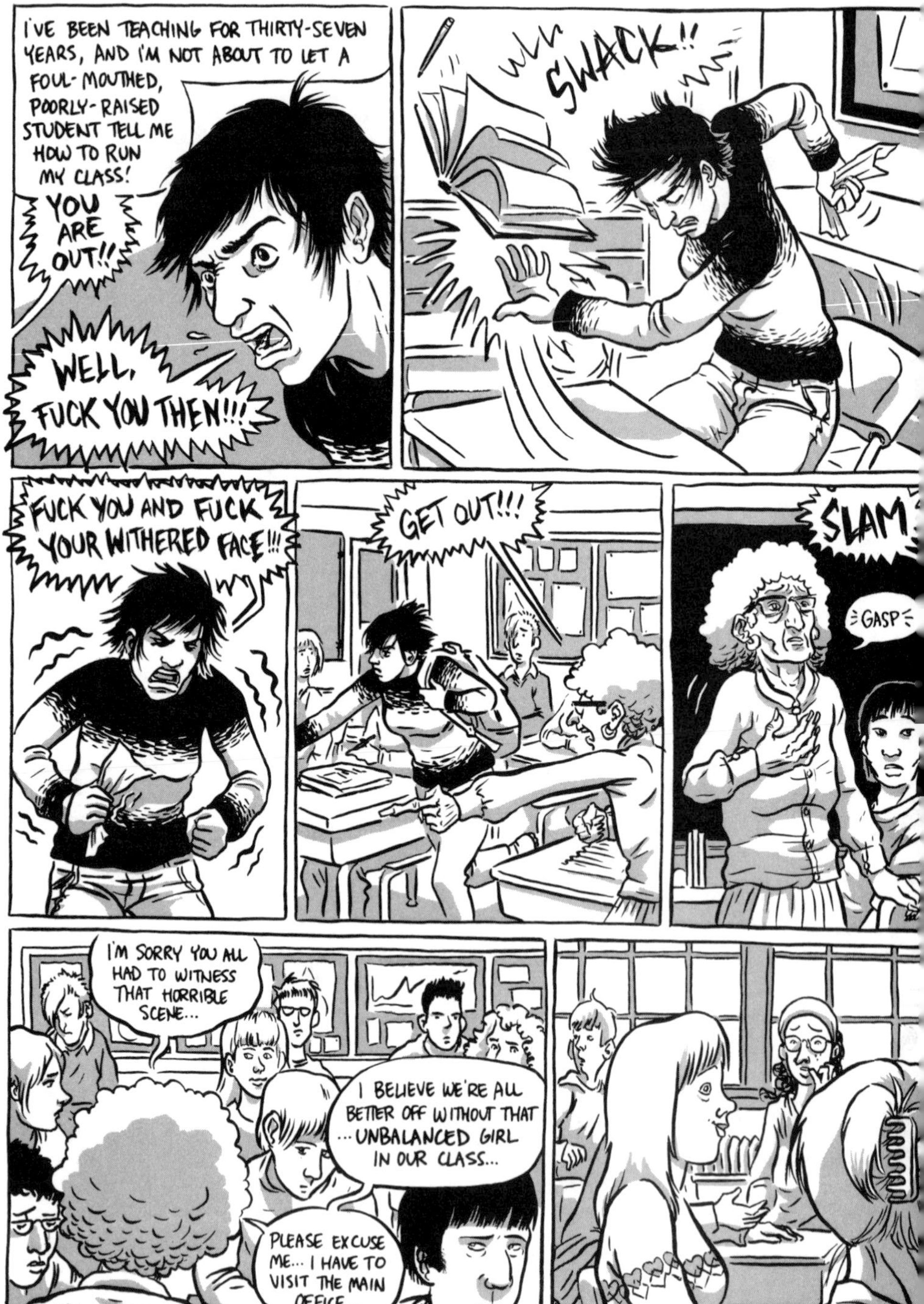
I'VE BEEN TEACHING FOR THIRTY-SEVEN YEARS, AND I'M NOT ABOUT TO LET A FOUL-MOUTHED, POORLY-RAISED STUDENT TELL ME HOW TO RUN MY CLASS!
YOU ARE OUT!!
WELL, FUCK YOU THEN!!!
SWACK!!
FUCK YOU AND FUCK YOUR WITHERED FACE!!!
GET OUT!!!
SLAM
GASP
I'M SORRY YOU ALL HAD TO WITNESS THAT HORRIBLE SCENE...
I BELIEVE WE'RE ALL BETTER OFF WITHOUT THAT ...UNBALANCED GIRL IN OUR CLASS...
PLEASE EXCUSE ME... I HAVE TO VISIT THE MAIN OFFICE...

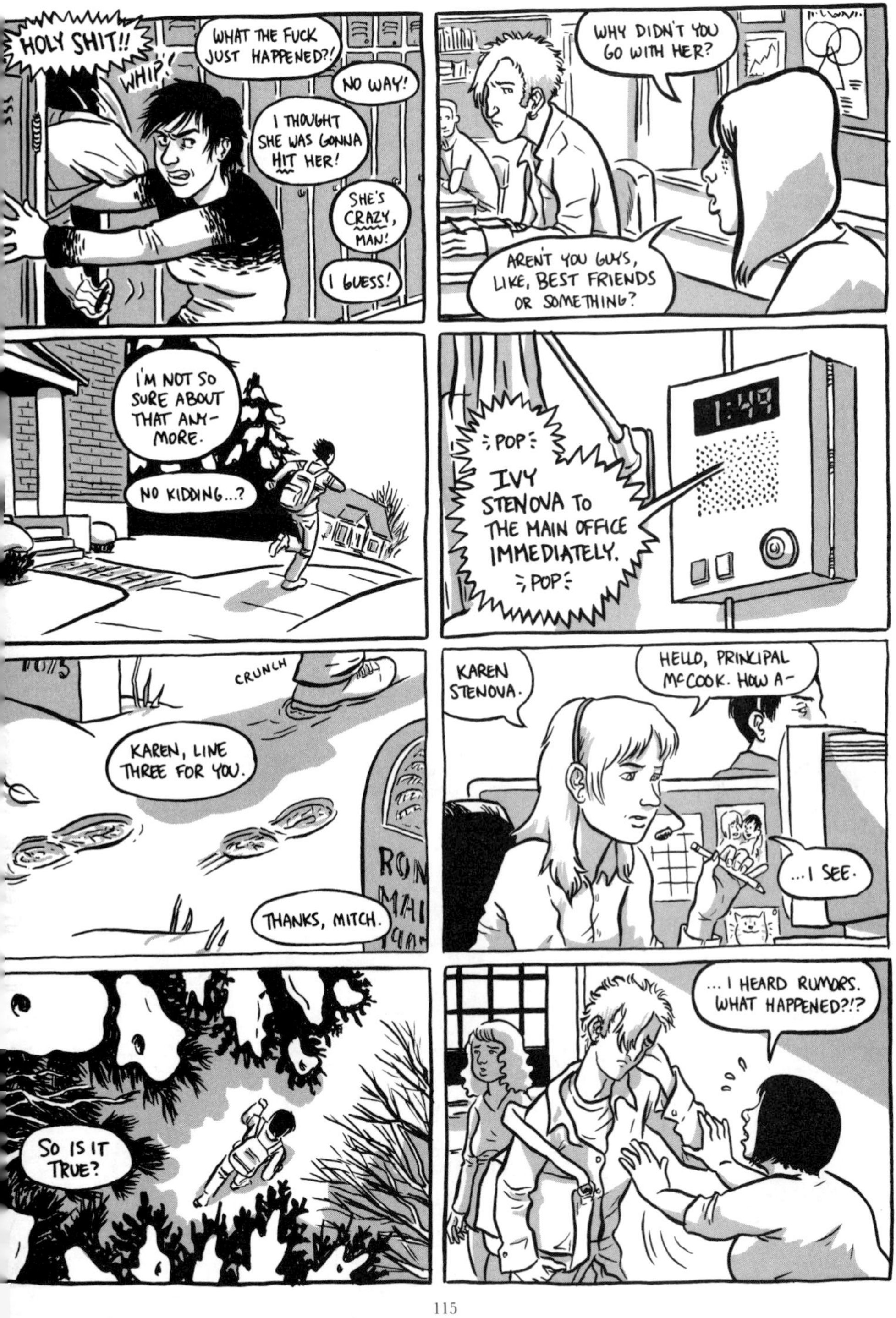

HOLY SHIT!!
WHIP
WHAT THE FUCK JUST HAPPENED?!
NO WAY!
I THOUGHT SHE WAS GONNA HIT HER!
SHE'S CRAZY, MAN!
I GUESS!
WHY DIDN'T YOU GO WITH HER?
AREN'T YOU GUYS, LIKE, BEST FRIENDS OR SOMETHING?
I'M NOT SO SURE ABOUT THAT ANY-MORE.
NO KIDDING...?
POP
IVY STENOVA TO THE MAIN OFFICE IMMEDIATELY.
POP
CRUNCH
KAREN, LINE THREE FOR YOU.
THANKS, MITCH.
KAREN STENOVA.
HELLO, PRINCIPAL McCOOK. HOW A-
...I SEE.
SO IS IT TRUE?
...I HEARD RUMORS. WHAT HAPPENED?!?

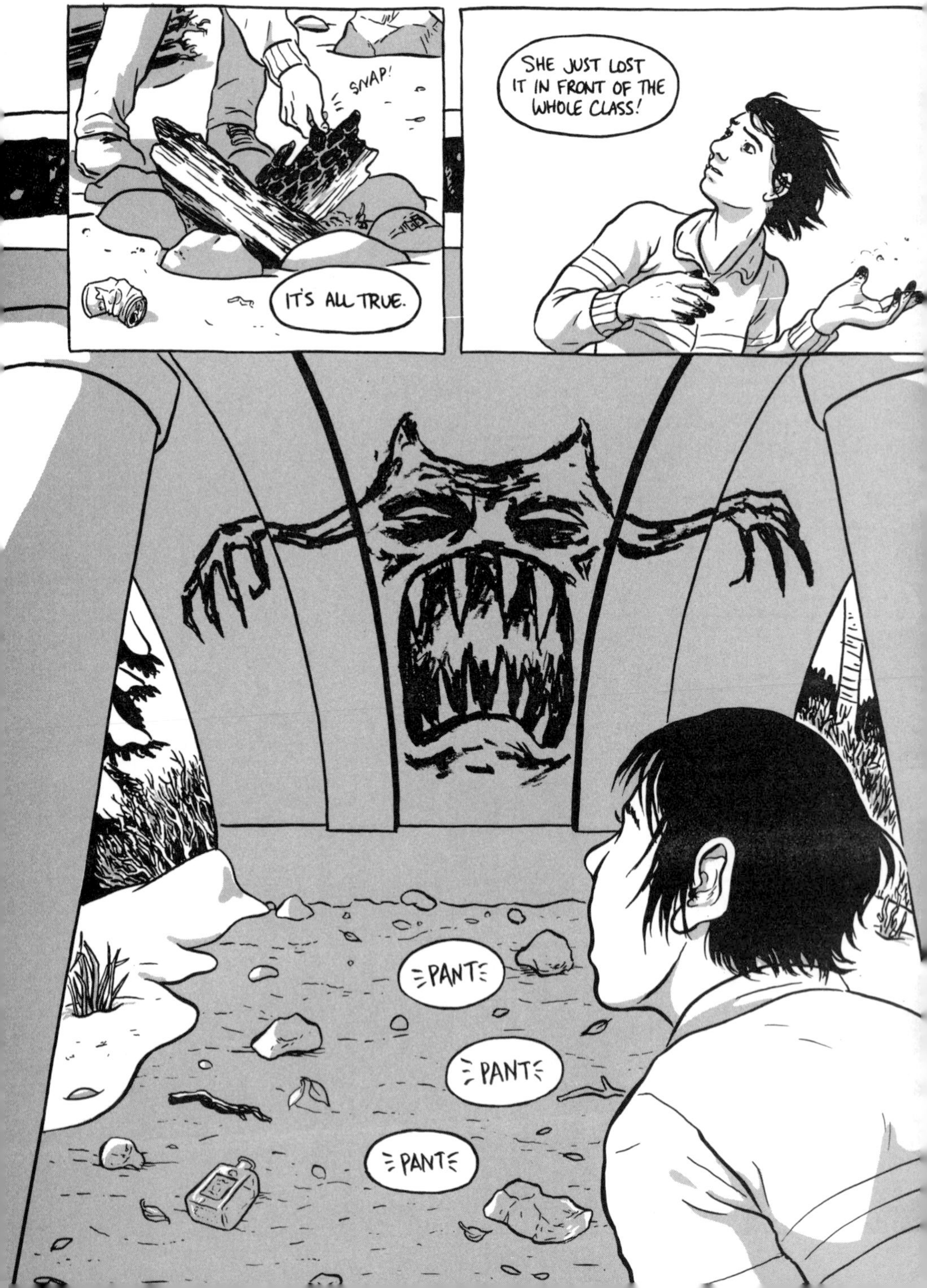
SNAP!
IT'S ALL TRUE.
SHE JUST LOST IT IN FRONT OF THE WHOLE CLASS!
PANT
PANT
PANT

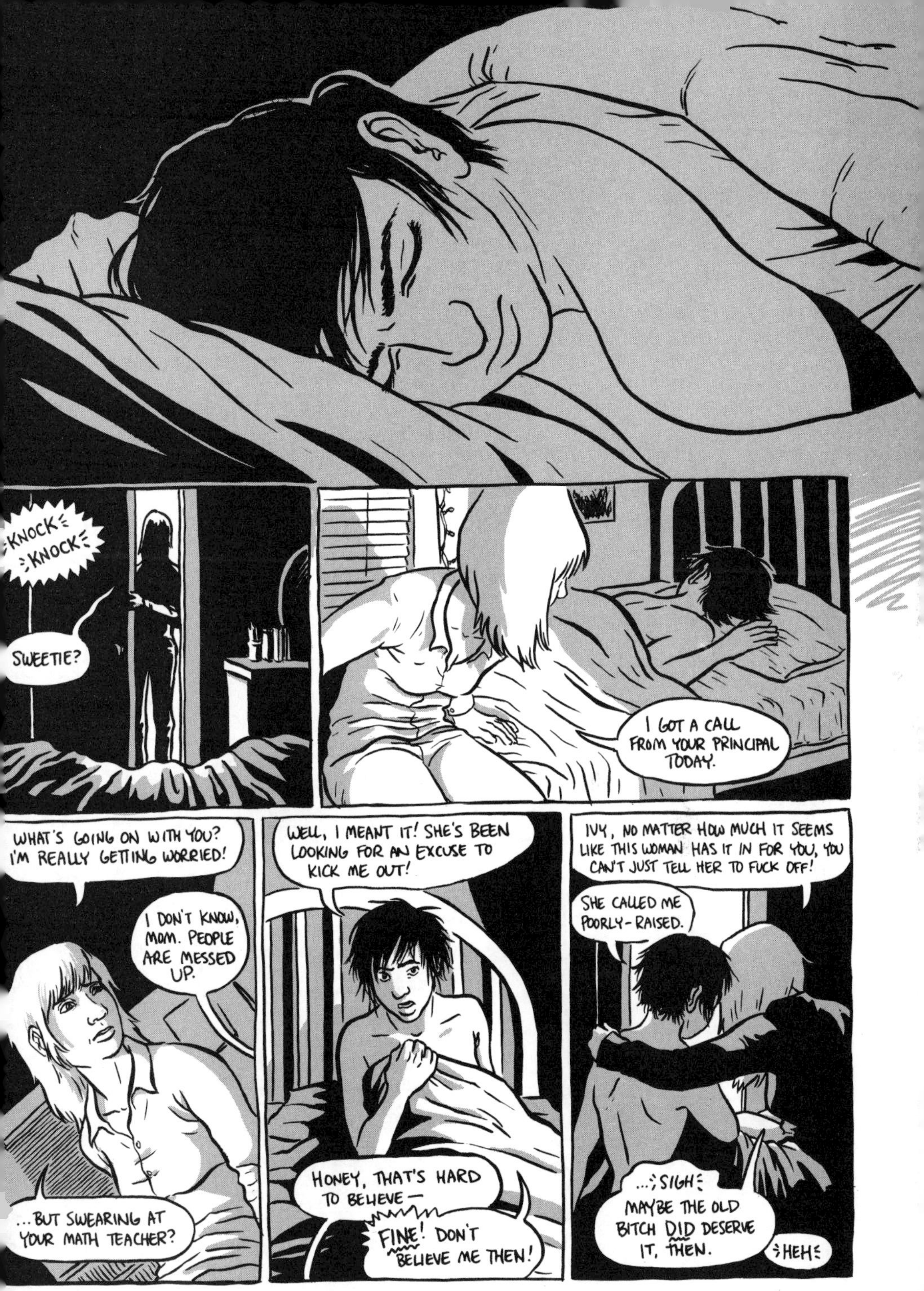

KNOCK KNOCK
SWEETIE?
I GOT A CALL FROM YOUR PRINCIPAL TODAY.
WHAT'S GOING ON WITH YOU? I'M REALLY GETTING WORRIED!
I DON'T KNOW, MOM. PEOPLE ARE MESSED UP.
...BUT SWEARING AT YOUR MATH TEACHER?
WELL, I MEANT IT! SHE'S BEEN LOOKING FOR AN EXCUSE TO KICK ME OUT!
HONEY, THAT'S HARD TO BELIEVE—
FINE! DON'T BELIEVE ME THEN!
IVY, NO MATTER HOW MUCH IT SEEMS LIKE THIS WOMAN HAS IT IN FOR YOU, YOU CAN'T JUST TELL HER TO FUCK OFF!
SHE CALLED ME POORLY-RAISED.
...SIGH
MAYBE THE OLD BITCH DID DESERVE IT, THEN.
HEH

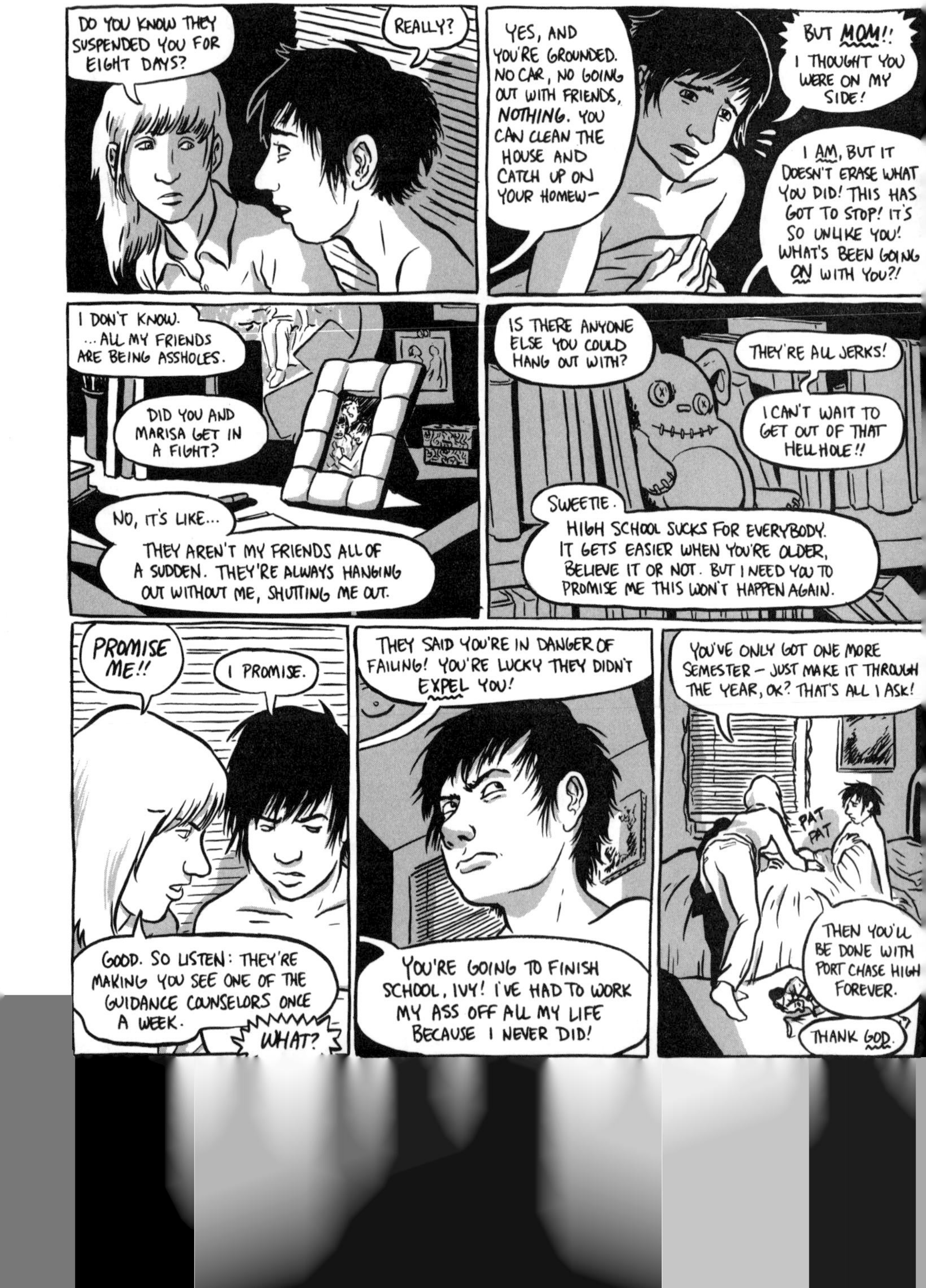
DO YOU KNOW THEY SUSPENDED YOU FOR EIGHT DAYS?
REALLY?
YES, AND YOU'RE GROUNDED. NO CAR, NO GOING OUT WITH FRIENDS, NOTHING. YOU CAN CLEAN THE HOUSE AND CATCH UP ON YOUR HOMEW—
BUT MOM!! I THOUGHT YOU WERE ON MY SIDE!
I AM, BUT IT DOESN'T ERASE WHAT YOU DID! THIS HAS GOT TO STOP! IT'S SO UNLIKE YOU! WHAT'S BEEN GOING ON WITH YOU?!
I DON'T KNOW. ...ALL MY FRIENDS ARE BEING ASSHOLES.
DID YOU AND MARISA GET IN A FIGHT?
NO, IT'S LIKE...
THEY AREN'T MY FRIENDS ALL OF A SUDDEN. THEY'RE ALWAYS HANGING OUT WITHOUT ME, SHUTTING ME OUT.
IS THERE ANYONE ELSE YOU COULD HANG OUT WITH?
THEY'RE ALL JERKS!
I CAN'T WAIT TO GET OUT OF THAT HELLHOLE!!
SWEETIE.
HIGH SCHOOL SUCKS FOR EVERYBODY. IT GETS EASIER WHEN YOU'RE OLDER, BELIEVE IT OR NOT. BUT I NEED YOU TO PROMISE ME THIS WON'T HAPPEN AGAIN.
PROMISE ME!!
I PROMISE.
GOOD. SO LISTEN: THEY'RE MAKING YOU SEE ONE OF THE GUIDANCE COUNSELORS ONCE A WEEK.
WHAT?
THEY SAID YOU'RE IN DANGER OF FAILING! YOU'RE LUCKY THEY DIDN'T EXPEL YOU!
YOU'RE GOING TO FINISH SCHOOL, IVY! I'VE HAD TO WORK MY ASS OFF ALL MY LIFE BECAUSE I NEVER DID!
YOU'VE ONLY GOT ONE MORE SEMESTER — JUST MAKE IT THROUGH THE YEAR, OK? THAT'S ALL I ASK!
PAT PAT
THEN YOU'LL BE DONE WITH PORT CHASE HIGH FOREVER.
THANK GOD.

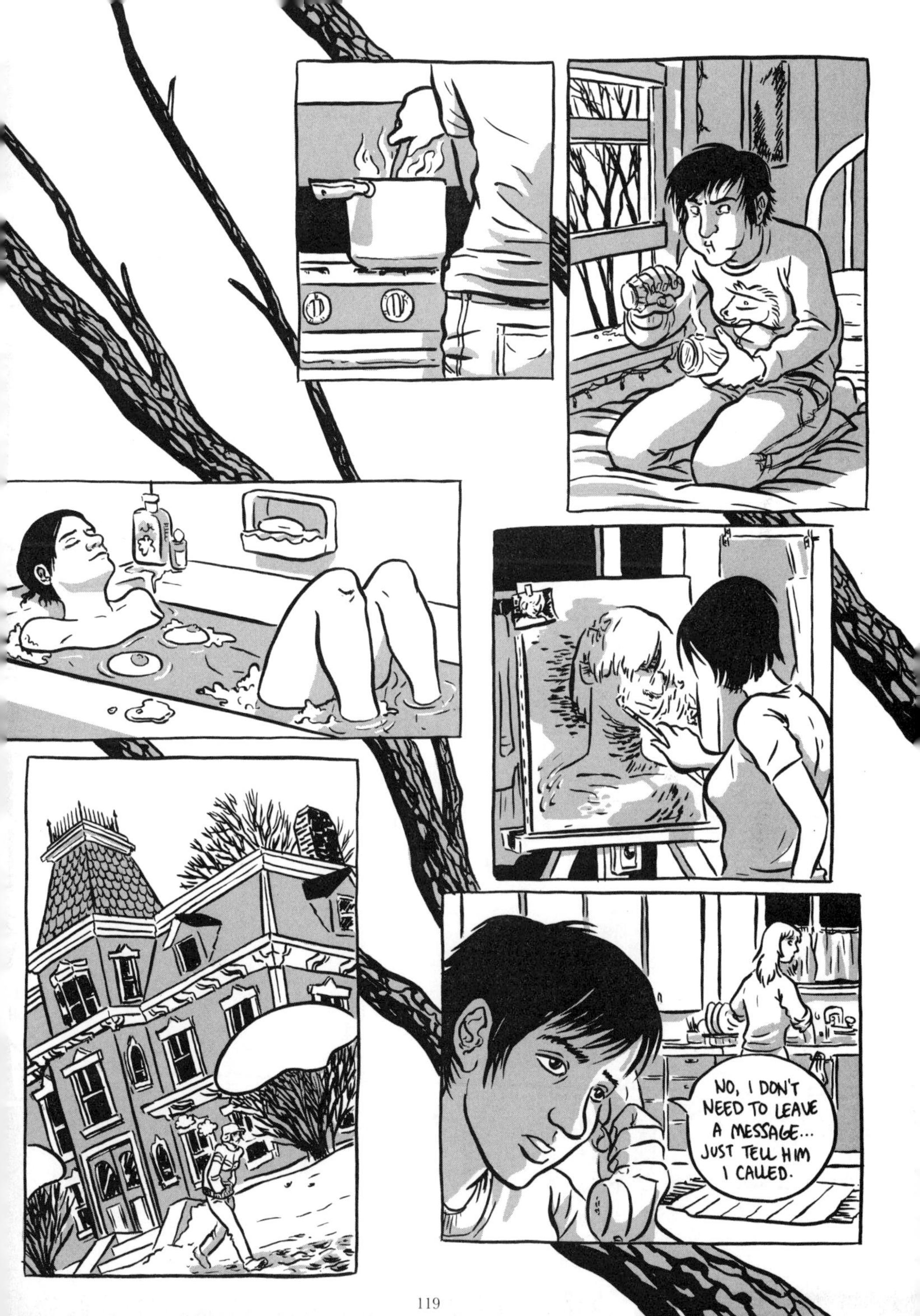
NO, I DON'T NEED TO LEAVE A MESSAGE... JUST TELL HIM I CALLED.

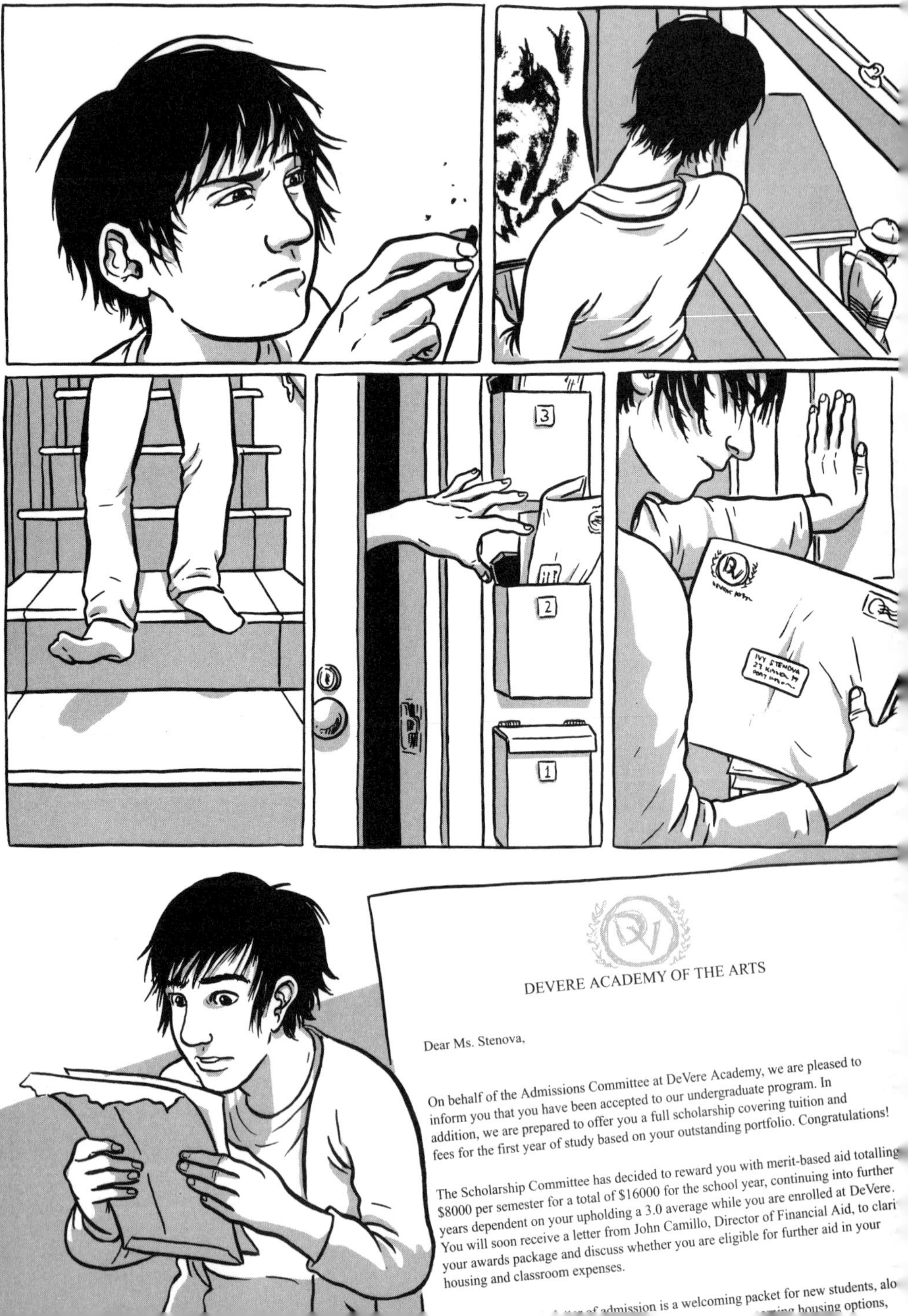
3
2
1
IVY STENOVA
DEVERE ACADEMY OF THE ARTS
Dear Ms. Stenova,
On behalf of the Admissions Committee at DeVere Academy, we are pleased to inform you that you have been accepted to our undergraduate program. In addition, we are prepared to offer you a full scholarship covering tuition and fees for the first year of study based on your outstanding portfolio. Congratulations!
The Scholarship Committee has decided to reward you with merit-based aid totalling $8000 per semester for a total of $16000 for the school year, continuing into further years dependent on your upholding a 3.0 average while you are enrolled at DeVere. You will soon receive a letter from John Camillo, Director of Financial Aid, to clari your awards package and discuss whether you are eligible for further aid in your housing and classroom expenses.
of admission is a welcoming packet for new students, alo
housing options,

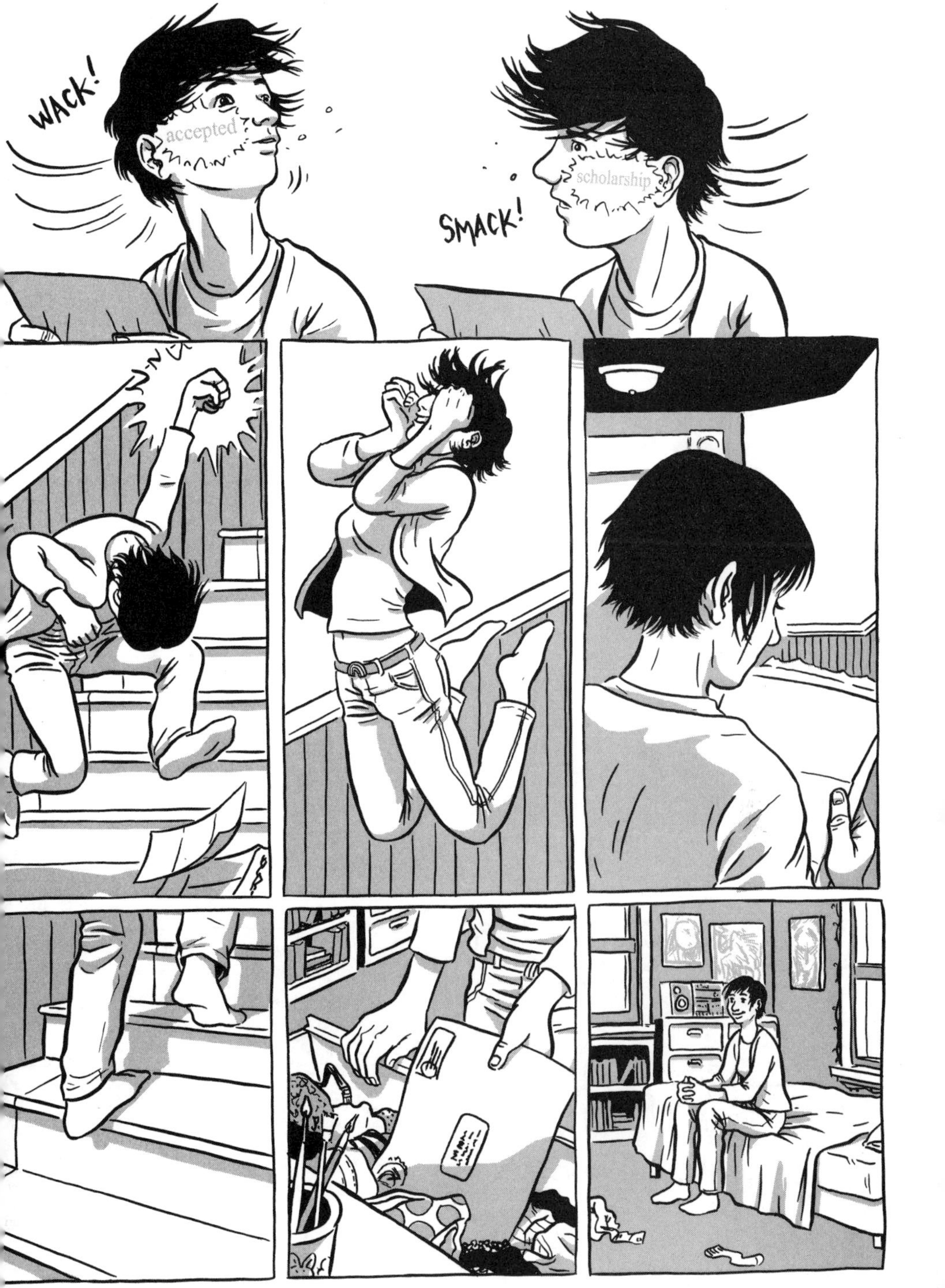
WACK!
accepted
scholarship
SMACK!

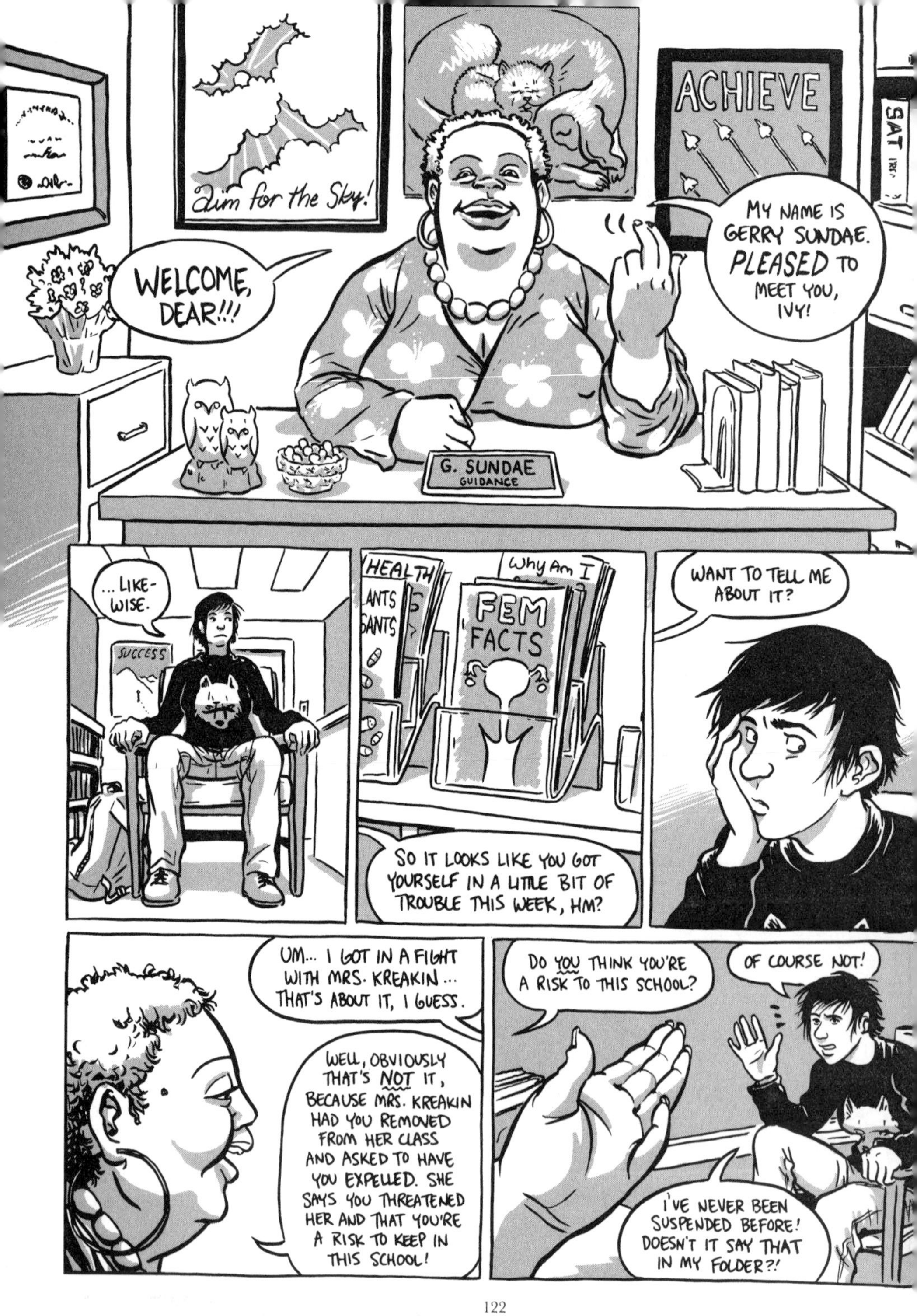
Aim for the Sky!
ACHIEVE
SAT
WELCOME, DEAR!!!
MY NAME IS GERRY SUNDAE. PLEASED TO MEET YOU, IVY!
G. SUNDAE
GUIDANCE
...LIKE-WISE.
SUCCESS
HEALTH
Why Am I
FEM FACTS
SO IT LOOKS LIKE YOU GOT YOURSELF IN A LITTLE BIT OF TROUBLE THIS WEEK, HM?
WANT TO TELL ME ABOUT IT?
UM... I GOT IN A FIGHT WITH MRS. KREAKIN... THAT'S ABOUT IT, I GUESS.
WELL, OBVIOUSLY THAT'S NOT IT, BECAUSE MRS. KREAKIN HAD YOU REMOVED FROM HER CLASS AND ASKED TO HAVE YOU EXPELLED. SHE SAYS YOU THREATENED HER AND THAT YOU'RE A RISK TO KEEP IN THIS SCHOOL!
DO YOU THINK YOU'RE A RISK TO THIS SCHOOL?
OF COURSE NOT!
I'VE NEVER BEEN SUSPENDED BEFORE! DOESN'T IT SAY THAT IN MY FOLDER?!

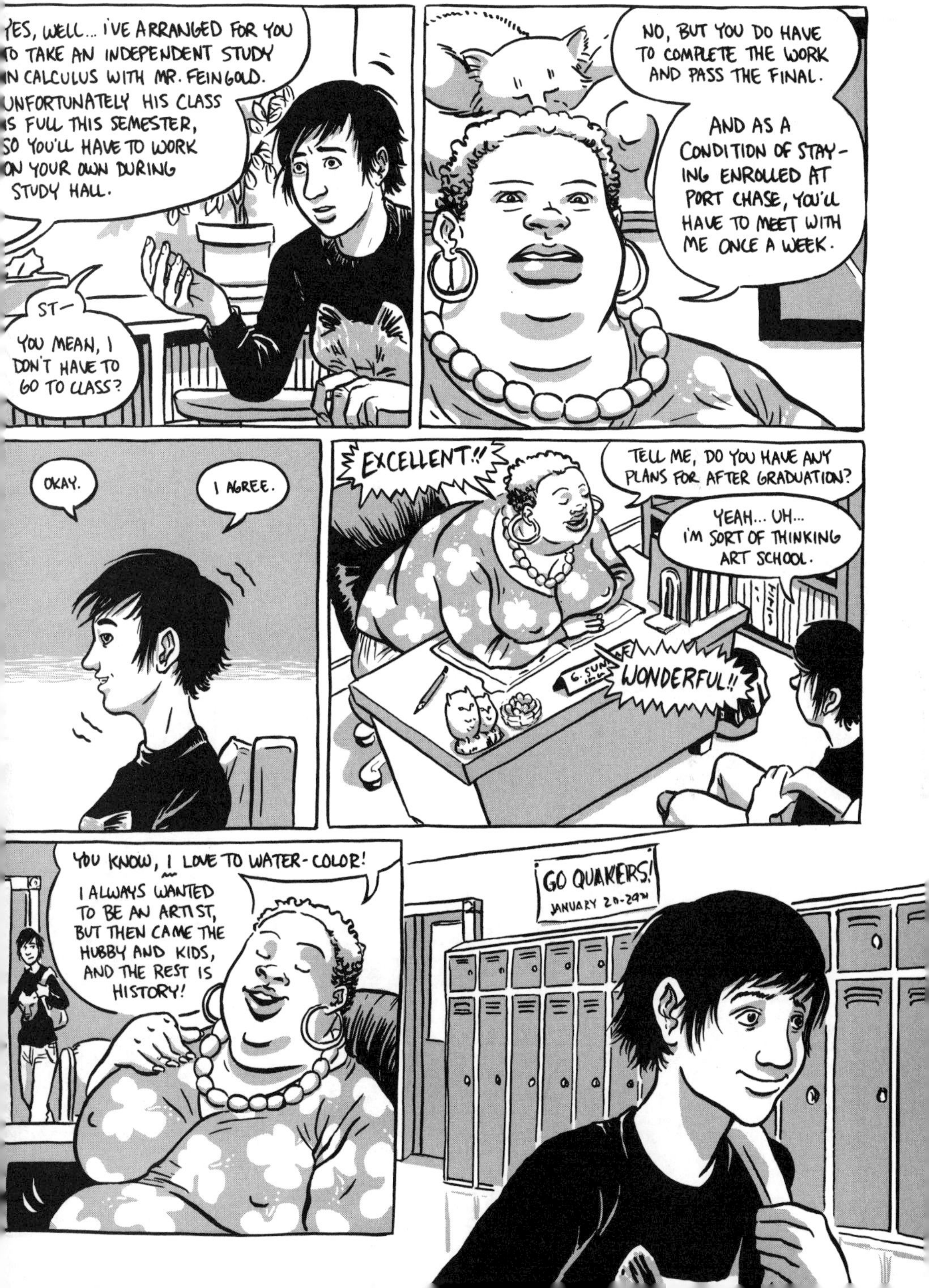
YES, WELL... I'VE ARRANGED FOR YOU TO TAKE AN INDEPENDENT STUDY IN CALCULUS WITH MR. FEINGOLD. UNFORTUNATELY HIS CLASS IS FULL THIS SEMESTER, SO YOU'LL HAVE TO WORK ON YOUR OWN DURING STUDY HALL.
ST—
YOU MEAN, I DON'T HAVE TO GO TO CLASS?
NO, BUT YOU DO HAVE TO COMPLETE THE WORK AND PASS THE FINAL.
AND AS A CONDITION OF STAYING ENROLLED AT PORT CHASE, YOU'LL HAVE TO MEET WITH ME ONCE A WEEK.
OKAY.
I AGREE.
EXCELLENT!!
TELL ME, DO YOU HAVE ANY PLANS FOR AFTER GRADUATION?
YEAH... UH... I'M SORT OF THINKING ART SCHOOL.
WONDERFUL!!
YOU KNOW, I LOVE TO WATER-COLOR!
I ALWAYS WANTED TO BE AN ARTIST, BUT THEN CAME THE HUBBY AND KIDS, AND THE REST IS HISTORY!
GO QUAKERS!
JANUARY 20-29TH

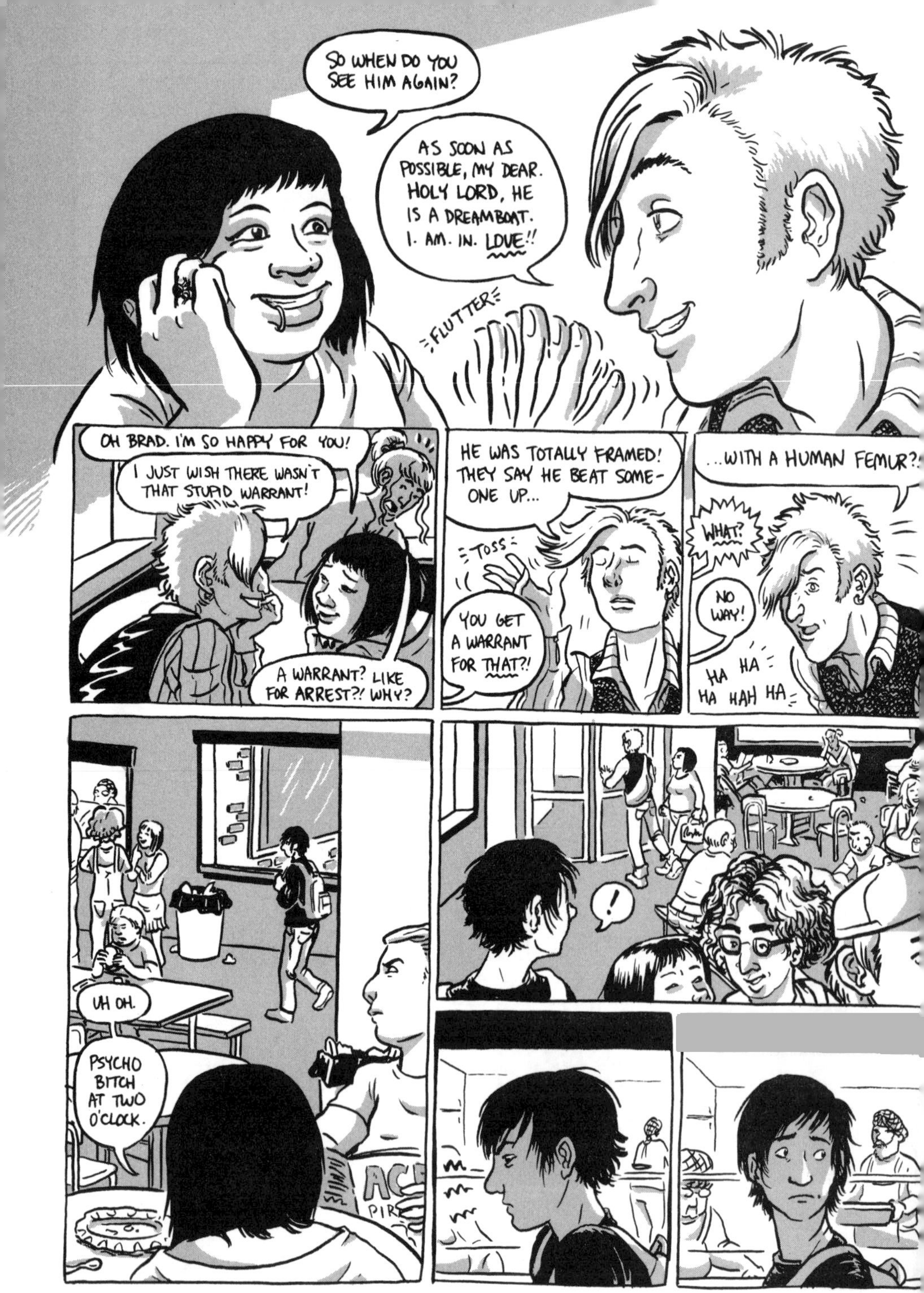

SO WHEN DO YOU SEE HIM AGAIN?
AS SOON AS POSSIBLE, MY DEAR. HOLY LORD, HE IS A DREAMBOAT. I. AM. IN. LOVE!!
FLUTTER
OH BRAD. I'M SO HAPPY FOR YOU!
I JUST WISH THERE WASN'T THAT STUPID WARRANT!
A WARRANT? LIKE FOR ARREST?! WHY?
HE WAS TOTALLY FRAMED! THEY SAY HE BEAT SOME-ONE UP...
TOSS
YOU GET A WARRANT FOR THAT?!
...WITH A HUMAN FEMUR?!
WHAT?
NO WAY!
HA HA HA HAH HA
UH OH.
PSYCHO BITCH AT TWO O'CLOCK.
!

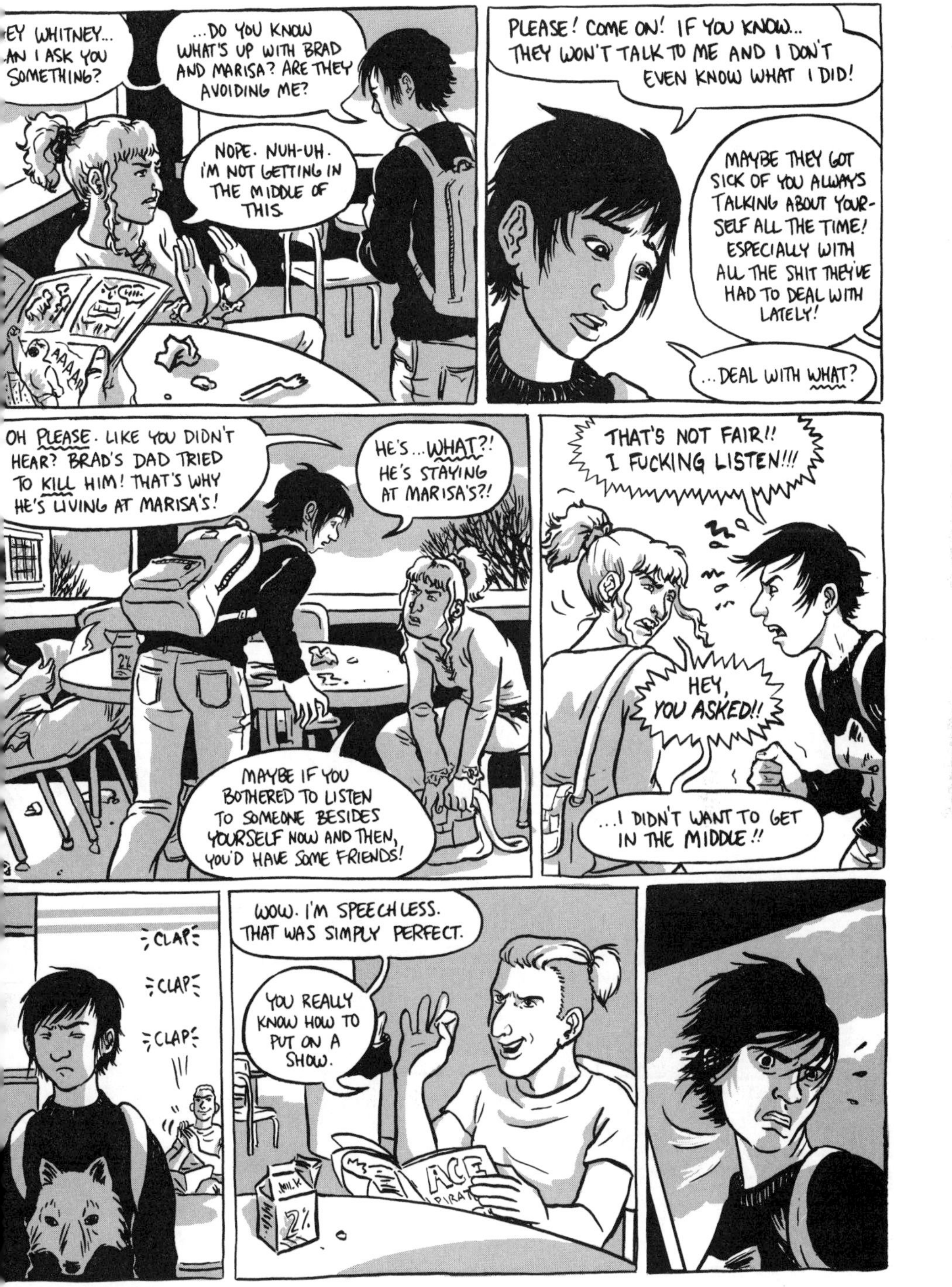
EY WHITNEY... AN I ASK YOU SOMETHING?
...DO YOU KNOW WHAT'S UP WITH BRAD AND MARISA? ARE THEY AVOIDING ME?
NOPE. NUH-UH. I'M NOT GETTING IN THE MIDDLE OF THIS.
AAAAA
PLEASE! COME ON! IF YOU KNOW... THEY WON'T TALK TO ME AND I DON'T EVEN KNOW WHAT I DID!
MAYBE THEY GOT SICK OF YOU ALWAYS TALKING ABOUT YOURSELF ALL THE TIME! ESPECIALLY WITH ALL THE SHIT THEY'VE HAD TO DEAL WITH LATELY!
...DEAL WITH WHAT?
OH PLEASE. LIKE YOU DIDN'T HEAR? BRAD'S DAD TRIED TO KILL HIM! THAT'S WHY HE'S LIVING AT MARISA'S!
HE'S...WHAT?! HE'S STAYING AT MARISA'S?!
MAYBE IF YOU BOTHERED TO LISTEN TO SOMEONE BESIDES YOURSELF NOW AND THEN, YOU'D HAVE SOME FRIENDS!
THAT'S NOT FAIR!! I FUCKING LISTEN!!!
HEY, YOU ASKED!!
...I DIDN'T WANT TO GET IN THE MIDDLE!!
CLAP
CLAP
CLAP
WOW. I'M SPEECHLESS. THAT WAS SIMPLY PERFECT.
YOU REALLY KNOW HOW TO PUT ON A SHOW.
MILK
2%
ACE

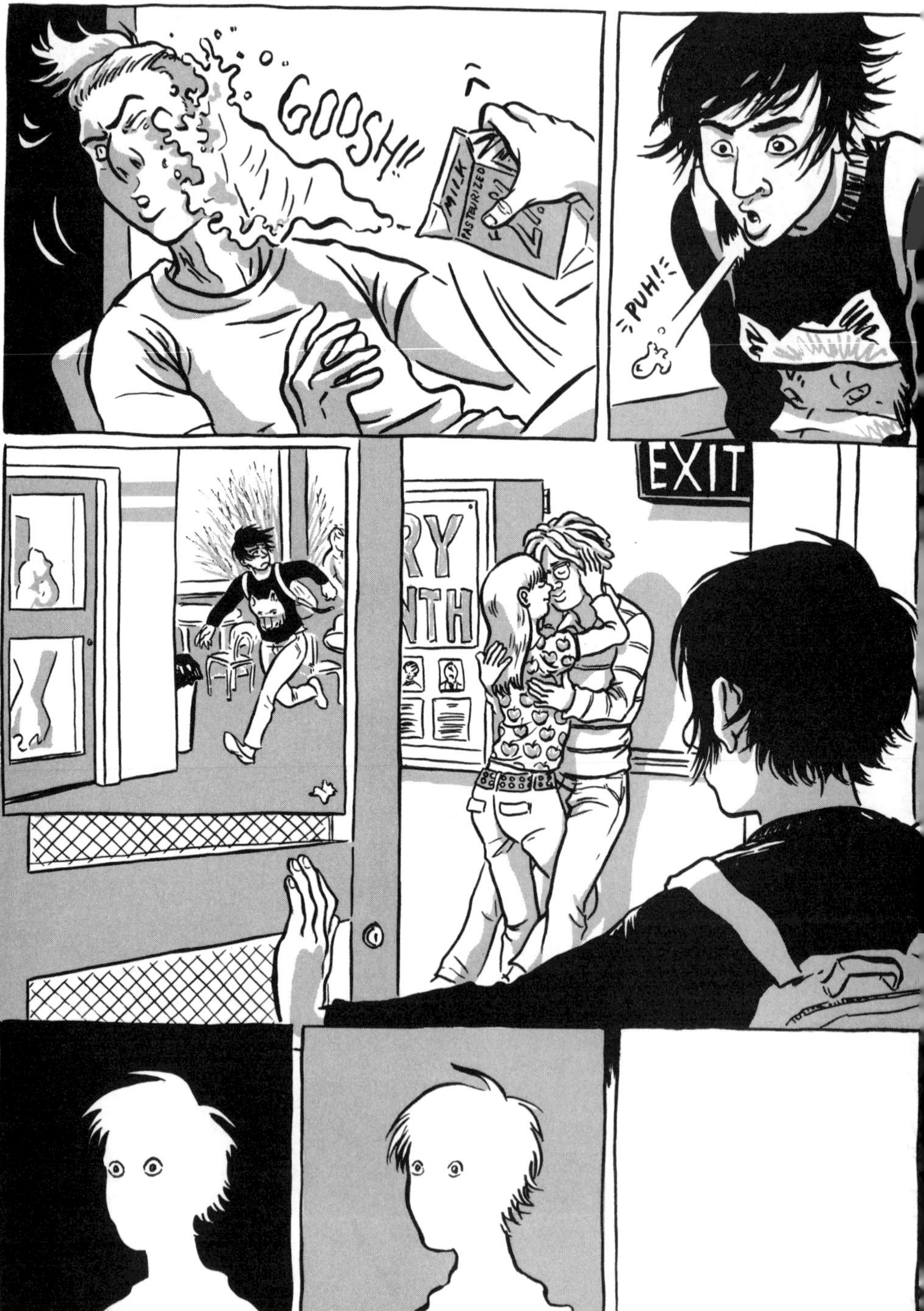
GOOSH!!
MILK
PASTEURIZED
PUH!
EXIT
RY
NTH

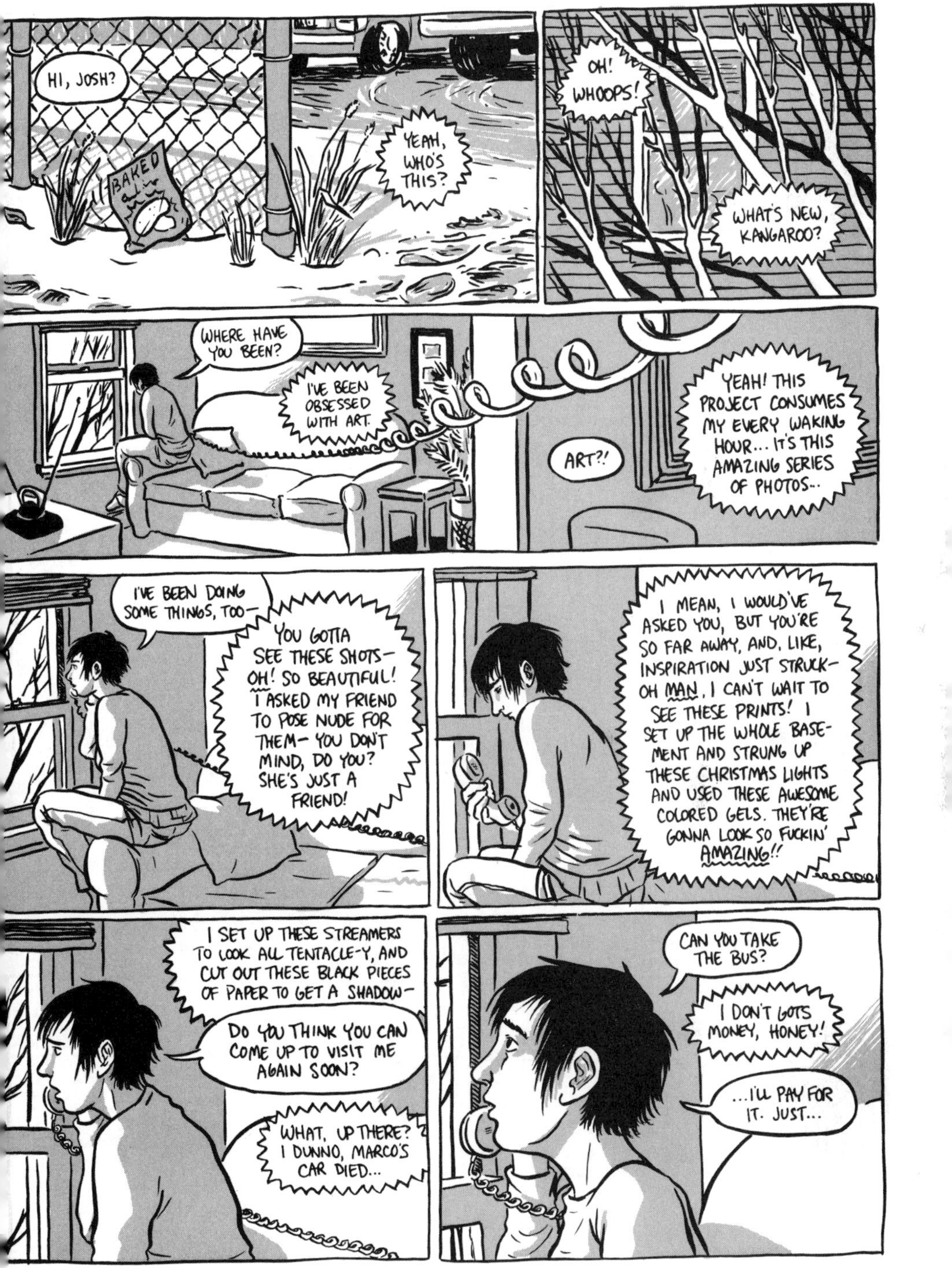
HI, JOSH?
YEAH, WHO'S THIS?
BAKED
OH! WHOOPS!
WHAT'S NEW, KANGAROO?
WHERE HAVE YOU BEEN?
I'VE BEEN OBSESSED WITH ART.
ART?!
YEAH! THIS PROJECT CONSUMES MY EVERY WAKING HOUR... IT'S THIS AMAZING SERIES OF PHOTOS..
I'VE BEEN DOING SOME THINGS, TOO—
YOU GOTTA SEE THESE SHOTS— OH! SO BEAUTIFUL! I ASKED MY FRIEND TO POSE NUDE FOR THEM— YOU DON'T MIND, DO YOU? SHE'S JUST A FRIEND!
I MEAN, I WOULD'VE ASKED YOU, BUT YOU'RE SO FAR AWAY, AND, LIKE, INSPIRATION JUST STRUCK— OH MAN, I CAN'T WAIT TO SEE THESE PRINTS! I SET UP THE WHOLE BASEMENT AND STRUNG UP THESE CHRISTMAS LIGHTS AND USED THESE AWESOME COLORED GELS. THEY'RE GONNA LOOK SO FUCKIN' AMAZING!!
I SET UP THESE STREAMERS TO LOOK ALL TENTACLE-Y, AND CUT OUT THESE BLACK PIECES OF PAPER TO GET A SHADOW—
DO YOU THINK YOU CAN COME UP TO VISIT ME AGAIN SOON?
WHAT, UP THERE? I DUNNO, MARCO'S CAR DIED...
CAN YOU TAKE THE BUS?
I DON'T GOTS MONEY, HONEY!
...I'LL PAY FOR IT. JUST...

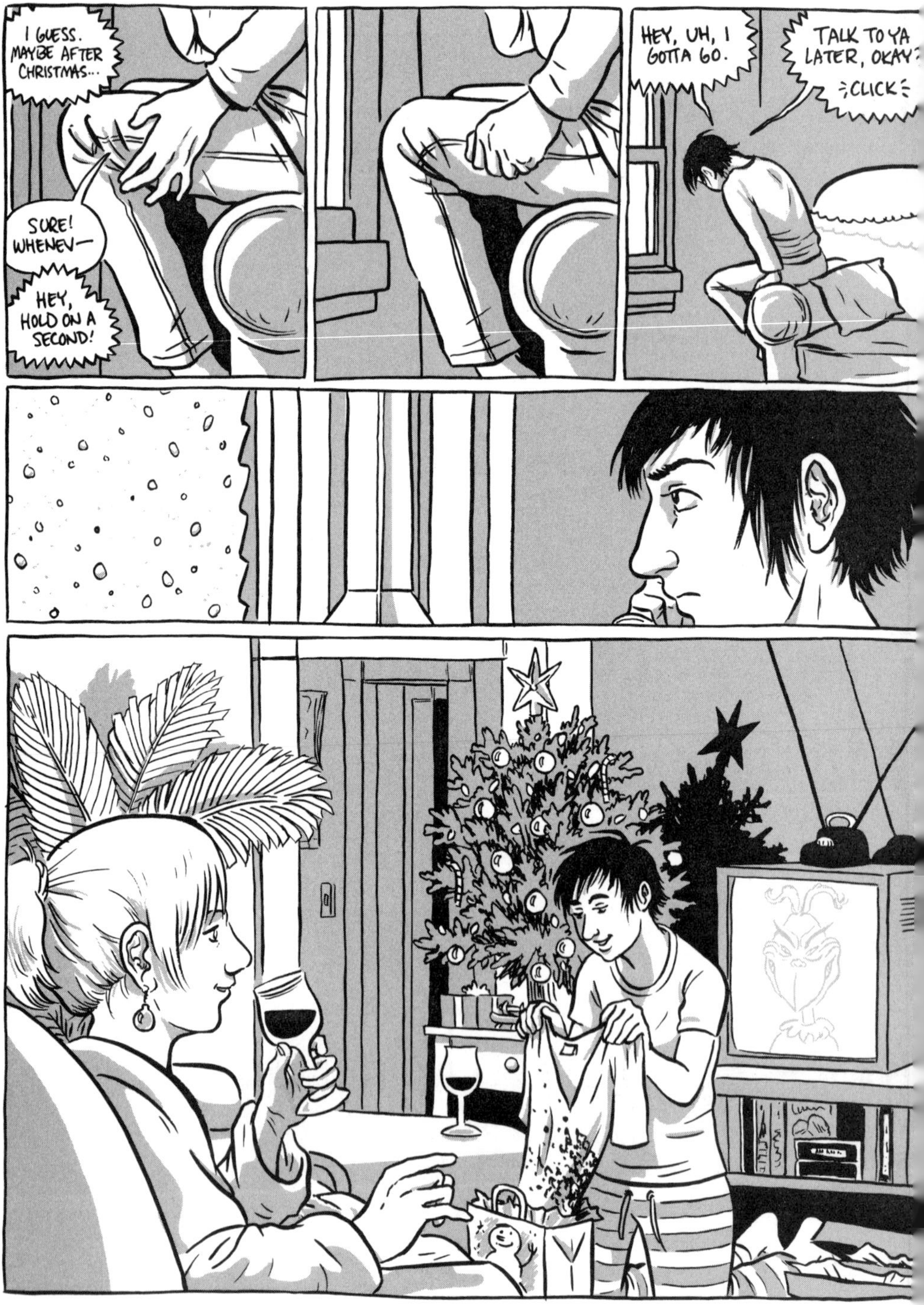
I GUESS. MAYBE AFTER CHRISTMAS...
SURE! WHENEV—
HEY, HOLD ON A SECOND!
HEY, UH, I GOTTA GO.
TALK TO YA LATER, OKAY?
CLICK

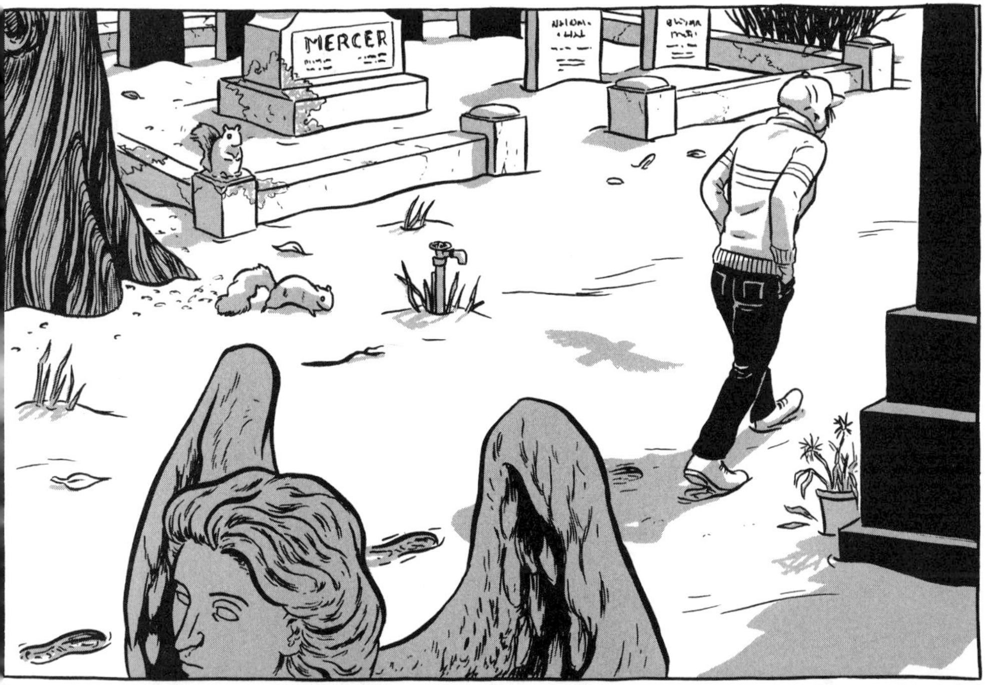
MERCER

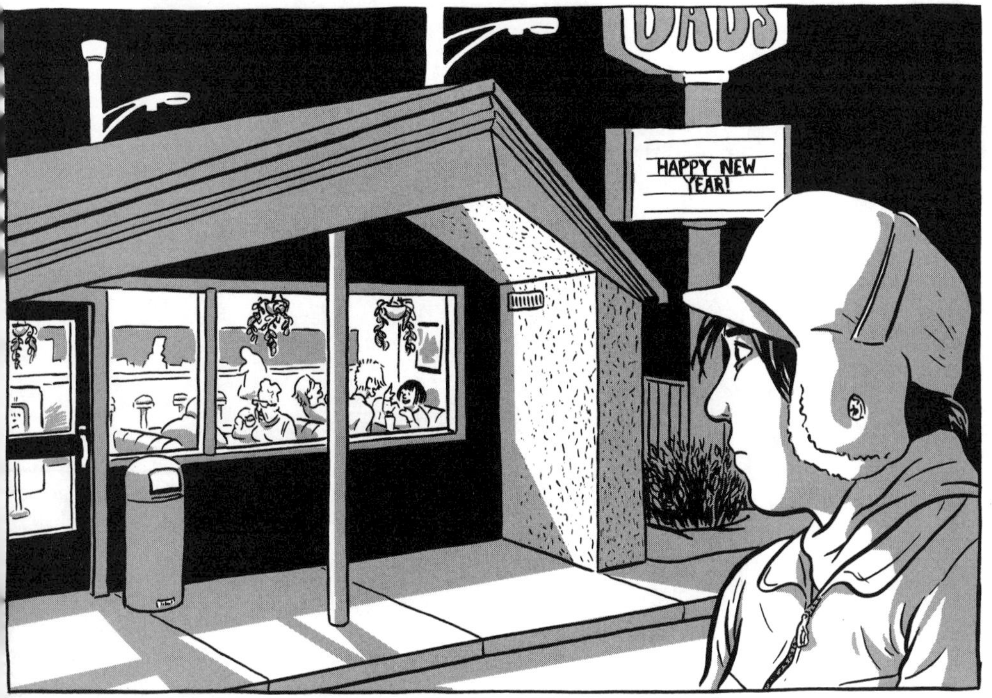
HAPPY NEW YEAR!

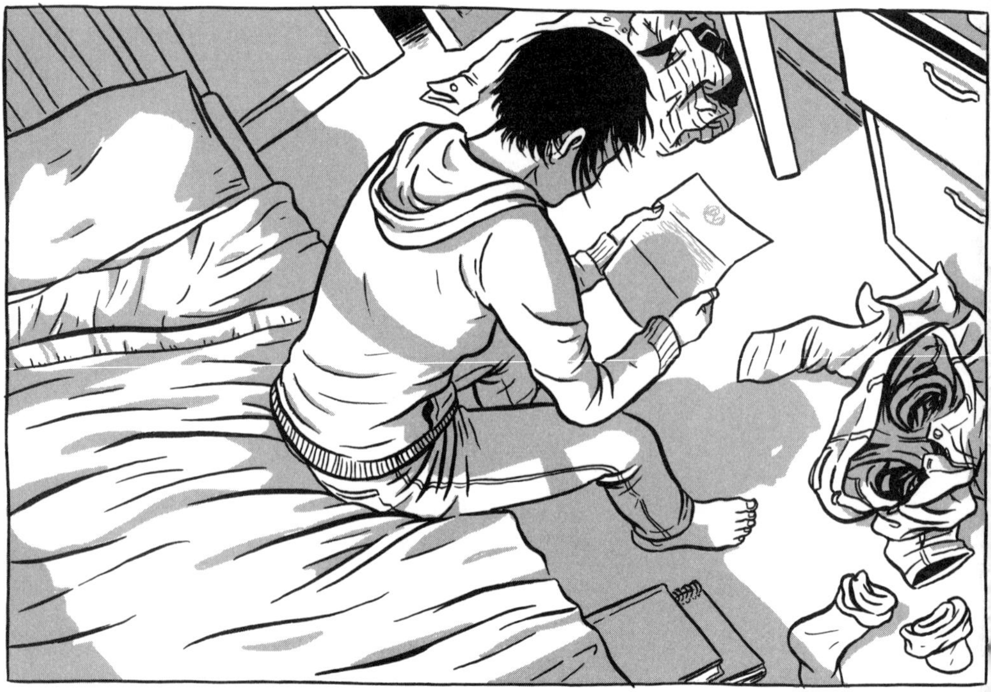

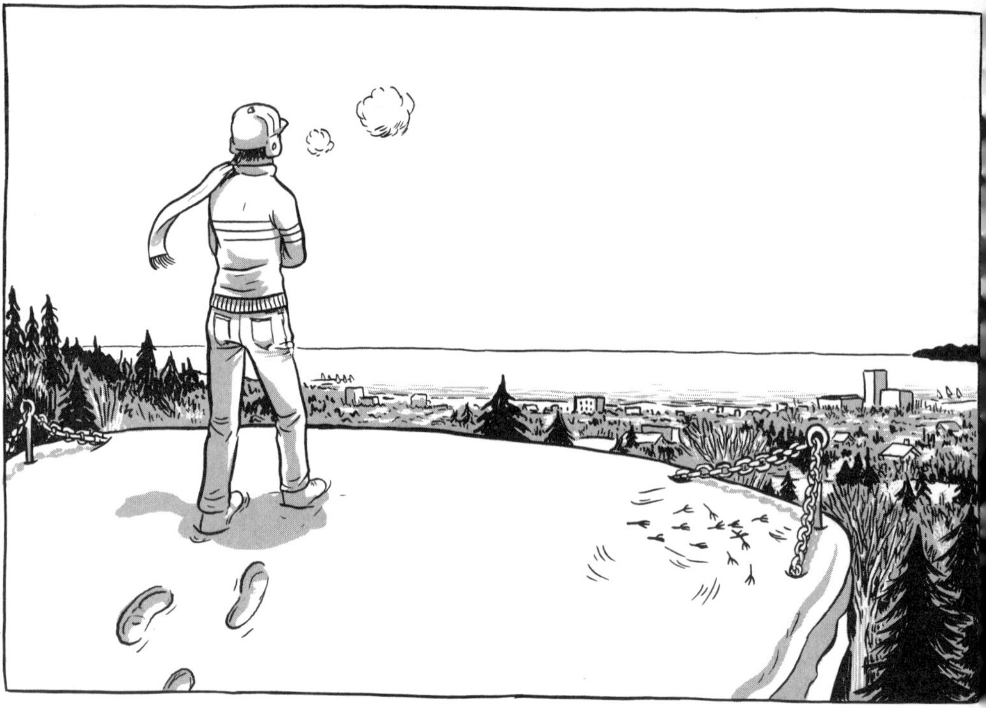

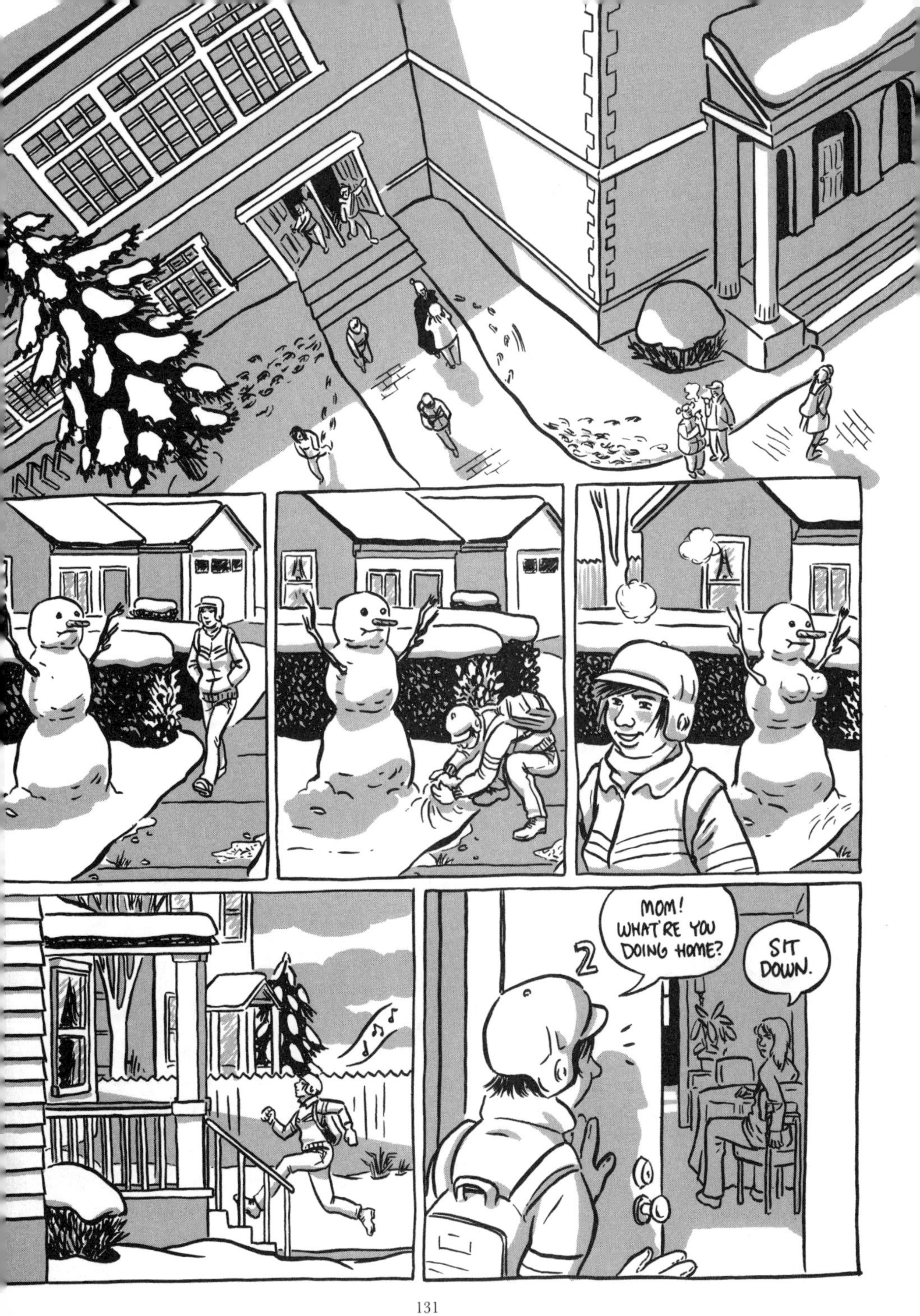

2
MOM! WHAT'RE YOU DOING HOME?
SIT DOWN.

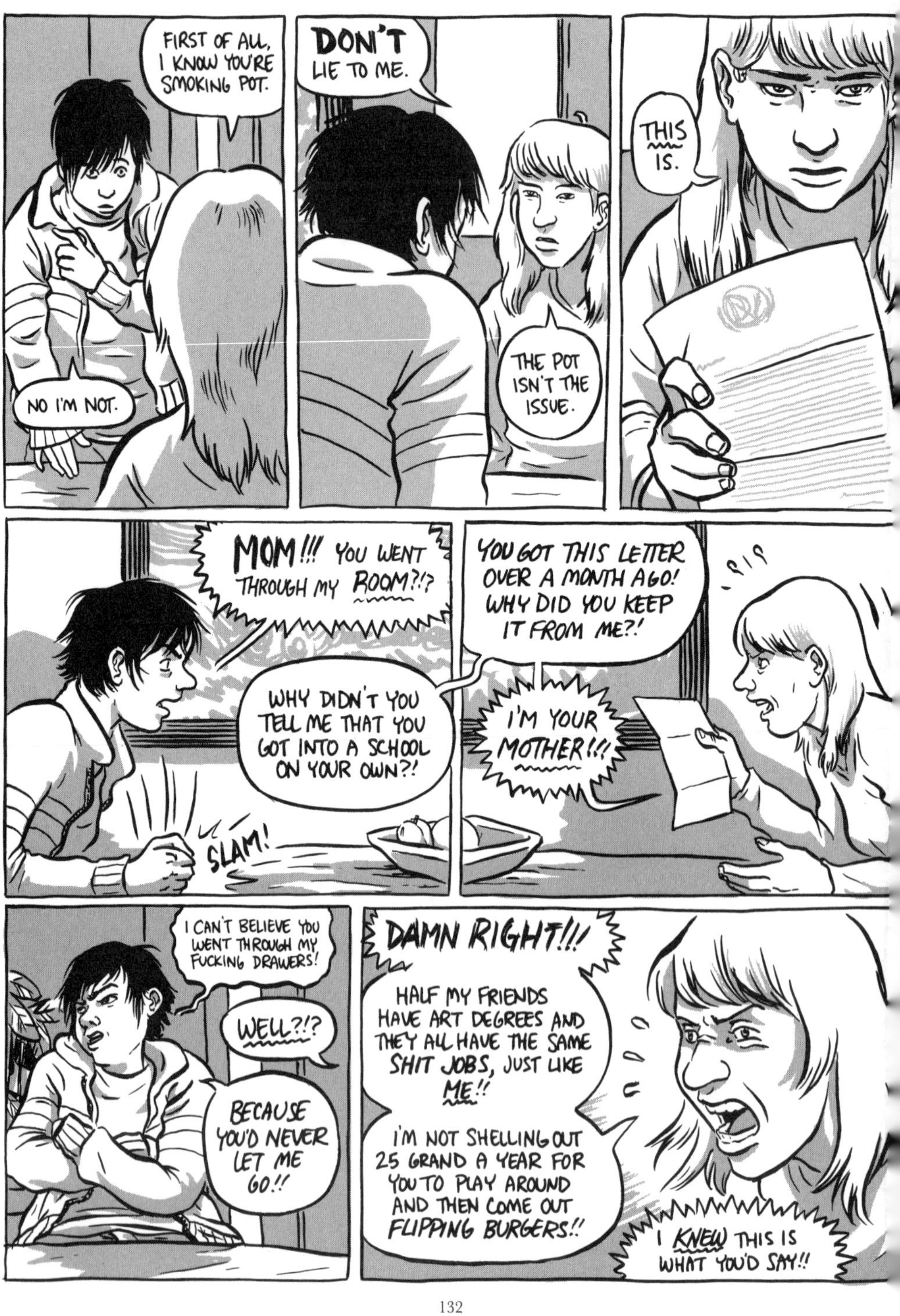
FIRST OF ALL, I KNOW YOU'RE SMOKING POT.
NO I'M NOT.
DON'T LIE TO ME.
THE POT ISN'T THE ISSUE.
THIS IS.
MOM!!! YOU WENT THROUGH MY ROOM?!?
WHY DIDN'T YOU TELL ME THAT YOU GOT INTO A SCHOOL ON YOUR OWN?!
SLAM!
YOU GOT THIS LETTER OVER A MONTH AGO! WHY DID YOU KEEP IT FROM ME?!
I'M YOUR MOTHER!!!
I CAN'T BELIEVE YOU WENT THROUGH MY FUCKING DRAWERS!
WELL?!?
BECAUSE YOU'D NEVER LET ME GO!!
DAMN RIGHT!!!
HALF MY FRIENDS HAVE ART DEGREES AND THEY ALL HAVE THE SAME SHIT JOBS, JUST LIKE ME!!
I'M NOT SHELLING OUT 25 GRAND A YEAR FOR YOU TO PLAY AROUND AND THEN COME OUT FLIPPING BURGERS!!
I KNEW THIS IS WHAT YOU'D SAY!!

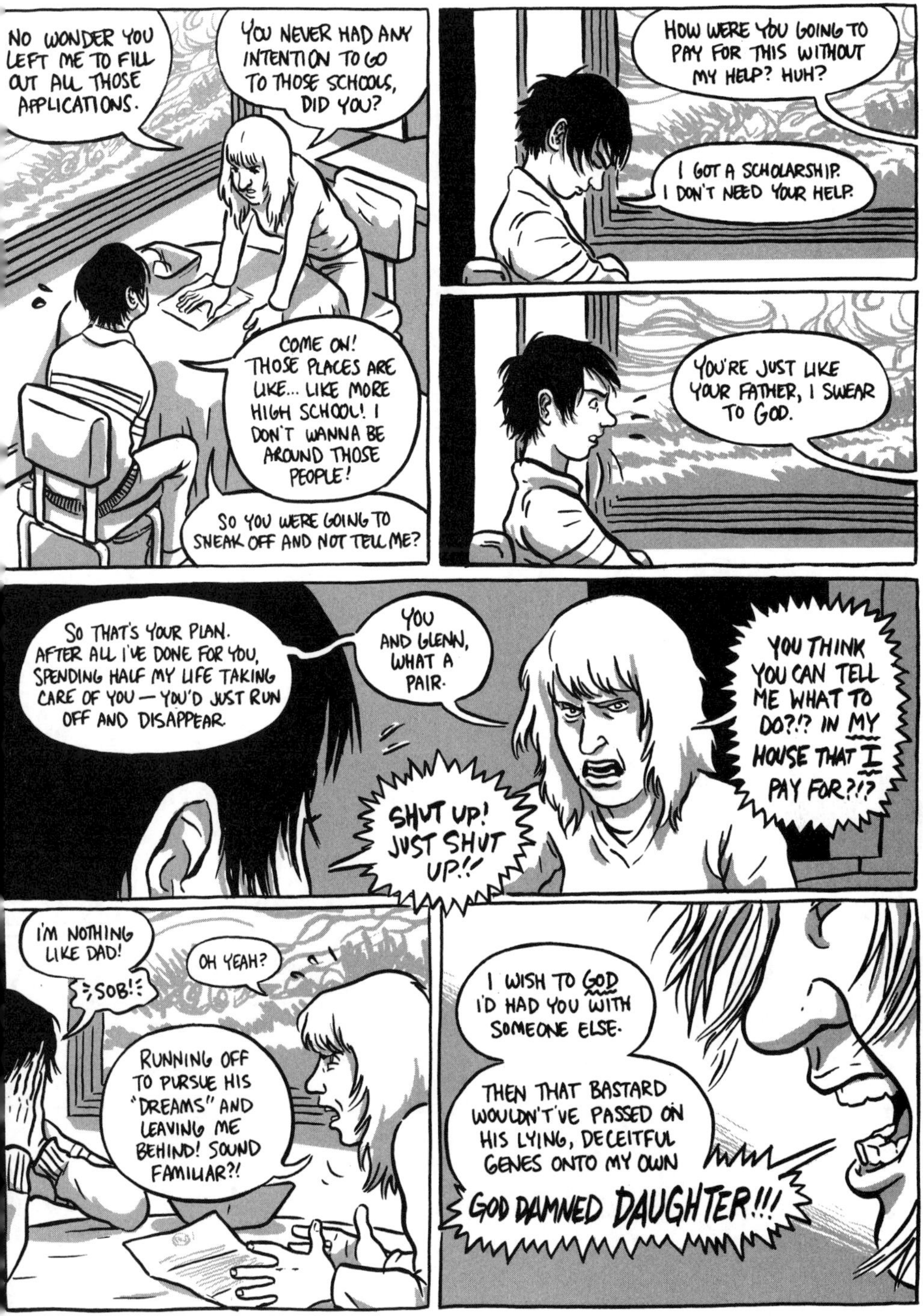
NO WONDER YOU LEFT ME TO FILL OUT ALL THOSE APPLICATIONS.
YOU NEVER HAD ANY INTENTION TO GO TO THOSE SCHOOLS, DID YOU?
COME ON! THOSE PLACES ARE LIKE... LIKE MORE HIGH SCHOOL! I DON'T WANNA BE AROUND THOSE PEOPLE!
SO YOU WERE GOING TO SNEAK OFF AND NOT TELL ME?
HOW WERE YOU GOING TO PAY FOR THIS WITHOUT MY HELP? HUH?
I GOT A SCHOLARSHIP. I DON'T NEED YOUR HELP.
YOU'RE JUST LIKE YOUR FATHER, I SWEAR TO GOD.
SO THAT'S YOUR PLAN. AFTER ALL I'VE DONE FOR YOU, SPENDING HALF MY LIFE TAKING CARE OF YOU — YOU'D JUST RUN OFF AND DISAPPEAR.
YOU AND GLENN, WHAT A PAIR.
YOU THINK YOU CAN TELL ME WHAT TO DO?!? IN MY HOUSE THAT I PAY FOR?!?
SHUT UP! JUST SHUT UP!!
I'M NOTHING LIKE DAD!
SOB!
OH YEAH?
RUNNING OFF TO PURSUE HIS "DREAMS" AND LEAVING ME BEHIND! SOUND FAMILIAR?!
I WISH TO GOD I'D HAD YOU WITH SOMEONE ELSE.
THEN THAT BASTARD WOULDN'T'VE PASSED ON HIS LYING, DECEITFUL GENES ONTO MY OWN
GOD DAMNED DAUGHTER!!!

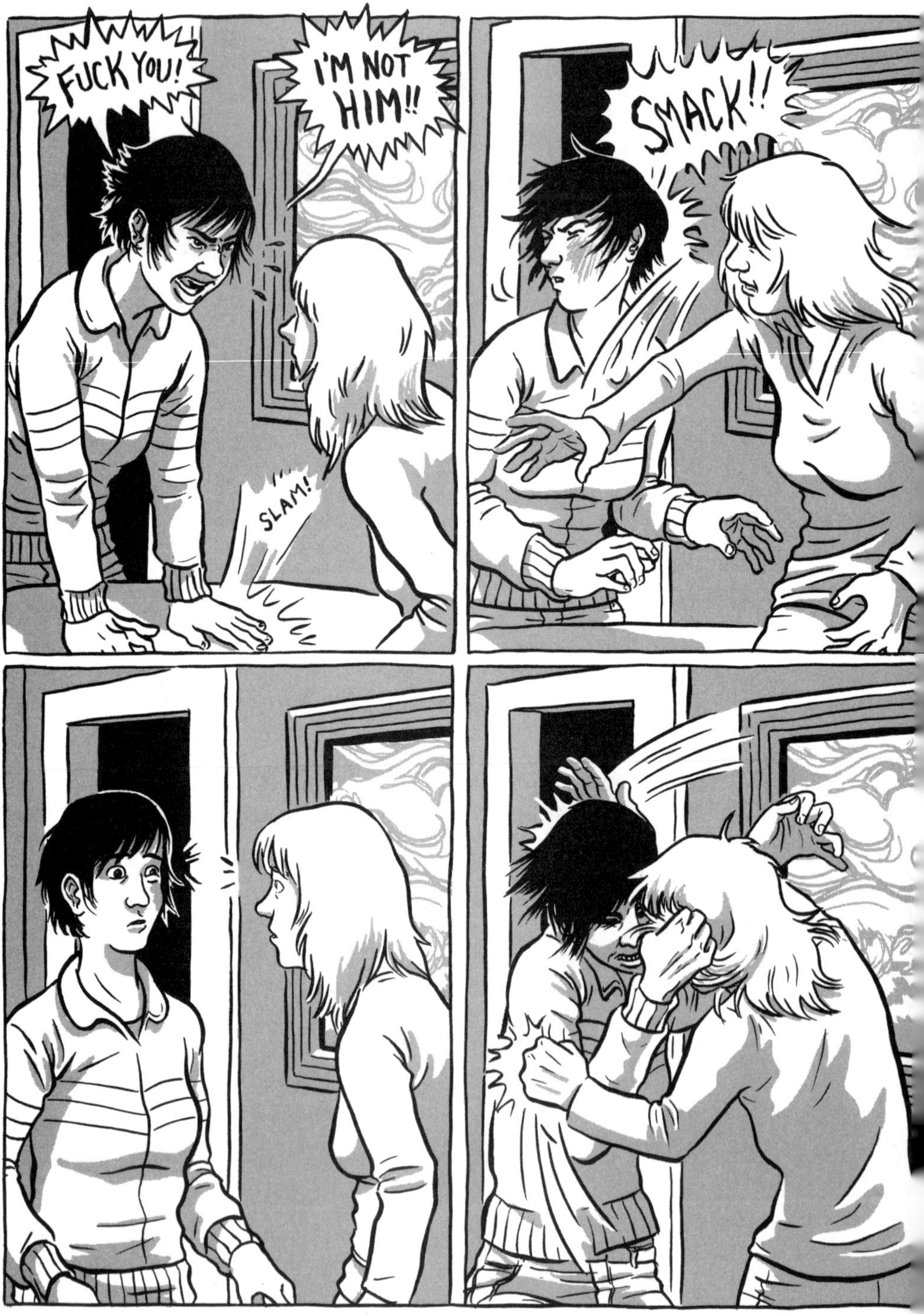
FUCK YOU!
I'M NOT HIM!!
SLAM!
SMACK!!

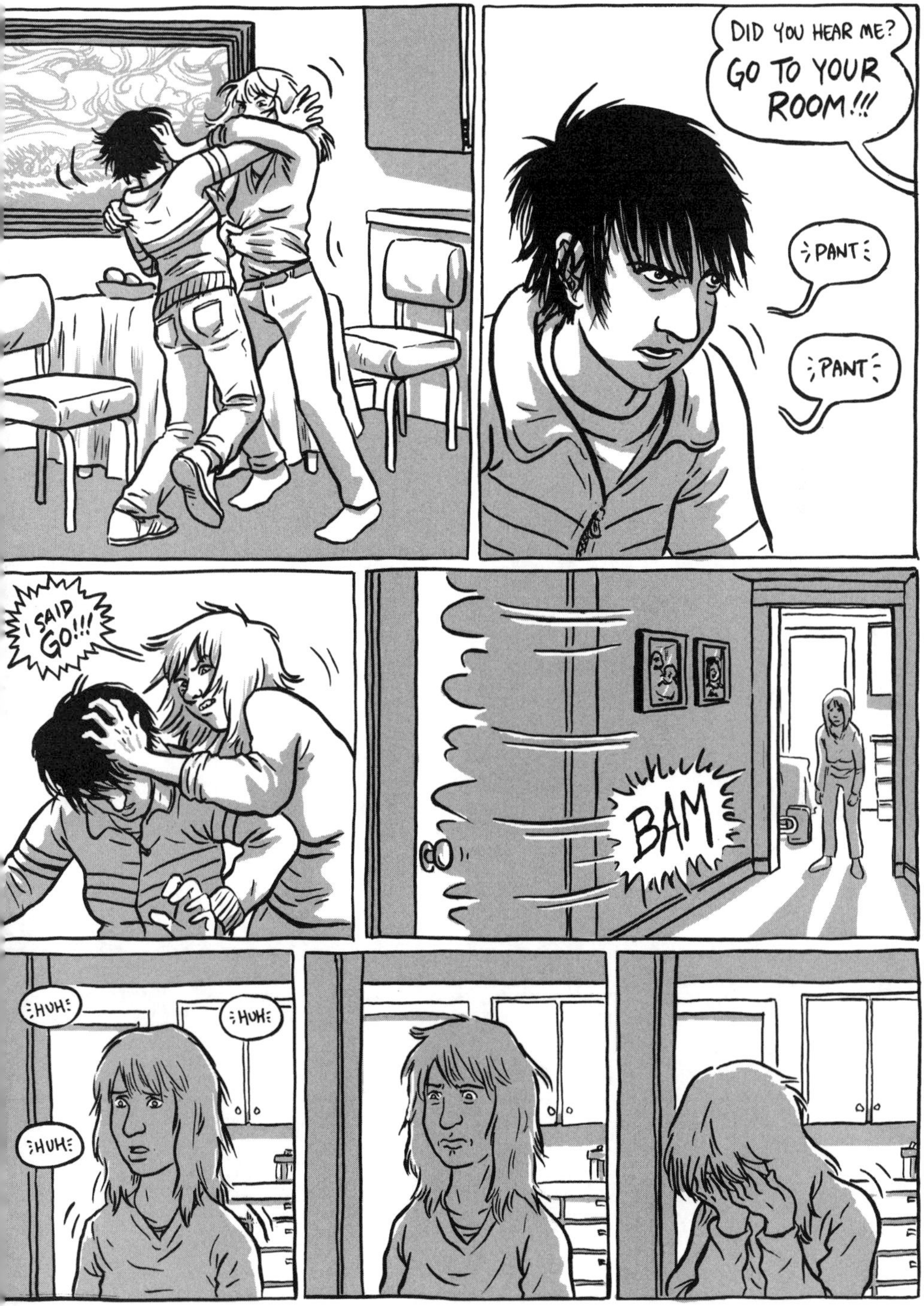
DID YOU HEAR ME? GO TO YOUR ROOM!!!
PANT
PANT
I SAID GO!!!
BAM
HUH
HUH
HUH

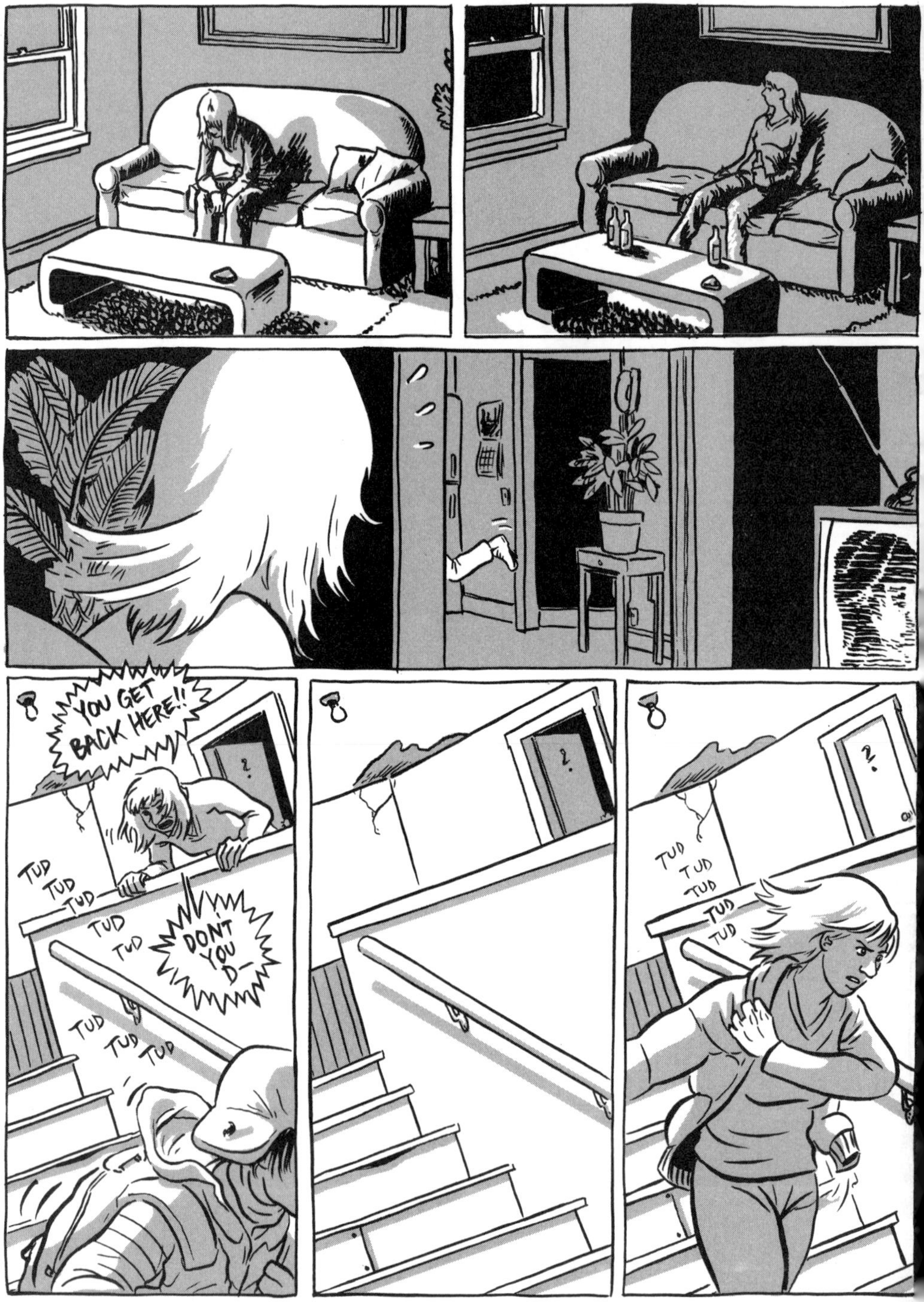
YOU GET BACK HERE!!
TUD TUD TUD
TUD TUD
DON'T YOU D—
TUD TUD TUD
TUD TUD TUD TUD TUD

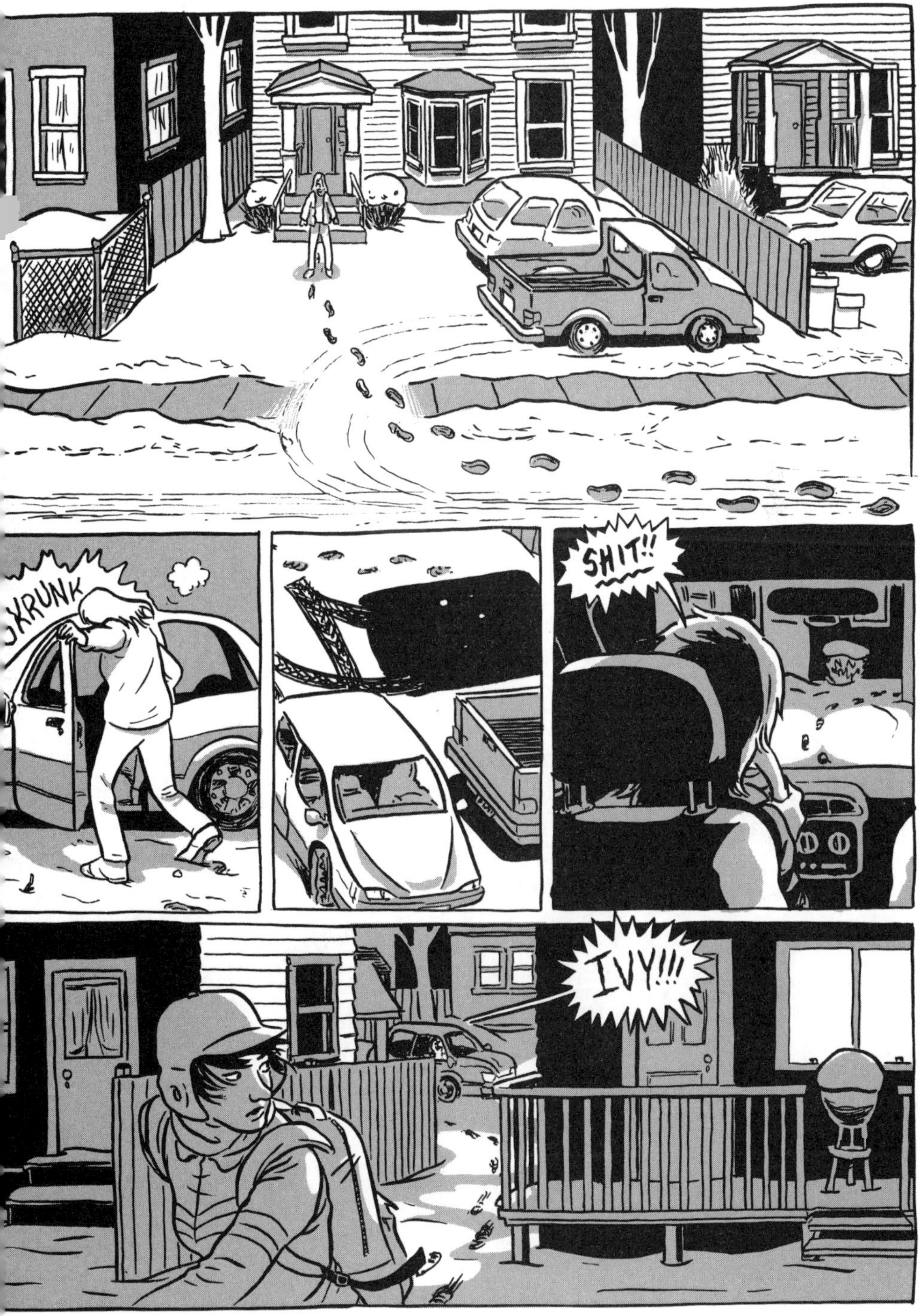
KRUNK
SHIT!!
IVY!!!

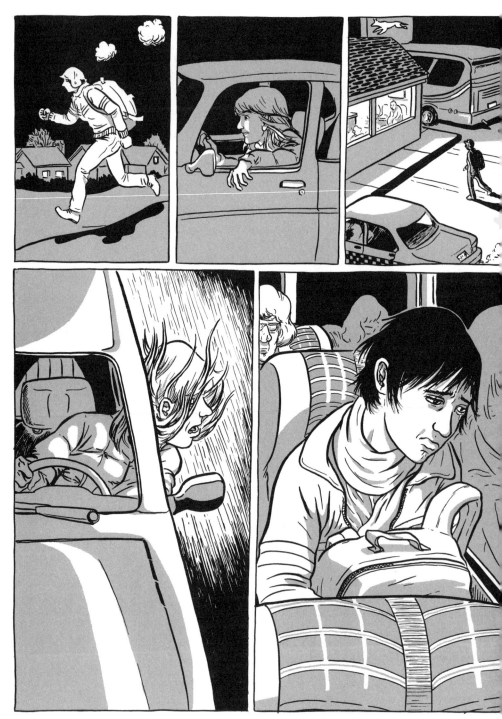

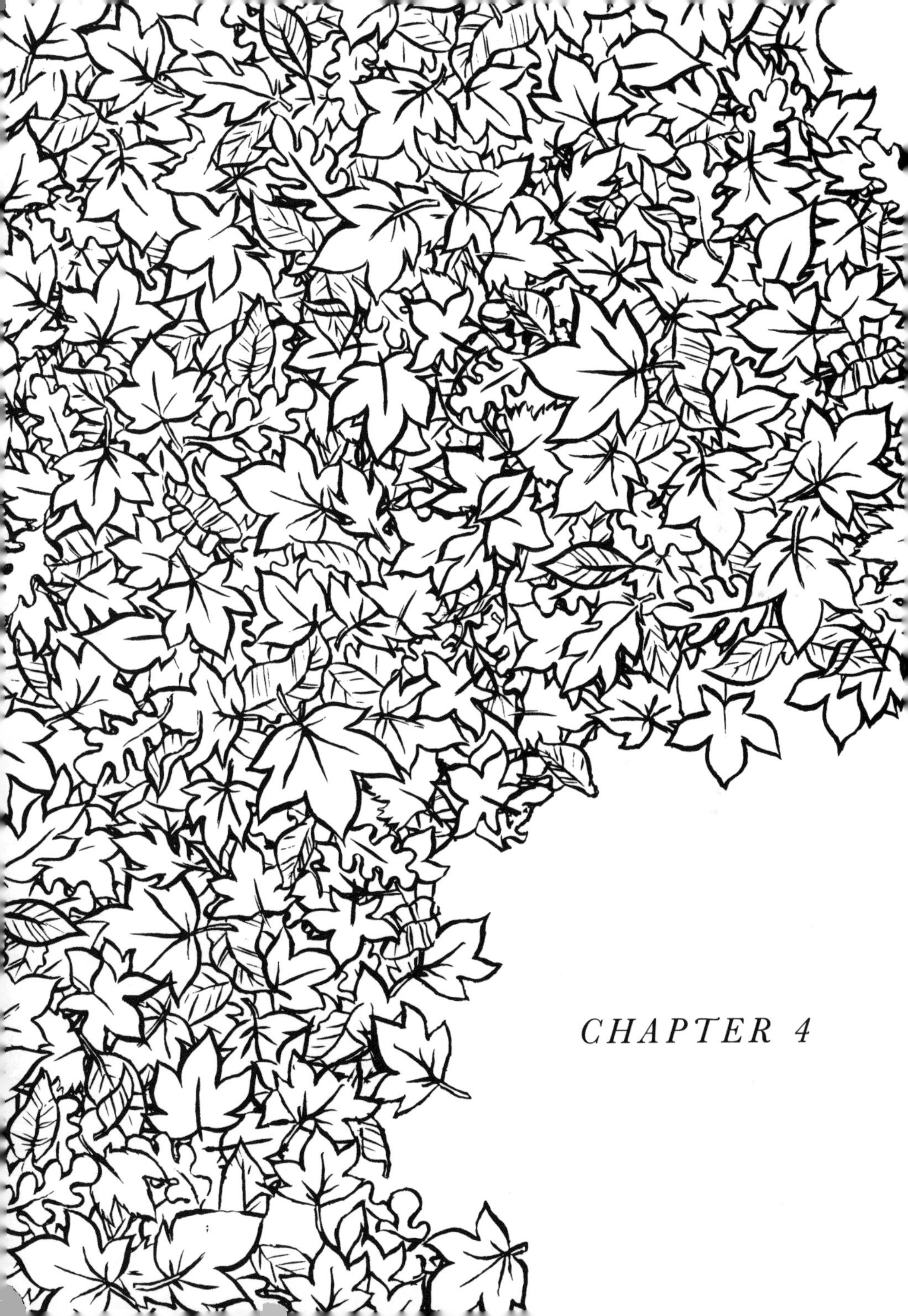

CHAPTER 4

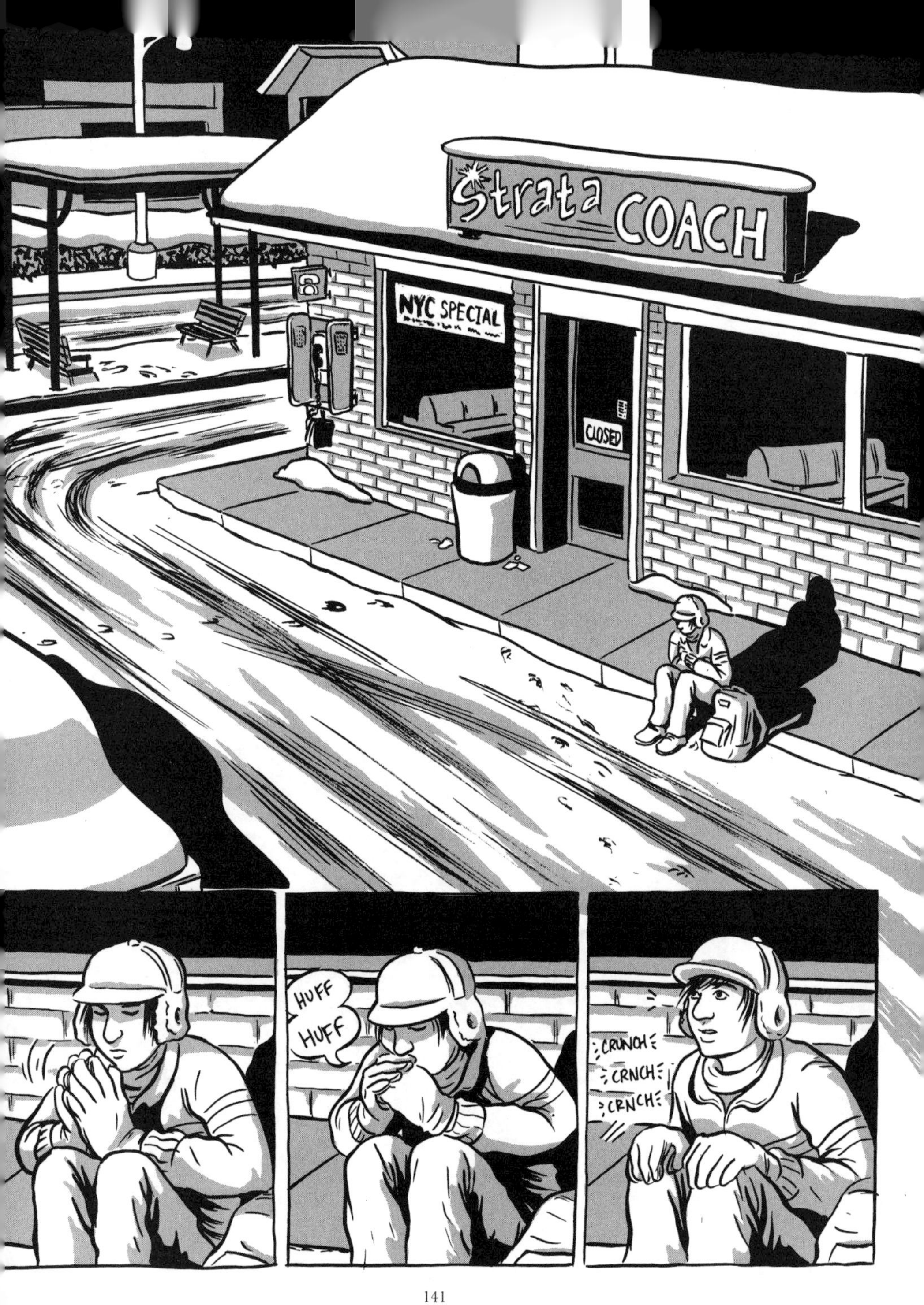
Strata COACH
NYC SPECIAL
CLOSED
HUFF
HUFF
CRUNCH
CRNCH
CRNCH

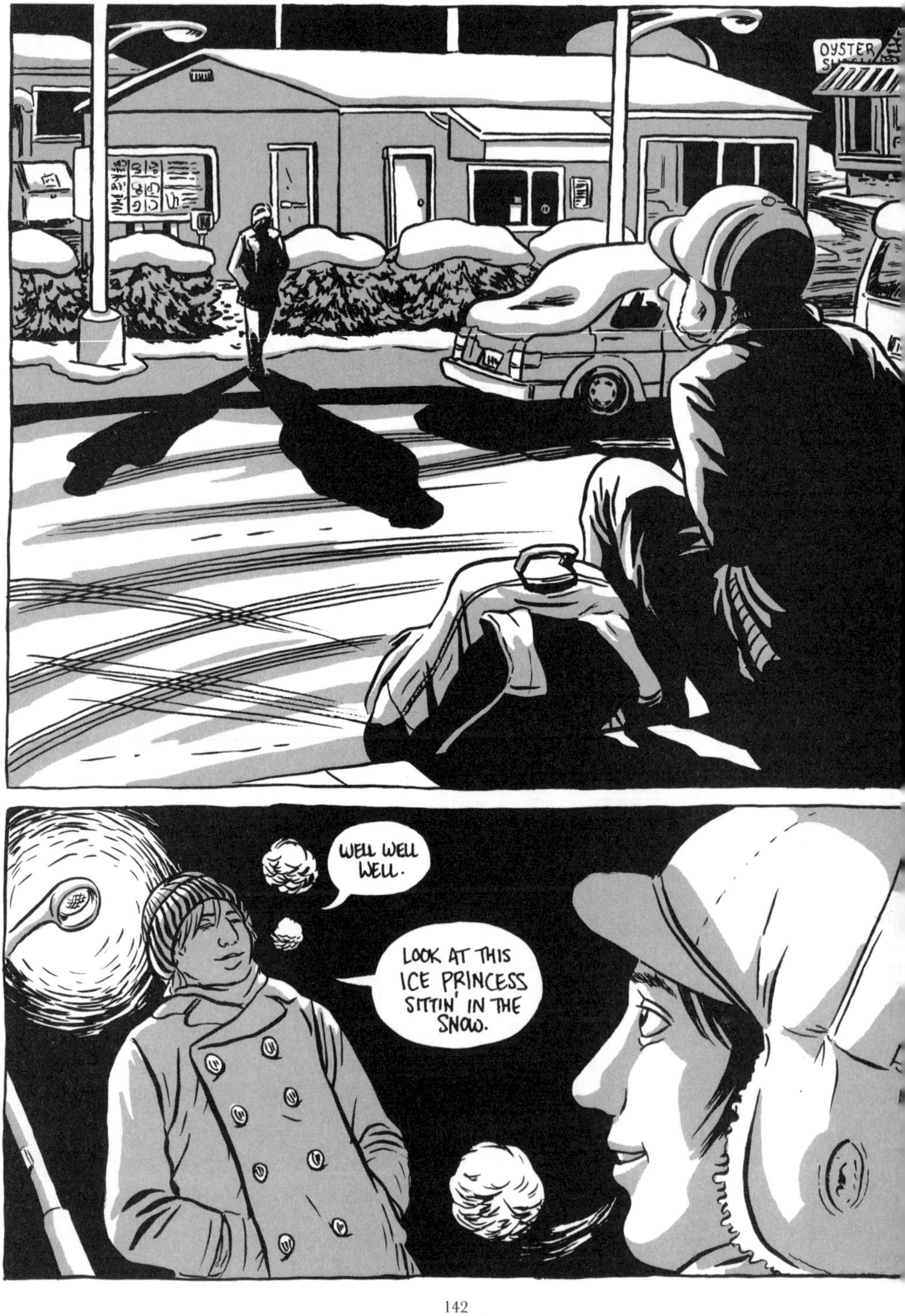
OYSTER
WELL WELL WELL.
LOOK AT THIS ICE PRINCESS SITTIN' IN THE SNOW.

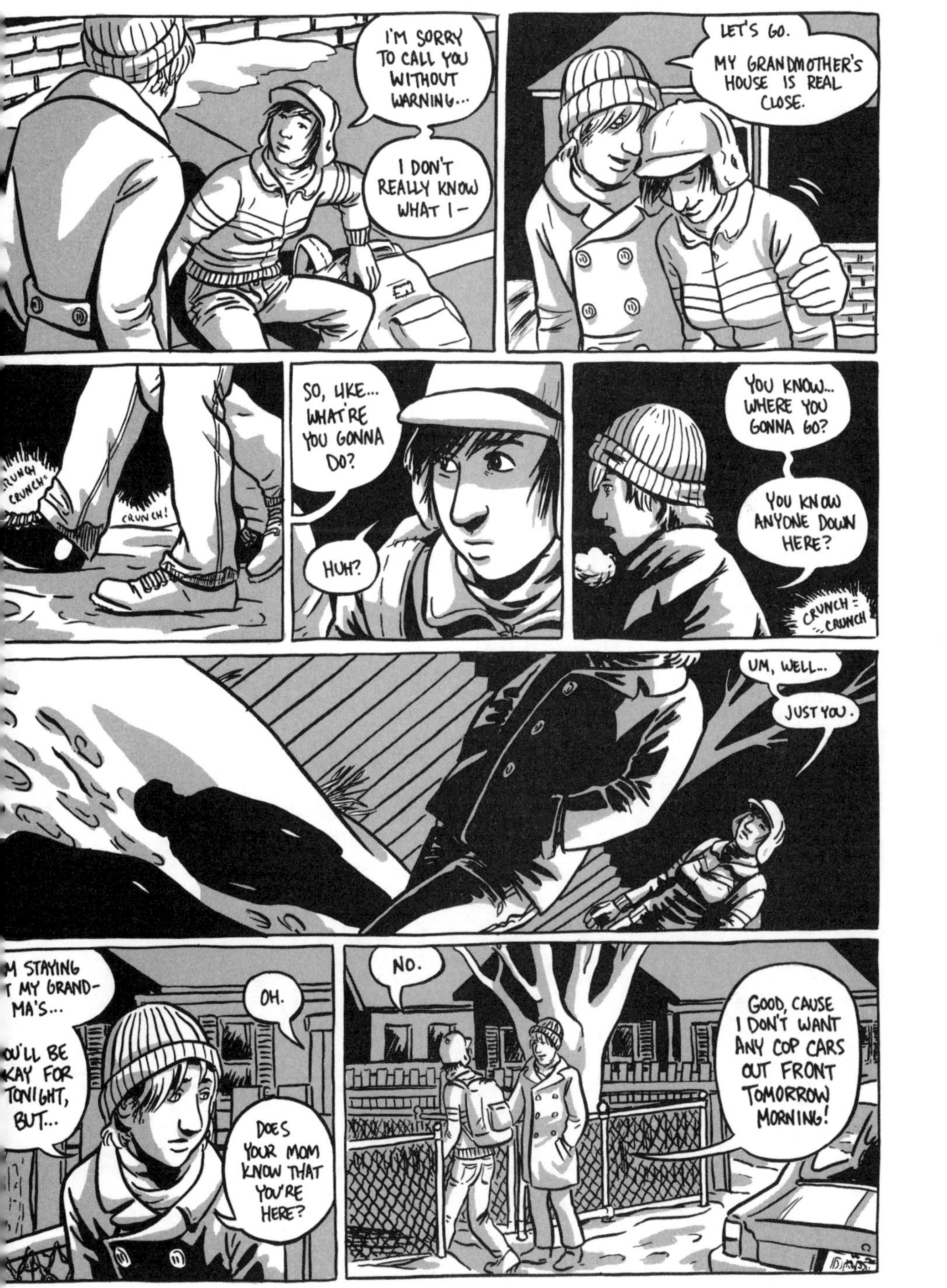
I'M SORRY TO CALL YOU WITHOUT WARNING...
I DON'T REALLY KNOW WHAT I—
LET'S GO.
MY GRANDMOTHER'S HOUSE IS REAL CLOSE.
CRUNCH CRUNCH
CRUNCH!
SO, LIKE... WHAT'RE YOU GONNA DO?
HUH?
YOU KNOW... WHERE YOU GONNA GO?
YOU KNOW ANYONE DOWN HERE?
CRUNCH CRUNCH
UM, WELL...
JUST YOU.
M STAYING T MY GRAND-MA'S...
OU'LL BE KAY FOR TONIGHT, BUT...
OH.
DOES YOUR MOM KNOW THAT YOU'RE HERE?
NO.
GOOD, CAUSE I DON'T WANT ANY COP CARS OUT FRONT TOMORROW MORNING!

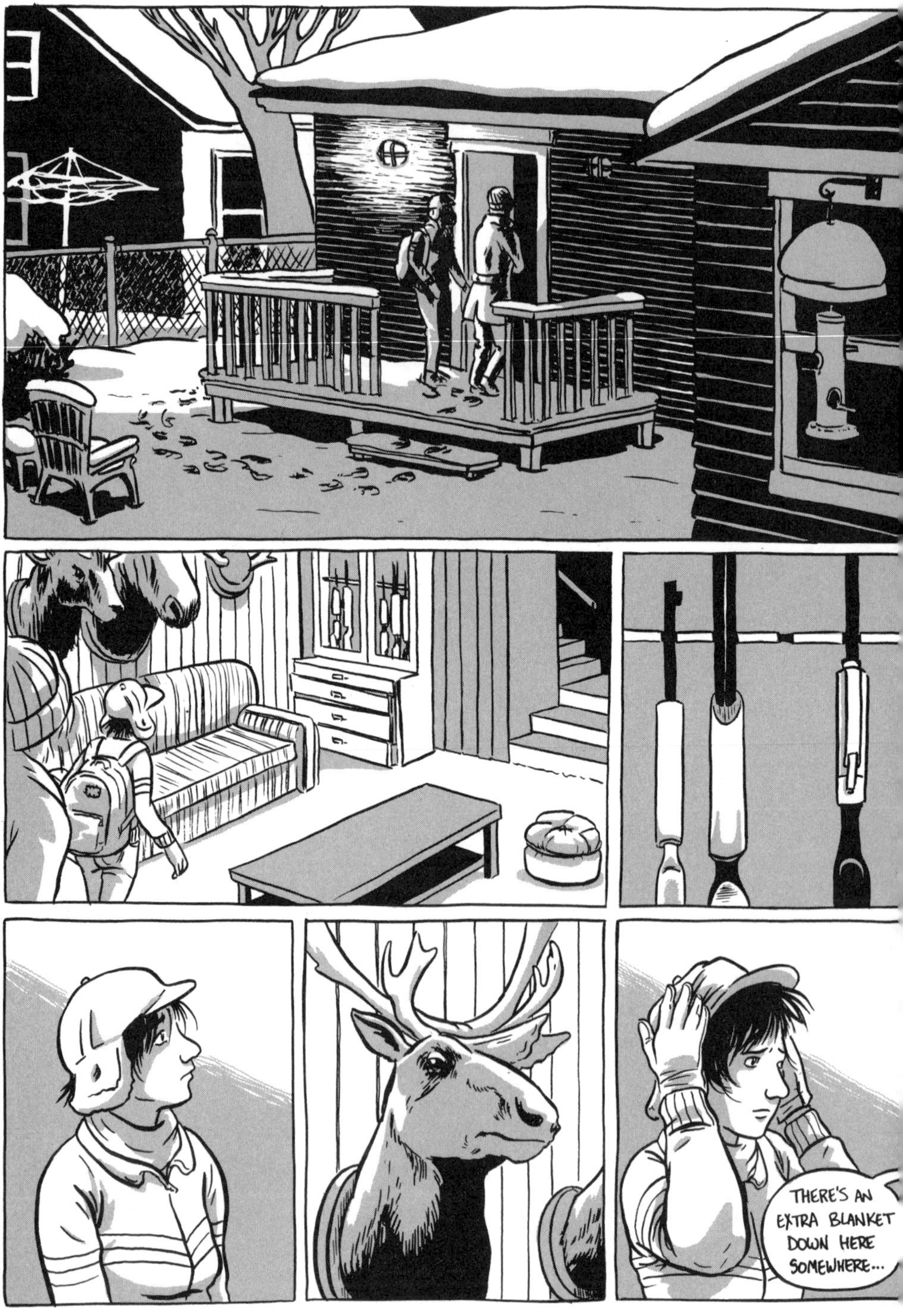
THERE'S AN EXTRA BLANKET DOWN HERE SOMEWHERE...

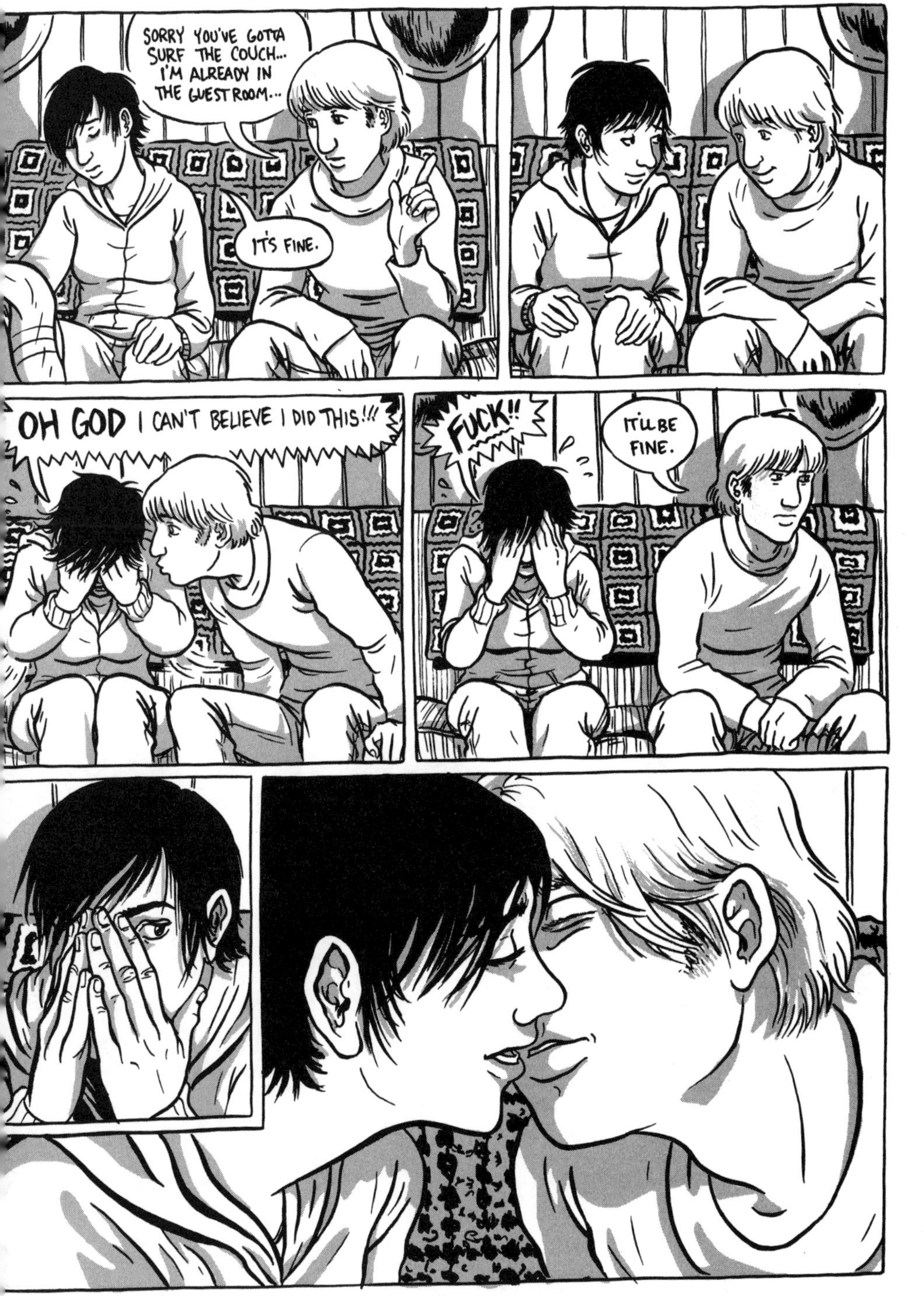
SORRY YOU'VE GOTTA SURF THE COUCH... I'M ALREADY IN THE GUEST ROOM...
IT'S FINE.
OH GOD I CAN'T BELIEVE I DID THIS!!!
FUCK!!
IT'LL BE FINE.

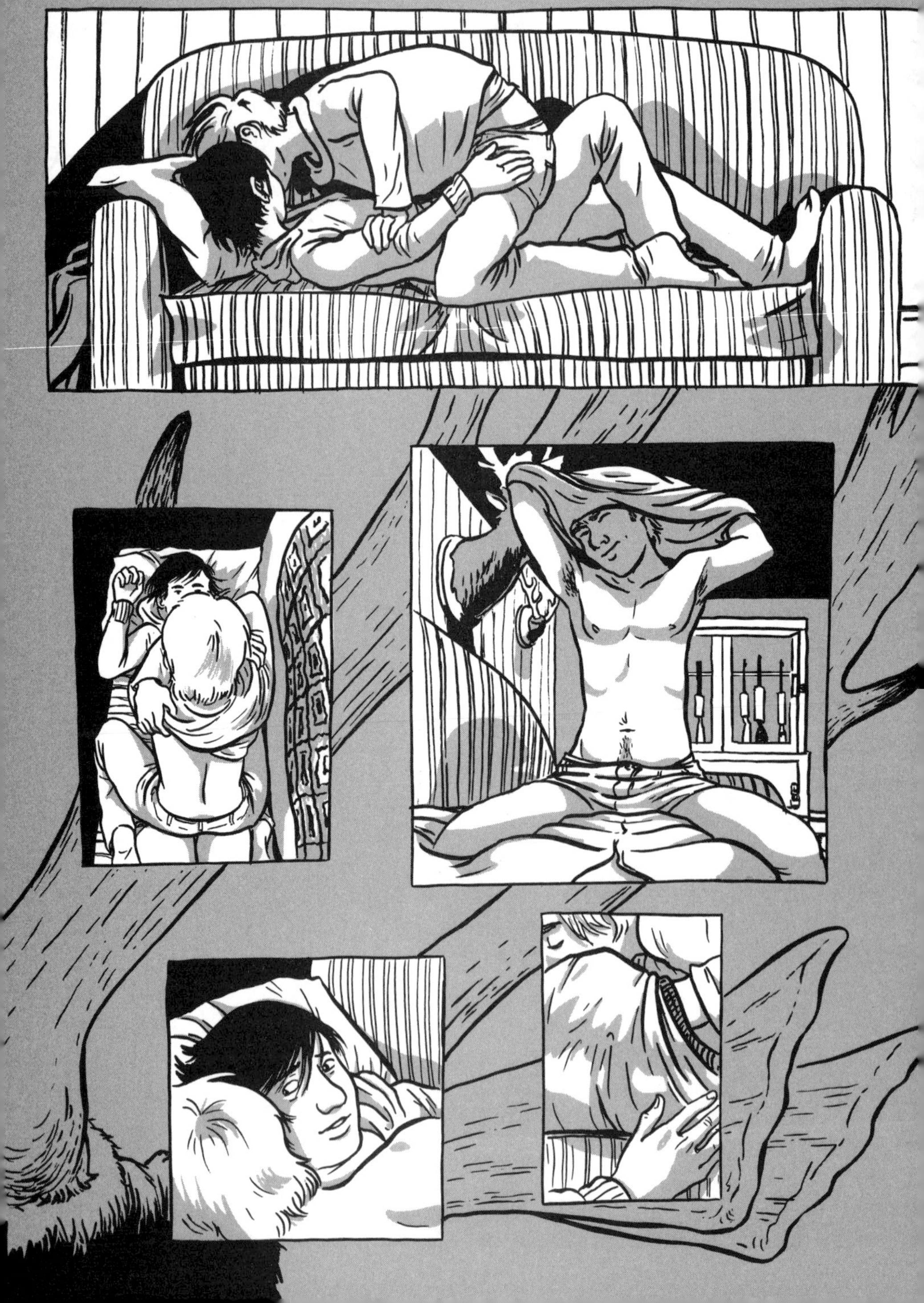

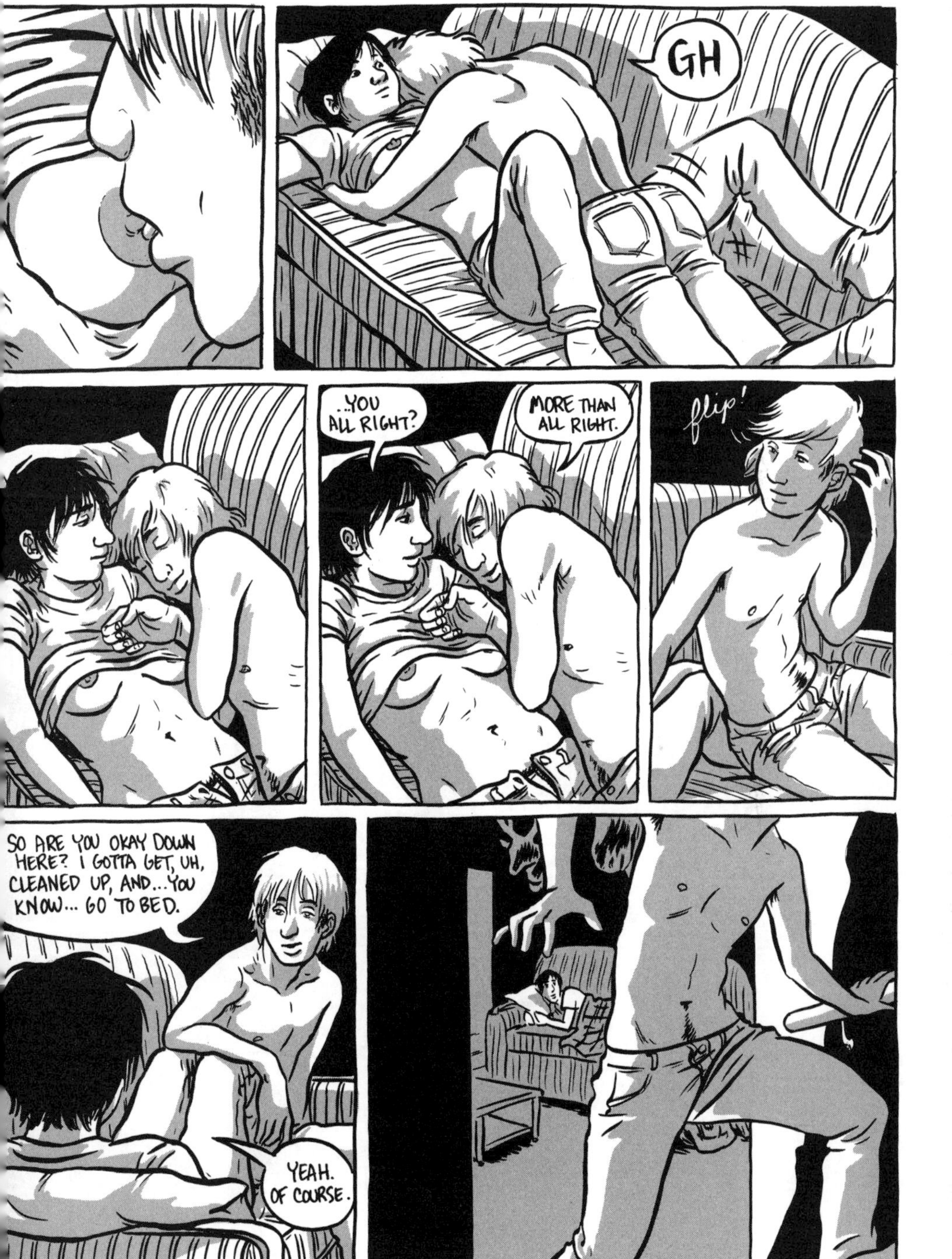
GH
..YOU ALL RIGHT?
MORE THAN ALL RIGHT.
flip!
SO ARE YOU OKAY DOWN HERE? I GOTTA GET, UH, CLEANED UP, AND... YOU KNOW... GO TO BED.
YEAH. OF COURSE.

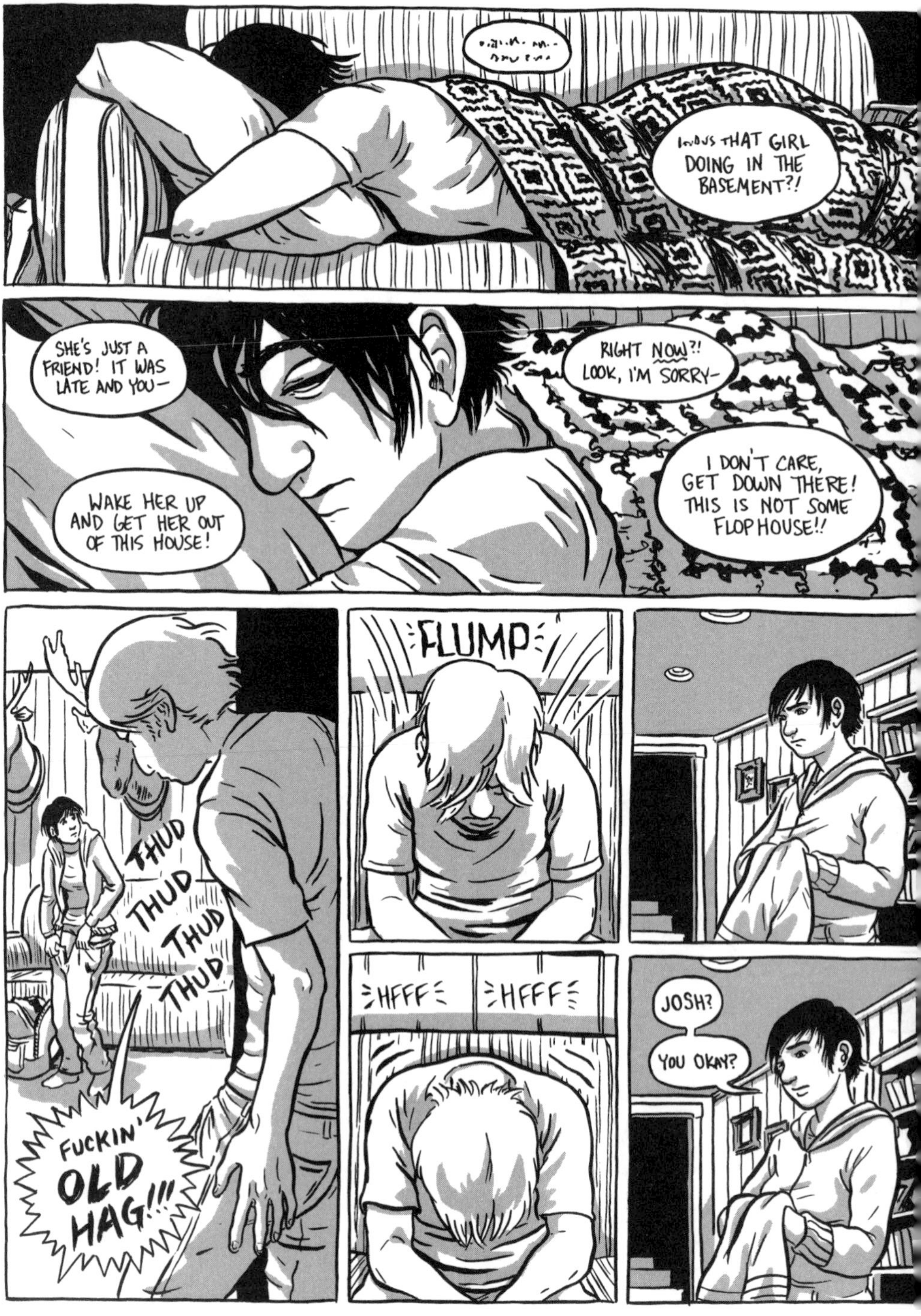
THAT GIRL DOING IN THE BASEMENT?!
SHE'S JUST A FRIEND! IT WAS LATE AND YOU—
RIGHT NOW?! LOOK, I'M SORRY—
WAKE HER UP AND GET HER OUT OF THIS HOUSE!
I DON'T CARE, GET DOWN THERE! THIS IS NOT SOME FLOPHOUSE!!
THUD
THUD
THUD
THUD
FUCKIN' OLD HAG!!!
FLUMP
HFFF
HFFF
JOSH?
YOU OKAY?

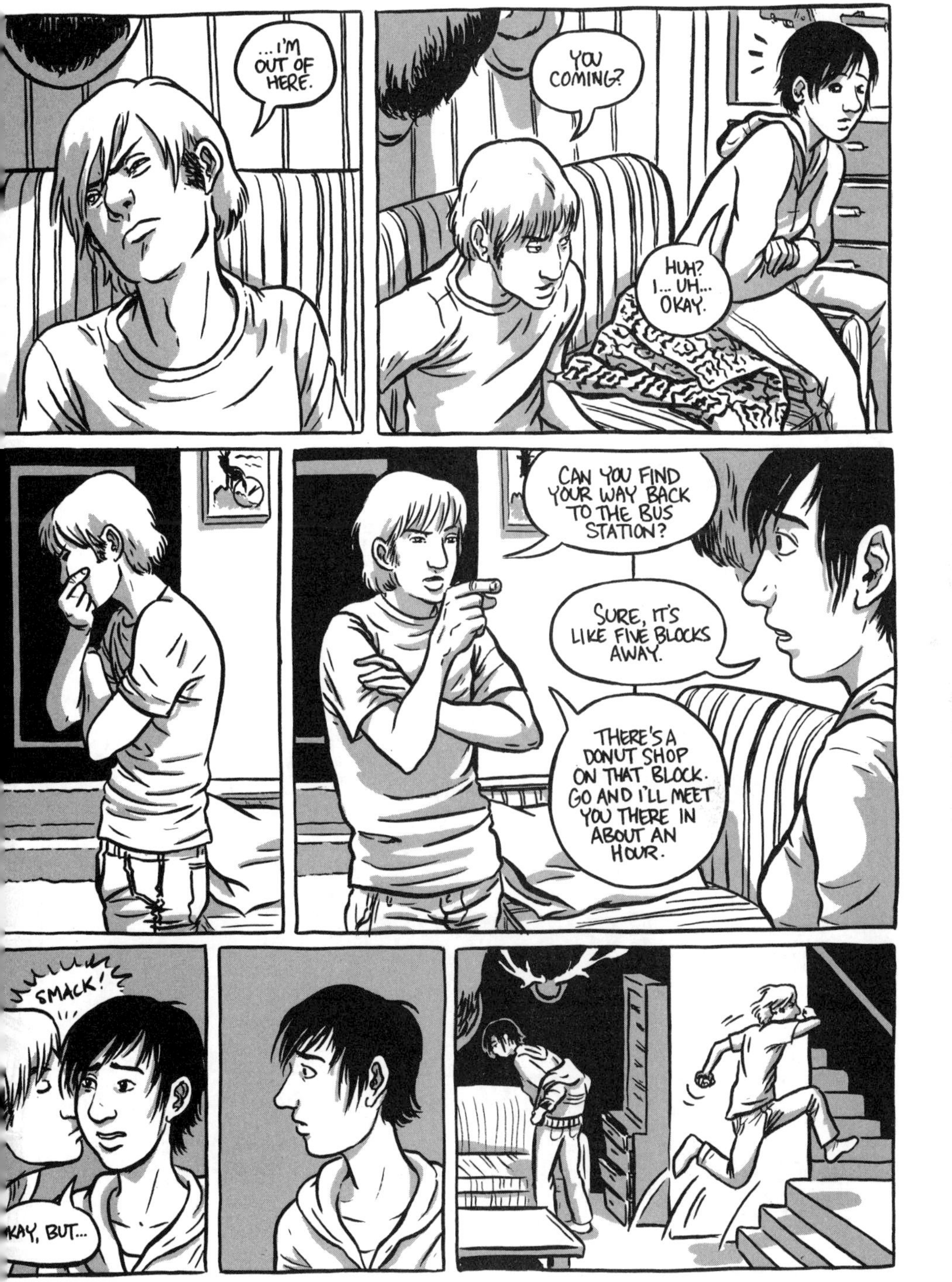
...I'M OUT OF HERE.
YOU COMING?
HUH? I... UH... OKAY.
CAN YOU FIND YOUR WAY BACK TO THE BUS STATION?
SURE, IT'S LIKE FIVE BLOCKS AWAY.
THERE'S A DONUT SHOP ON THAT BLOCK. GO AND I'LL MEET YOU THERE IN ABOUT AN HOUR.
SMACK!
KAY, BUT...

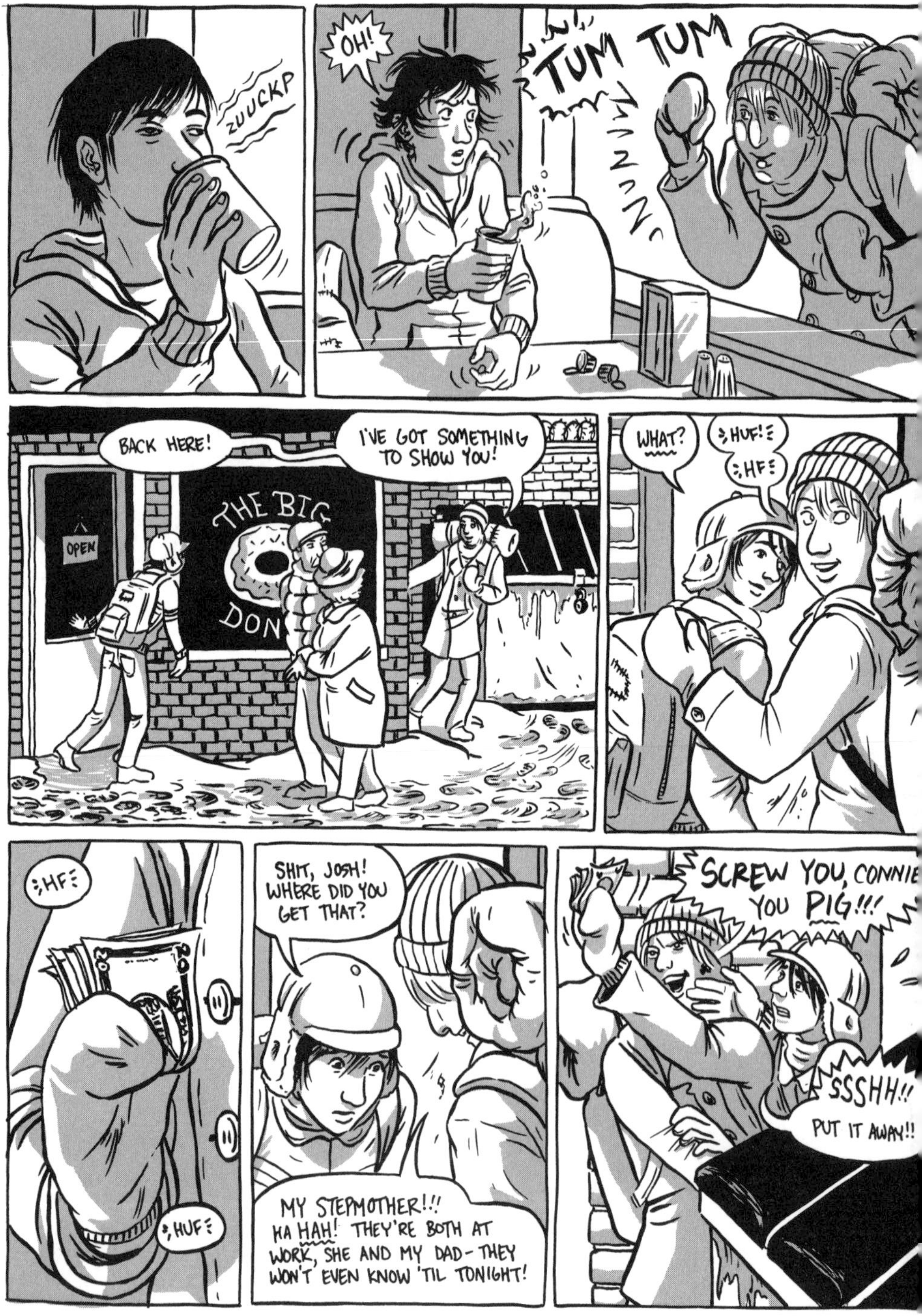

ZUUCKP
OH!
TUM TUM
BACK HERE!
I'VE GOT SOMETHING TO SHOW YOU!
THE BIG DON
OPEN
WHAT?
HUF!
HF
HF
HUF
SHIT, JOSH! WHERE DID YOU GET THAT?
MY STEPMOTHER!!! HA HAH! THEY'RE BOTH AT WORK, SHE AND MY DAD - THEY WON'T EVEN KNOW 'TIL TONIGHT!
SCREW YOU, CONNIE YOU PIG!!!
SSSHH!! PUT IT AWAY!!

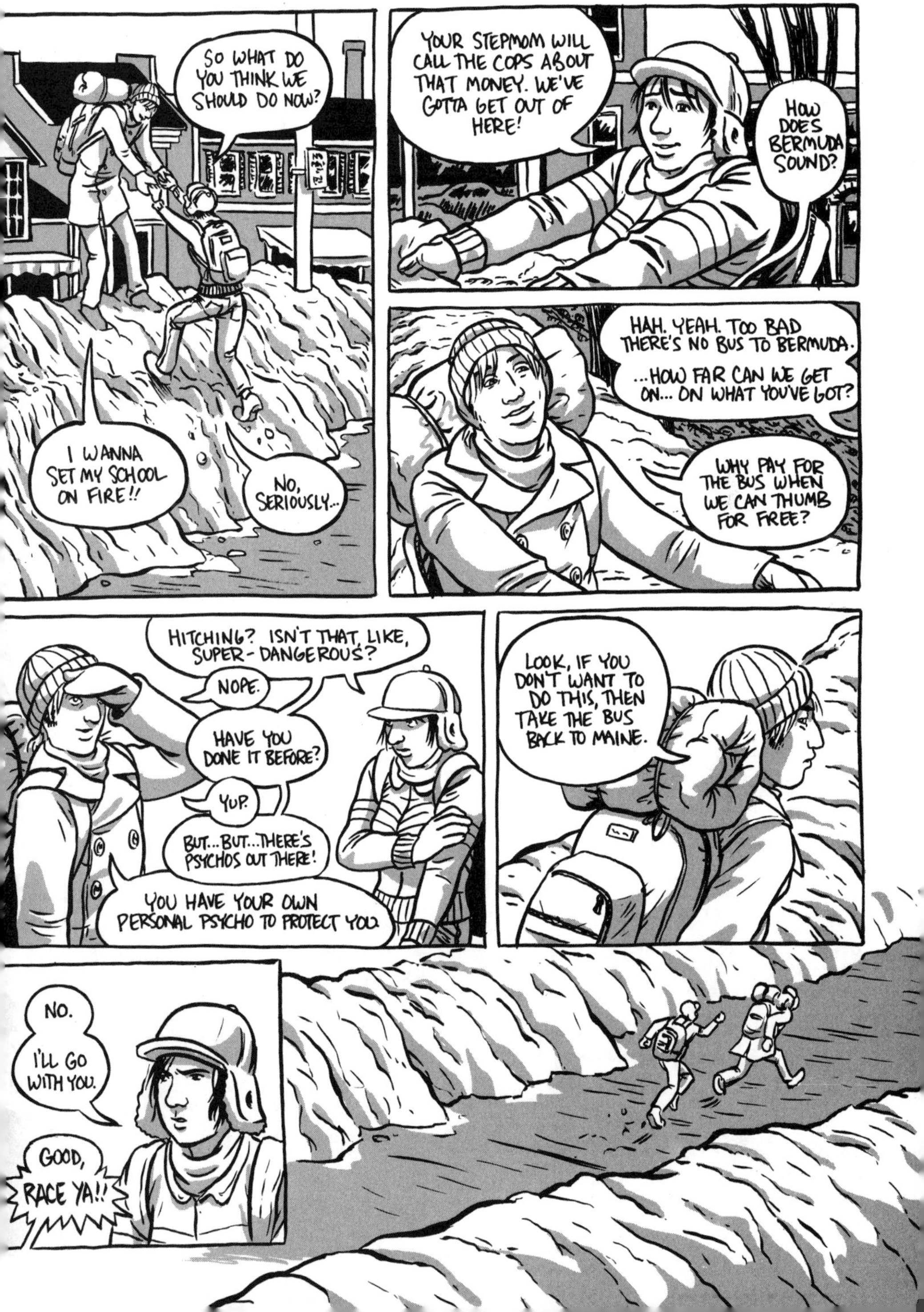
SO WHAT DO YOU THINK WE SHOULD DO NOW?
I WANNA SET MY SCHOOL ON FIRE!!
NO, SERIOUSLY...
YOUR STEPMOM WILL CALL THE COPS ABOUT THAT MONEY. WE'VE GOTTA GET OUT OF HERE!
HOW DOES BERMUDA SOUND?
HAH. YEAH. TOO BAD THERE'S NO BUS TO BERMUDA.
...HOW FAR CAN WE GET ON... ON WHAT YOU'VE GOT?
WHY PAY FOR THE BUS WHEN WE CAN THUMB FOR FREE?
HITCHING? ISN'T THAT, LIKE, SUPER-DANGEROUS?
NOPE.
HAVE YOU DONE IT BEFORE?
YUP.
BUT...BUT...THERE'S PSYCHOS OUT THERE!
YOU HAVE YOUR OWN PERSONAL PSYCHO TO PROTECT YOU.
LOOK, IF YOU DON'T WANT TO DO THIS, THEN TAKE THE BUS BACK TO MAINE.
NO.
I'LL GO WITH YOU.
GOOD,
RACE YA!!

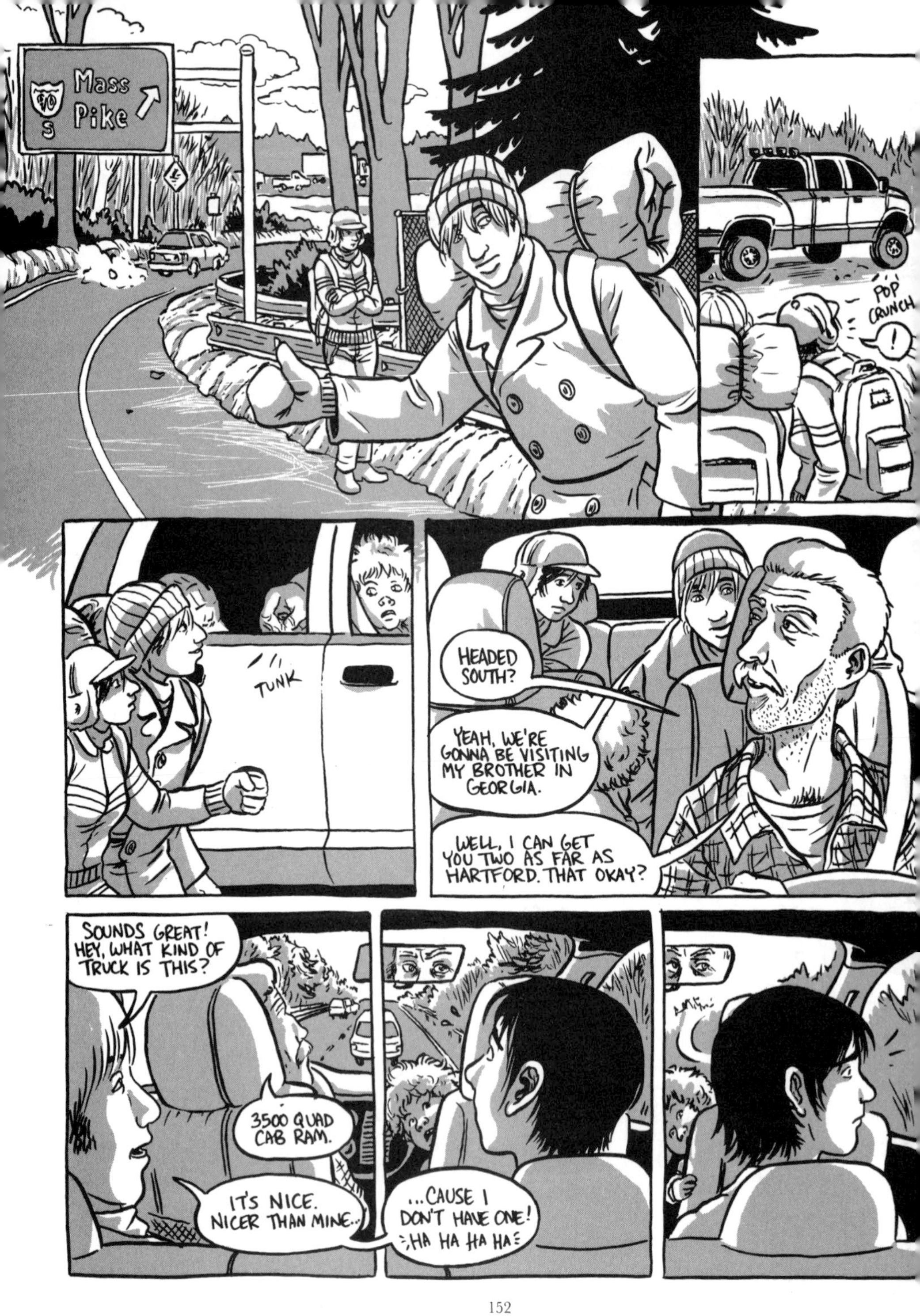
Mass Pike
POP
CRUNCH
!
TUNK
HEADED SOUTH?
YEAH, WE'RE GONNA BE VISITING MY BROTHER IN GEORGIA.
WELL, I CAN GET YOU TWO AS FAR AS HARTFORD. THAT OKAY?
SOUNDS GREAT! HEY, WHAT KIND OF TRUCK IS THIS?
3500 QUAD CAB RAM.
IT'S NICE. NICER THAN MINE...
...CAUSE I DON'T HAVE ONE! HA HA HA HA

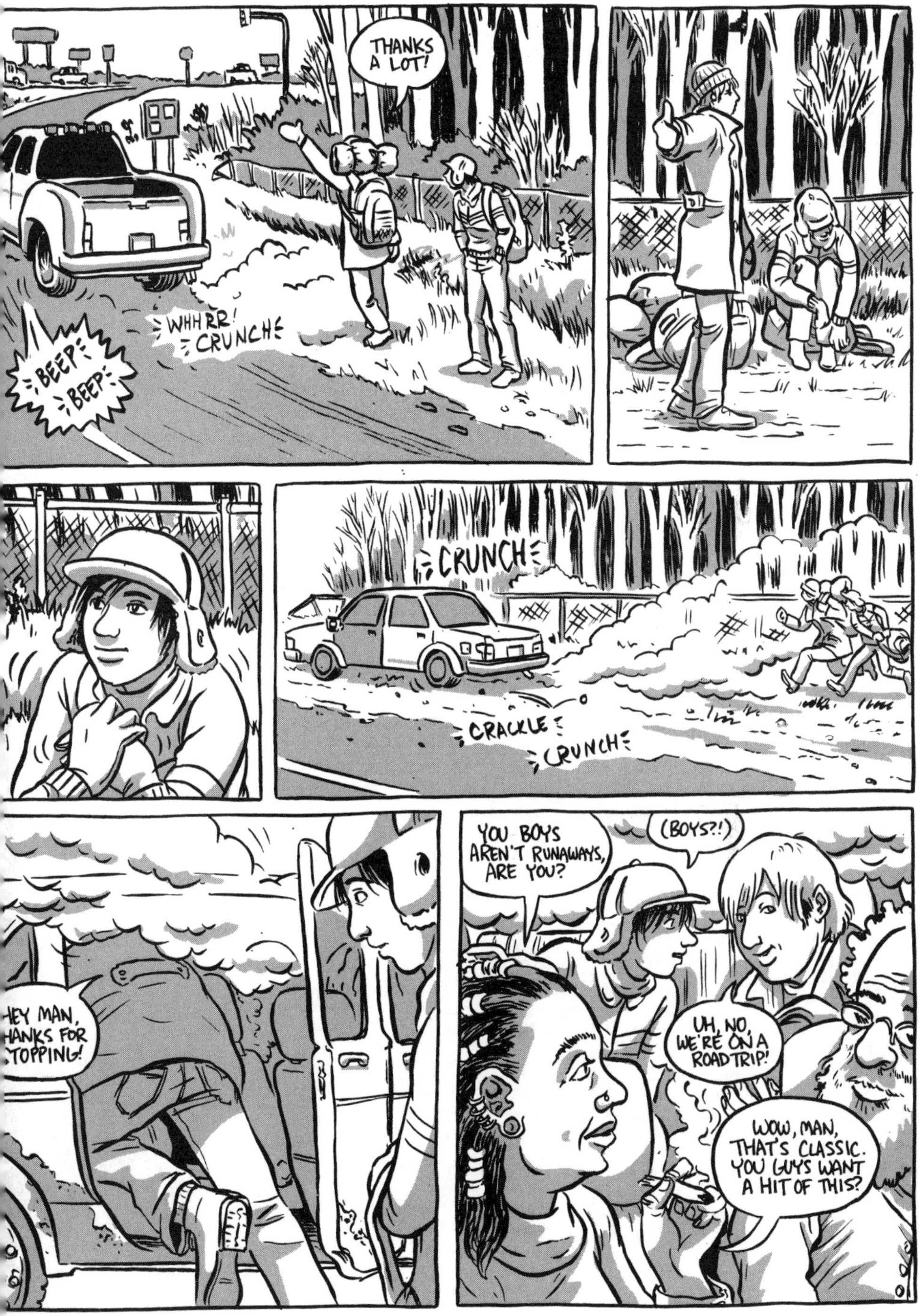
THANKS A LOT!
WHHRR!
CRUNCH
BEEP BEEP
CRUNCH
CRACKLE
CRUNCH
HEY MAN, THANKS FOR STOPPING!
YOU BOYS AREN'T RUNAWAYS, ARE YOU?
(BOYS?!)
UH, NO, WE'RE ON A ROAD TRIP!
WOW, MAN, THAT'S CLASSIC. YOU GUYS WANT A HIT OF THIS?

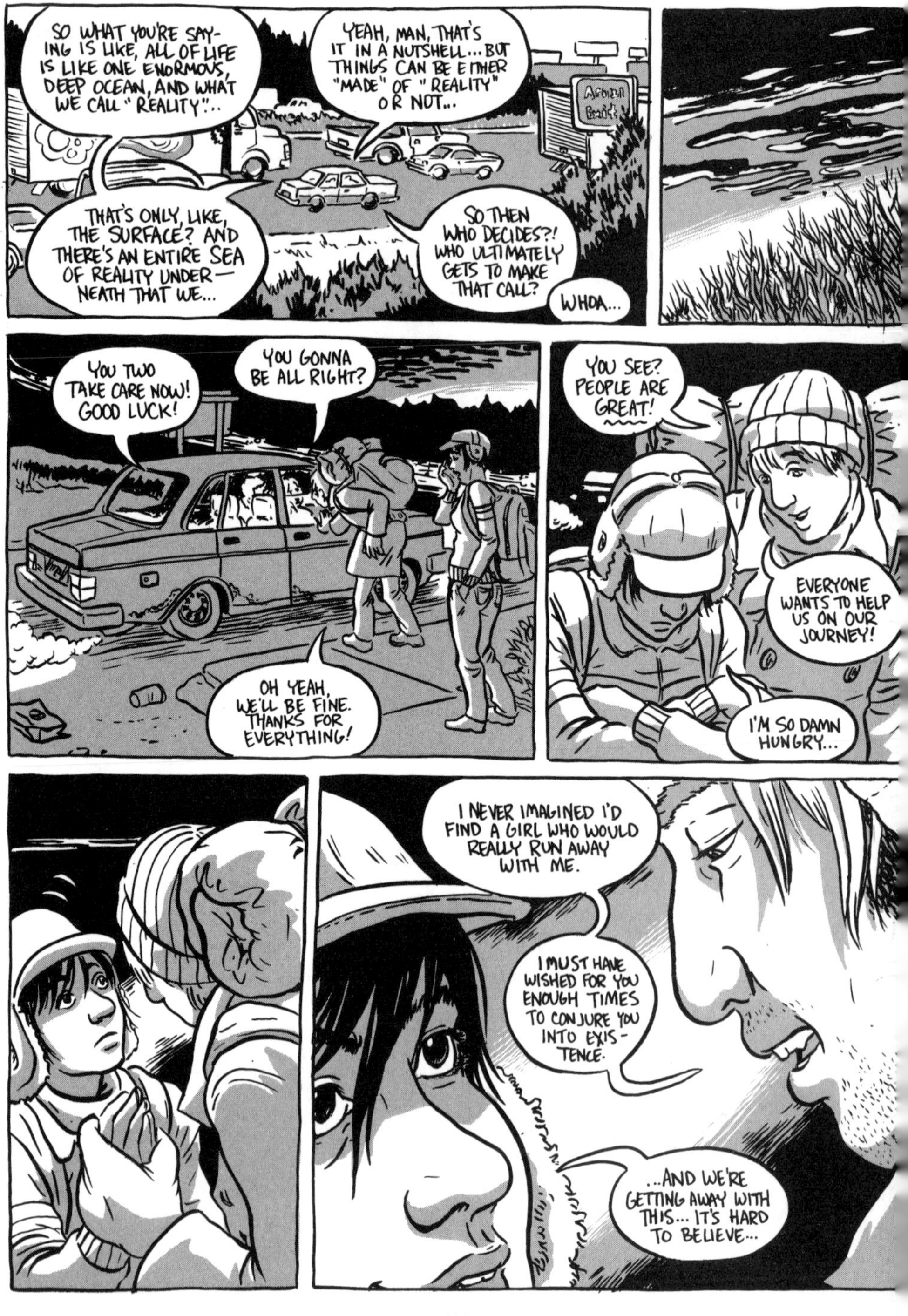

SO WHAT YOU'RE SAYING IS LIKE, ALL OF LIFE IS LIKE ONE ENORMOUS, DEEP OCEAN, AND WHAT WE CALL "REALITY"...
YEAH, MAN, THAT'S IT IN A NUTSHELL... BUT THINGS CAN BE EITHER "MADE" OF "REALITY" OR NOT...
THAT'S ONLY, LIKE, THE SURFACE? AND THERE'S AN ENTIRE SEA OF REALITY UNDERNEATH THAT WE...
SO THEN WHO DECIDES?! WHO ULTIMATELY GETS TO MAKE THAT CALL?
WHOA...
YOU TWO TAKE CARE NOW! GOOD LUCK!
YOU GONNA BE ALL RIGHT?
OH YEAH, WE'LL BE FINE. THANKS FOR EVERYTHING!
YOU SEE? PEOPLE ARE GREAT!
EVERYONE WANTS TO HELP US ON OUR JOURNEY!
I'M SO DAMN HUNGRY...
I NEVER IMAGINED I'D FIND A GIRL WHO WOULD REALLY RUN AWAY WITH ME.
I MUST HAVE WISHED FOR YOU ENOUGH TIMES TO CONJURE YOU INTO EXISTENCE.
...AND WE'RE GETTING AWAY WITH THIS... IT'S HARD TO BELIEVE...

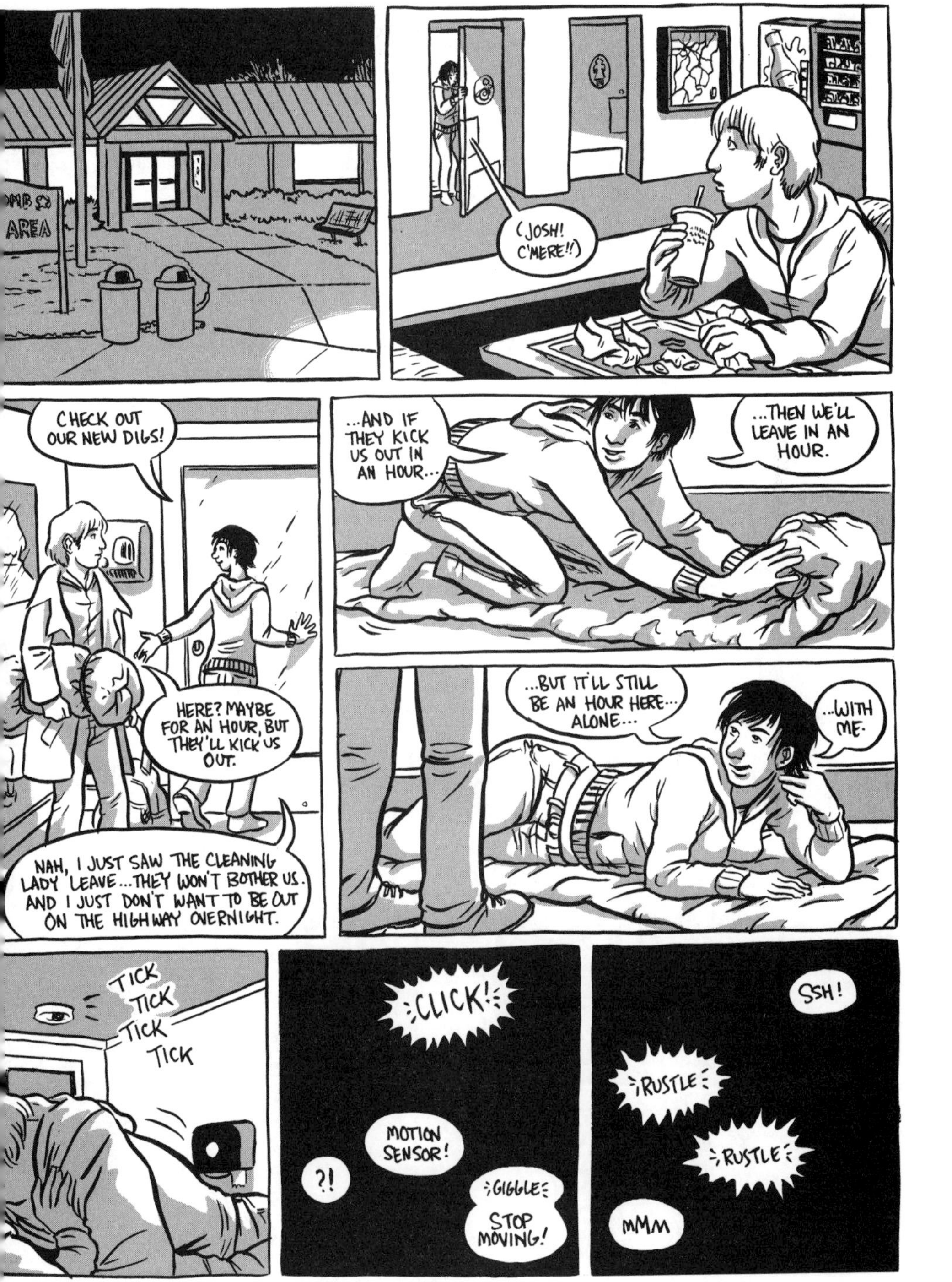

(JOSH! C'MERE!!)
CHECK OUT OUR NEW DIGS!
HERE? MAYBE FOR AN HOUR, BUT THEY'LL KICK US OUT.
NAH, I JUST SAW THE CLEANING LADY LEAVE... THEY WON'T BOTHER US. AND I JUST DON'T WANT TO BE OUT ON THE HIGHWAY OVERNIGHT.
...AND IF THEY KICK US OUT IN AN HOUR...
...THEN WE'LL LEAVE IN AN HOUR.
...BUT IT'LL STILL BE AN HOUR HERE... ALONE...
...WITH ME.
TICK
TICK
TICK
TICK
CLICK!
MOTION SENSOR!
?!
GIGGLE
STOP MOVING!
SSH!
RUSTLE
RUSTLE
MMM

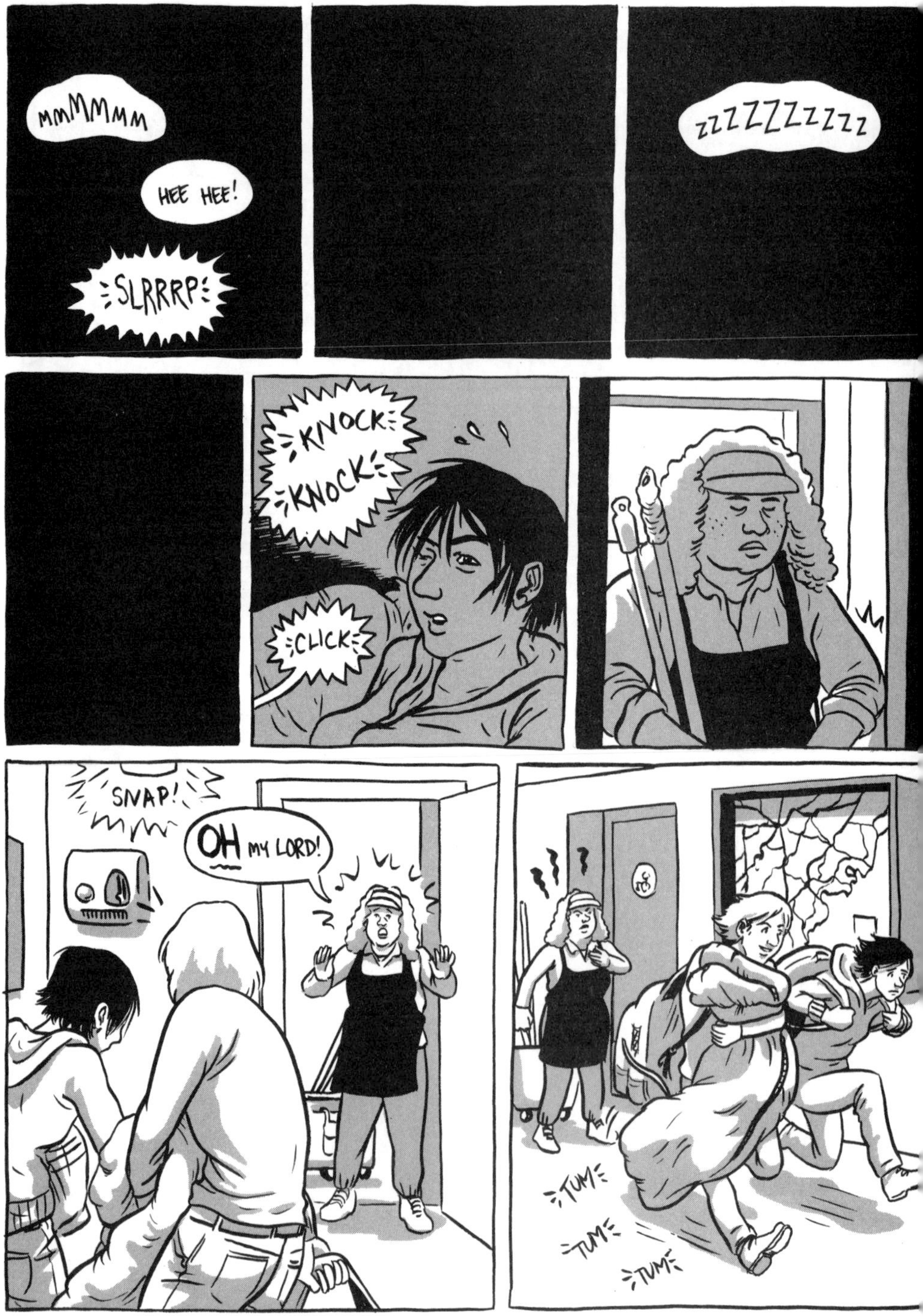
MMMMMMM
HEE HEE!
SLRRRP
ZZZZZZZZZZZ
KNOCK
KNOCK
CLICK
SNAP!
OH MY LORD!
TUM
TUM
TUM

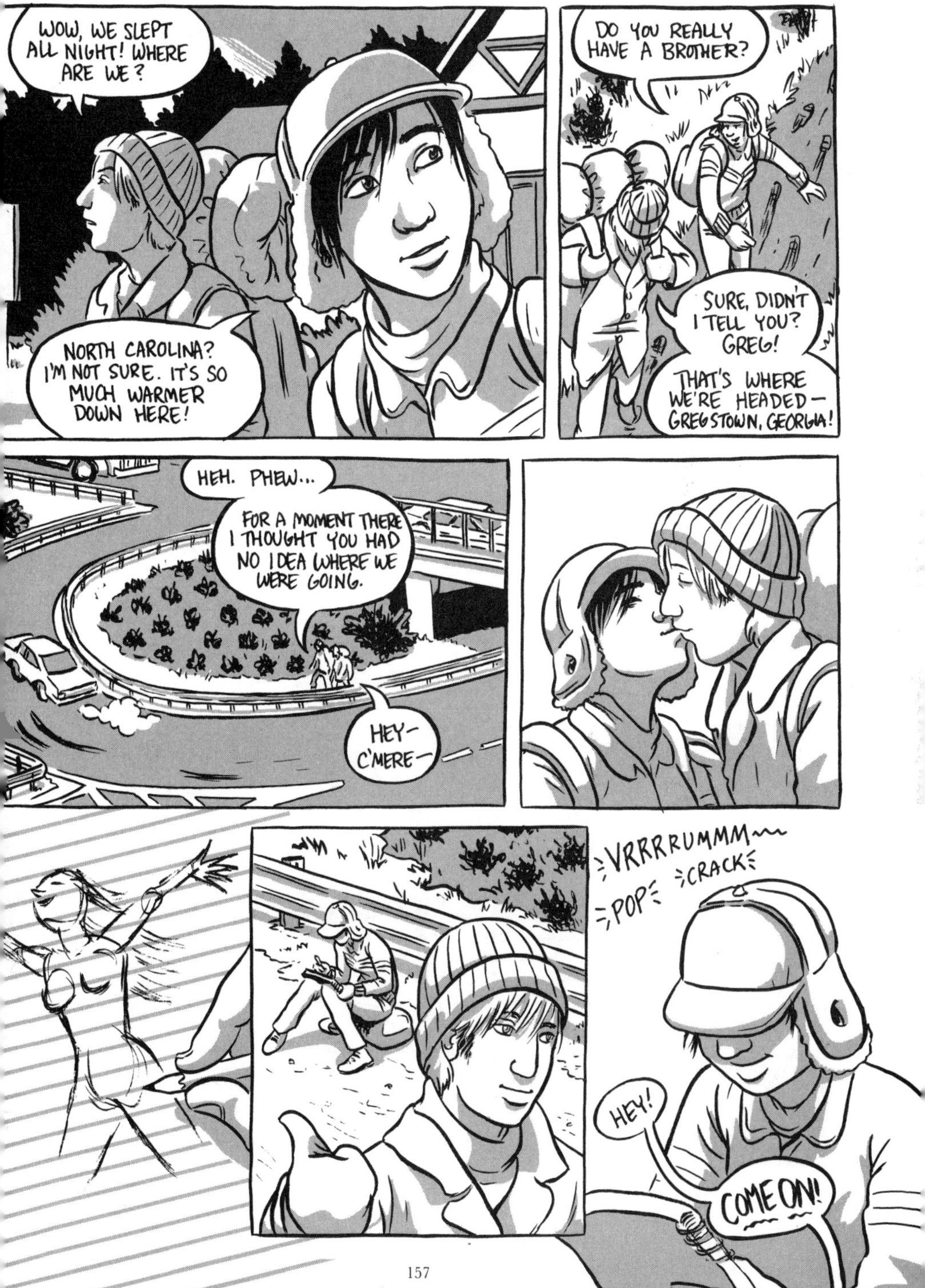
WOW, WE SLEPT ALL NIGHT! WHERE ARE WE?
NORTH CAROLINA? I'M NOT SURE. IT'S SO MUCH WARMER DOWN HERE!
DO YOU REALLY HAVE A BROTHER?
SURE, DIDN'T I TELL YOU? GREG!
THAT'S WHERE WE'RE HEADED— GREGSTOWN, GEORGIA!
HEH. PHEW...
FOR A MOMENT THERE I THOUGHT YOU HAD NO IDEA WHERE WE WERE GOING.
HEY— C'MERE—
VRRRRUMMM
POP
CRACK
HEY!
COME ON!

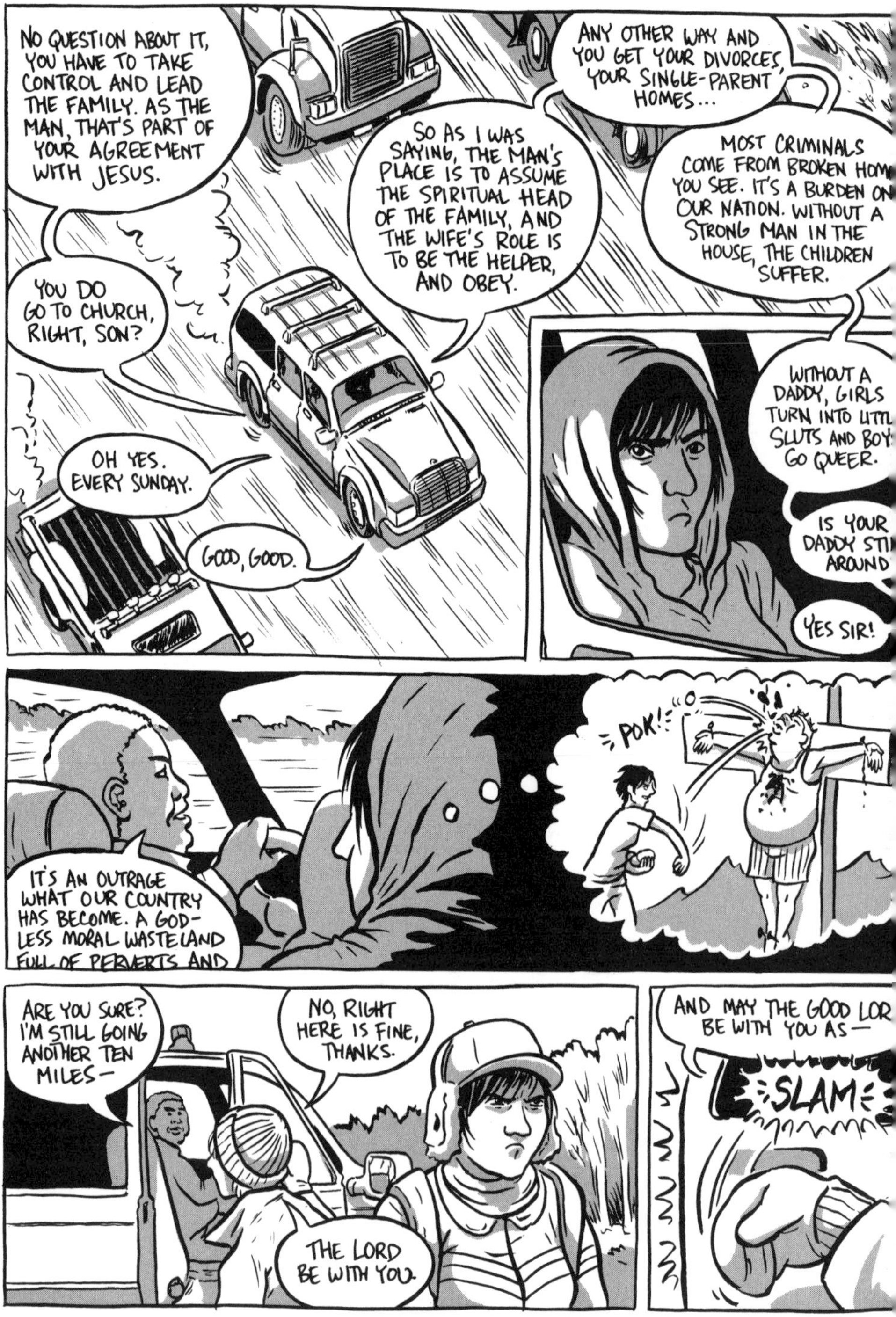
NO QUESTION ABOUT IT, YOU HAVE TO TAKE CONTROL AND LEAD THE FAMILY. AS THE MAN, THAT'S PART OF YOUR AGREEMENT WITH JESUS.
YOU DO GO TO CHURCH, RIGHT, SON?
OH YES. EVERY SUNDAY.
GOOD, GOOD.
SO AS I WAS SAYING, THE MAN'S PLACE IS TO ASSUME THE SPIRITUAL HEAD OF THE FAMILY, AND THE WIFE'S ROLE IS TO BE THE HELPER, AND OBEY.
ANY OTHER WAY AND YOU GET YOUR DIVORCES, YOUR SINGLE-PARENT HOMES...
MOST CRIMINALS COME FROM BROKEN HOM YOU SEE. IT'S A BURDEN ON OUR NATION. WITHOUT A STRONG MAN IN THE HOUSE, THE CHILDREN SUFFER.
WITHOUT A DADDY, GIRLS TURN INTO LITTL SLUTS AND BOY GO QUEER.
IS YOUR DADDY STI AROUND
YES SIR!
IT'S AN OUTRAGE WHAT OUR COUNTRY HAS BECOME. A GOD-LESS MORAL WASTELAND FULL OF PERVERTS AND
POK!
ARE YOU SURE? I'M STILL GOING ANOTHER TEN MILES—
NO, RIGHT HERE IS FINE, THANKS.
THE LORD BE WITH YOU.
AND MAY THE GOOD LOR BE WITH YOU AS—
SLAM

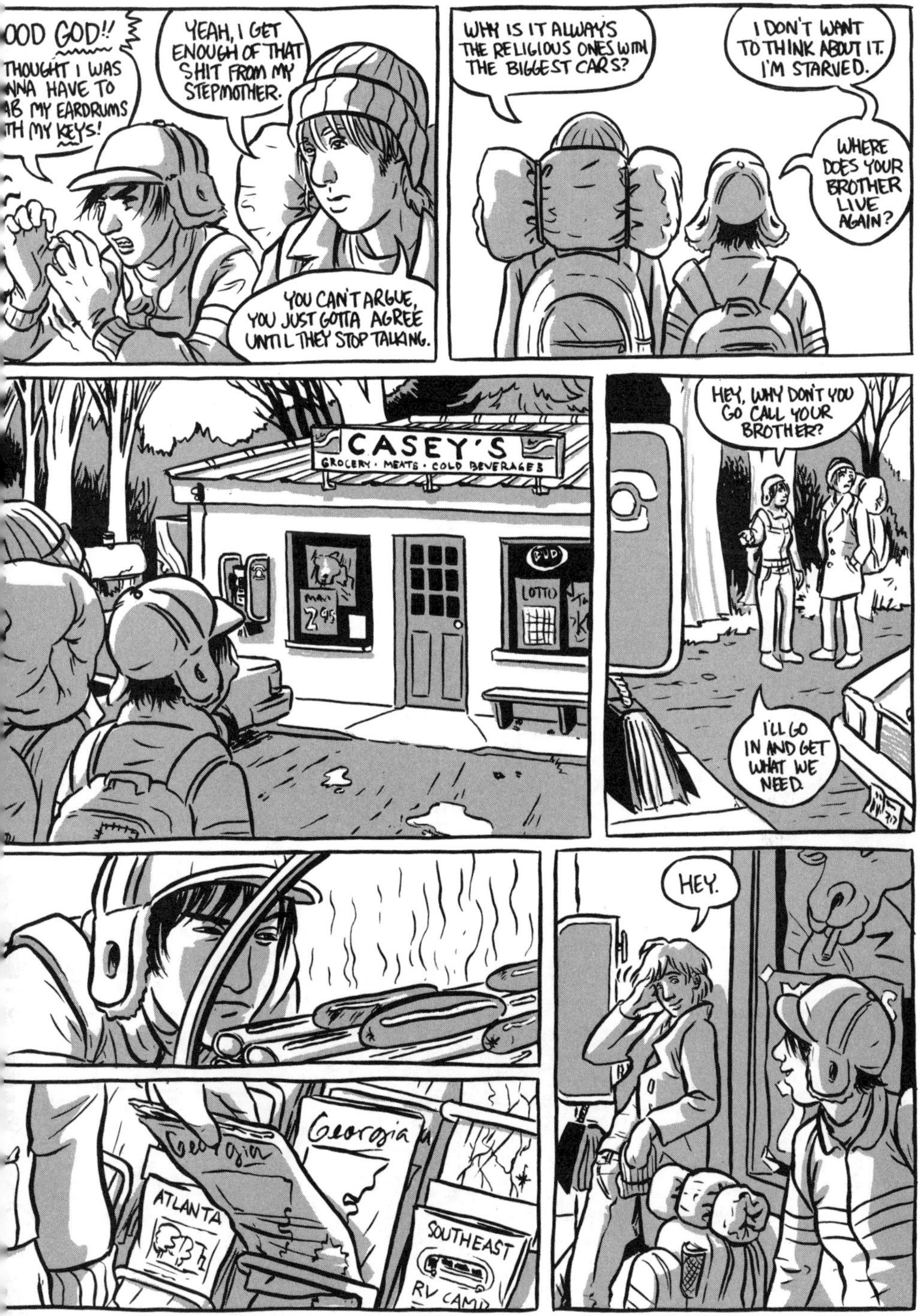
OOD GOD!! THOUGHT I WAS NNA HAVE TO AB MY EARDRUMS TH MY KEYS!
YEAH, I GET ENOUGH OF THAT SHIT FROM MY STEPMOTHER.
YOU CAN'T ARGUE, YOU JUST GOTTA AGREE UNTIL THEY STOP TALKING.
WHY IS IT ALWAYS THE RELIGIOUS ONES WITH THE BIGGEST CARS?
I DON'T WANT TO THINK ABOUT IT. I'M STARVED.
WHERE DOES YOUR BROTHER LIVE AGAIN?
CASEY'S
GROCERY · MEATS · COLD BEVERAGES
BUD
LOTTO
HEY, WHY DON'T YOU GO CALL YOUR BROTHER?
I'LL GO IN AND GET WHAT WE NEED.
HEY.
Georgia
Georgia
ATLANTA
SOUTHEAST
RV CAMP

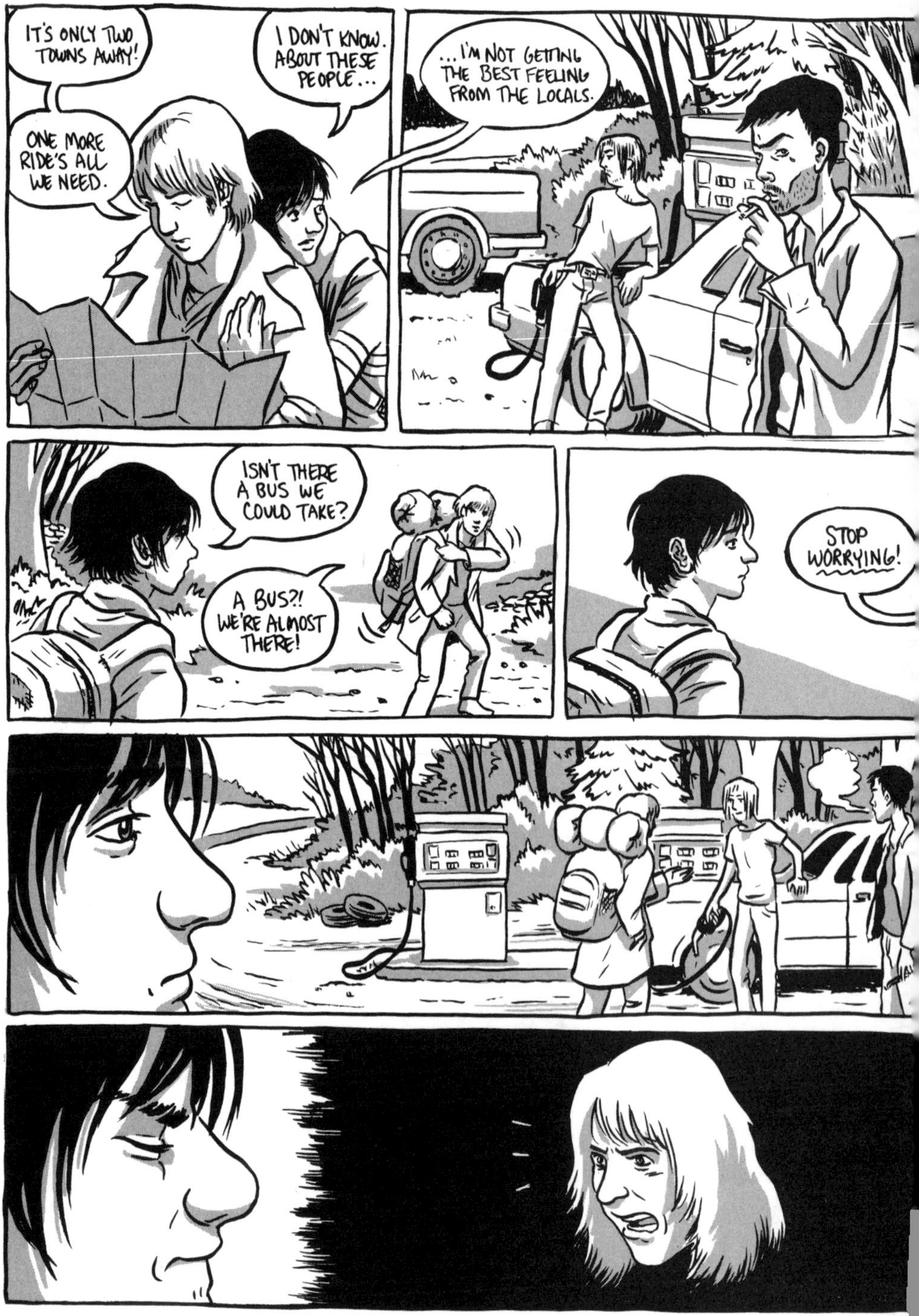
IT'S ONLY TWO TOWNS AWAY!
ONE MORE RIDE'S ALL WE NEED.
I DON'T KNOW. ABOUT THESE PEOPLE...
...I'M NOT GETTING THE BEST FEELING FROM THE LOCALS.
ISN'T THERE A BUS WE COULD TAKE?
A BUS?! WE'RE ALMOST THERE!
STOP WORRYING!

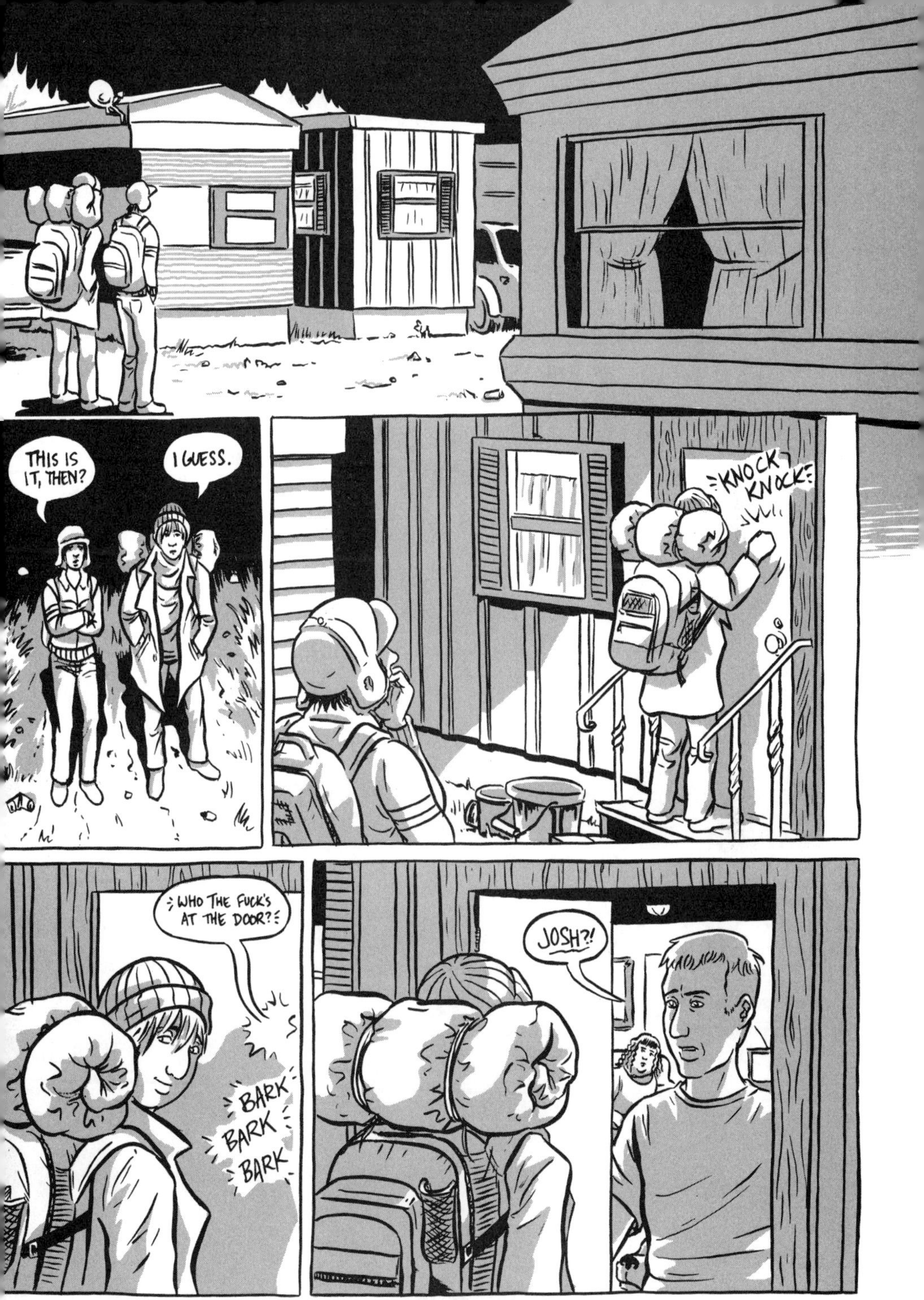
THIS IS IT, THEN?
I GUESS.
KNOCK KNOCK
WHO THE FUCK'S AT THE DOOR?
BARK BARK BARK
JOSH?!

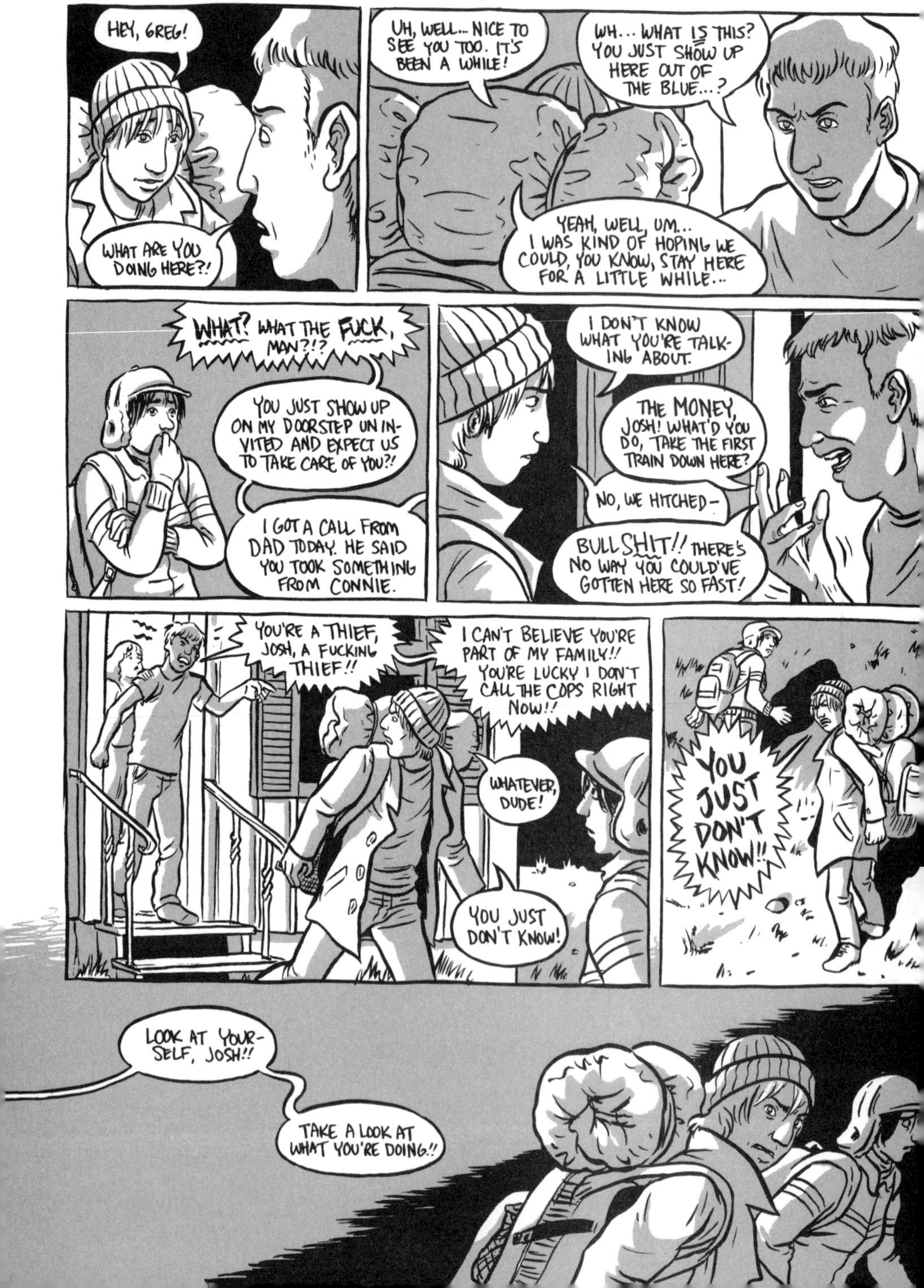
HEY, GREG!
WHAT ARE YOU DOING HERE?!
UH, WELL... NICE TO SEE YOU TOO. IT'S BEEN A WHILE!
WH... WHAT IS THIS? YOU JUST SHOW UP HERE OUT OF THE BLUE...?
YEAH, WELL, UM... I WAS KIND OF HOPING WE COULD, YOU KNOW, STAY HERE FOR A LITTLE WHILE...
WHAT? WHAT THE FUCK, MAN?!?
YOU JUST SHOW UP ON MY DOORSTEP UNINVITED AND EXPECT US TO TAKE CARE OF YOU?!
I GOT A CALL FROM DAD TODAY. HE SAID YOU TOOK SOMETHING FROM CONNIE.
I DON'T KNOW WHAT YOU'RE TALKING ABOUT.
THE MONEY, JOSH! WHAT'D YOU DO, TAKE THE FIRST TRAIN DOWN HERE?
NO, WE HITCHED—
BULLSHIT!! THERE'S NO WAY YOU COULD'VE GOTTEN HERE SO FAST!
YOU'RE A THIEF, JOSH, A FUCKING THIEF!!
I CAN'T BELIEVE YOU'RE PART OF MY FAMILY!! YOU'RE LUCKY I DON'T CALL THE COPS RIGHT NOW!!
WHATEVER, DUDE!
YOU JUST DON'T KNOW!
YOU JUST DON'T KNOW!!
LOOK AT YOURSELF, JOSH!!
TAKE A LOOK AT WHAT YOU'RE DOING!!

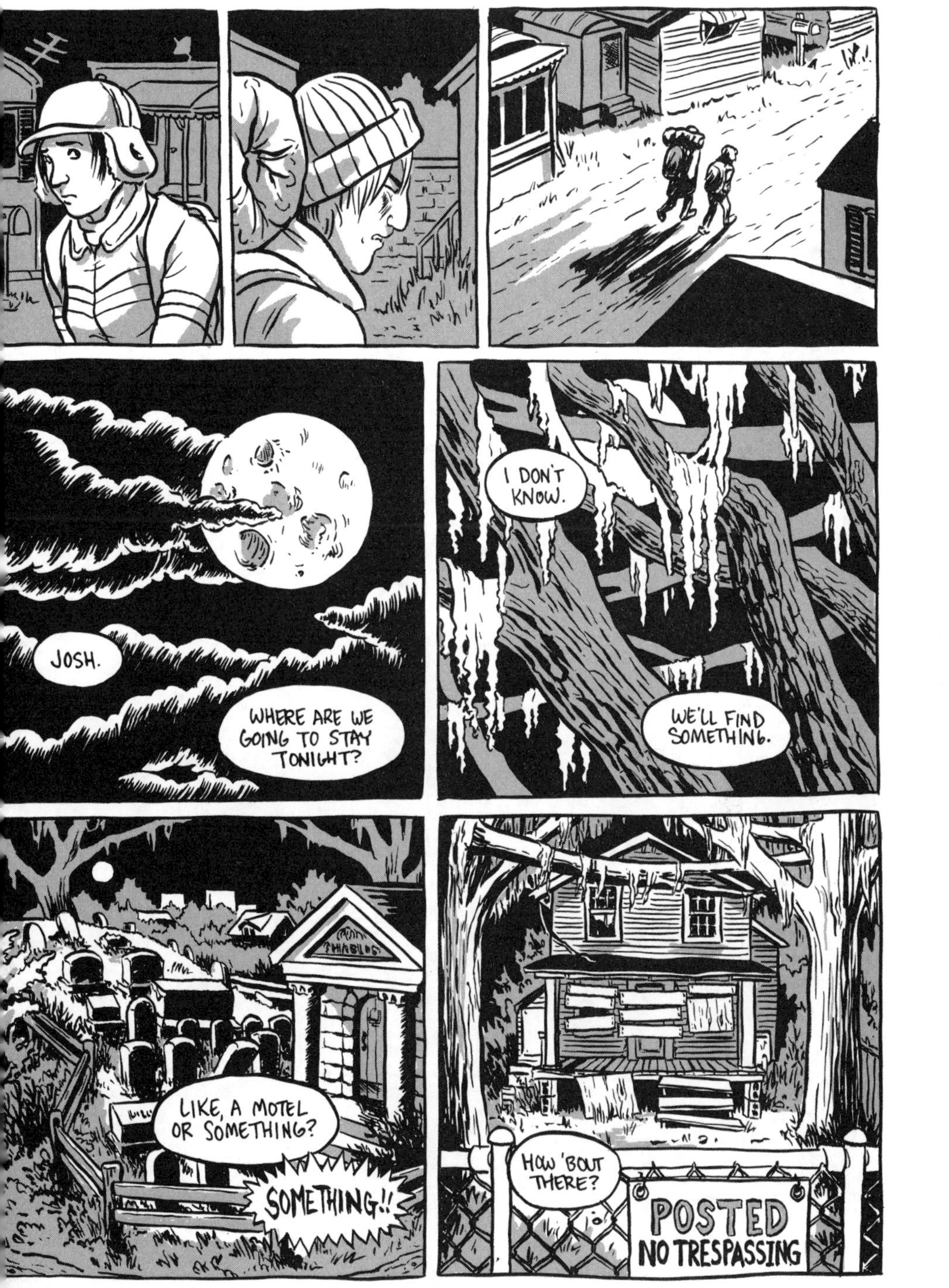
JOSH.
WHERE ARE WE GOING TO STAY TONIGHT?
I DON'T KNOW.
WE'LL FIND SOMETHING.
LIKE, A MOTEL OR SOMETHING?
SOMETHING!!
HOW 'BOUT THERE?
POSTED
NO TRESPASSING

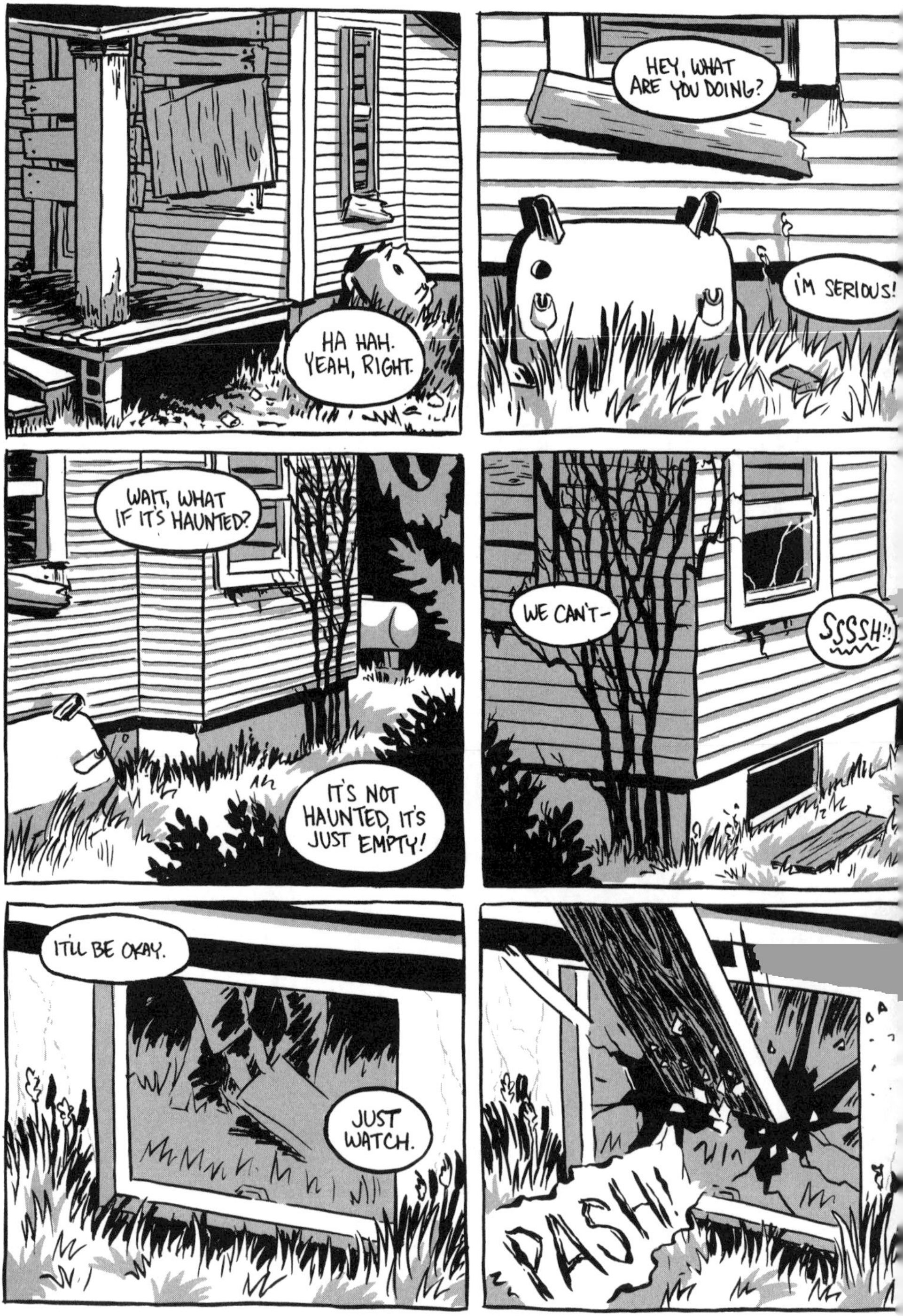
HA HAH. YEAH, RIGHT.
HEY, WHAT ARE YOU DOING?
I'M SERIOUS!
WAIT, WHAT IF IT'S HAUNTED?
IT'S NOT HAUNTED, IT'S JUST EMPTY!
WE CAN'T-
SSSSH!!
IT'LL BE OKAY.
JUST WATCH.
PASH!

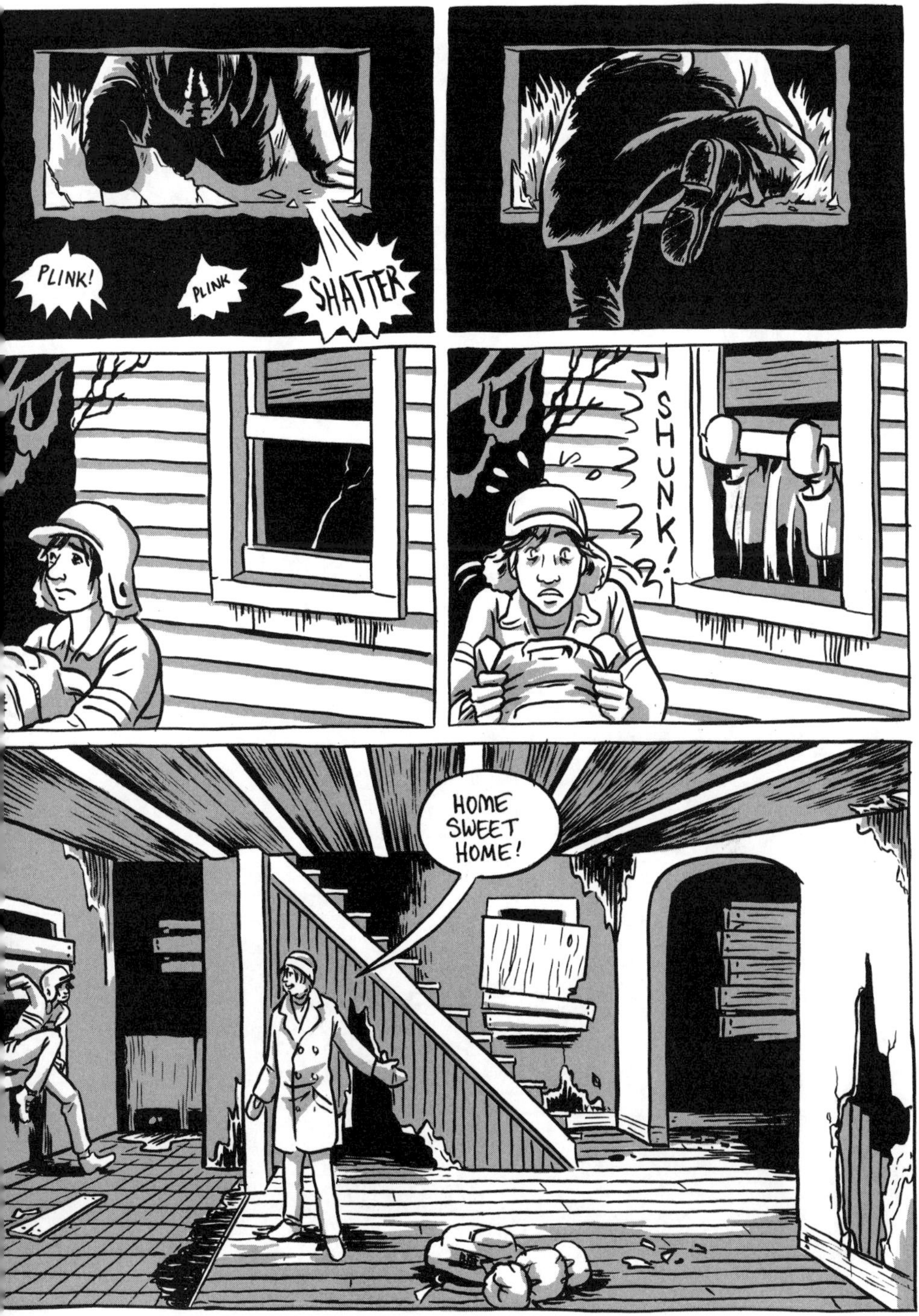
PLINK!
PLINK
SHATTER
SHUNK!
HOME SWEET HOME!

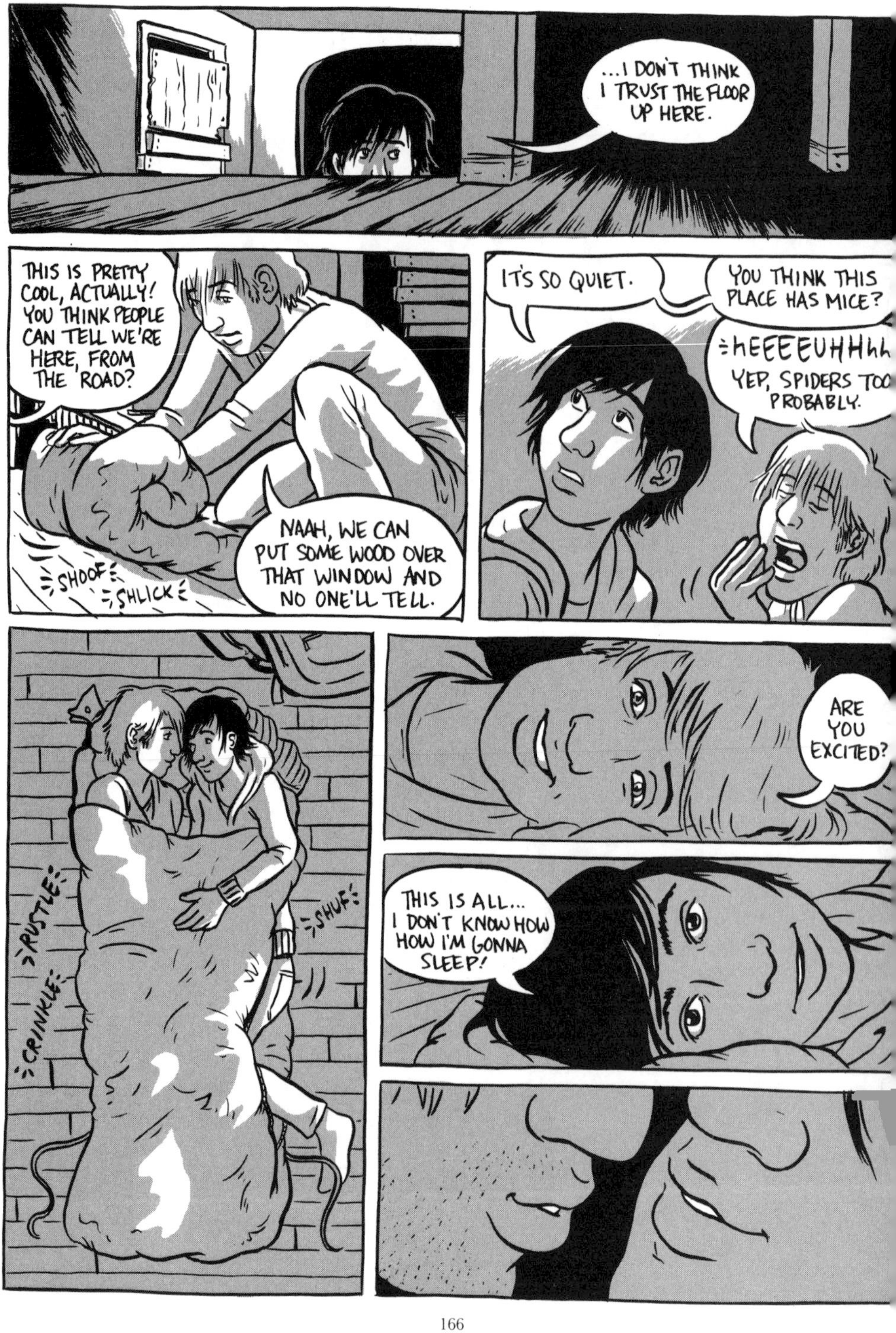
...I DON'T THINK I TRUST THE FLOOR UP HERE.
THIS IS PRETTY COOL, ACTUALLY! YOU THINK PEOPLE CAN TELL WE'RE HERE, FROM THE ROAD?
SHOOF
SHLICK
NAAH, WE CAN PUT SOME WOOD OVER THAT WINDOW AND NO ONE'LL TELL.
IT'S SO QUIET.
YOU THINK THIS PLACE HAS MICE?
HEEEEUHHHh
YEP, SPIDERS TOO PROBABLY.
RUSTLE
CRINKLE
SHUF
ARE YOU EXCITED?
THIS IS ALL... I DON'T KNOW HOW HOW I'M GONNA SLEEP!

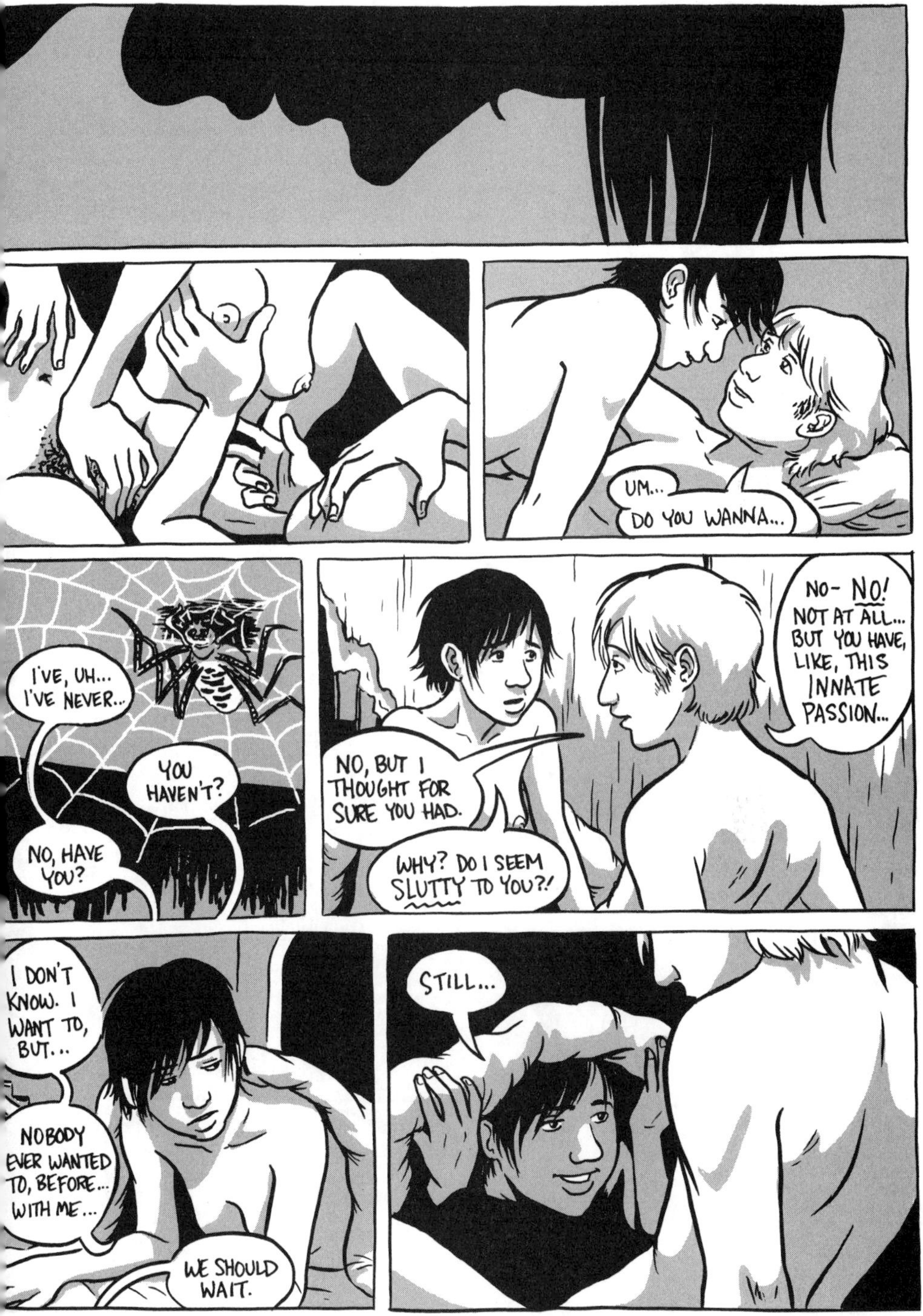
UM... DO YOU WANNA...
I'VE, UH... I'VE NEVER...
YOU HAVEN'T?
NO, HAVE YOU?
NO, BUT I THOUGHT FOR SURE YOU HAD.
WHY? DO I SEEM SLUTTY TO YOU?!
NO- NO! NOT AT ALL... BUT YOU HAVE, LIKE, THIS INNATE PASSION...
I DON'T KNOW. I WANT TO, BUT...
NOBODY EVER WANTED TO, BEFORE... WITH ME...
WE SHOULD WAIT.
STILL...

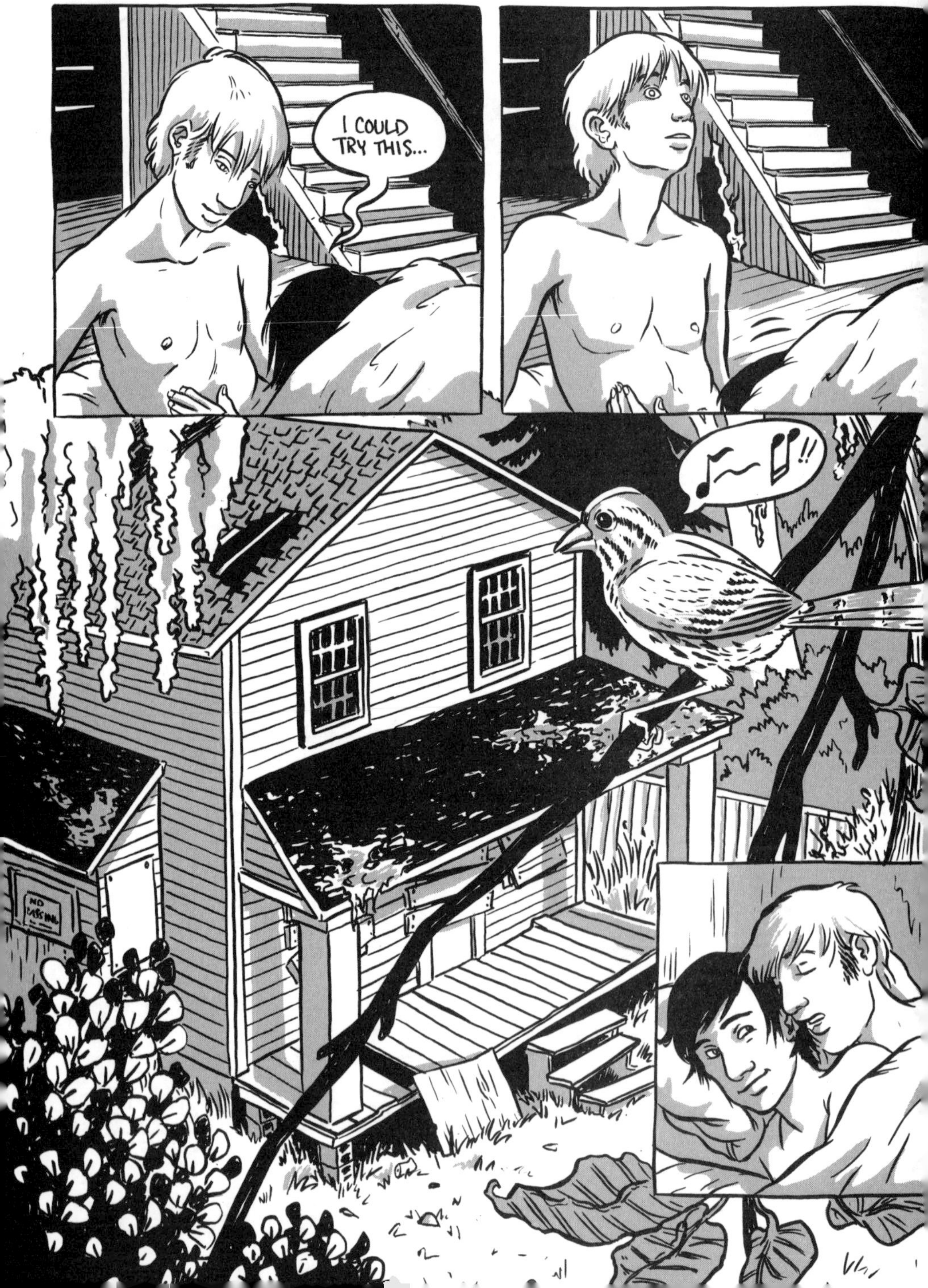
I COULD TRY THIS...

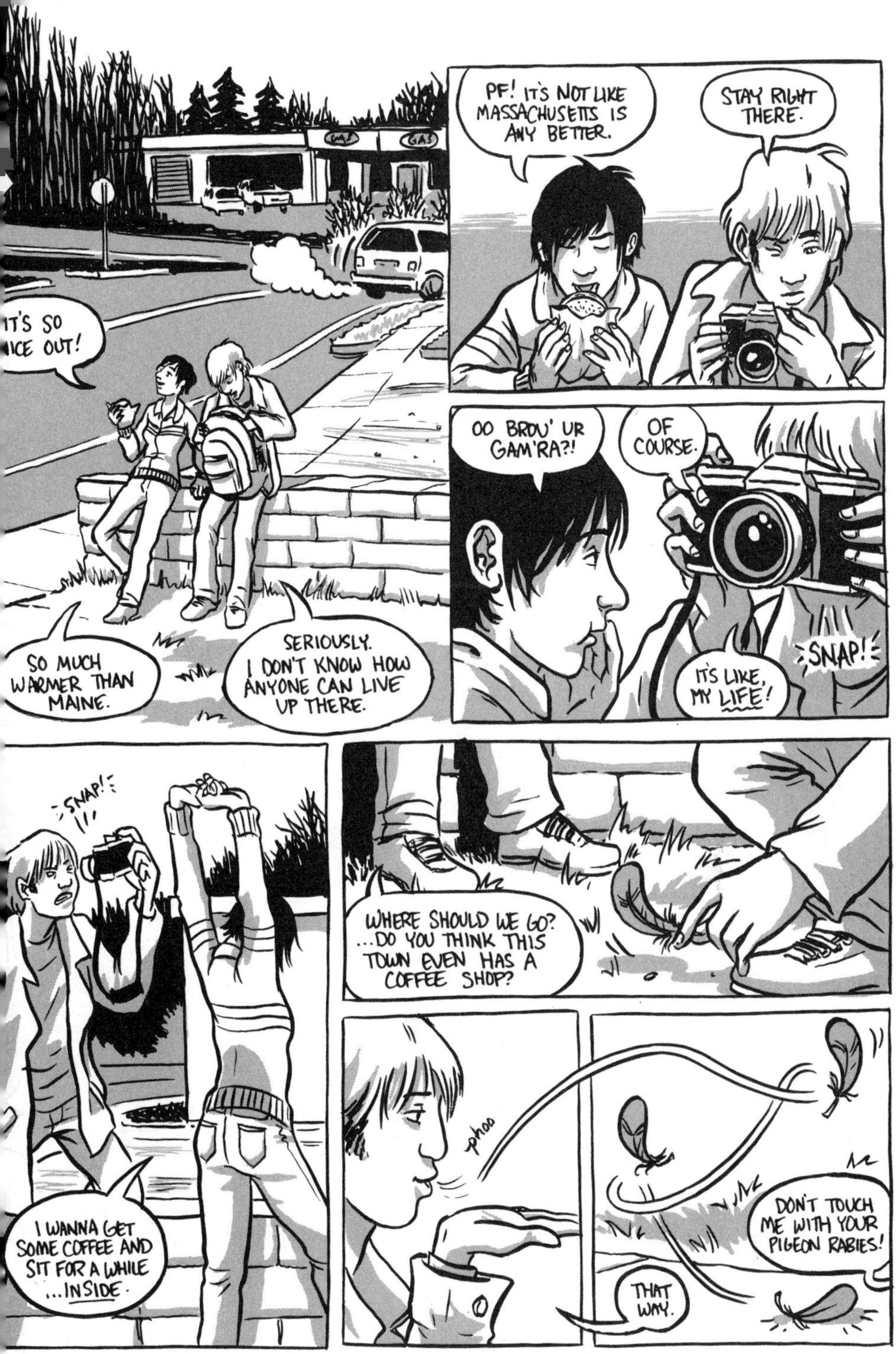

IT'S SO
NICE OUT!
SO MUCH WARMER THAN MAINE.
SERIOUSLY. I DON'T KNOW HOW ANYONE CAN LIVE UP THERE.
PF! IT'S NOT LIKE MASSACHUSETTS IS ANY BETTER.
STAY RIGHT THERE.
OO BROU' UR GAM'RA?!
OF COURSE.
IT'S LIKE, MY LIFE!
SNAP!
SNAP!
I WANNA GET SOME COFFEE AND SIT FOR A WHILE ...INSIDE.
WHERE SHOULD WE GO? ...DO YOU THINK THIS TOWN EVEN HAS A COFFEE SHOP?
phoo
THAT WAY.
DON'T TOUCH ME WITH YOUR PIGEON RABIES!

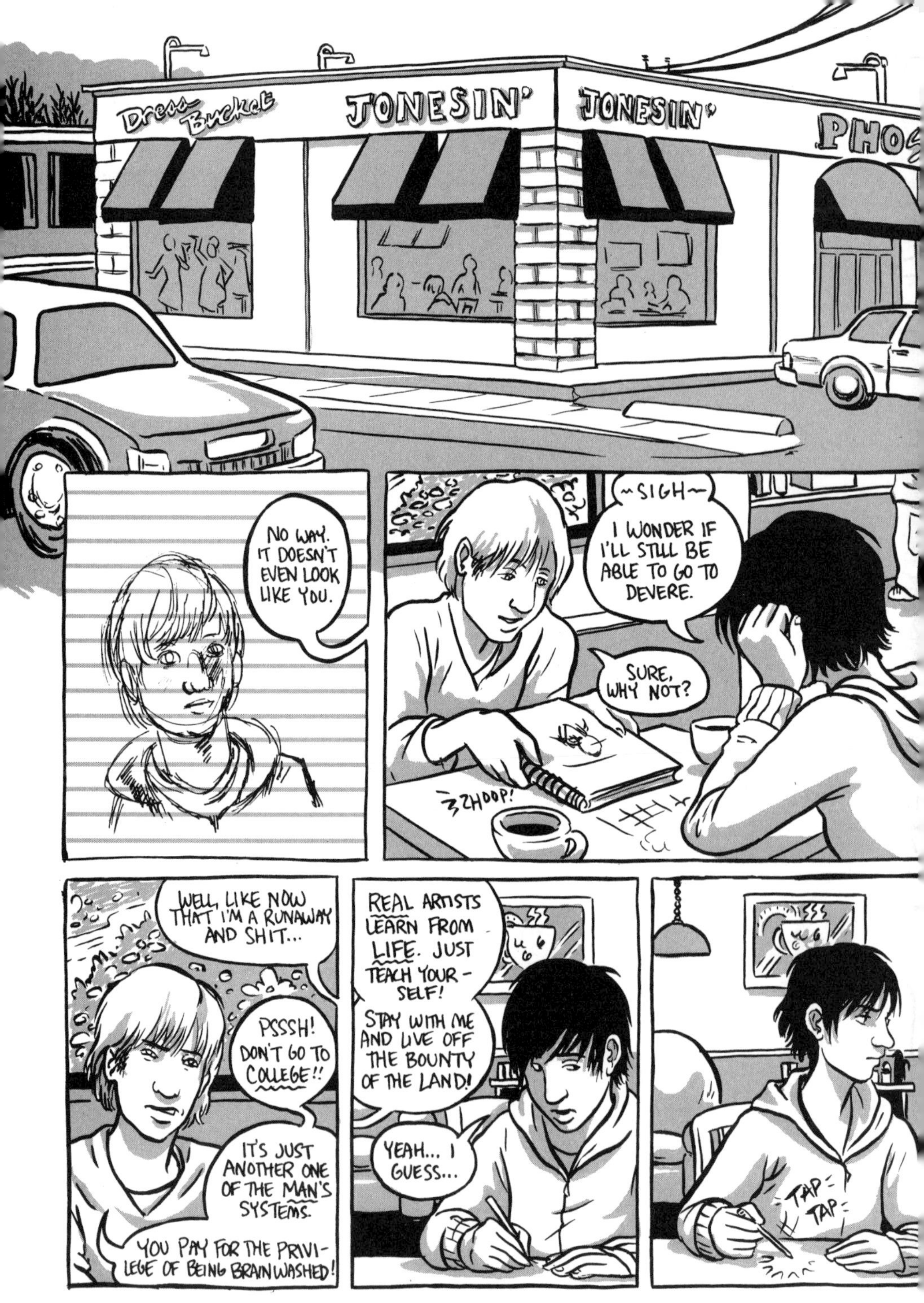
Dress Bucket
JONESIN'
JONESIN'
PHO
NO WAY. IT DOESN'T EVEN LOOK LIKE YOU.
~SIGH~
I WONDER IF I'LL STILL BE ABLE TO GO TO DEVERE.
SURE, WHY NOT?
ZHOOP!
WELL, LIKE NOW THAT I'M A RUNAWAY AND SHIT...
PSSSH! DON'T GO TO COLLEGE!!
IT'S JUST ANOTHER ONE OF THE MAN'S SYSTEMS.
YOU PAY FOR THE PRIVI-LEGE OF BEING BRAINWASHED!
REAL ARTISTS LEARN FROM LIFE. JUST TEACH YOUR-SELF!
STAY WITH ME AND LIVE OFF THE BOUNTY OF THE LAND!
YEAH... I GUESS...
TAP TAP

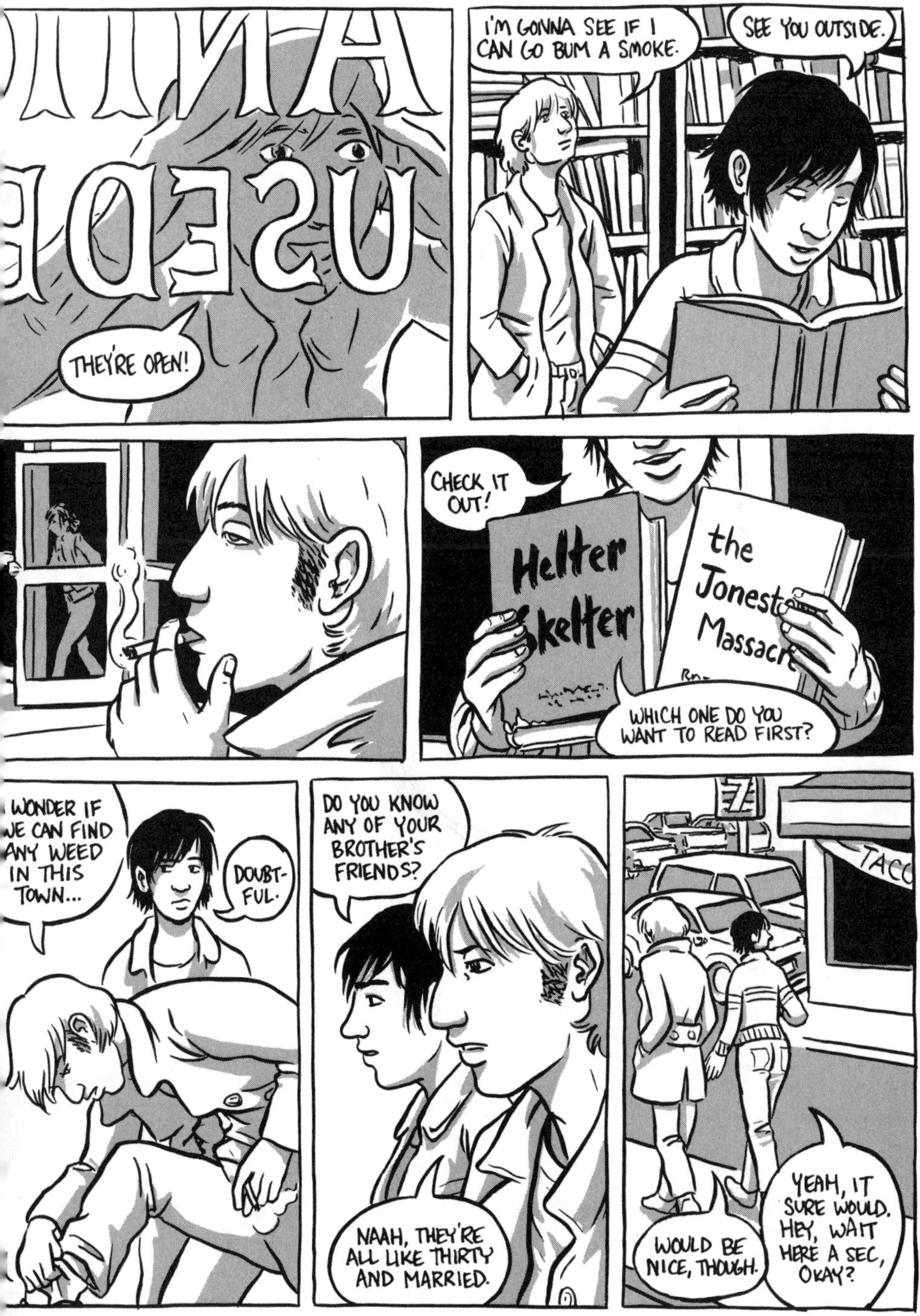
THEY'RE OPEN!
I'M GONNA SEE IF I CAN GO BUM A SMOKE.
SEE YOU OUTSIDE.
CHECK IT OUT!
Helter Skelter
WHICH ONE DO YOU WANT TO READ FIRST?
I WONDER IF WE CAN FIND ANY WEED IN THIS TOWN...
DOUBT-FUL.
DO YOU KNOW ANY OF YOUR BROTHER'S FRIENDS?
NAAH, THEY'RE ALL LIKE THIRTY AND MARRIED.
WOULD BE NICE, THOUGH.
YEAH, IT SURE WOULD. HEY, WAIT HERE A SEC, OKAY?

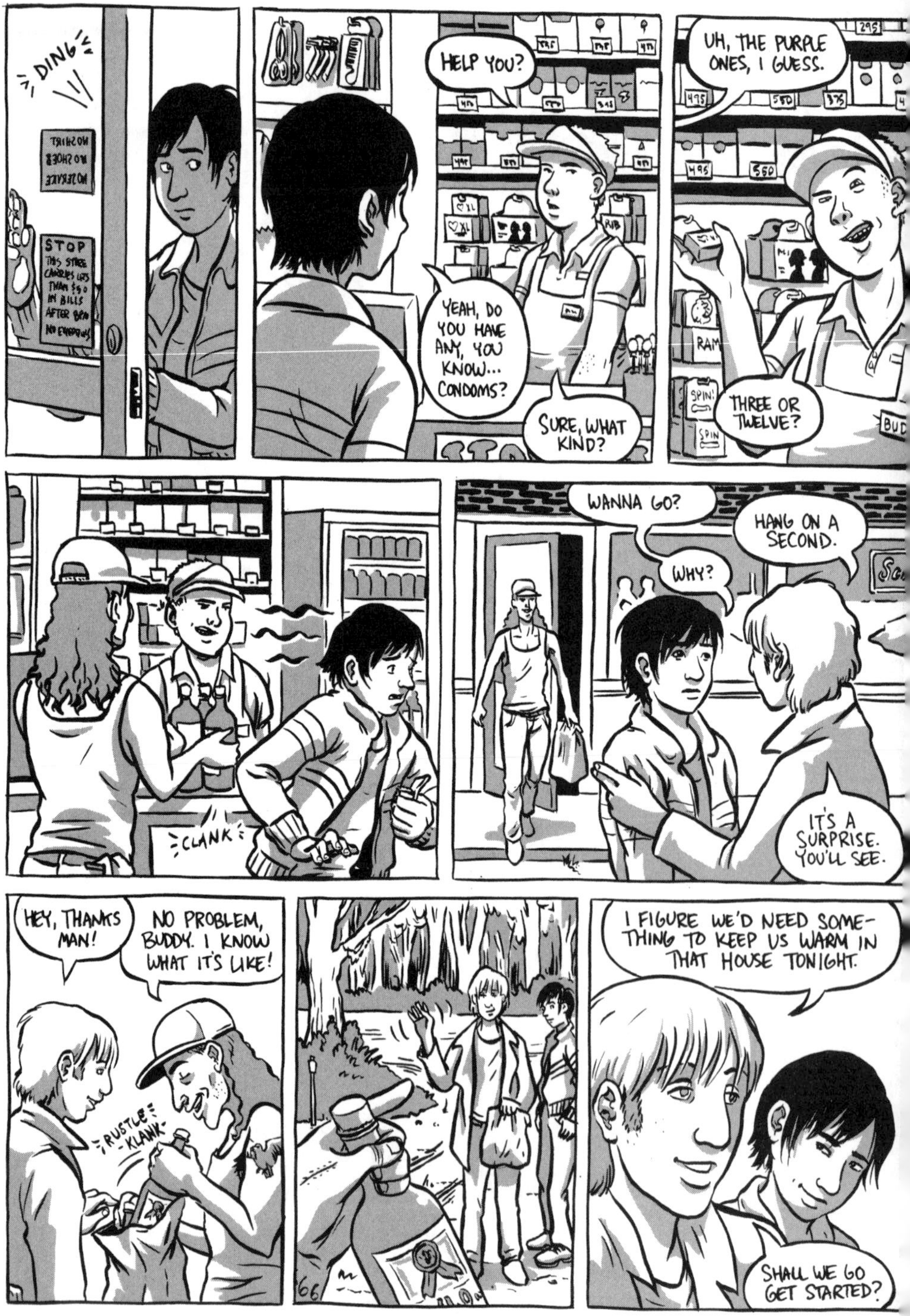
DING
NO SHIRT
NO SHOES
NO SERVICE
STOP
THIS STORE CARRIES LESS THAN $50 IN BILLS AFTER 8PM
NO EXCEPTIONS
HELP YOU?
YEAH, DO YOU HAVE ANY, YOU KNOW... CONDOMS?
SURE, WHAT KIND?
UH, THE PURPLE ONES, I GUESS.
THREE OR TWELVE?
CLANK
WANNA GO?
HANG ON A SECOND.
WHY?
IT'S A SURPRISE. YOU'LL SEE.
HEY, THANKS MAN!
NO PROBLEM, BUDDY. I KNOW WHAT IT'S LIKE!
RUSTLE-KLANK
I FIGURE WE'D NEED SOMETHING TO KEEP US WARM IN THAT HOUSE TONIGHT.
SHALL WE GO GET STARTED?

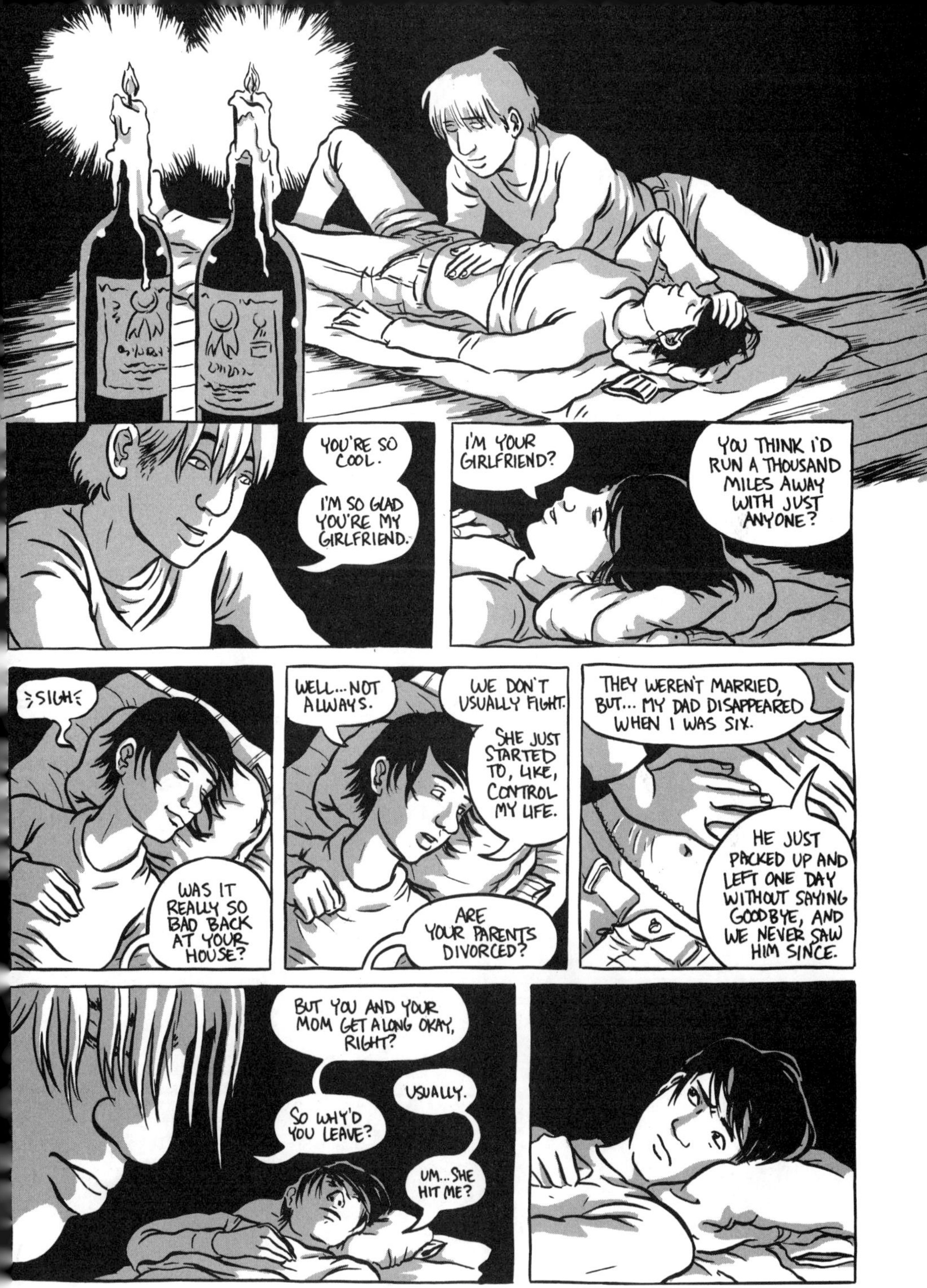
YOU'RE SO COOL.
I'M SO GLAD YOU'RE MY GIRLFRIEND.
I'M YOUR GIRLFRIEND?
YOU THINK I'D RUN A THOUSAND MILES AWAY WITH JUST ANYONE?
SIGH
WAS IT REALLY SO BAD BACK AT YOUR HOUSE?
WELL... NOT ALWAYS.
WE DON'T USUALLY FIGHT.
SHE JUST STARTED TO, LIKE, CONTROL MY LIFE.
ARE YOUR PARENTS DIVORCED?
THEY WEREN'T MARRIED, BUT... MY DAD DISAPPEARED WHEN I WAS SIX.
HE JUST PACKED UP AND LEFT ONE DAY WITHOUT SAYING GOODBYE, AND WE NEVER SAW HIM SINCE.
BUT YOU AND YOUR MOM GET ALONG OKAY, RIGHT?
USUALLY.
SO WHY'D YOU LEAVE?
UM... SHE HIT ME?

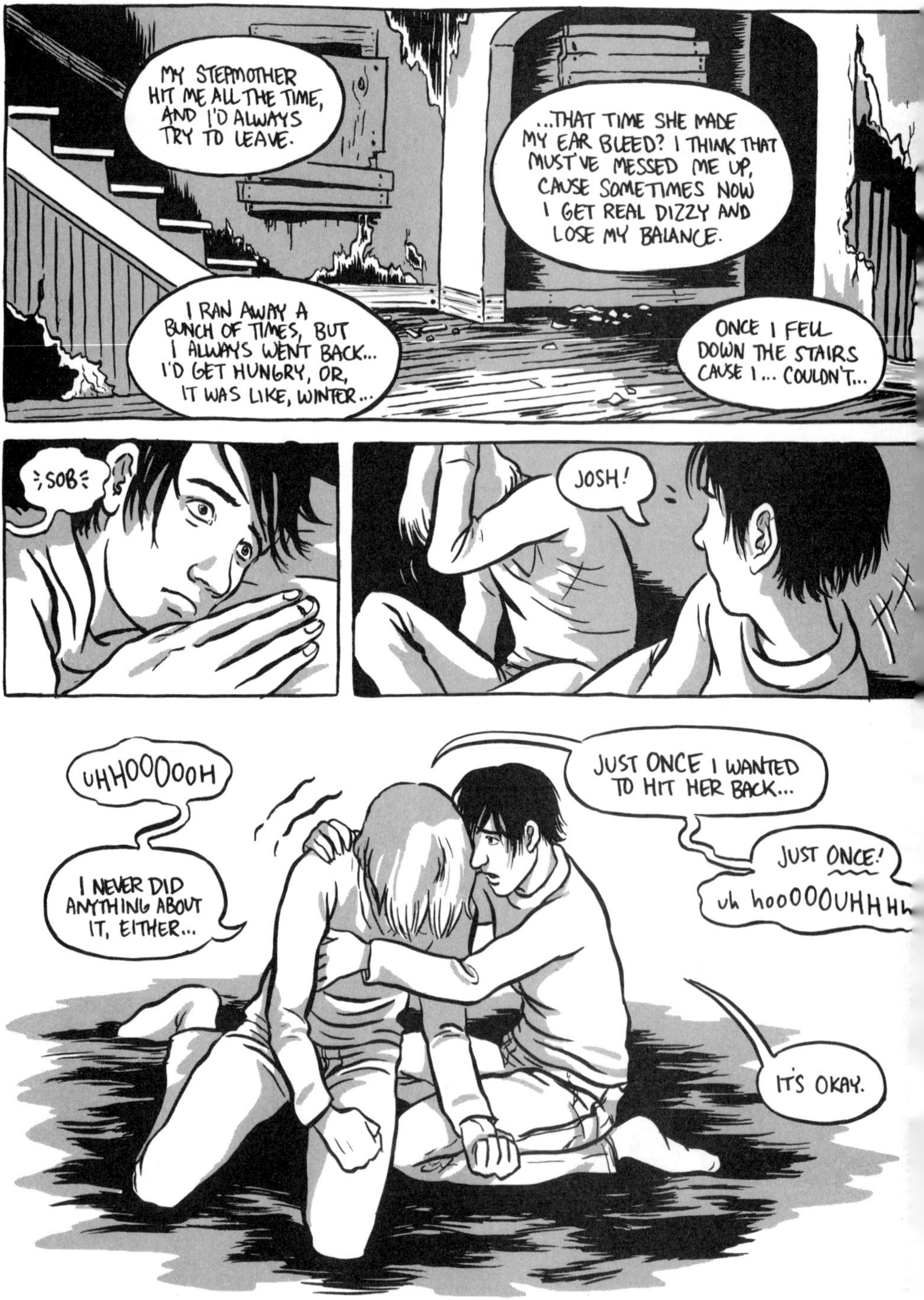
MY STEPMOTHER HIT ME ALL THE TIME, AND I'D ALWAYS TRY TO LEAVE.
I RAN AWAY A BUNCH OF TIMES, BUT I ALWAYS WENT BACK... I'D GET HUNGRY, OR, IT WAS LIKE, WINTER...
...THAT TIME SHE MADE MY EAR BLEED? I THINK THAT MUST'VE MESSED ME UP, CAUSE SOMETIMES NOW I GET REAL DIZZY AND LOSE MY BALANCE.
ONCE I FELL DOWN THE STAIRS CAUSE I... COULDN'T...
SOB
JOSH!
UHHOOOOOH
I NEVER DID ANYTHING ABOUT IT, EITHER...
JUST ONCE I WANTED TO HIT HER BACK...
JUST ONCE!
uh hooOOOUHHHH
IT'S OKAY.

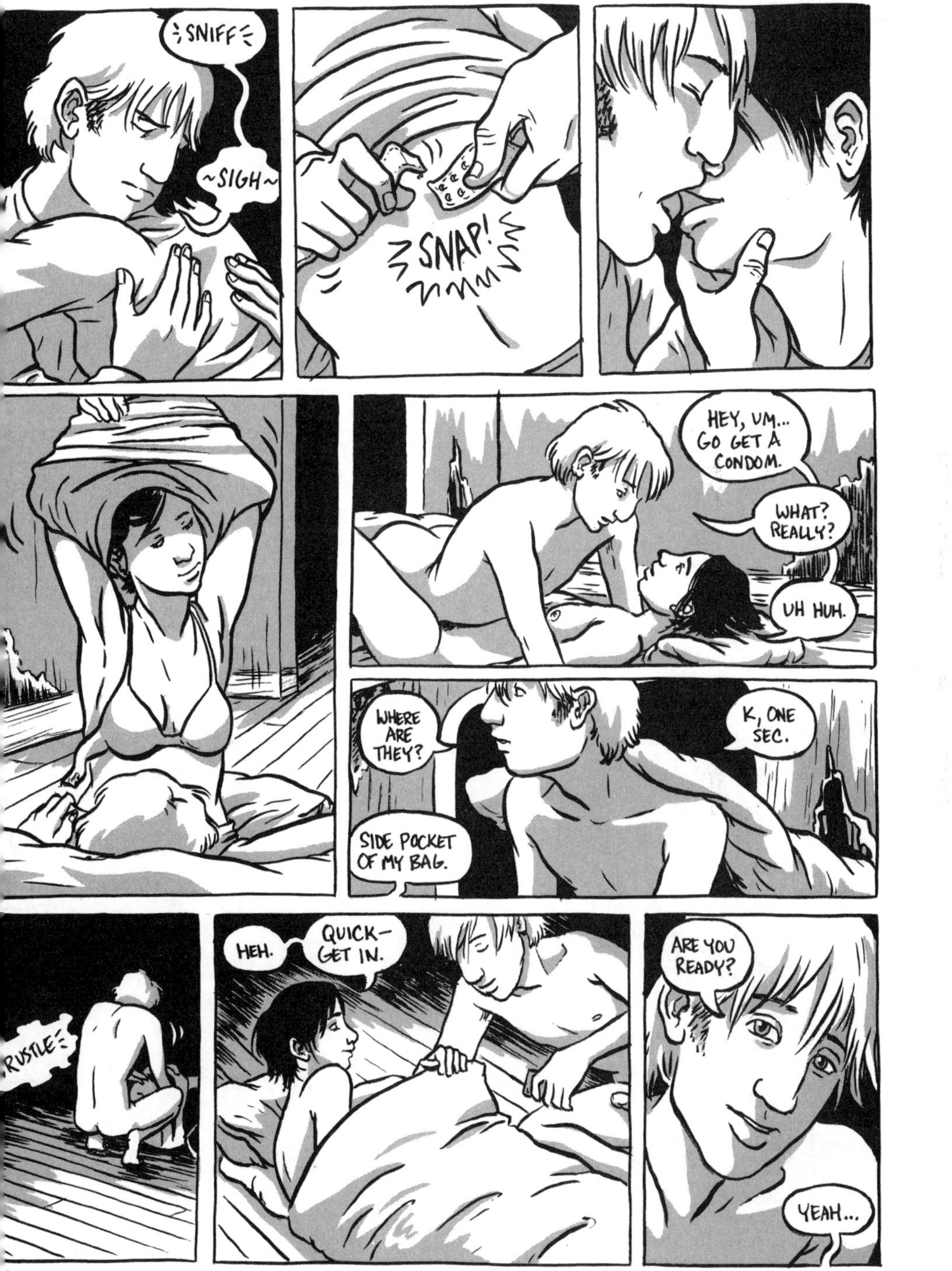
SNIFF
~SIGH~
SNAP!
HEY, UM... GO GET A CONDOM.
WHAT? REALLY?
UH HUH.
WHERE ARE THEY?
K, ONE SEC.
SIDE POCKET OF MY BAG.
RUSTLE
HEH.
QUICK— GET IN.
ARE YOU READY?
YEAH...

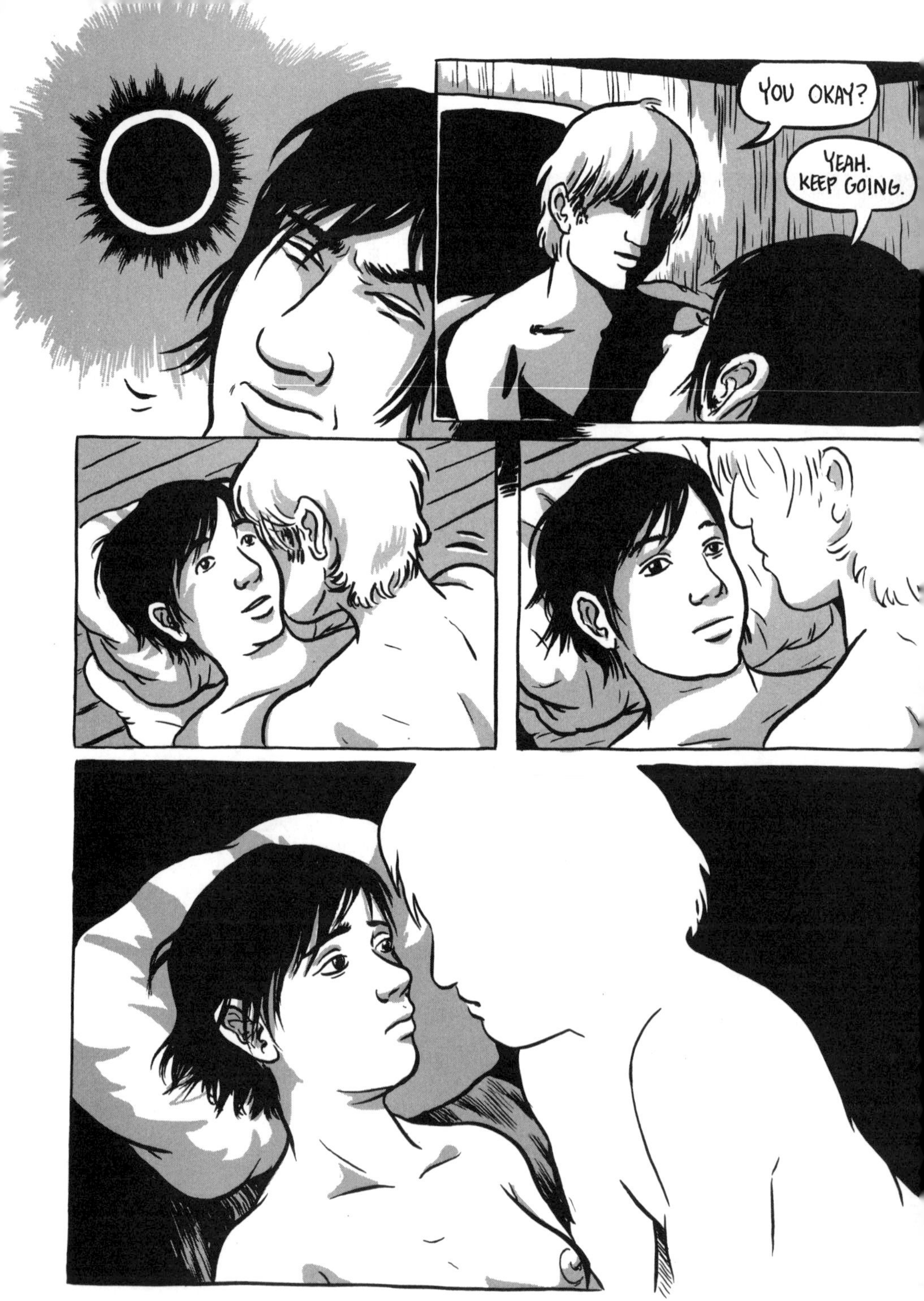
YOU OKAY?
YEAH. KEEP GOING.

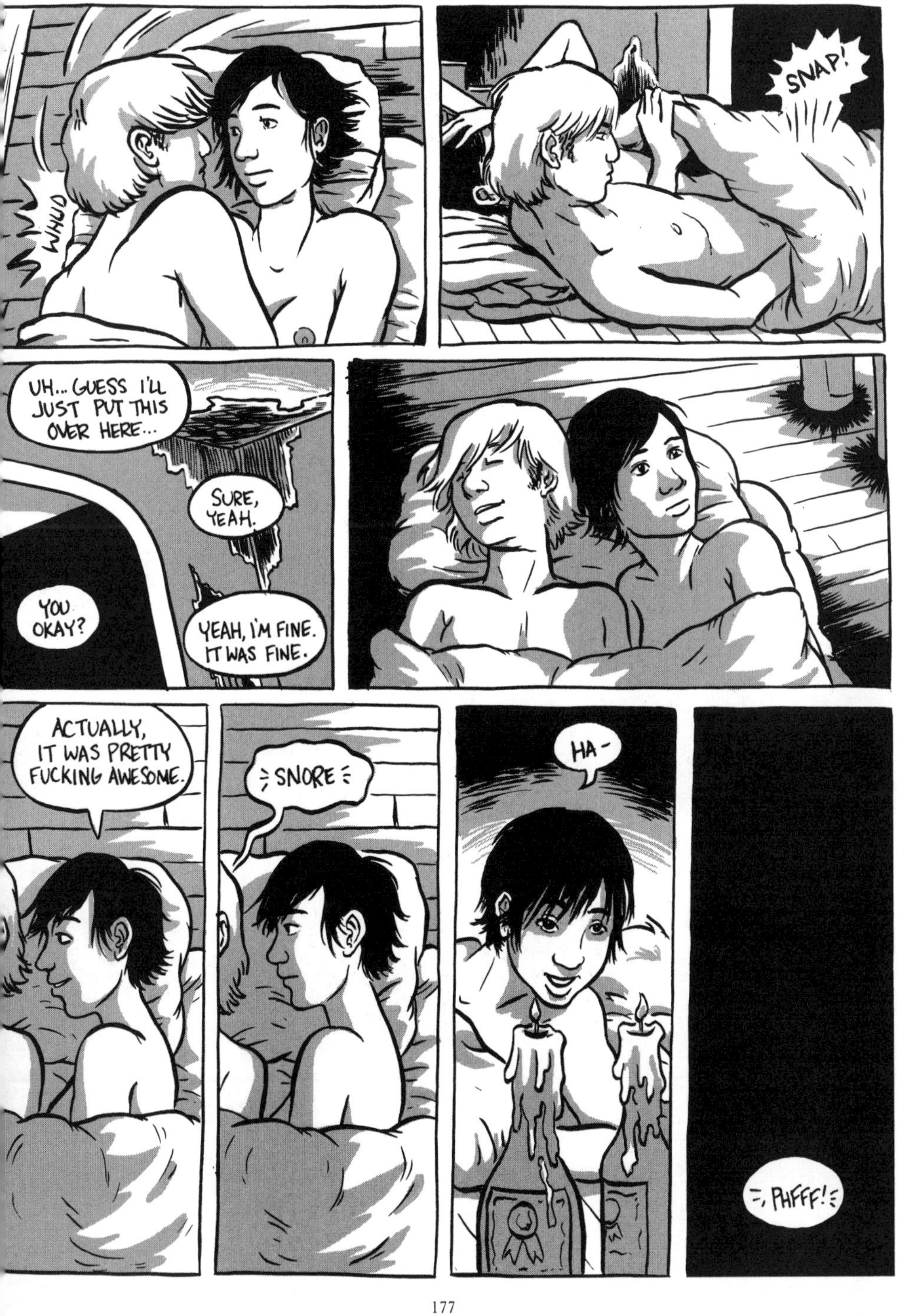
WHUD
SNAP!
UH... GUESS I'LL JUST PUT THIS OVER HERE...
SURE, YEAH.
YOU OKAY?
YEAH, I'M FINE. IT WAS FINE.
ACTUALLY, IT WAS PRETTY FUCKING AWESOME.
SNORE
HA-
PHFFF!

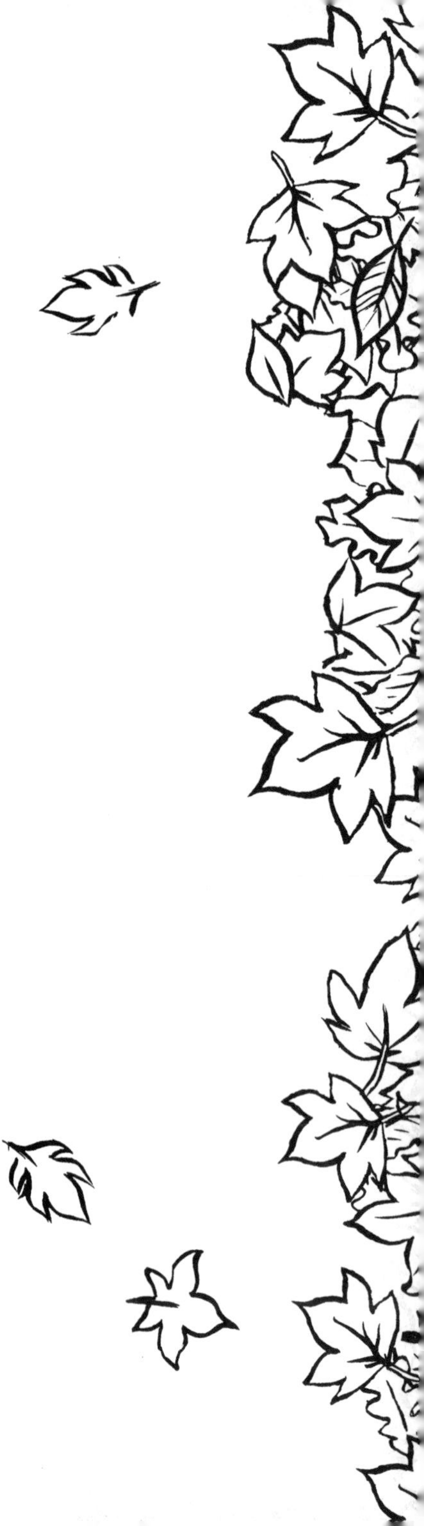

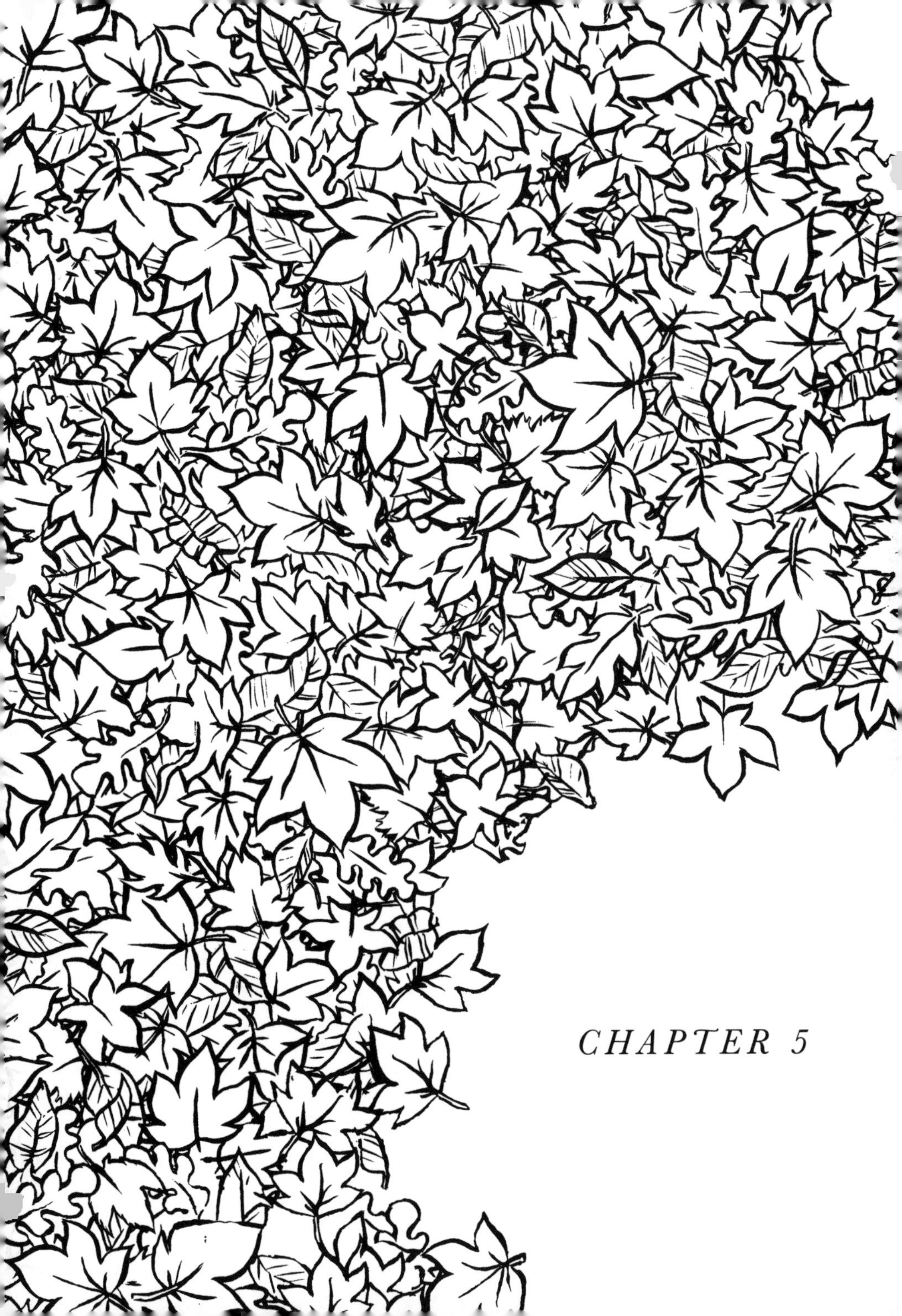

CHAPTER 5

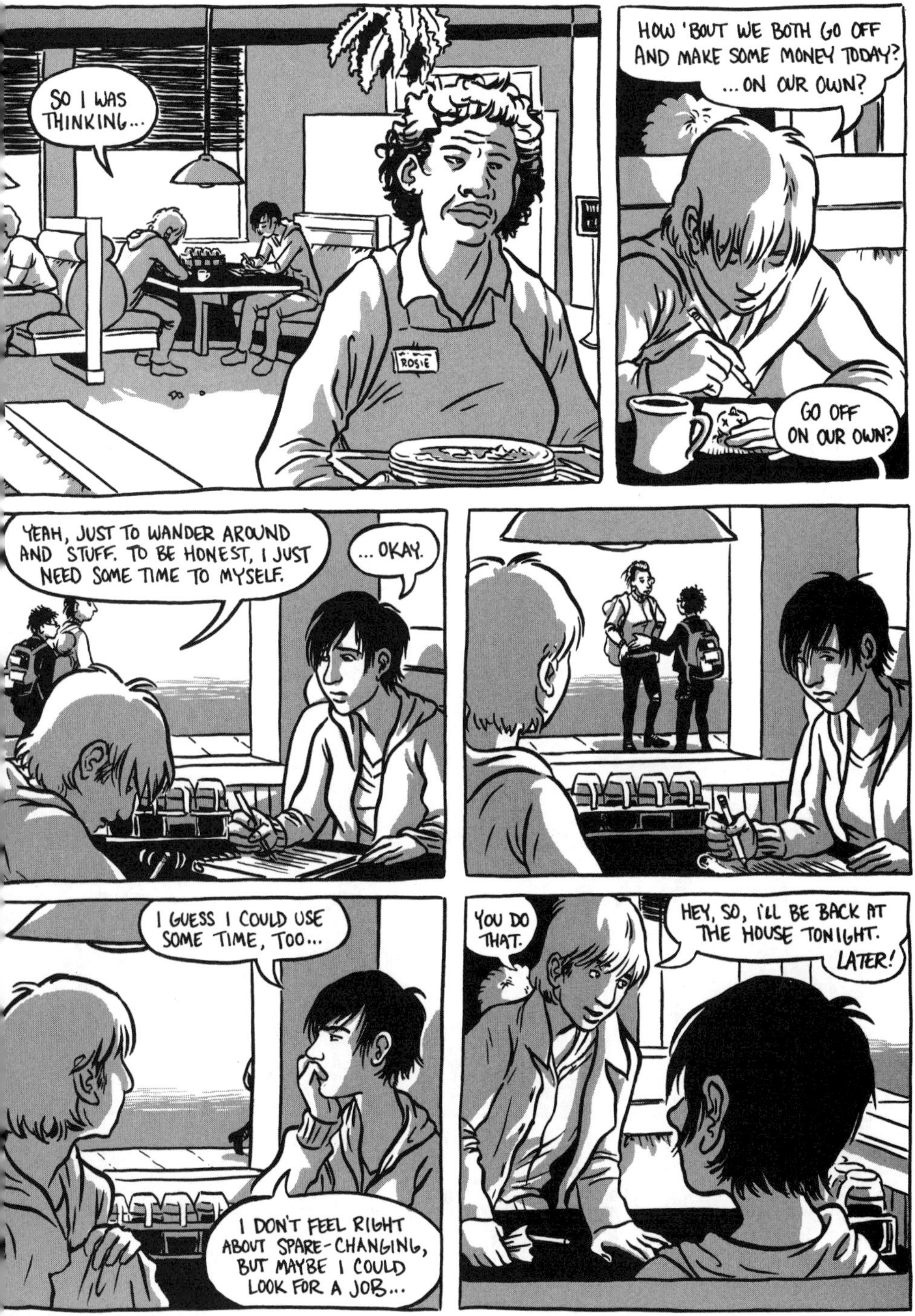
SO I WAS THINKING...
HOW 'BOUT WE BOTH GO OFF AND MAKE SOME MONEY TODAY?
...ON OUR OWN?
GO OFF ON OUR OWN?
ROSIE
YEAH, JUST TO WANDER AROUND AND STUFF. TO BE HONEST, I JUST NEED SOME TIME TO MYSELF.
...OKAY.
I GUESS I COULD USE SOME TIME, TOO...
I DON'T FEEL RIGHT ABOUT SPARE-CHANGING, BUT MAYBE I COULD LOOK FOR A JOB...
YOU DO THAT.
HEY, SO, I'LL BE BACK AT THE HOUSE TONIGHT.
LATER!

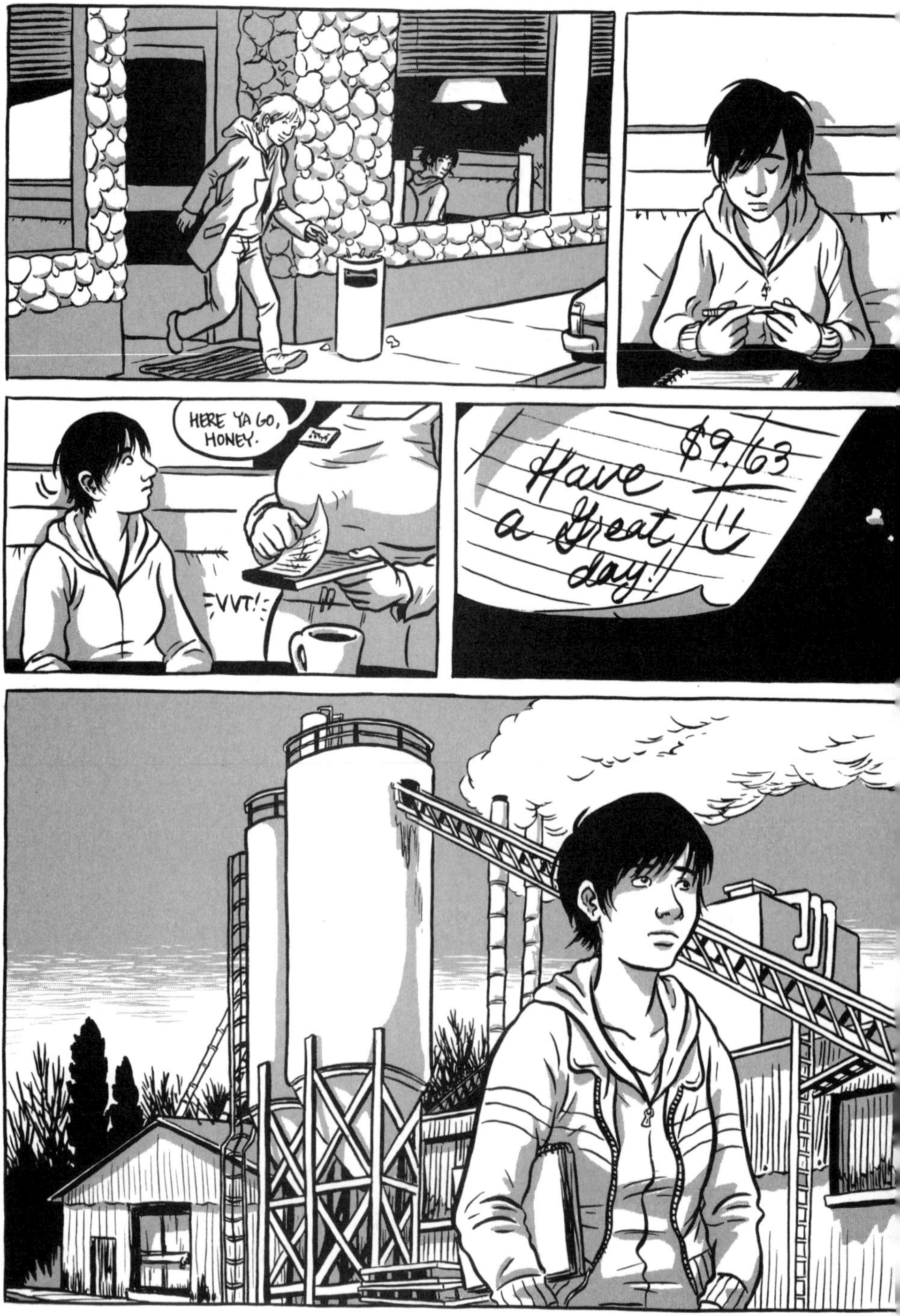
HERE YA GO, HONEY.
VVT!
$9.63
Have a Great day!

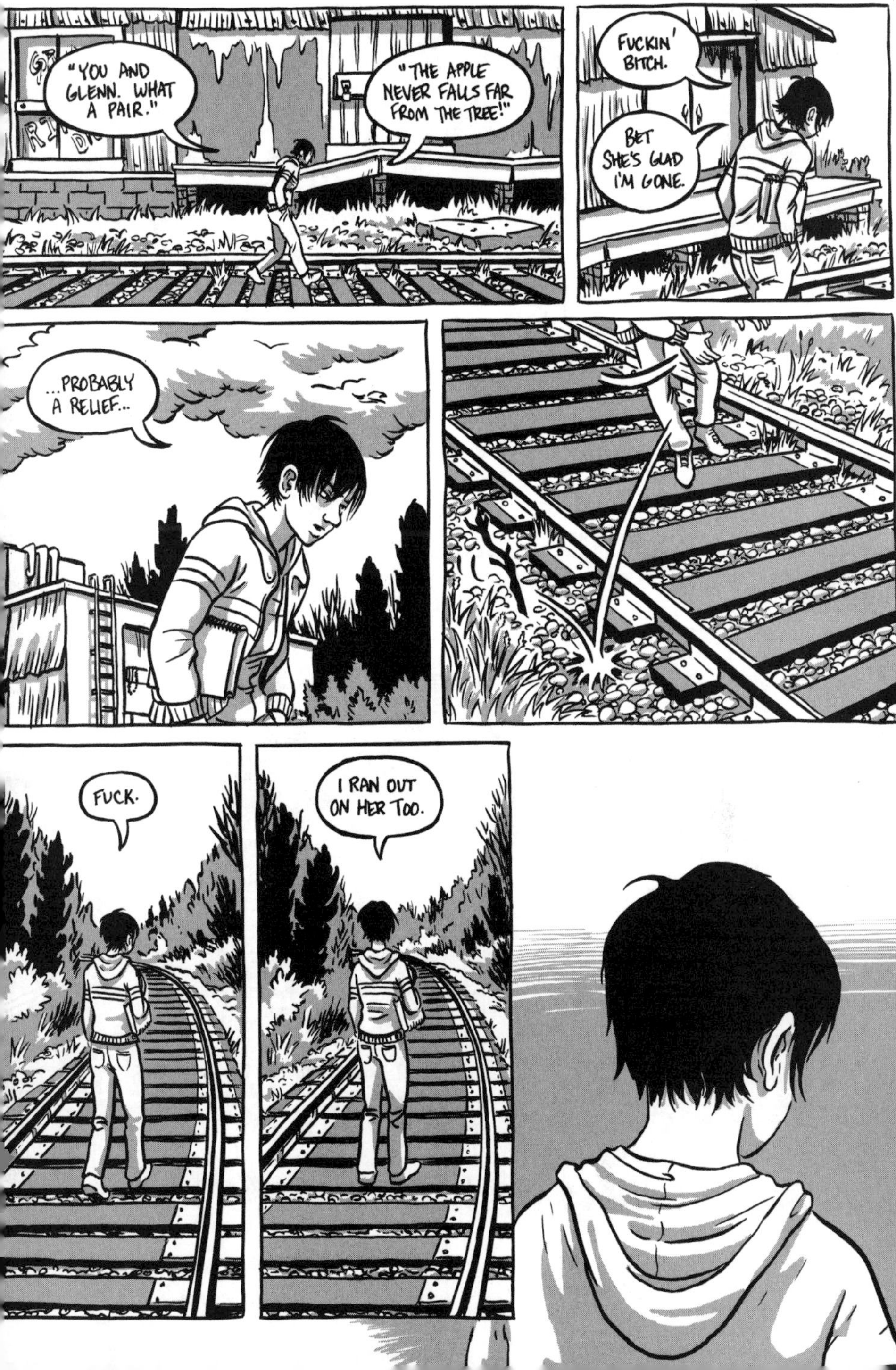
"YOU AND GLENN. WHAT A PAIR."
"THE APPLE NEVER FALLS FAR FROM THE TREE!"
FUCKIN' BITCH.
BET SHE'S GLAD I'M GONE.
...PROBABLY A RELIEF...
FUCK.
I RAN OUT ON HER TOO.

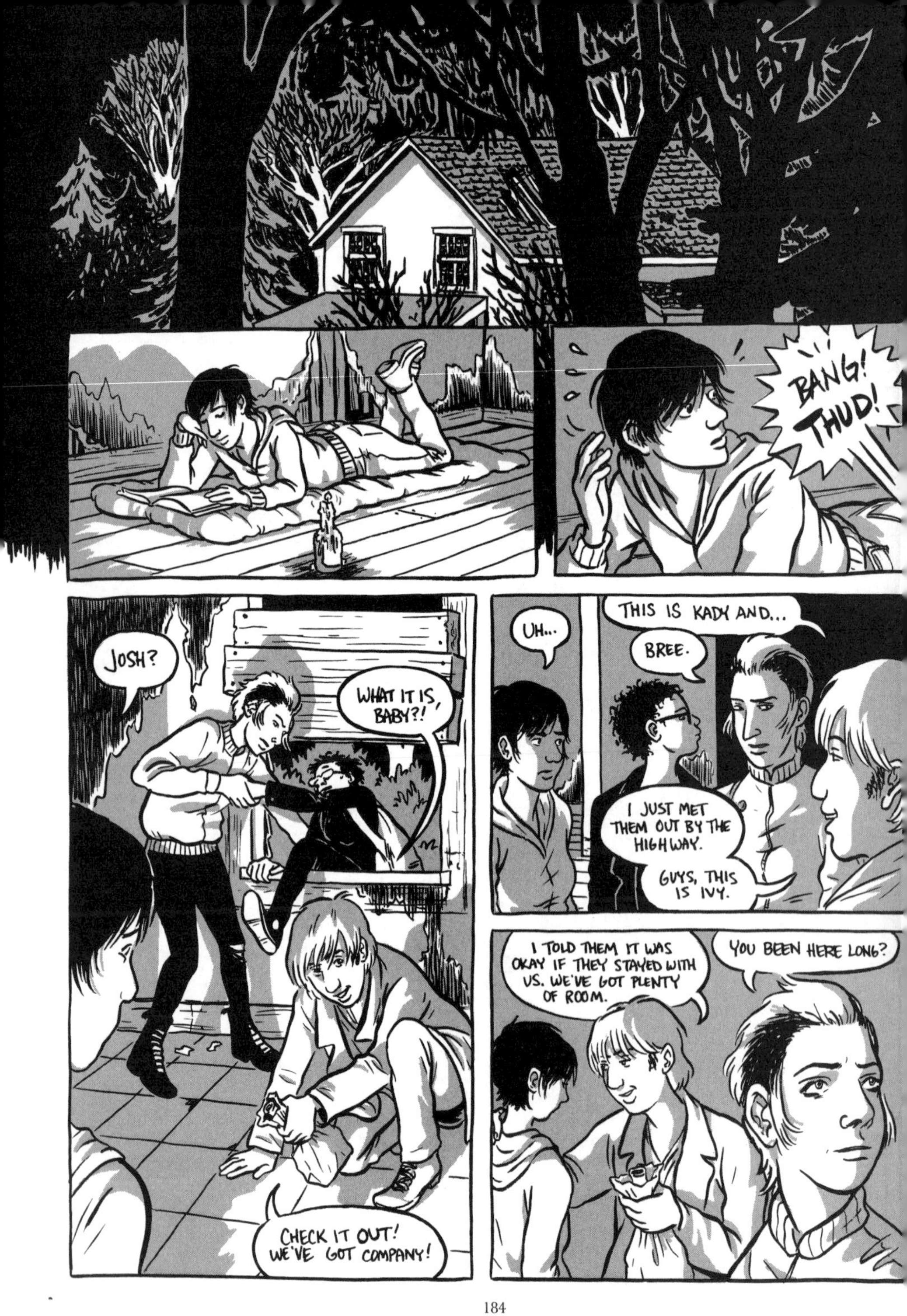
BANG! THUD!
JOSH?
WHAT IT IS, BABY?!
CHECK IT OUT! WE'VE GOT COMPANY!
UH...
THIS IS KADY AND...
BREE.
I JUST MET THEM OUT BY THE HIGHWAY.
GUYS, THIS IS IVY.
I TOLD THEM IT WAS OKAY IF THEY STAYED WITH US. WE'VE GOT PLENTY OF ROOM.
YOU BEEN HERE LONG?

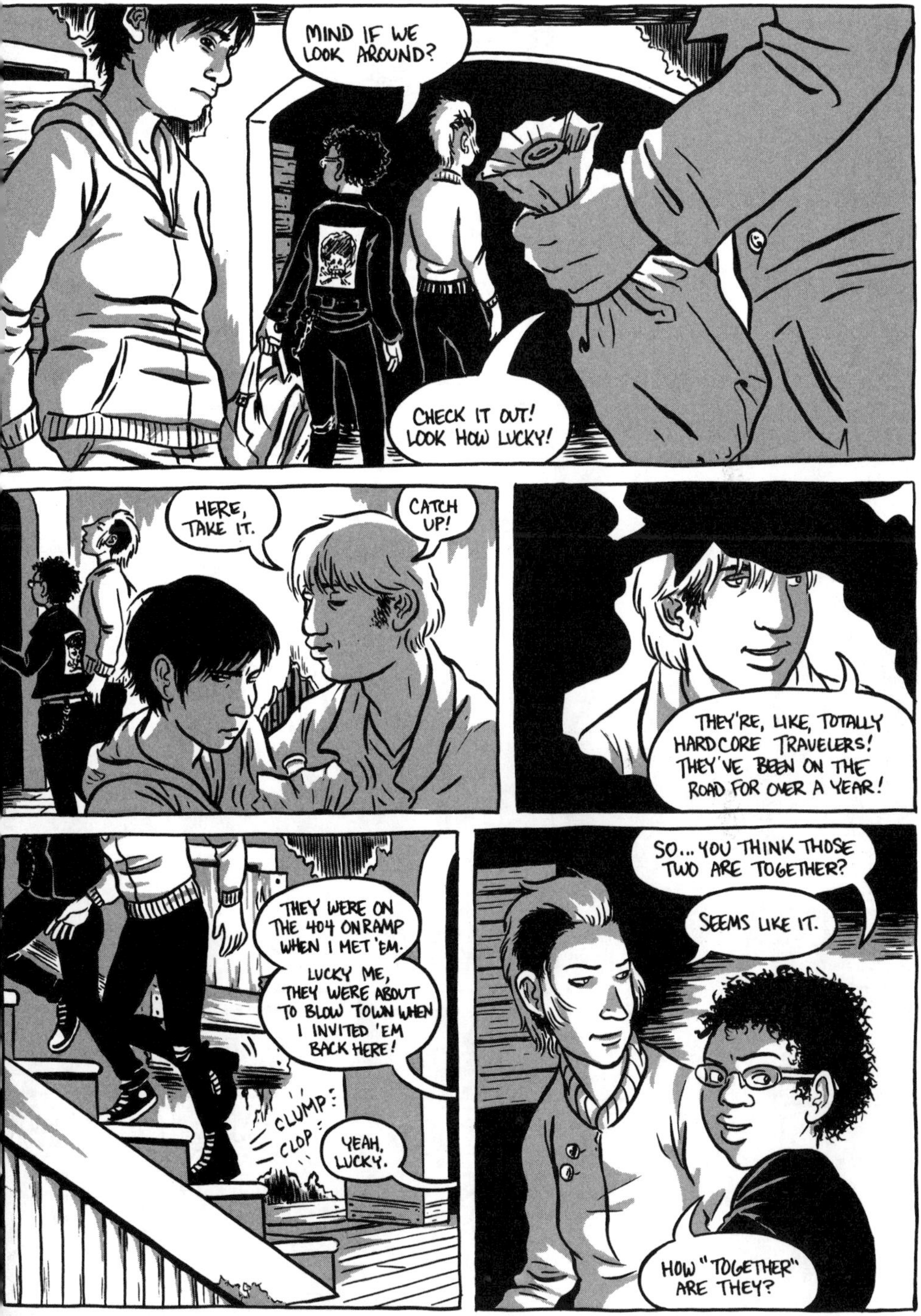
MIND IF WE LOOK AROUND?
CHECK IT OUT! LOOK HOW LUCKY!
HERE, TAKE IT.
CATCH UP!
THEY'RE, LIKE, TOTALLY HARDCORE TRAVELERS! THEY'VE BEEN ON THE ROAD FOR OVER A YEAR!
THEY WERE ON THE 404 ONRAMP WHEN I MET 'EM.
LUCKY ME, THEY WERE ABOUT TO BLOW TOWN WHEN I INVITED 'EM BACK HERE!
CLUMP
CLOP
YEAH, LUCKY.
SO... YOU THINK THOSE TWO ARE TOGETHER?
SEEMS LIKE IT.
HOW "TOGETHER" ARE THEY?

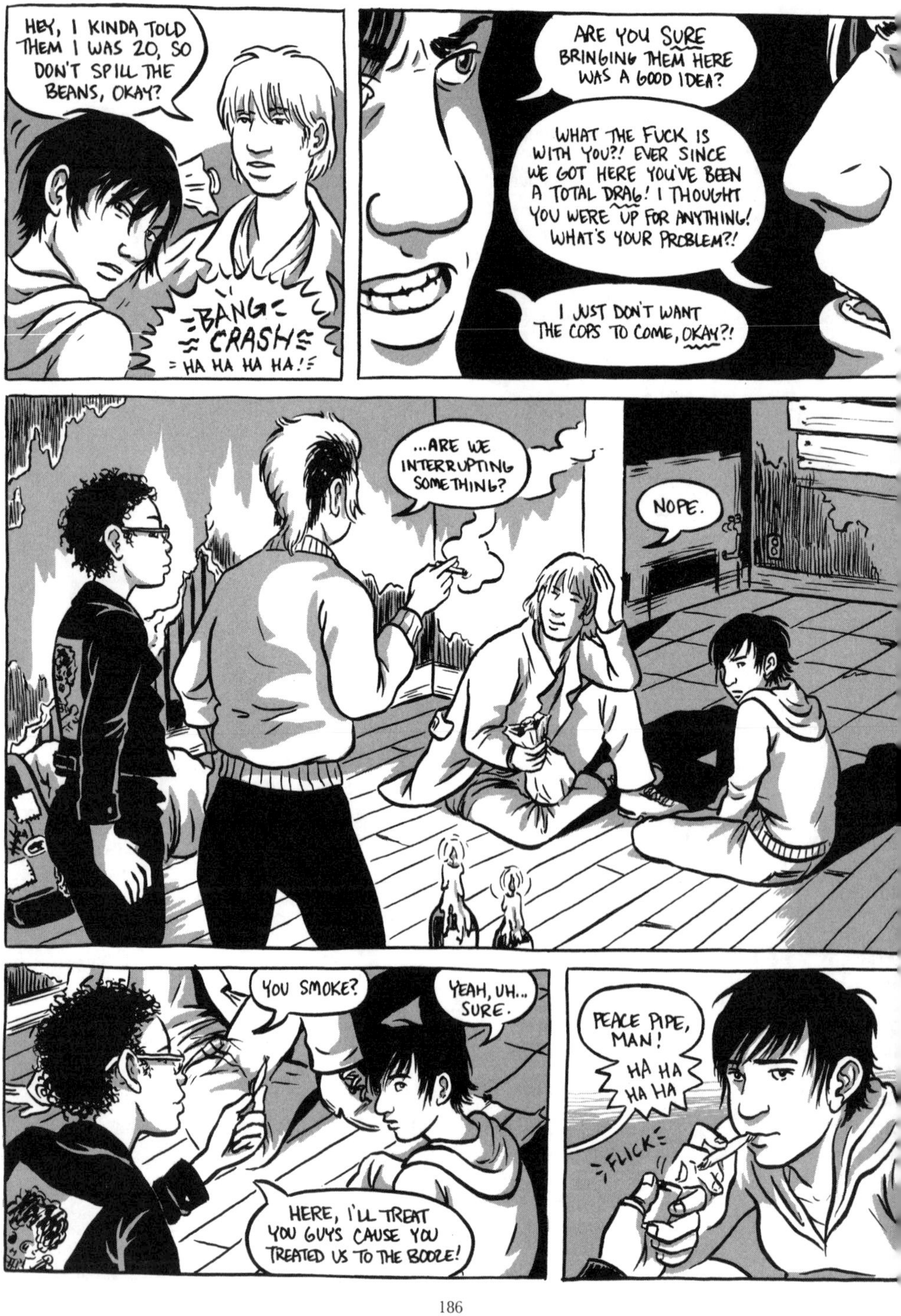
HEY, I KINDA TOLD THEM I WAS 20, SO DON'T SPILL THE BEANS, OKAY?
BANG CRASH
HA HA HA HA!
ARE YOU SURE BRINGING THEM HERE WAS A GOOD IDEA?
WHAT THE FUCK IS WITH YOU?! EVER SINCE WE GOT HERE YOU'VE BEEN A TOTAL DRAG! I THOUGHT YOU WERE UP FOR ANYTHING! WHAT'S YOUR PROBLEM?!
I JUST DON'T WANT THE COPS TO COME, OKAY?!
...ARE WE INTERRUPTING SOMETHING?
NOPE.
YOU SMOKE?
YEAH, UH... SURE.
HERE, I'LL TREAT YOU GUYS CAUSE YOU TREATED US TO THE BOOZE!
PEACE PIPE, MAN!
HA HA HA HA
FLICK

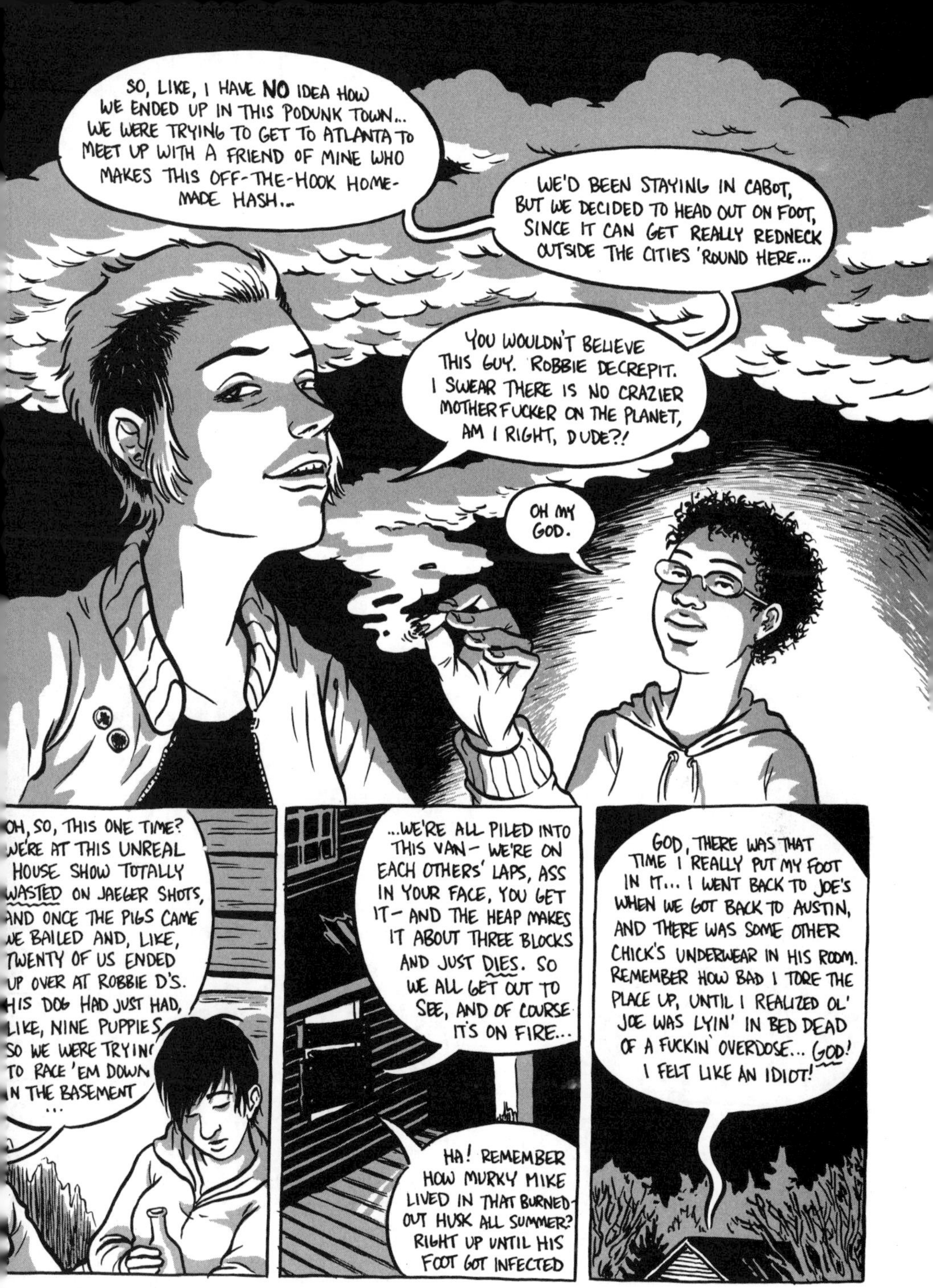
SO, LIKE, I HAVE NO IDEA HOW WE ENDED UP IN THIS PODUNK TOWN... WE WERE TRYING TO GET TO ATLANTA TO MEET UP WITH A FRIEND OF MINE WHO MAKES THIS OFF-THE-HOOK HOME-MADE HASH...
WE'D BEEN STAYING IN CABOT, BUT WE DECIDED TO HEAD OUT ON FOOT, SINCE IT CAN GET REALLY REDNECK OUTSIDE THE CITIES 'ROUND HERE...
YOU WOULDN'T BELIEVE THIS GUY. ROBBIE DECREPIT. I SWEAR THERE IS NO CRAZIER MOTHERFUCKER ON THE PLANET, AM I RIGHT, DUDE?!
OH MY GOD.
OH, SO, THIS ONE TIME? WE'RE AT THIS UNREAL HOUSE SHOW TOTALLY WASTED ON JAEGER SHOTS, AND ONCE THE PIGS CAME WE BAILED AND, LIKE, TWENTY OF US ENDED UP OVER AT ROBBIE D'S. HIS DOG HAD JUST HAD, LIKE, NINE PUPPIES SO WE WERE TRYING TO RACE 'EM DOWN IN THE BASEMENT ...
...WE'RE ALL PILED INTO THIS VAN– WE'RE ON EACH OTHERS' LAPS, ASS IN YOUR FACE, YOU GET IT– AND THE HEAP MAKES IT ABOUT THREE BLOCKS AND JUST DIES. SO WE ALL GET OUT TO SEE, AND OF COURSE IT'S ON FIRE...
HA! REMEMBER HOW MURKY MIKE LIVED IN THAT BURNED-OUT HUSK ALL SUMMER? RIGHT UP UNTIL HIS FOOT GOT INFECTED
GOD, THERE WAS THAT TIME I REALLY PUT MY FOOT IN IT... I WENT BACK TO JOE'S WHEN WE GOT BACK TO AUSTIN, AND THERE WAS SOME OTHER CHICK'S UNDERWEAR IN HIS ROOM. REMEMBER HOW BAD I TORE THE PLACE UP, UNTIL I REALIZED OL' JOE WAS LYIN' IN BED DEAD OF A FUCKIN' OVERDOSE... GOD! I FELT LIKE AN IDIOT!

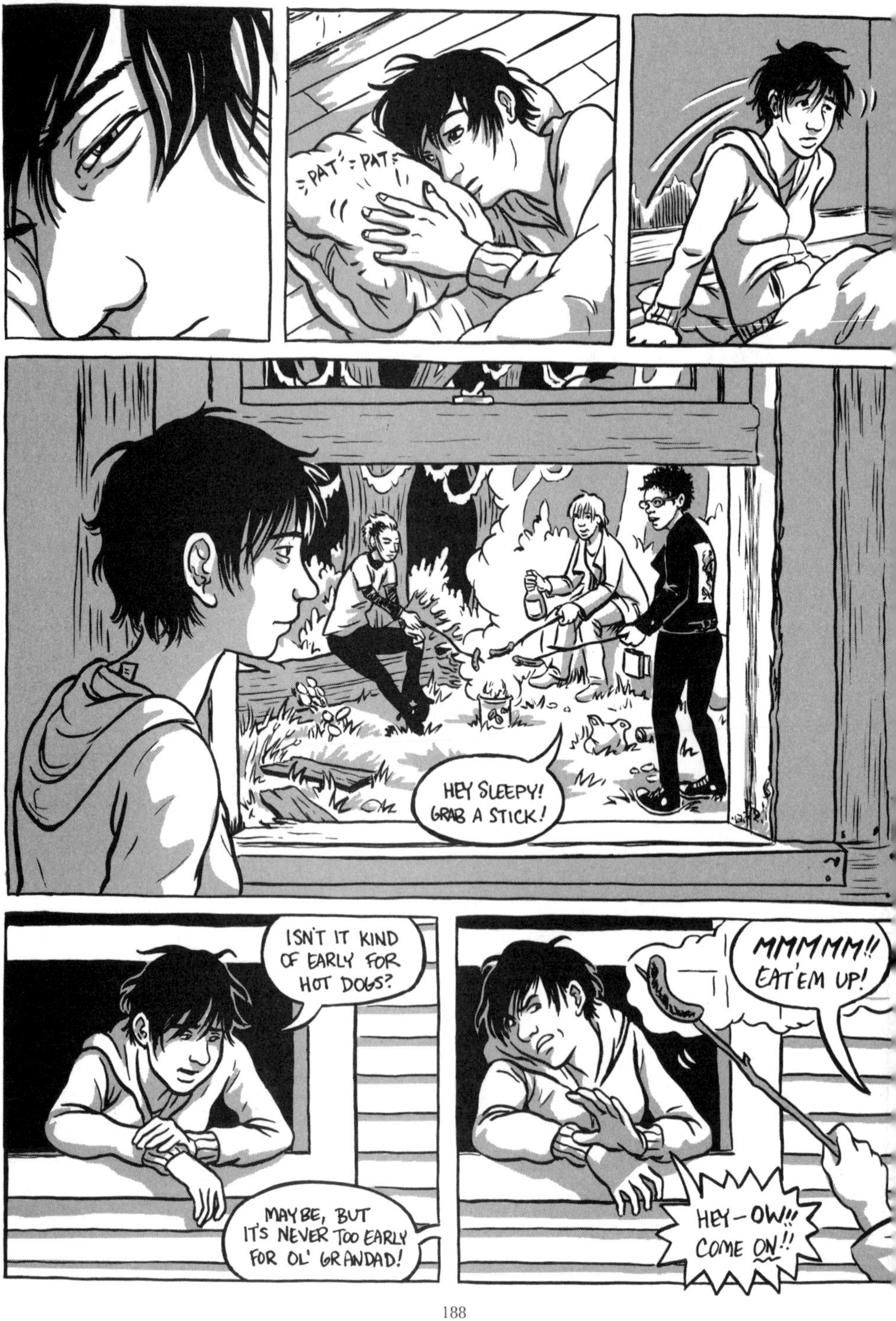

PAT PAT
HEY SLEEPY! GRAB A STICK!
ISN'T IT KIND OF EARLY FOR HOT DOGS?
MAYBE, BUT IT'S NEVER TOO EARLY FOR OL' GRANDAD!
MMMMM!! EAT'EM UP!
HEY-OW!! COME ON!!

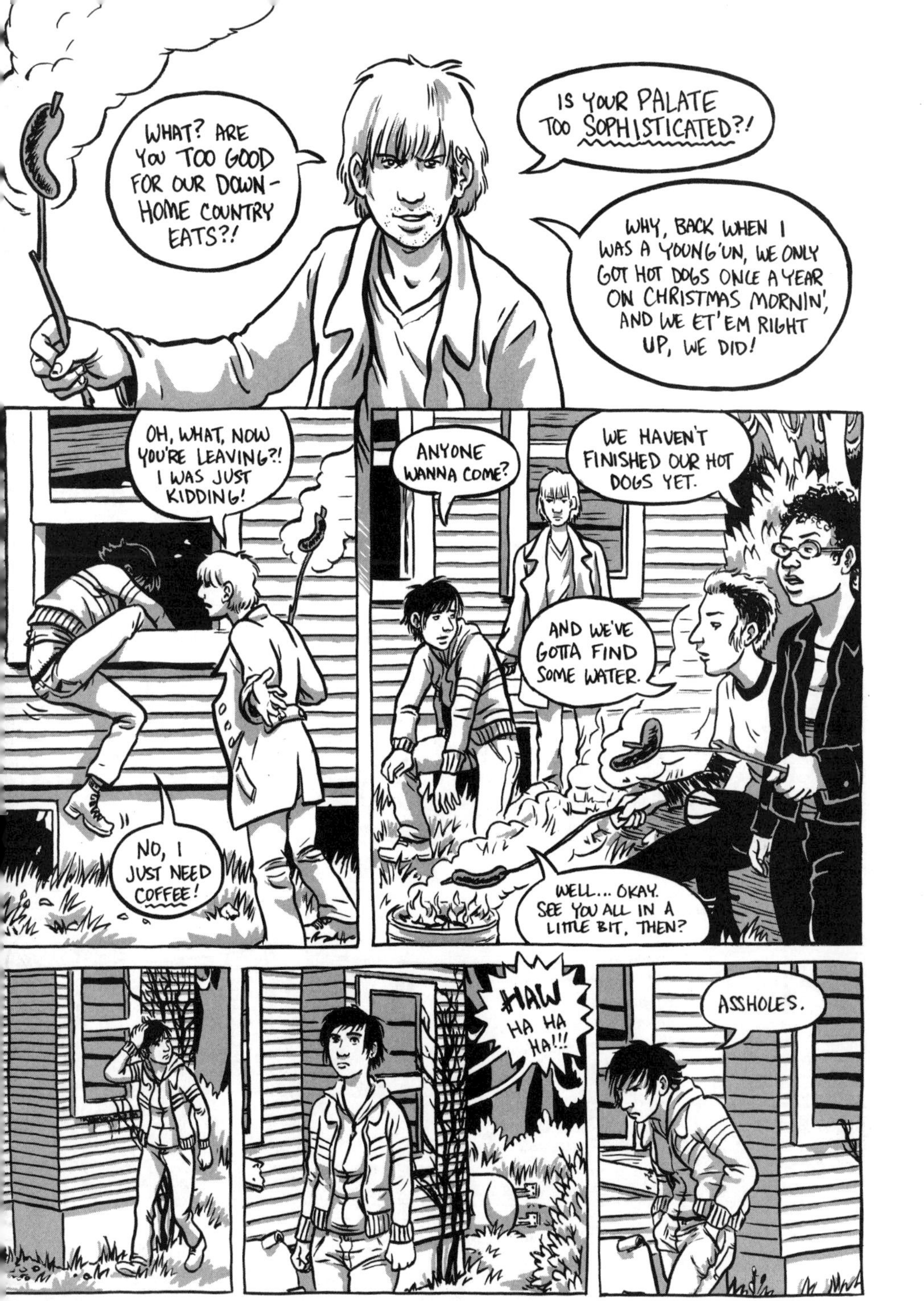
WHAT? ARE YOU TOO GOOD FOR OUR DOWN-HOME COUNTRY EATS?!
IS YOUR PALATE TOO SOPHISTICATED?!
WHY, BACK WHEN I WAS A YOUNG'UN, WE ONLY GOT HOT DOGS ONCE A YEAR ON CHRISTMAS MORNIN', AND WE ET'EM RIGHT UP, WE DID!
OH, WHAT, NOW YOU'RE LEAVING?! I WAS JUST KIDDING!
NO, I JUST NEED COFFEE!
ANYONE WANNA COME?
WE HAVEN'T FINISHED OUR HOT DOGS YET.
AND WE'VE GOTTA FIND SOME WATER.
WELL... OKAY. SEE YOU ALL IN A LITTLE BIT, THEN?
HAW HA HA HA!!!
ASSHOLES.

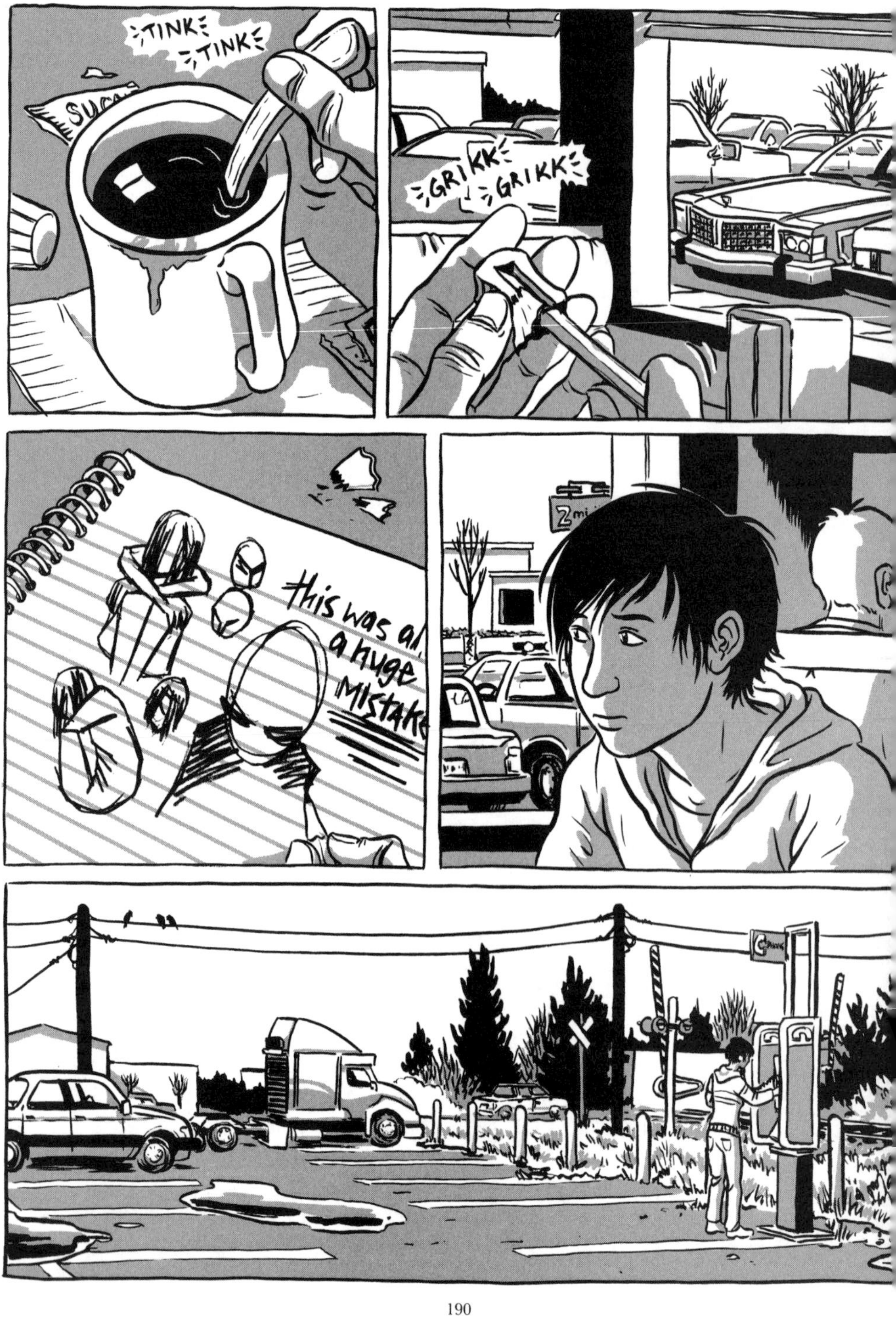
TINK
TINK
GRIKK
GRIKK
this was a
a huge
Mistak

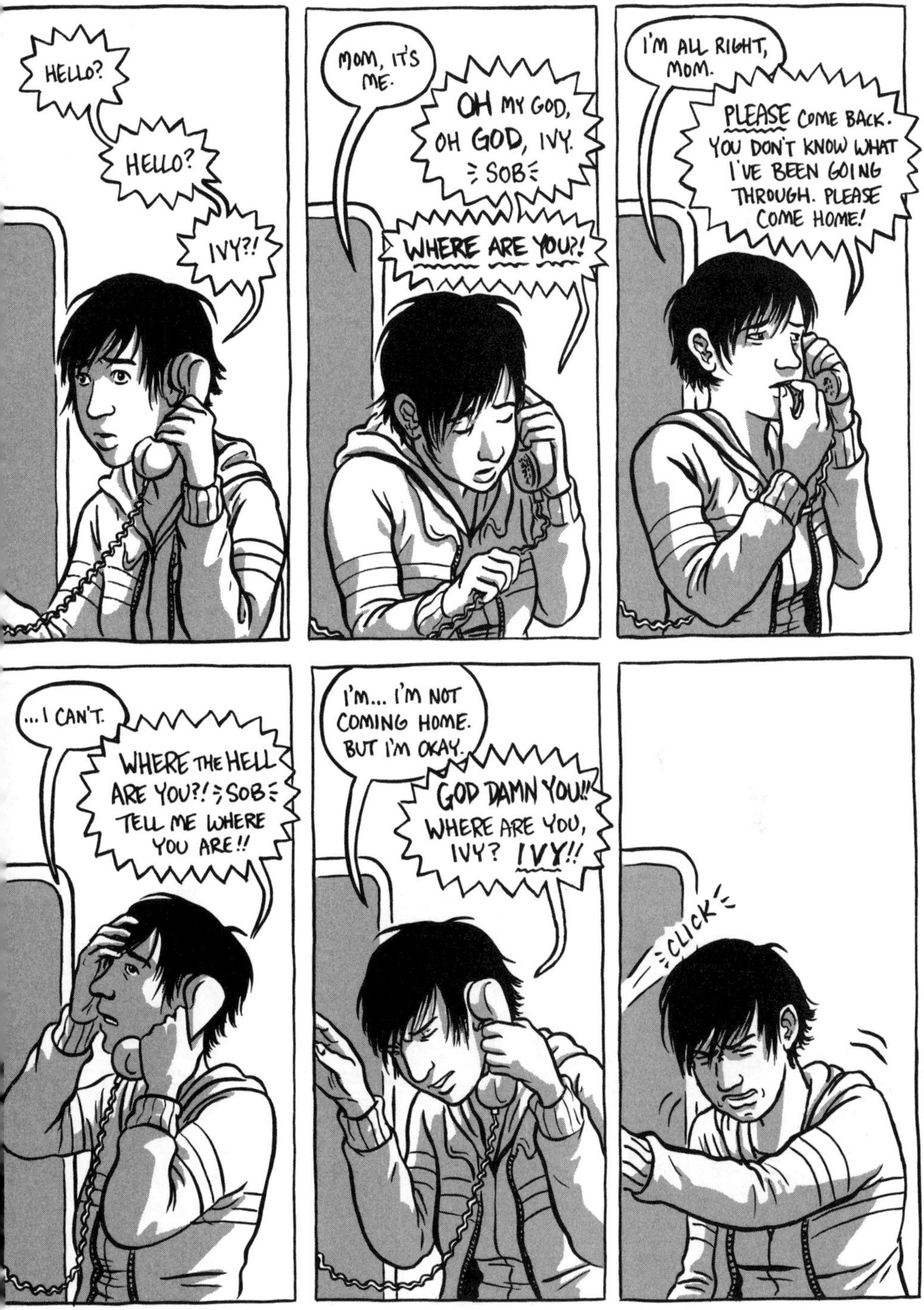
HELLO?
HELLO?
IVY?!
MOM, IT'S ME.
OH MY GOD, OH GOD, IVY. SOB
WHERE ARE YOU?!
I'M ALL RIGHT, MOM.
PLEASE COME BACK. YOU DON'T KNOW WHAT I'VE BEEN GOING THROUGH. PLEASE COME HOME!
...I CAN'T.
WHERE THE HELL ARE YOU?! SOB TELL ME WHERE YOU ARE!!
I'M... I'M NOT COMING HOME. BUT I'M OKAY.
GOD DAMN YOU!! WHERE ARE YOU, IVY? IVY!!
CLICK

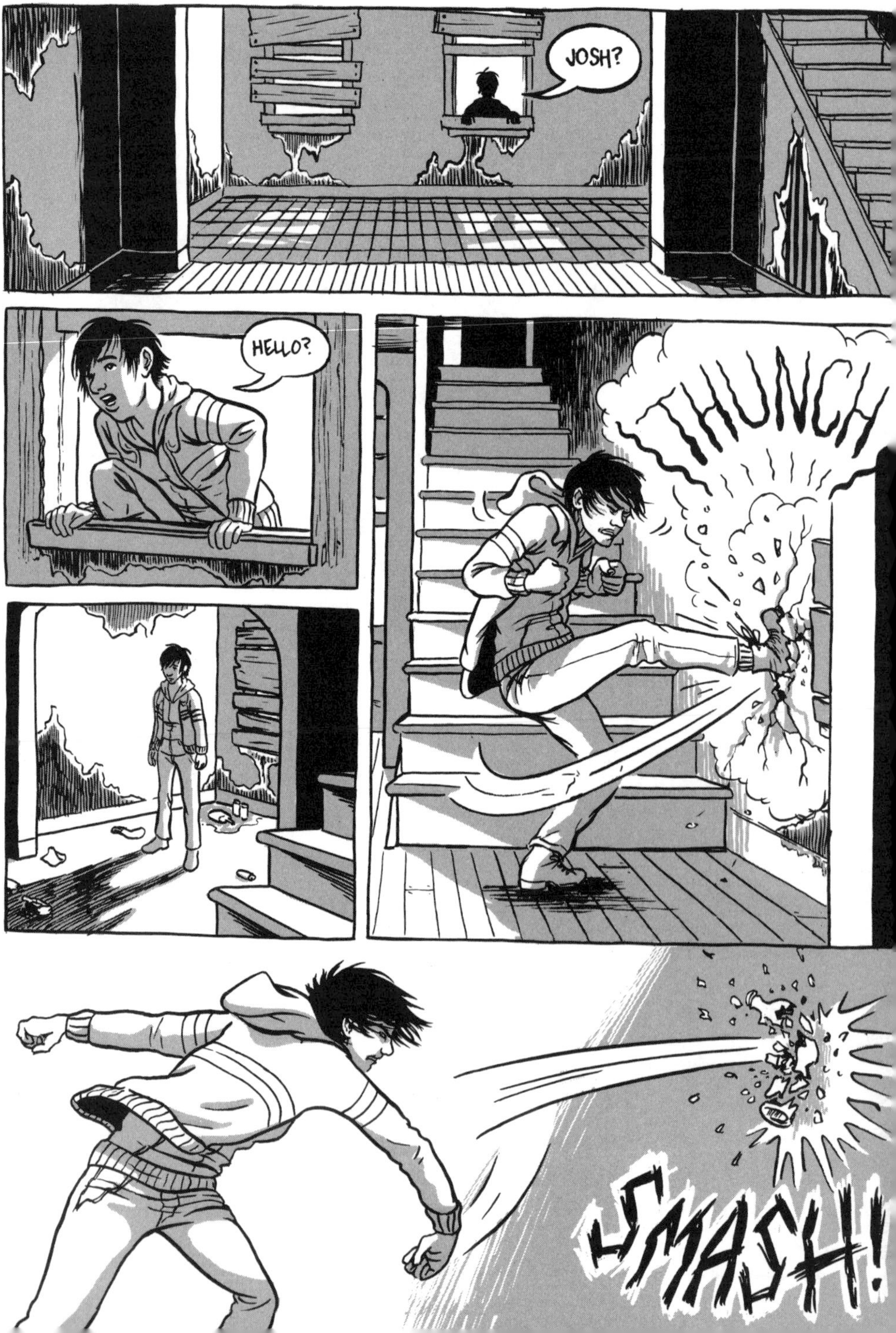
JOSH?
HELLO?
THUNCH
SMASH!

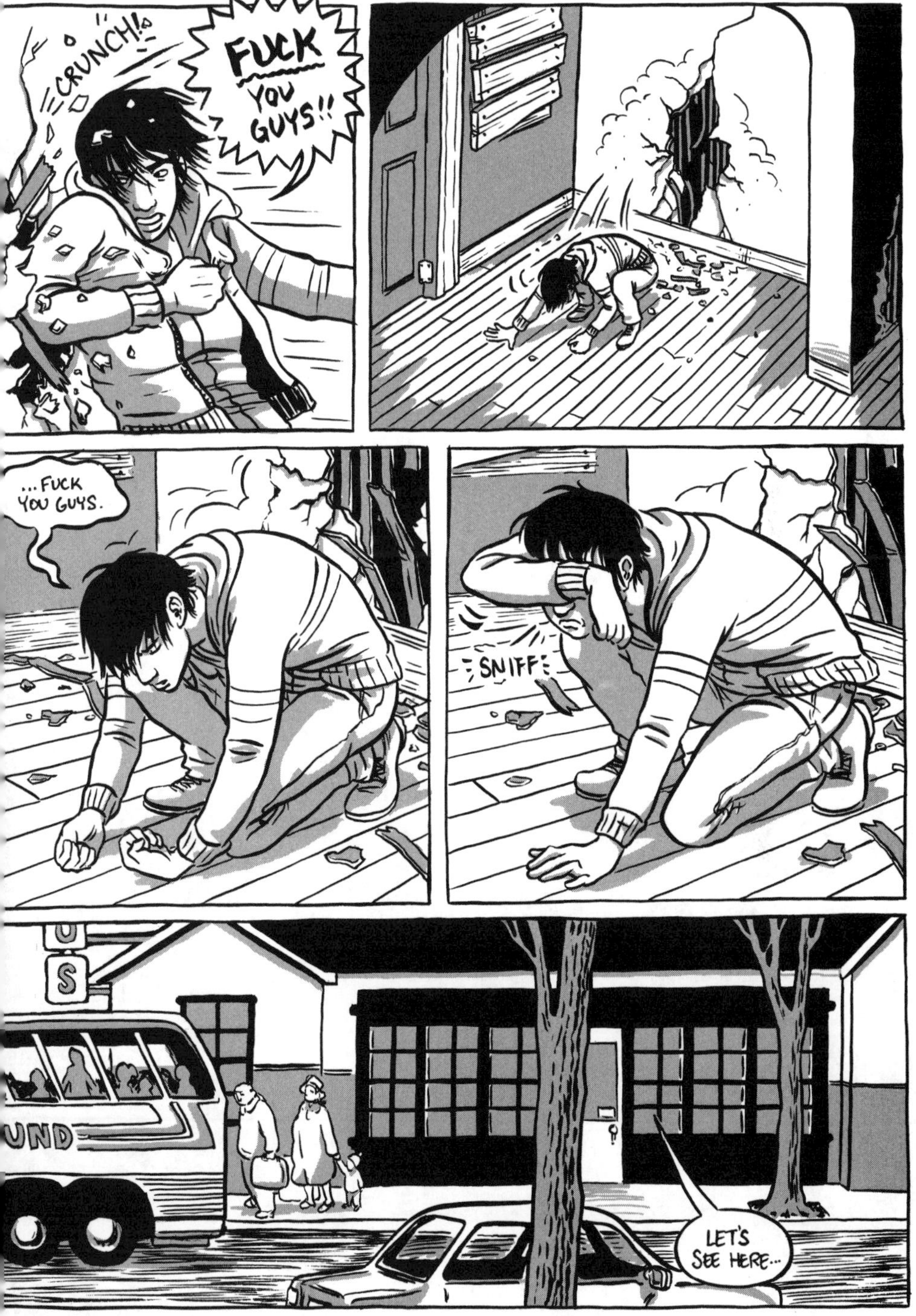
CRUNCH!
FUCK YOU GUYS!!
...FUCK YOU GUYS.
SNIFF
US
UND
LET'S SEE HERE...

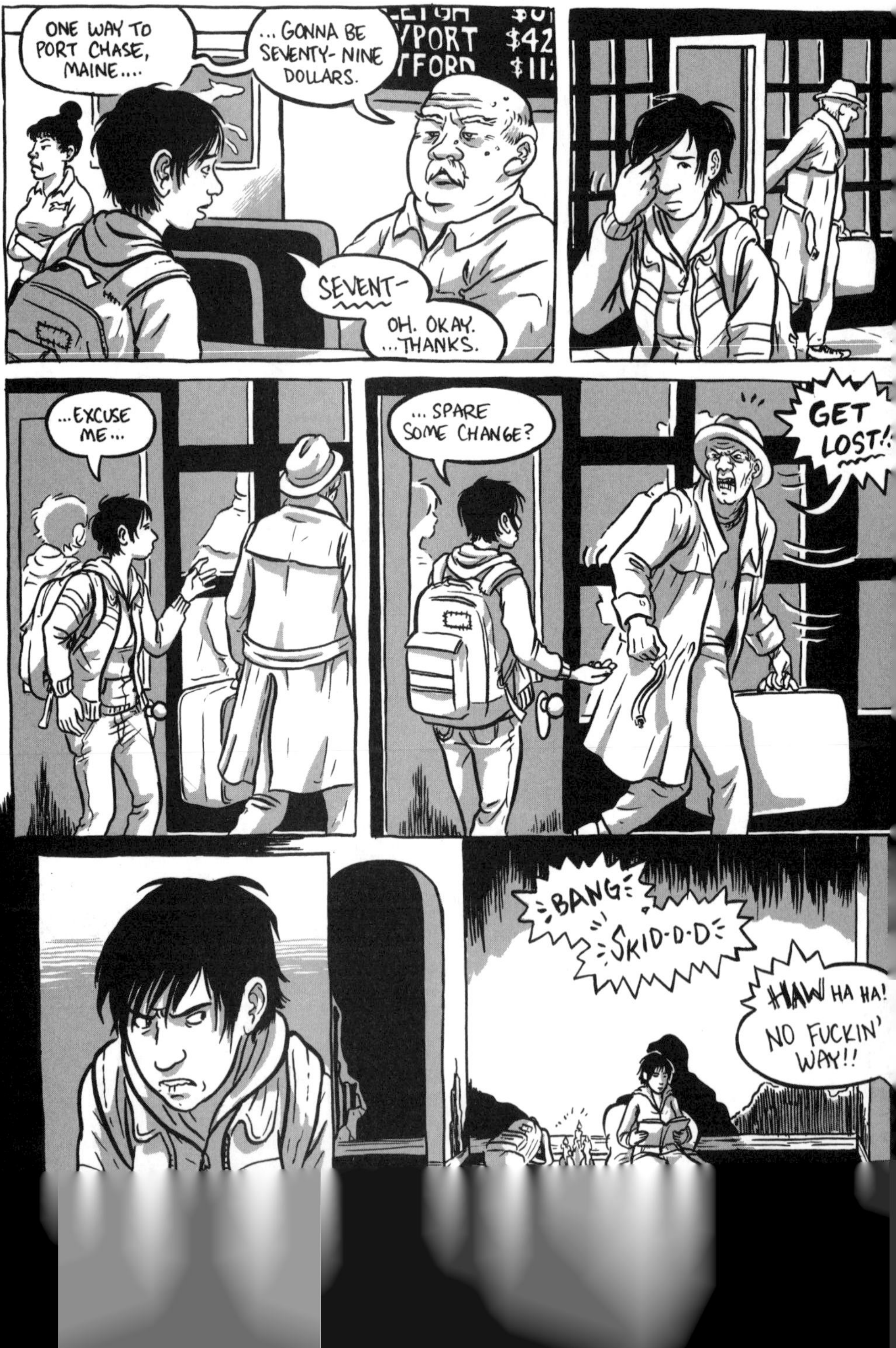

ONE WAY TO PORT CHASE, MAINE....
... GONNA BE SEVENTY-NINE DOLLARS.
SEVENT-
OH. OKAY. ...THANKS.
...EXCUSE ME...
... SPARE SOME CHANGE?
GET LOST!
BANG
SKID-D-D
HAW HA HA! NO FUCKIN' WAY!!

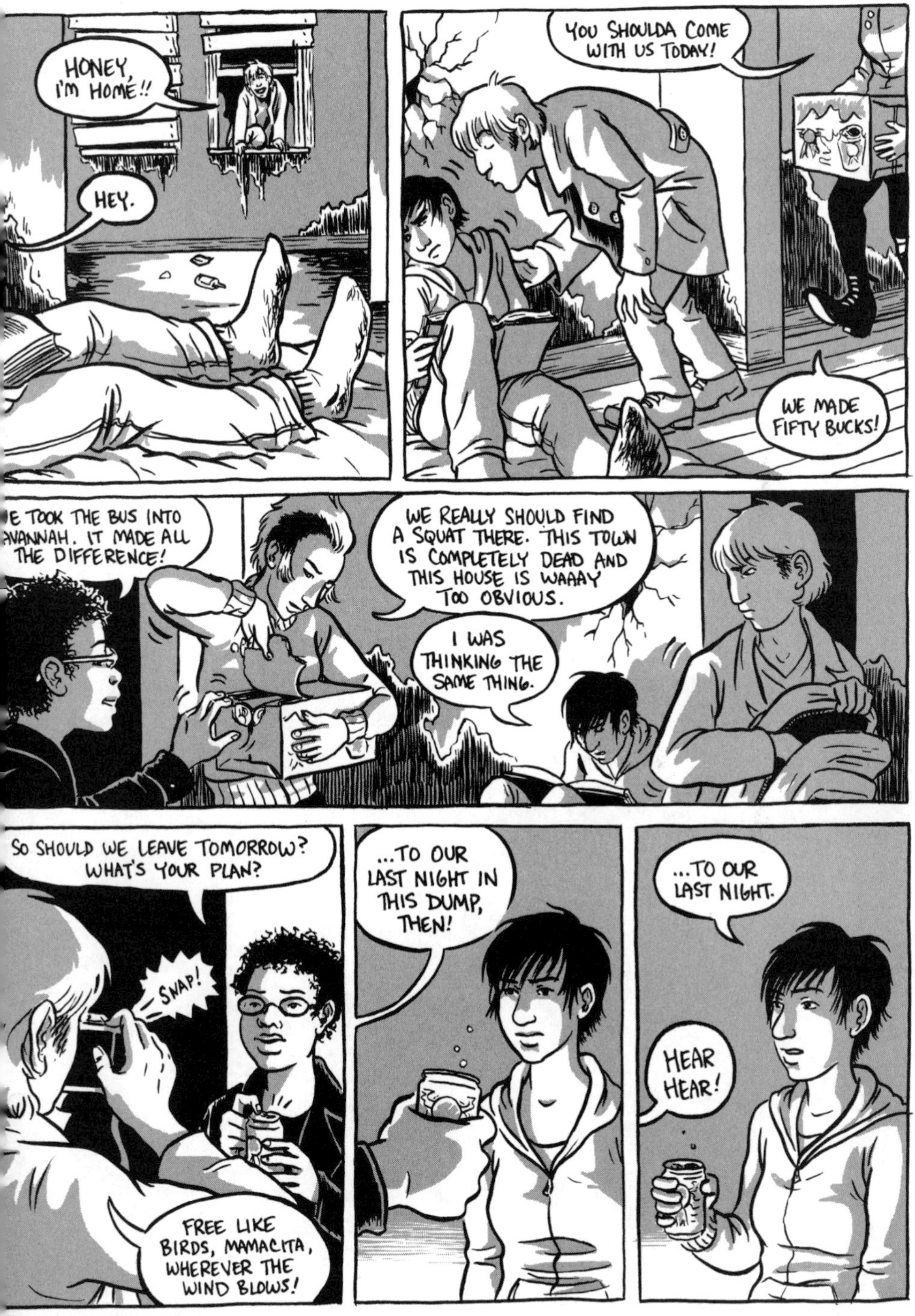
HONEY, I'M HOME!!
HEY.
YOU SHOULDA COME WITH US TODAY!
WE MADE FIFTY BUCKS!
E TOOK THE BUS INTO AVANNAH. IT MADE ALL THE DIFFERENCE!
WE REALLY SHOULD FIND A SQUAT THERE. THIS TOWN IS COMPLETELY DEAD AND THIS HOUSE IS WAAAY TOO OBVIOUS.
I WAS THINKING THE SAME THING.
SO SHOULD WE LEAVE TOMORROW? WHAT'S YOUR PLAN?
SNAP!
FREE LIKE BIRDS, MAMACITA, WHEREVER THE WIND BLOWS!
...TO OUR LAST NIGHT IN THIS DUMP, THEN!
...TO OUR LAST NIGHT.
HEAR HEAR!

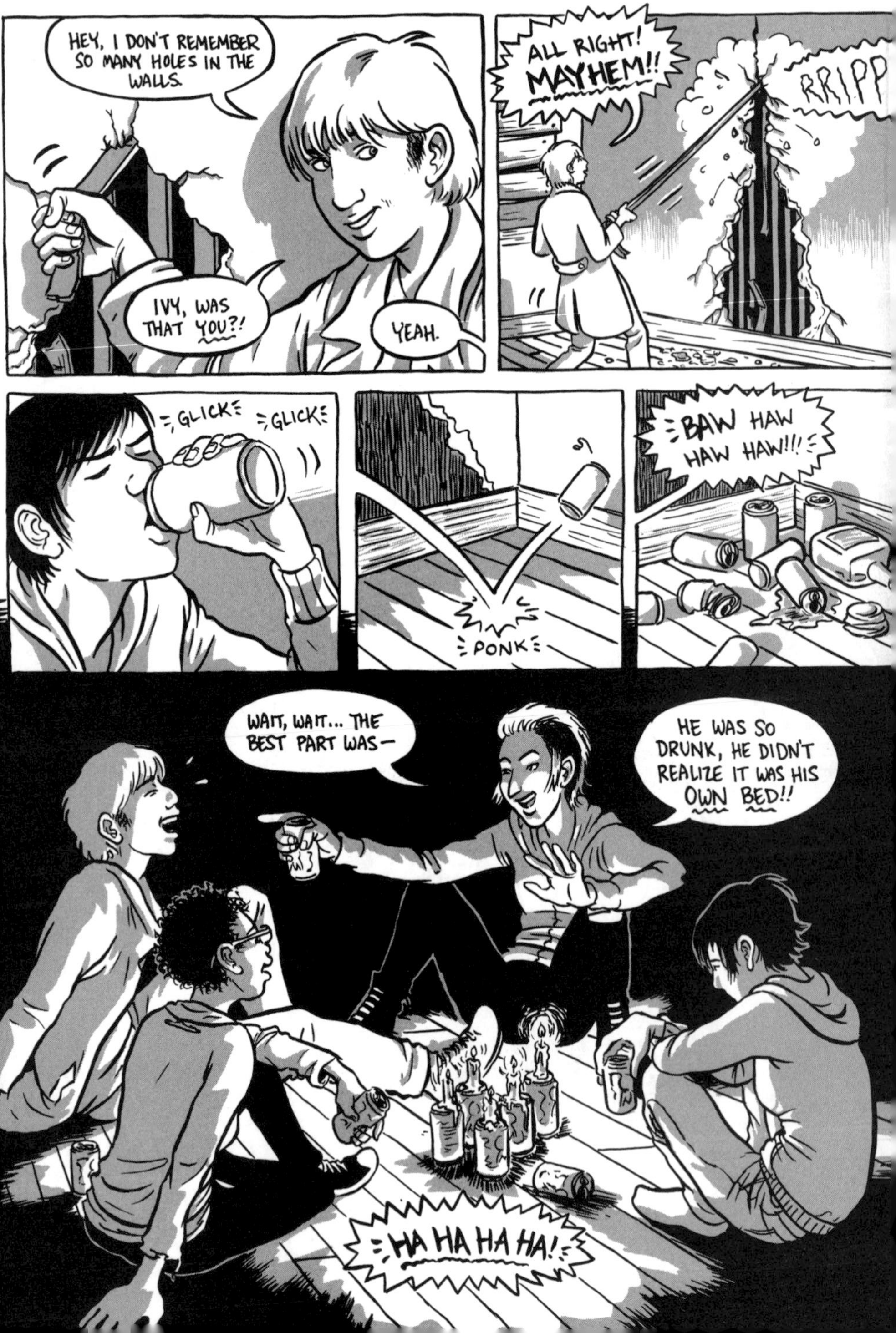
HEY, I DON'T REMEMBER SO MANY HOLES IN THE WALLS.
IVY, WAS THAT YOU?!
YEAH.
ALL RIGHT! MAYHEM!!
RRIPP
GLICK
GLICK
PONK
BAW HAW HAW HAW!!!
WAIT, WAIT... THE BEST PART WAS—
HE WAS SO DRUNK, HE DIDN'T REALIZE IT WAS HIS OWN BED!!
HA HA HA HA!

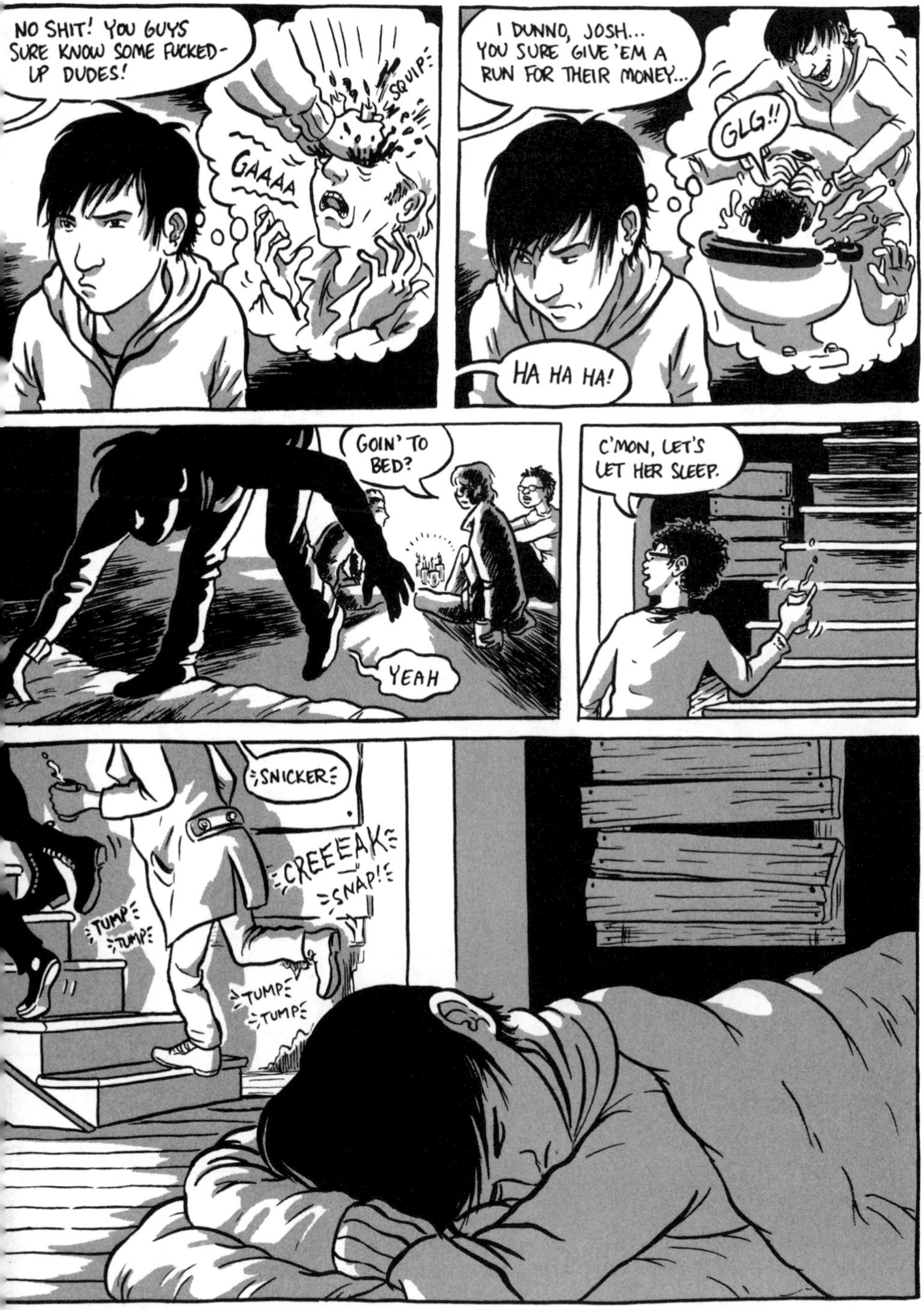

NO SHIT! YOU GUYS SURE KNOW SOME FUCKED-UP DUDES!
SQUIP
GAAAA
I DUNNO, JOSH... YOU SURE GIVE 'EM A RUN FOR THEIR MONEY...
GLG!!
HA HA HA!
GOIN' TO BED?
YEAH
C'MON, LET'S LET HER SLEEP.
SNICKER
CREEEAK
SNAP!
TUMP
TUMP
TUMP
TUMP

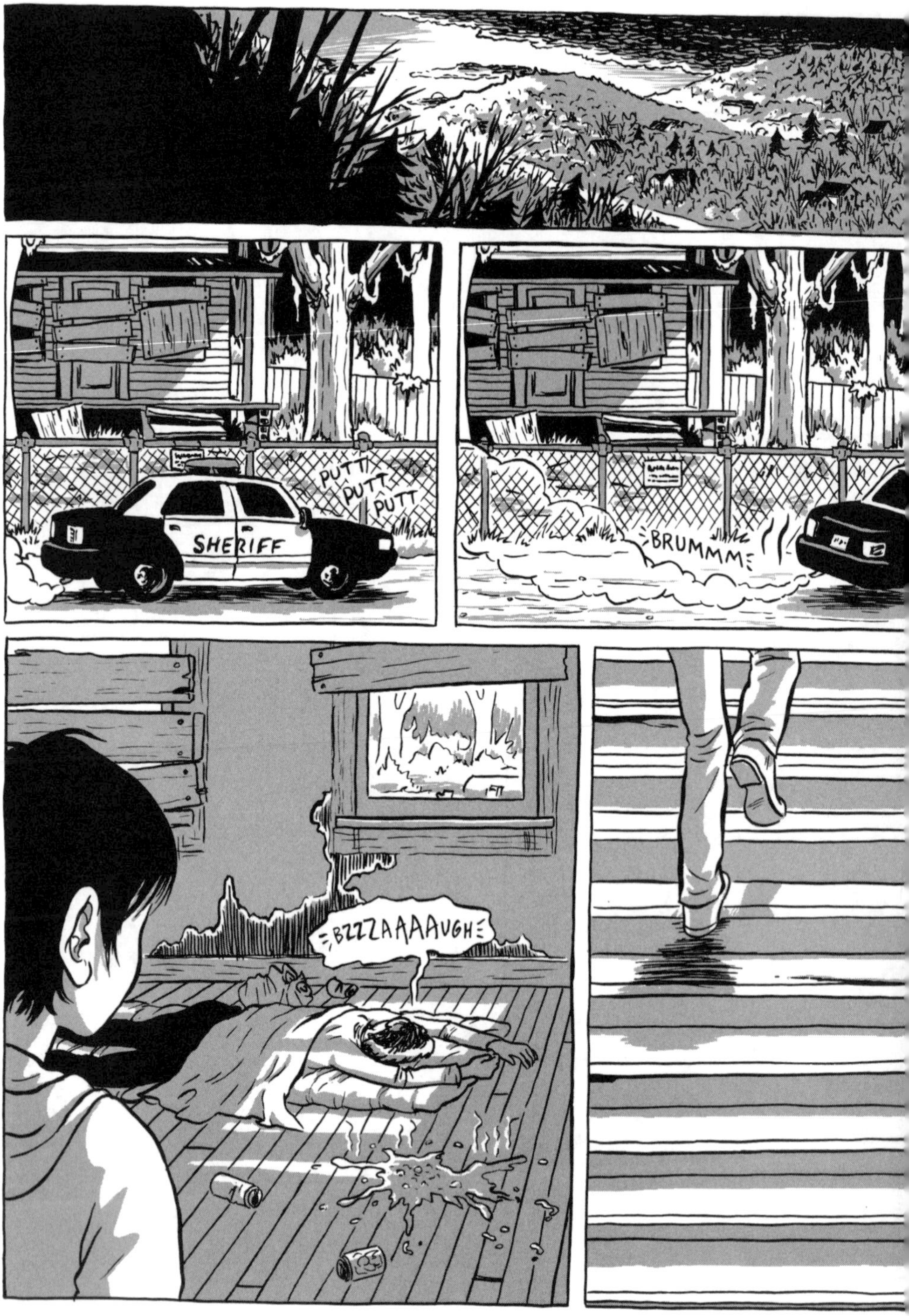

SHERIFF
PUTT PUTT PUTT
BRUMMM
BZZZAAAAUGH

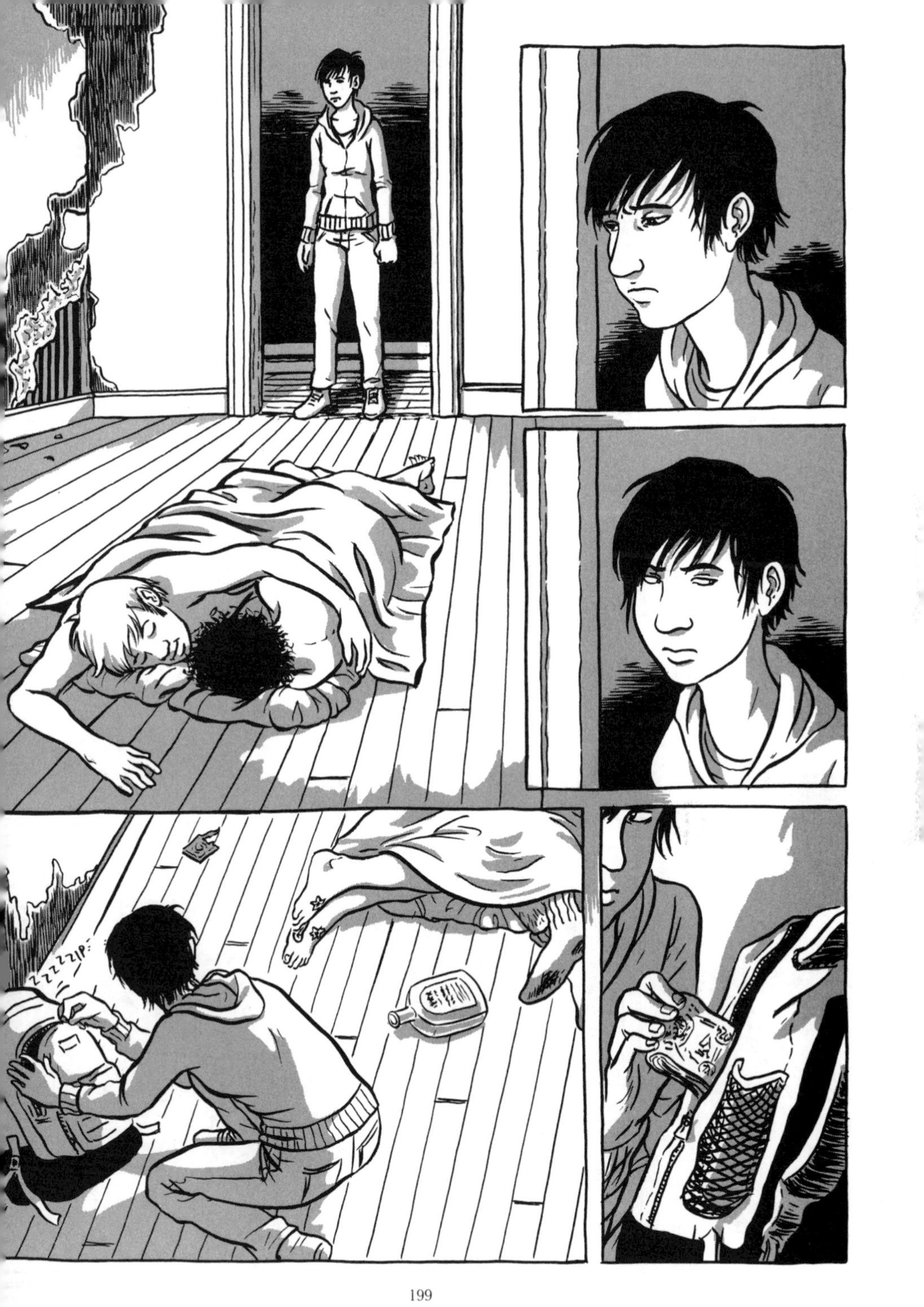
ZZZZZZIP

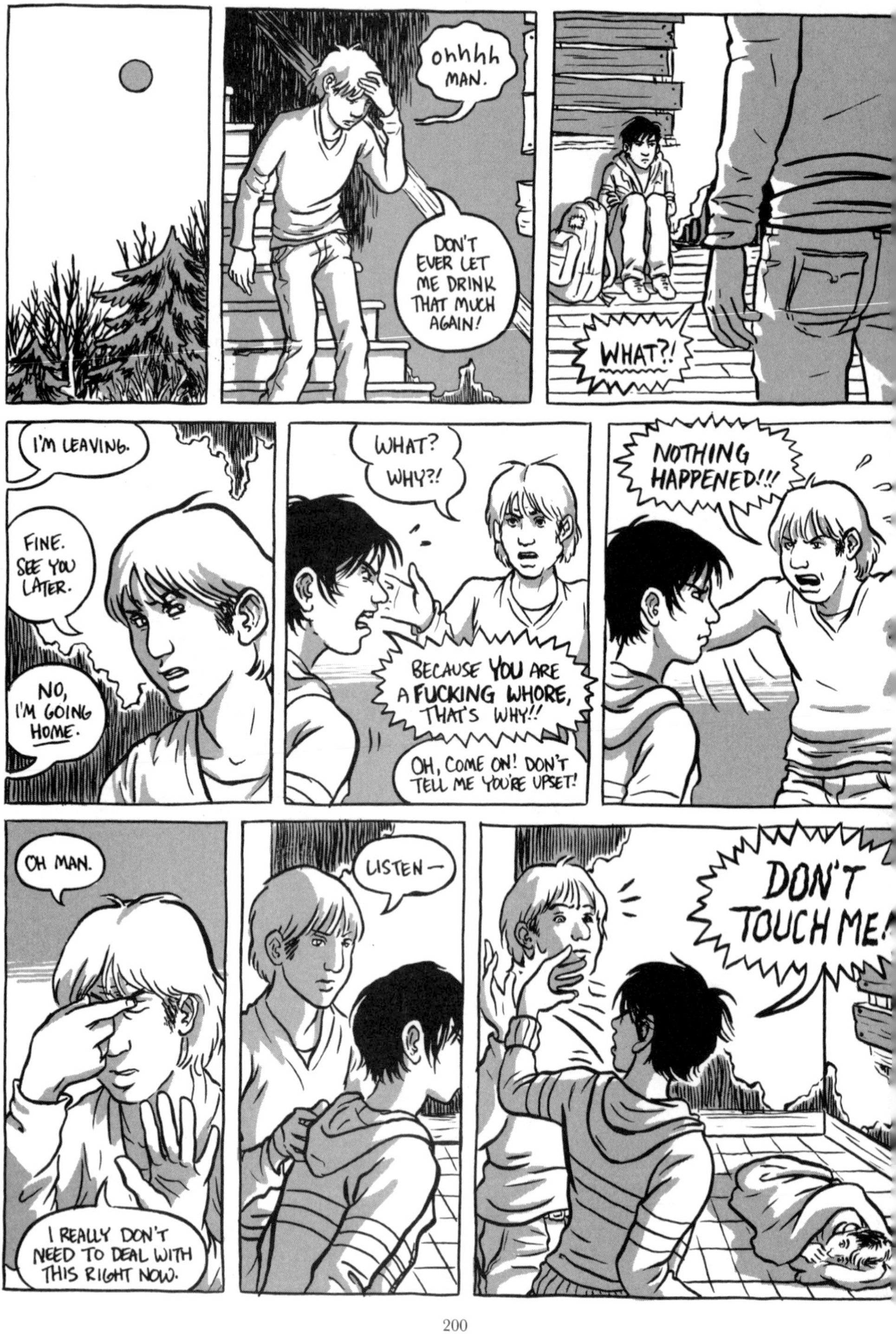
ohhhh MAN.
DON'T EVER LET ME DRINK THAT MUCH AGAIN!
WHAT?!
I'M LEAVING.
FINE. SEE YOU LATER.
NO, I'M GOING HOME.
WHAT? WHY?!
BECAUSE YOU ARE A FUCKING WHORE, THAT'S WHY!!
OH, COME ON! DON'T TELL ME YOU'RE UPSET!
NOTHING HAPPENED!!!
OH MAN.
I REALLY DON'T NEED TO DEAL WITH THIS RIGHT NOW.
LISTEN—
DON'T TOUCH ME!

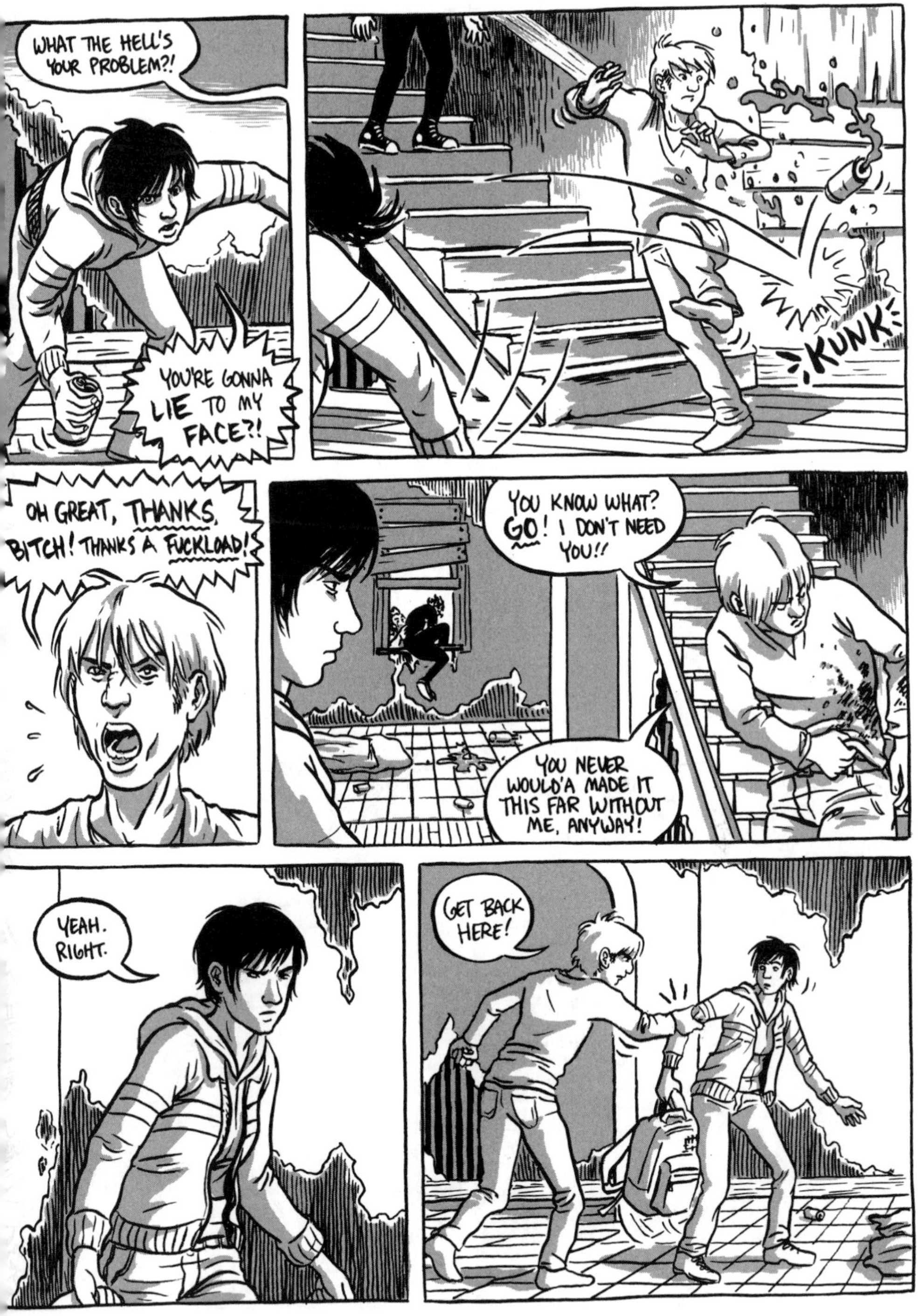
WHAT THE HELL'S YOUR PROBLEM?!
YOU'RE GONNA LIE TO MY FACE?!
KUNK
OH GREAT, THANKS, BITCH! THANKS A FUCKLOAD!
YOU KNOW WHAT? GO! I DON'T NEED YOU!!
YOU NEVER WOULD'A MADE IT THIS FAR WITHOUT ME, ANYWAY!
YEAH. RIGHT.
GET BACK HERE!

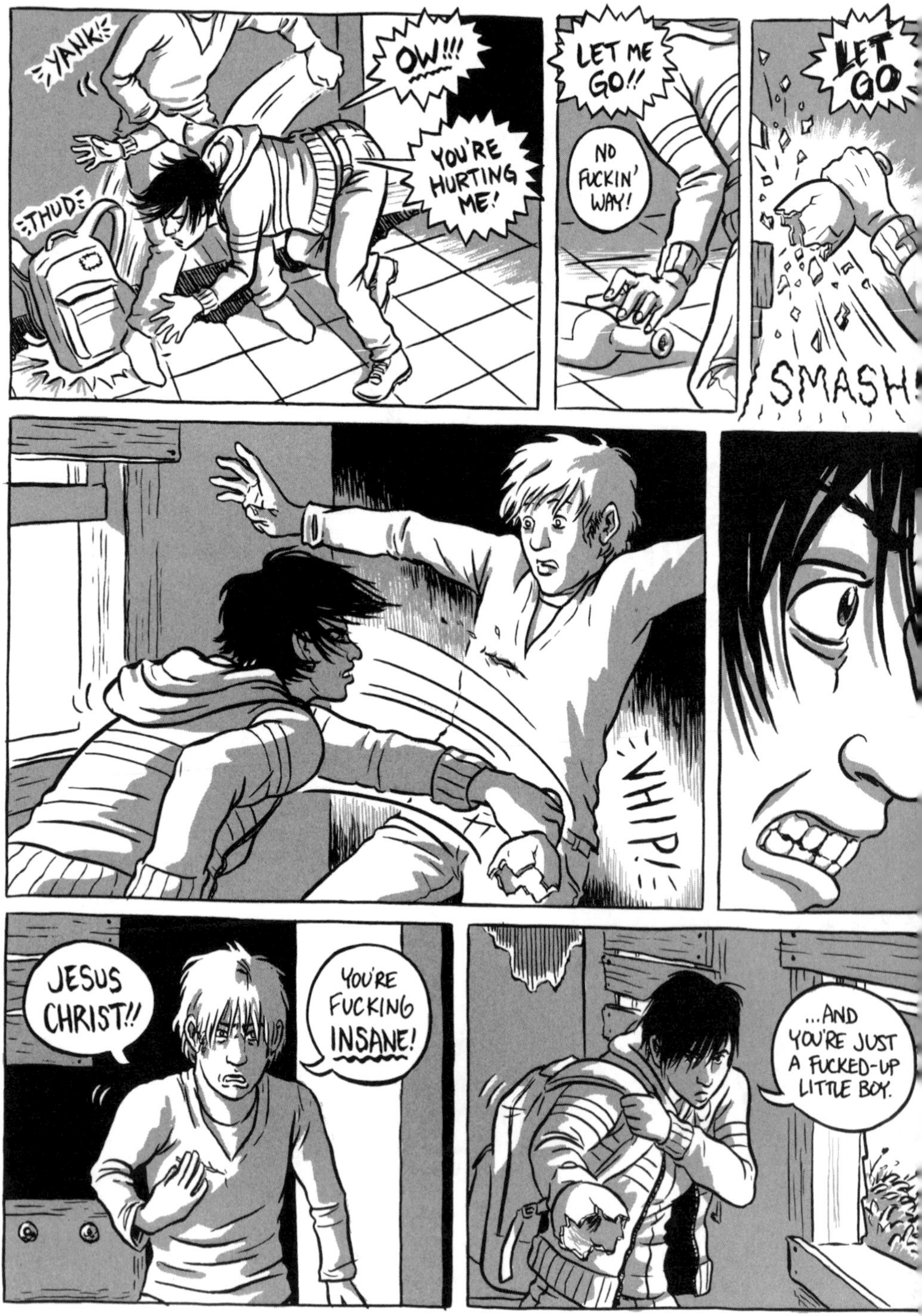
YANK!
THUD
OW!!!
YOU'RE HURTING ME!
LET ME GO!!
NO FUCKIN' WAY!
LET GO
SMASH
WHIP!
JESUS CHRIST!!
YOU'RE FUCKING INSANE!
...AND YOU'RE JUST A FUCKED-UP LITTLE BOY.

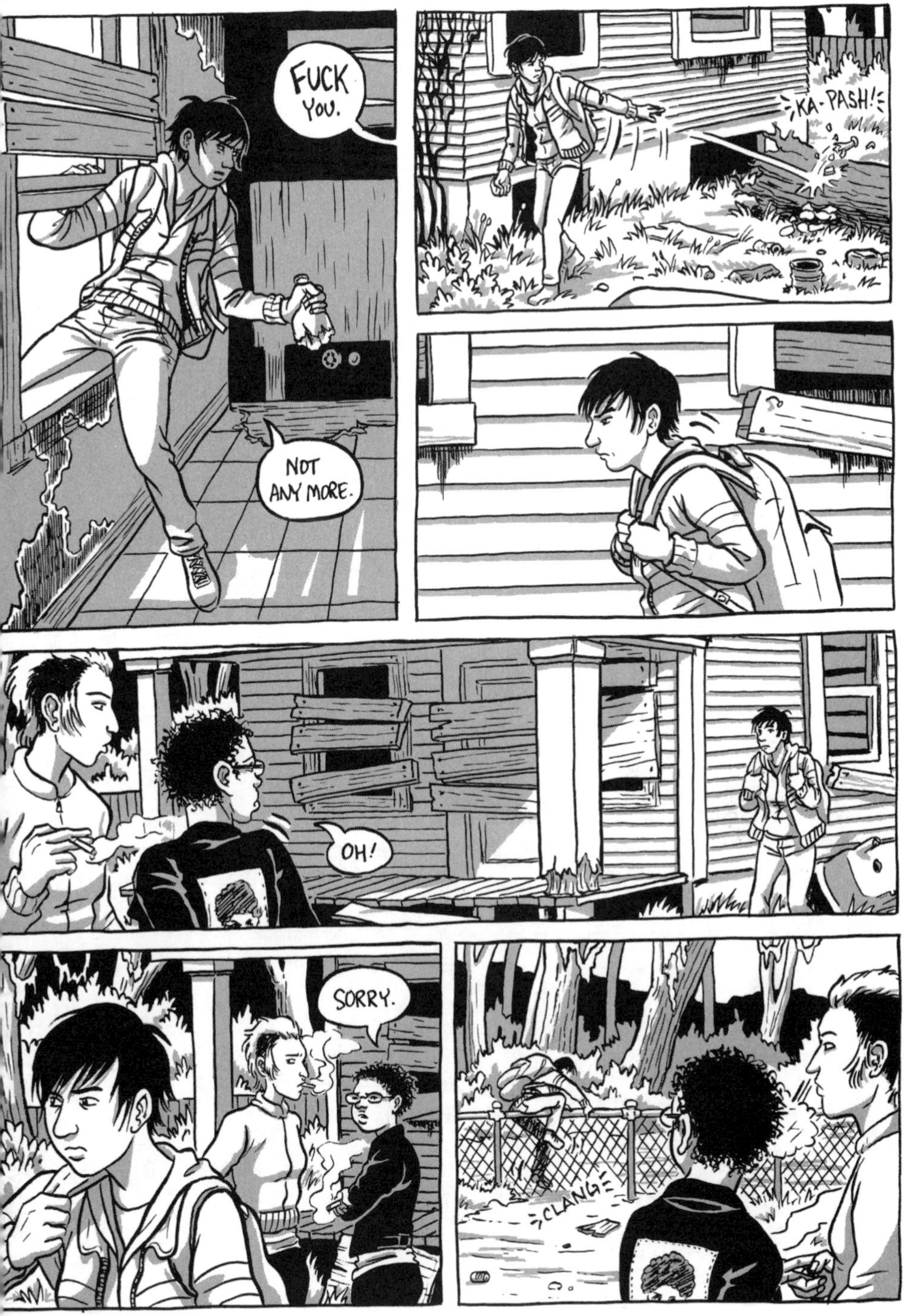
FUCK YOU.
NOT ANY MORE.
KA-PASH!
OH!
SORRY.
CLANG

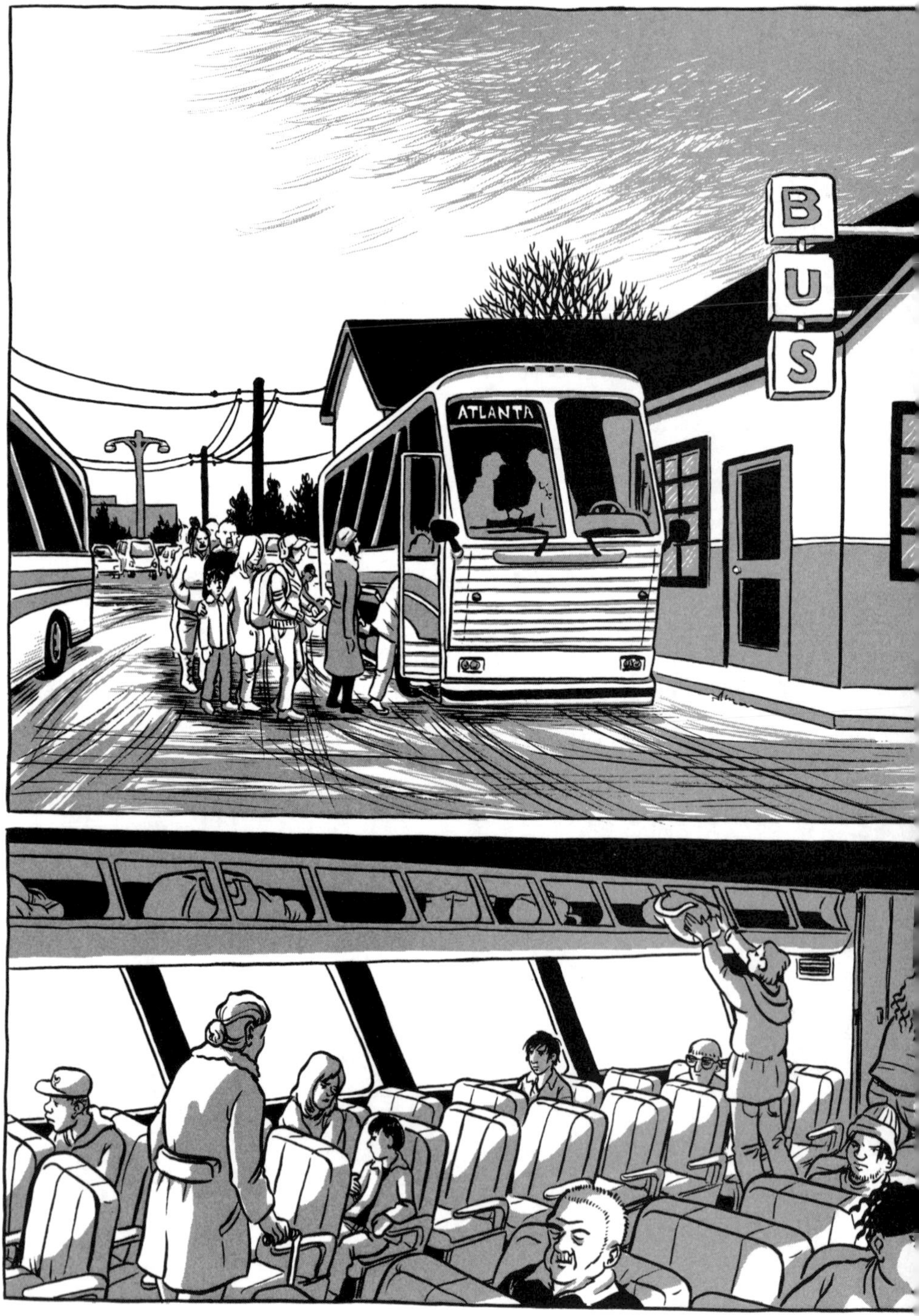
BUS
ATLANTA

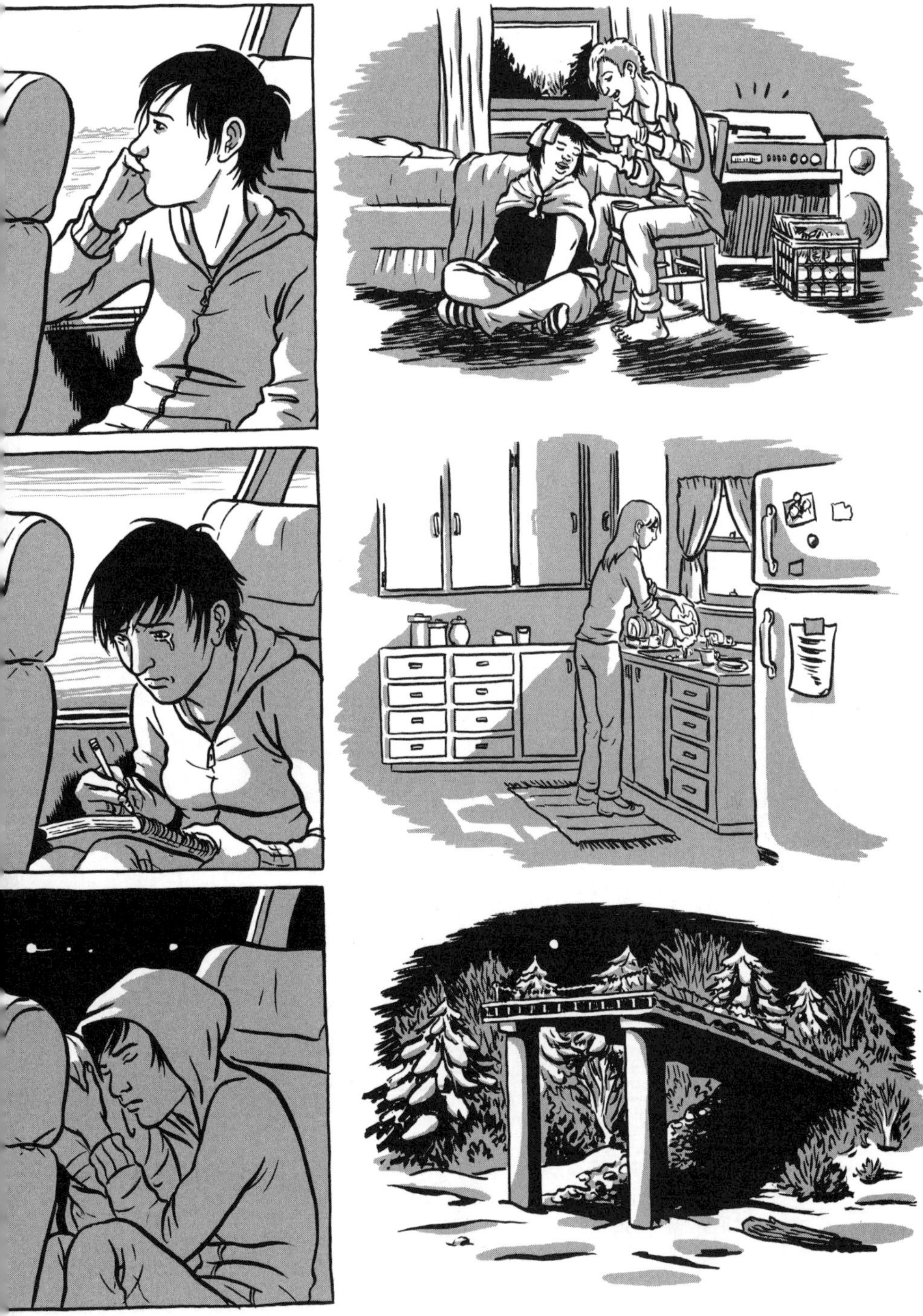

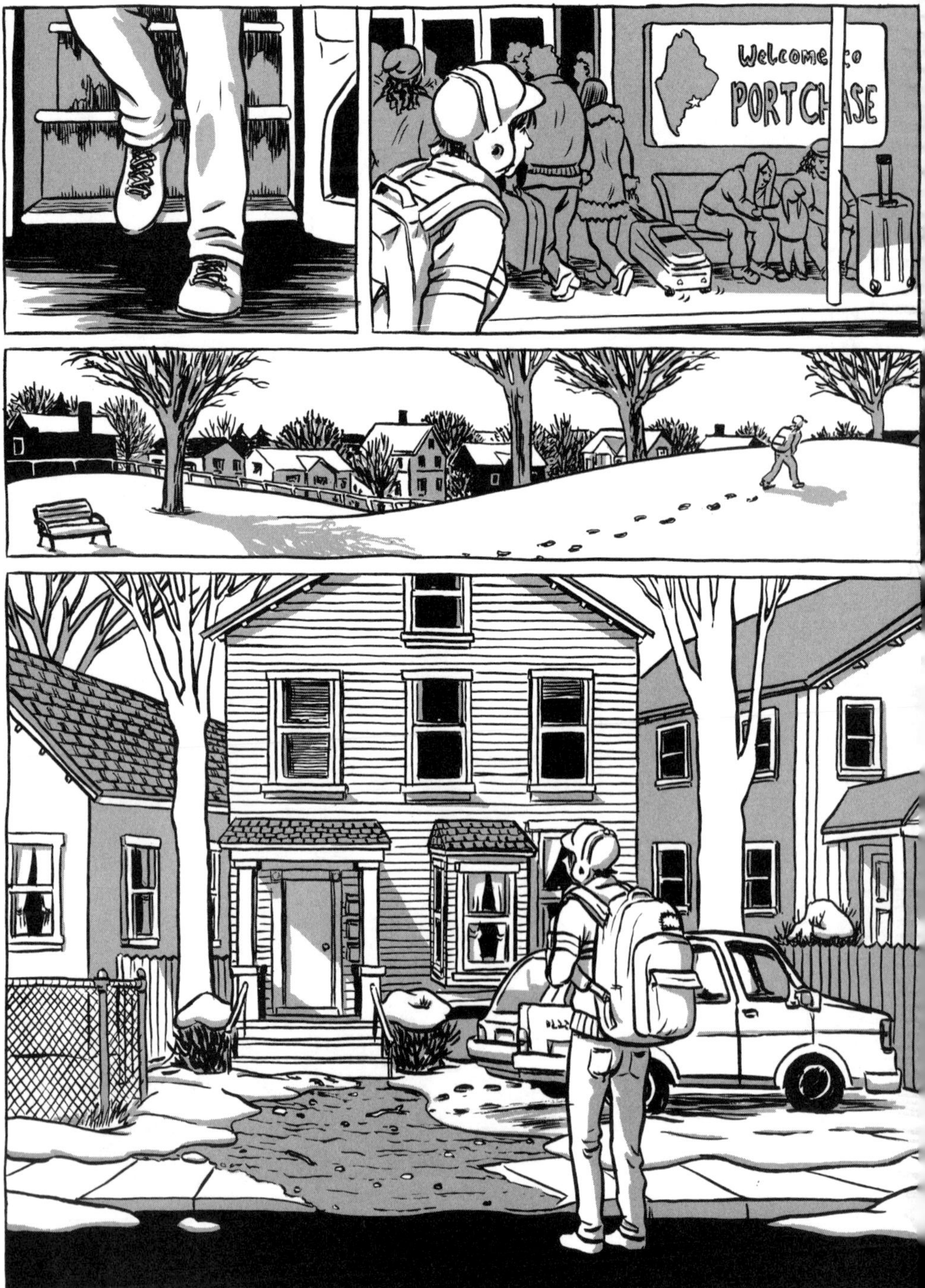
Welcome to
PORTCHASE

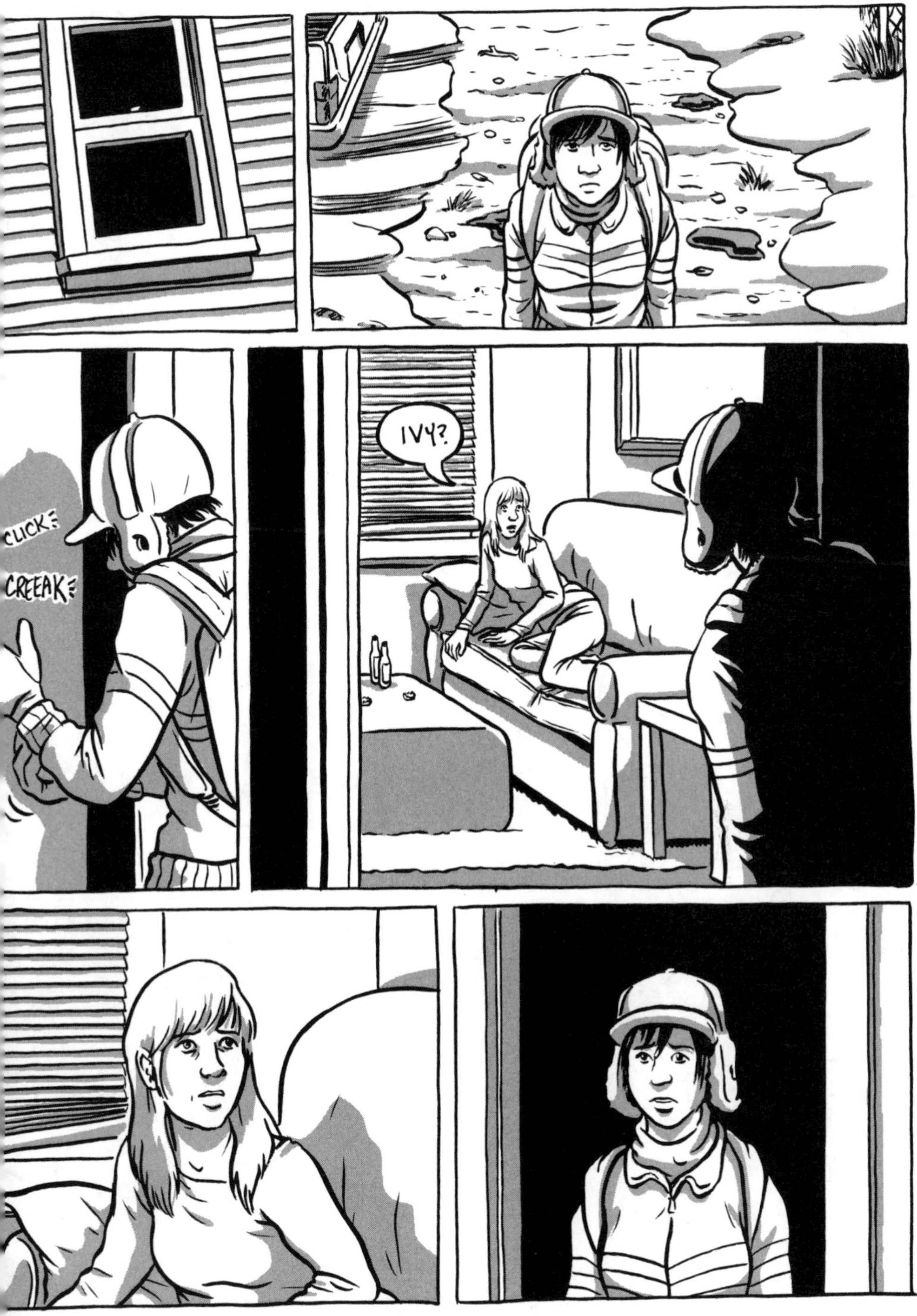
CLICK
CREEAK
IVY?

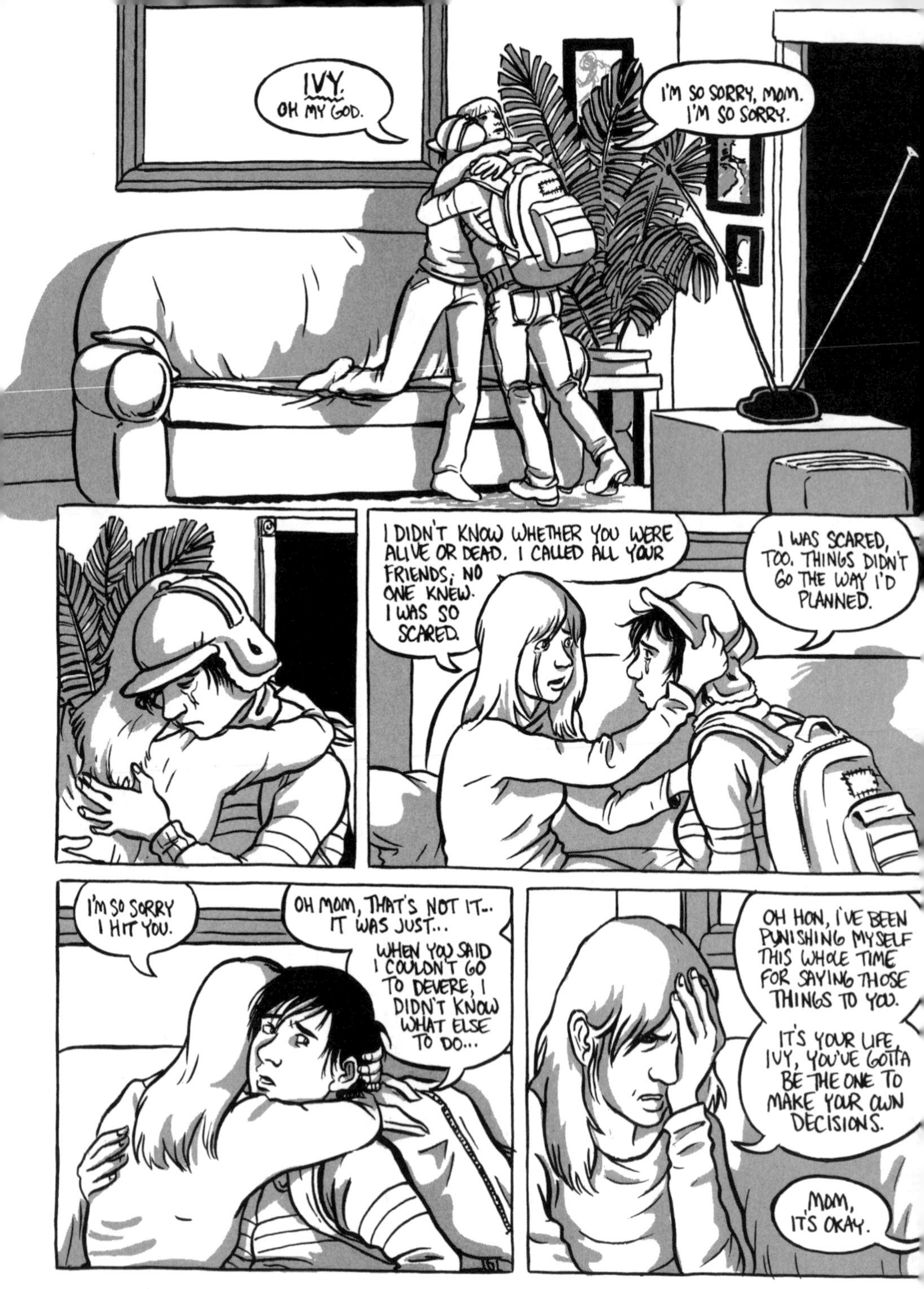

IVY. OH MY GOD.
I'M SO SORRY, MOM. I'M SO SORRY.
I DIDN'T KNOW WHETHER YOU WERE ALIVE OR DEAD. I CALLED ALL YOUR FRIENDS; NO ONE KNEW. I WAS SO SCARED.
I WAS SCARED, TOO. THINGS DIDN'T GO THE WAY I'D PLANNED.
I'M SO SORRY I HIT YOU.
OH MOM, THAT'S NOT IT.. IT WAS JUST...
WHEN YOU SAID I COULDN'T GO TO DEVERE, I DIDN'T KNOW WHAT ELSE TO DO...
OH HON, I'VE BEEN PUNISHING MYSELF THIS WHOLE TIME FOR SAYING THOSE THINGS TO YOU.
IT'S YOUR LIFE, IVY, YOU'VE GOTTA BE THE ONE TO MAKE YOUR OWN DECISIONS.
MOM, IT'S OKAY.

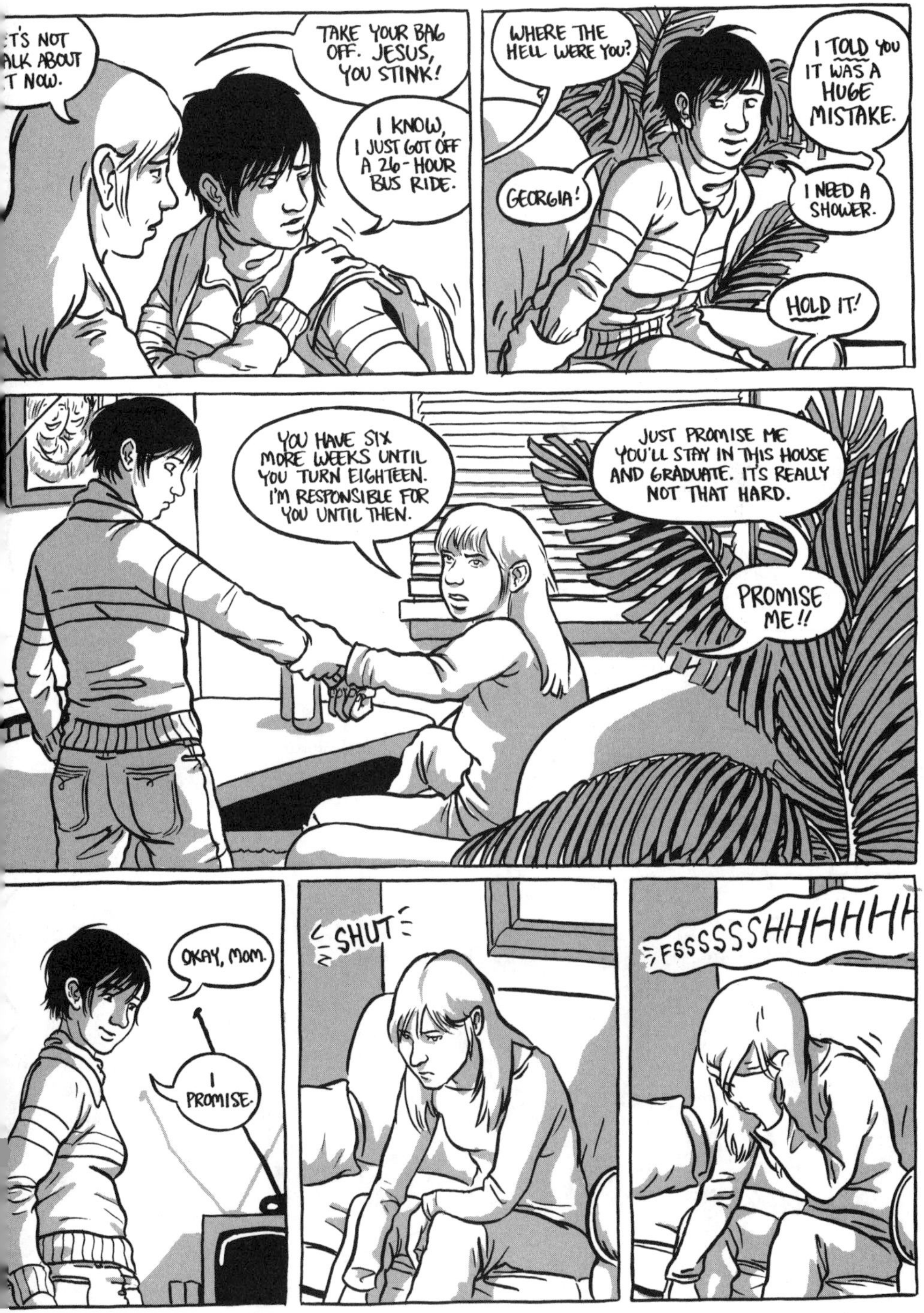

'T'S NOT
ALK ABOUT
T NOW.
TAKE YOUR BAG OFF. JESUS, YOU STINK!
I KNOW, I JUST GOT OFF A 26-HOUR BUS RIDE.
WHERE THE HELL WERE YOU?
GEORGIA!
I TOLD YOU IT WAS A HUGE MISTAKE.
I NEED A SHOWER.
HOLD IT!
YOU HAVE SIX MORE WEEKS UNTIL YOU TURN EIGHTEEN. I'M RESPONSIBLE FOR YOU UNTIL THEN.
JUST PROMISE ME YOU'LL STAY IN THIS HOUSE AND GRADUATE. IT'S REALLY NOT THAT HARD.
PROMISE ME!!
OKAY, MOM.
I PROMISE.
SHUT
FSSSSSSHHHHHH

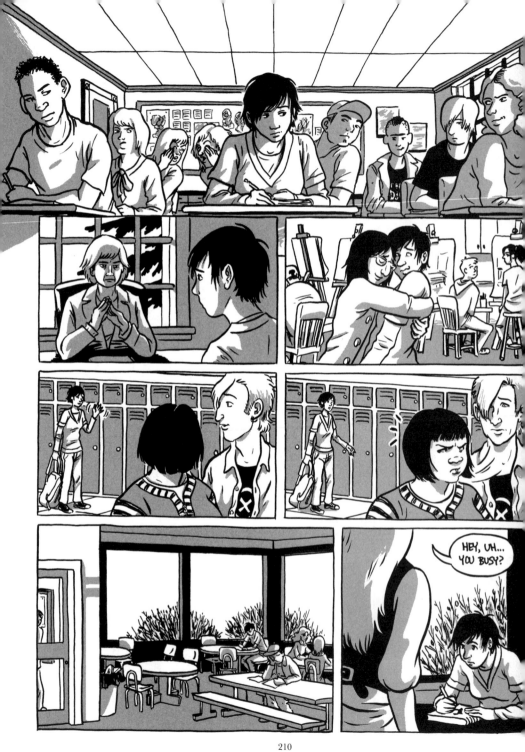

HEY, UH...
YOU BUSY?

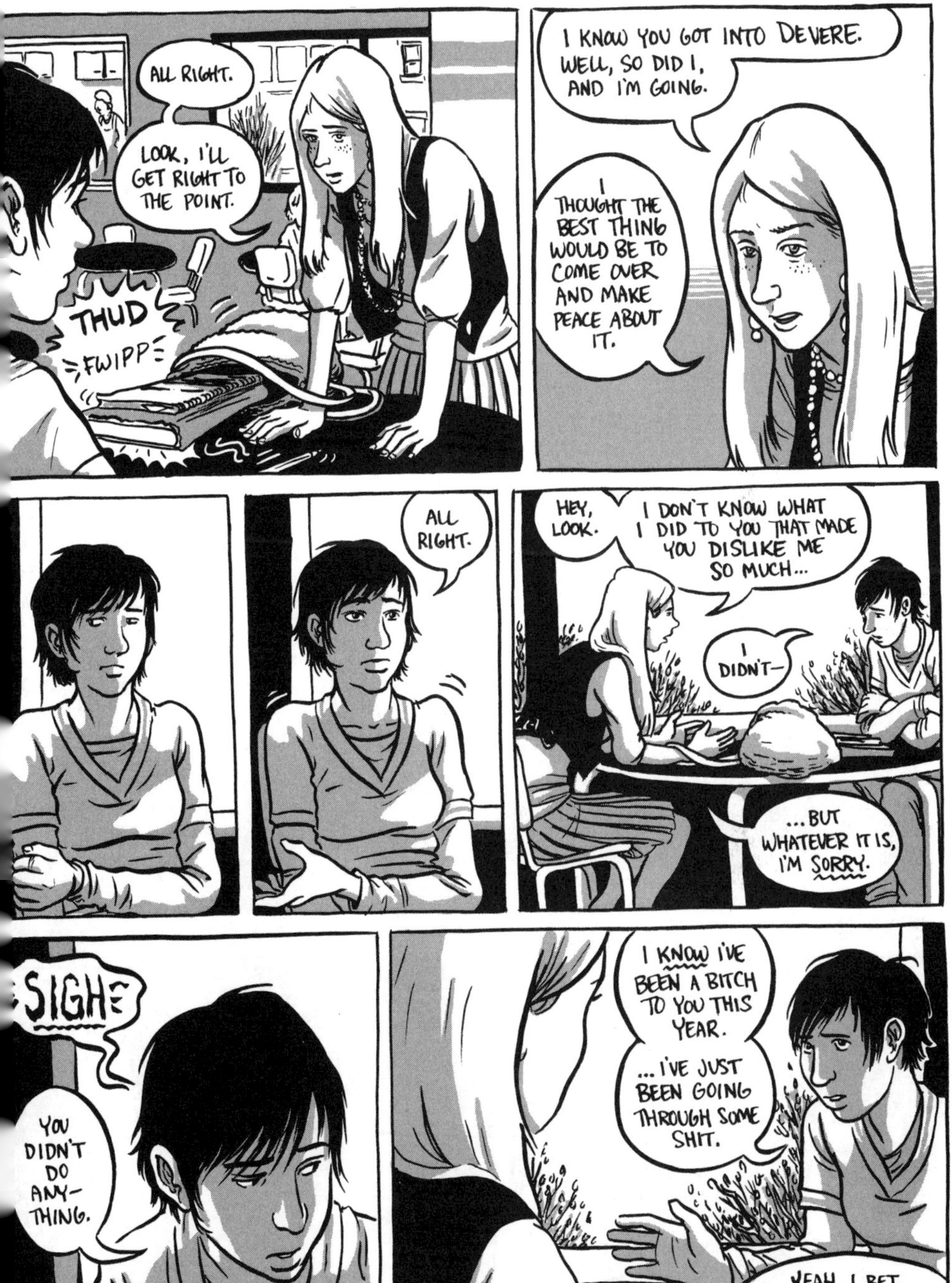
ALL RIGHT.
LOOK, I'LL GET RIGHT TO THE POINT.
THUD
FWIPP
I KNOW YOU GOT INTO DEVERE. WELL, SO DID I, AND I'M GOING.
I THOUGHT THE BEST THING WOULD BE TO COME OVER AND MAKE PEACE ABOUT IT.
ALL RIGHT.
HEY, LOOK.
I DON'T KNOW WHAT I DID TO YOU THAT MADE YOU DISLIKE ME SO MUCH...
I DIDN'T—
...BUT WHATEVER IT IS, I'M SORRY.
SIGH
YOU DIDN'T DO ANY-THING.
I KNOW I'VE BEEN A BITCH TO YOU THIS YEAR.
...I'VE JUST BEEN GOING THROUGH SOME SHIT.
YEAH, I BET. PEOPLE'R SAYING YOU RAN OFF TO NEW YORK.

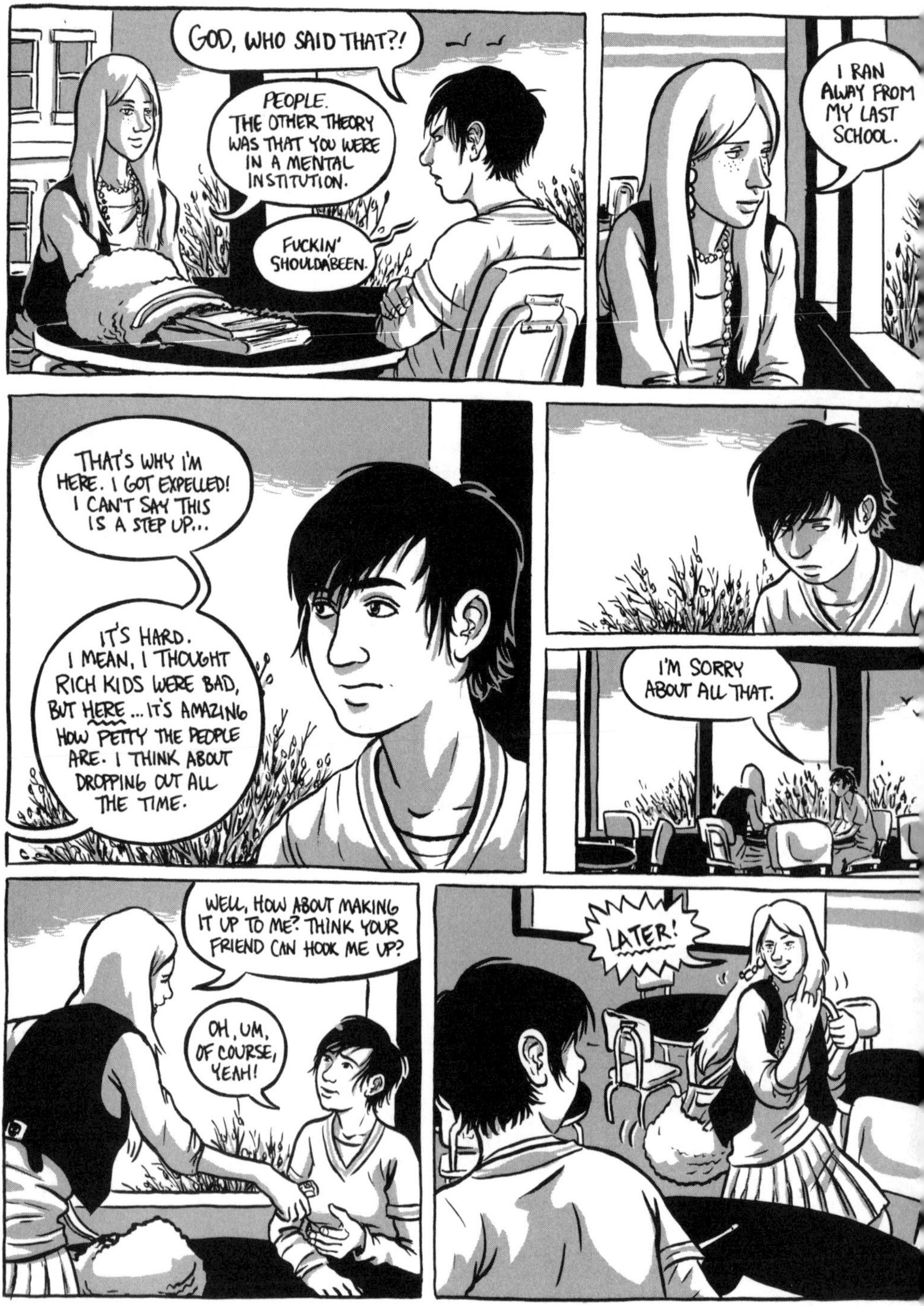
GOD, WHO SAID THAT?!
PEOPLE. THE OTHER THEORY WAS THAT YOU WERE IN A MENTAL INSTITUTION.
FUCKIN' SHOULDA'BEEN.
I RAN AWAY FROM MY LAST SCHOOL.
THAT'S WHY I'M HERE. I GOT EXPELLED! I CAN'T SAY THIS IS A STEP UP...
IT'S HARD. I MEAN, I THOUGHT RICH KIDS WERE BAD, BUT HERE... IT'S AMAZING HOW PETTY THE PEOPLE ARE. I THINK ABOUT DROPPING OUT ALL THE TIME.
I'M SORRY ABOUT ALL THAT.
WELL, HOW ABOUT MAKING IT UP TO ME? THINK YOUR FRIEND CAN HOOK ME UP?
OH, UM, OF COURSE, YEAH!
LATER!

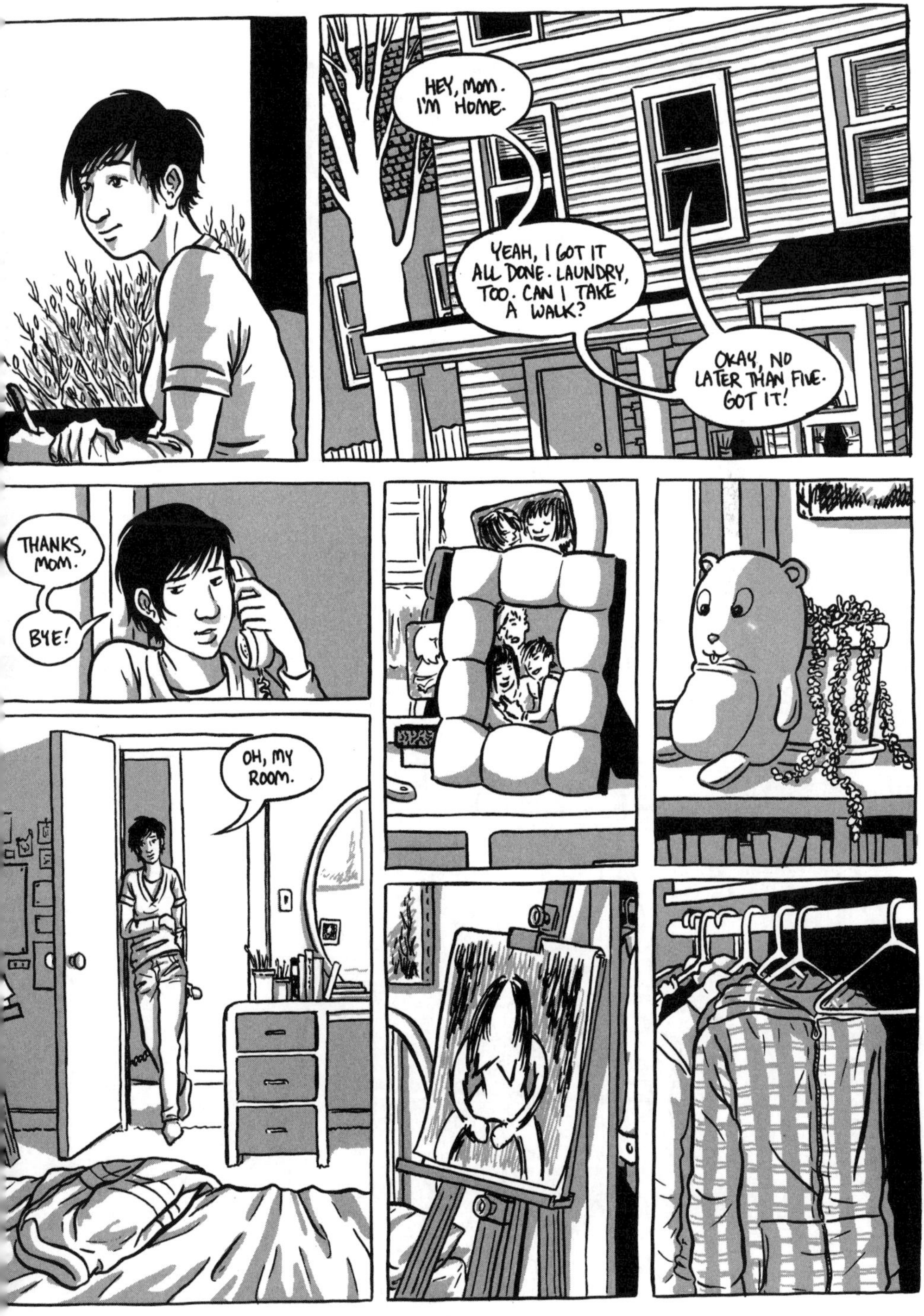
HEY, MOM. I'M HOME.
YEAH, I GOT IT ALL DONE. LAUNDRY, TOO. CAN I TAKE A WALK?
OKAY, NO LATER THAN FIVE. GOT IT!
THANKS, MOM.
BYE!
OH, MY ROOM.

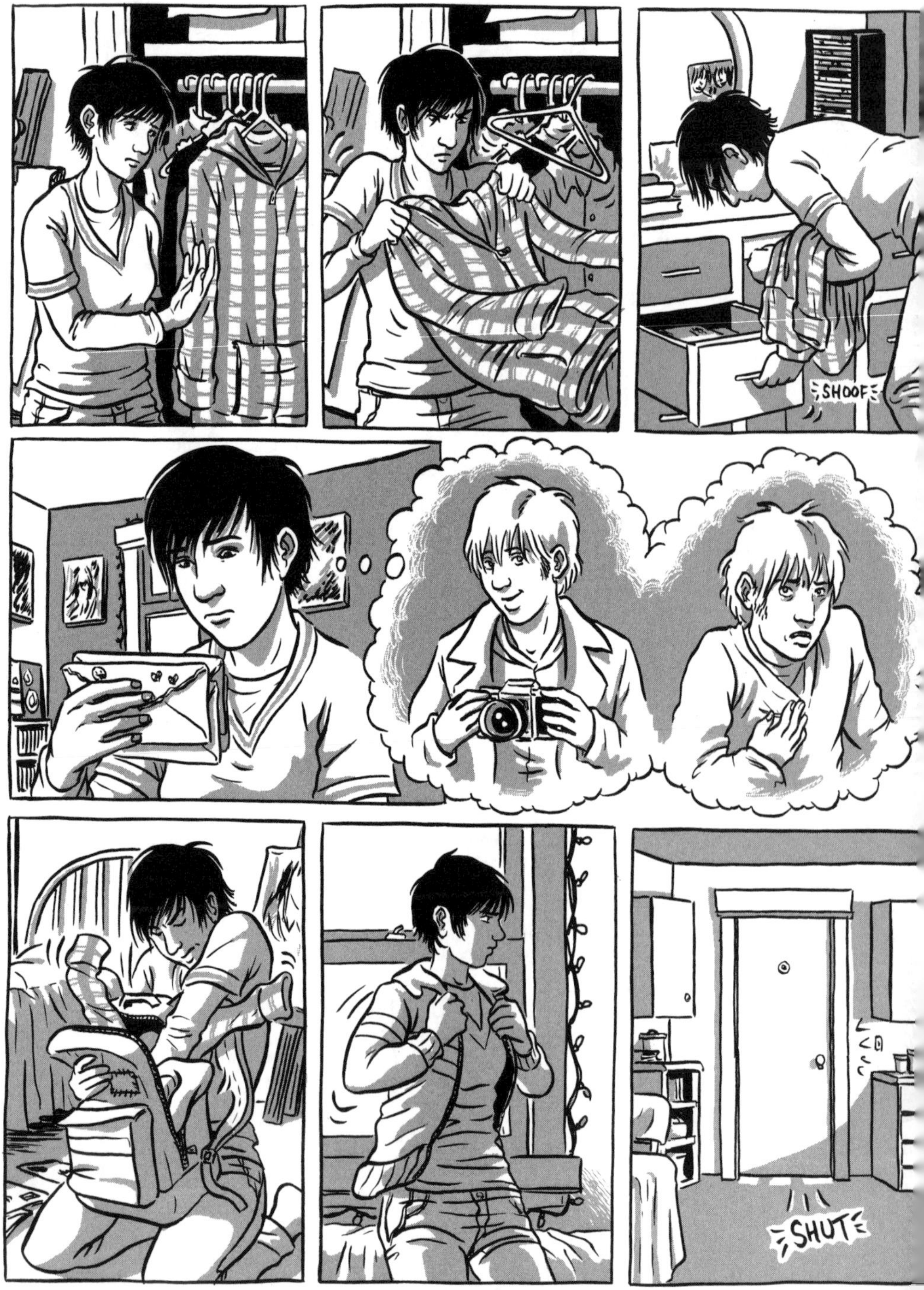
SHOOF
SHUT

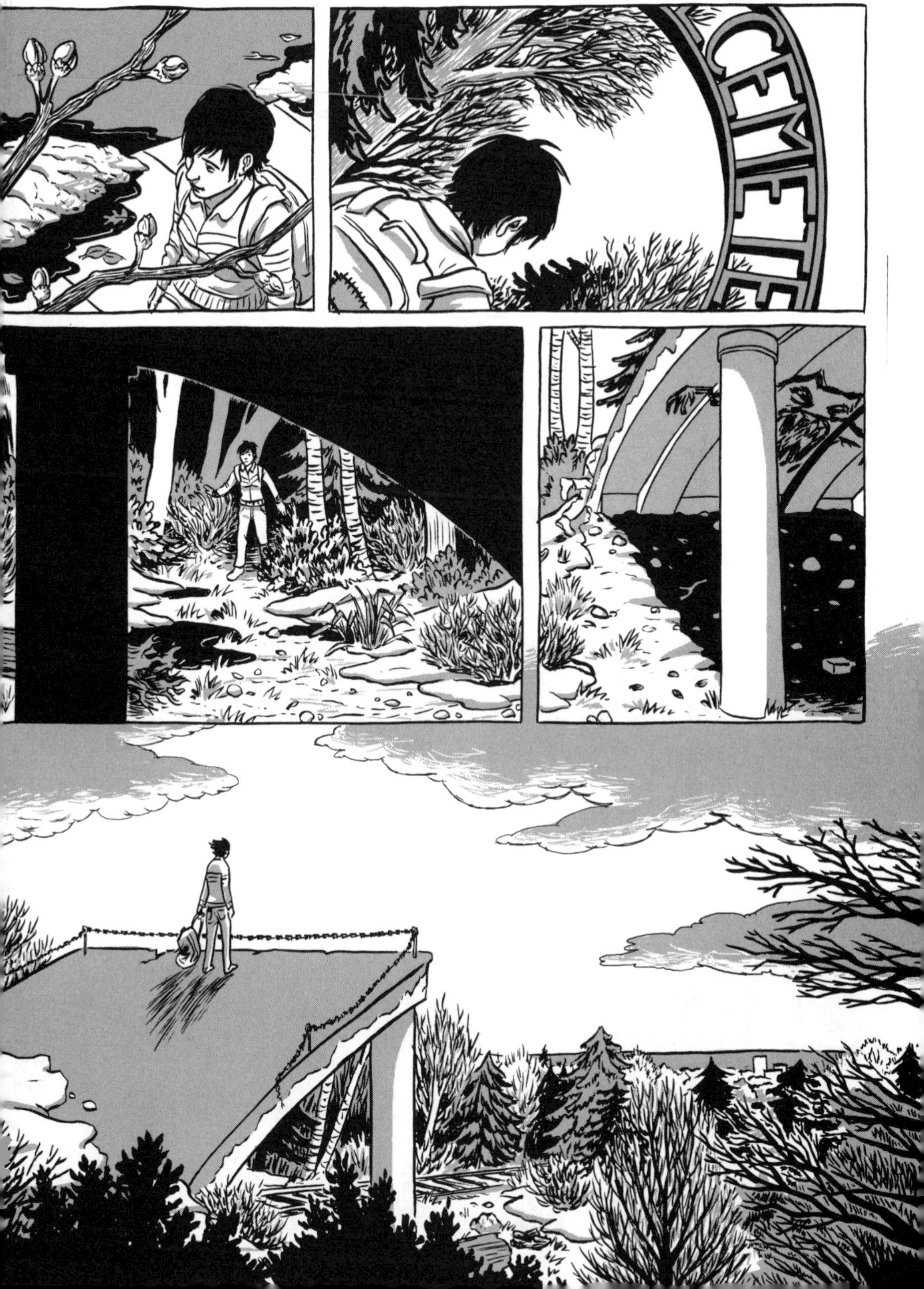
CEMETE

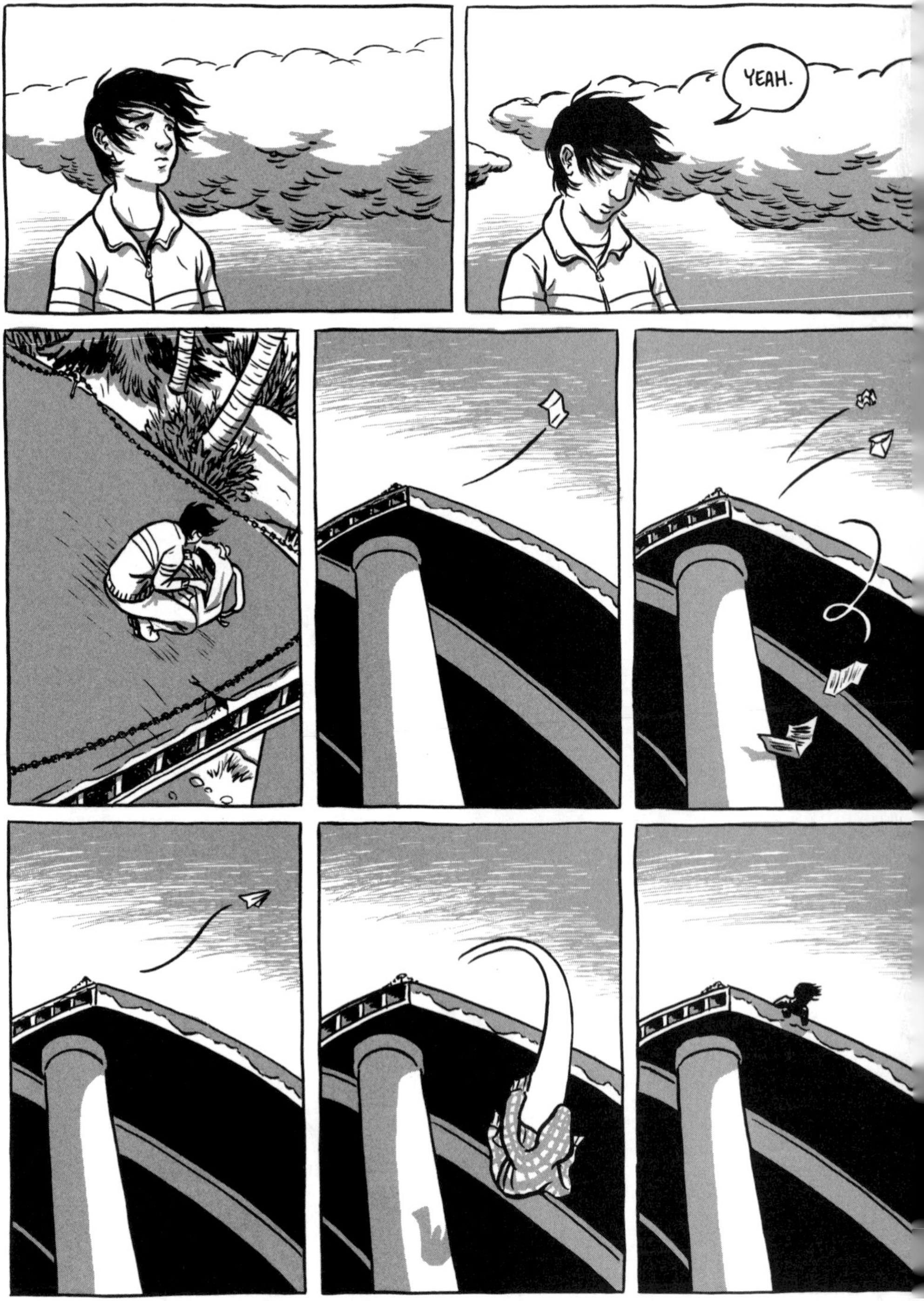
YEAH.

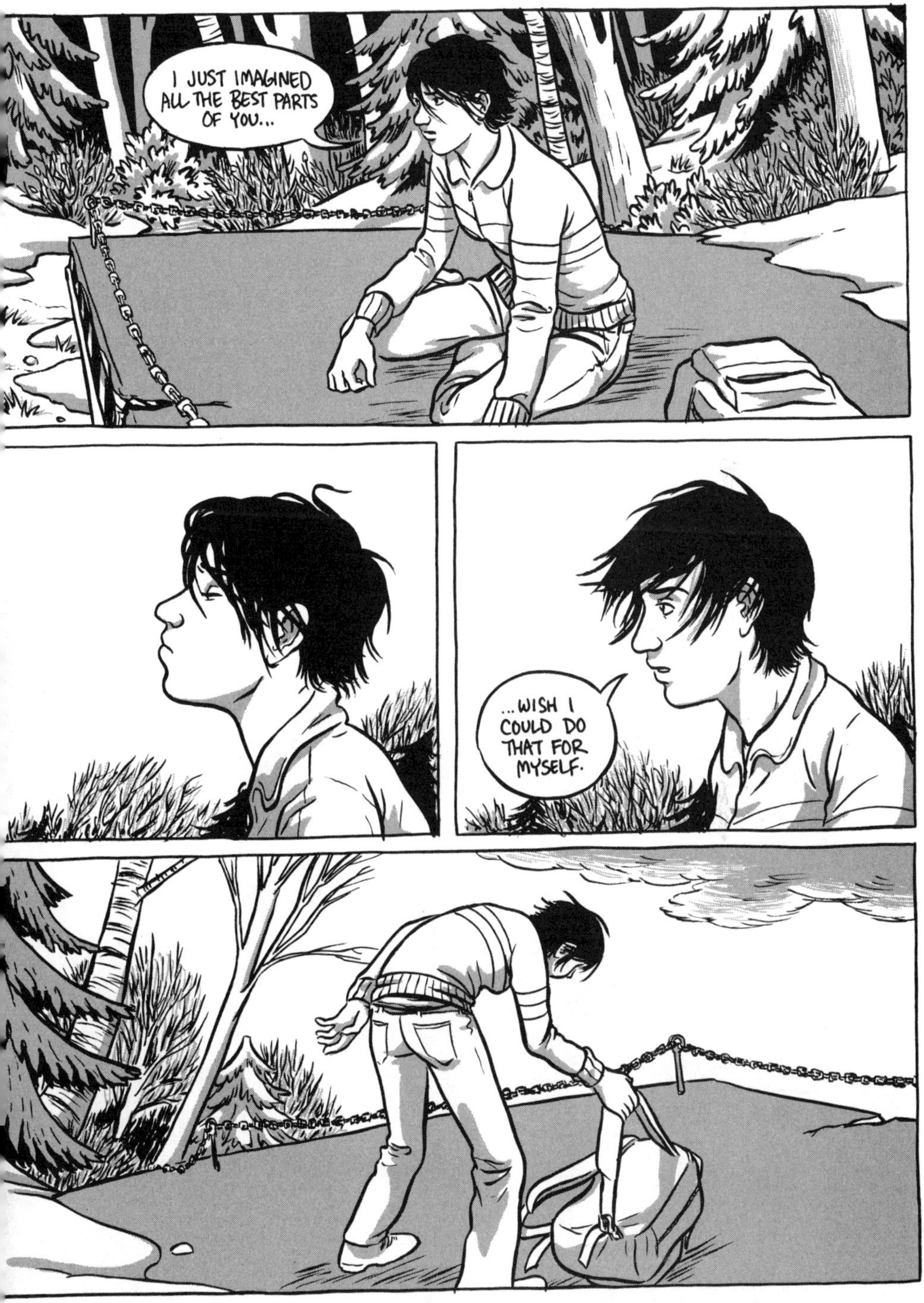
I JUST IMAGINED ALL THE BEST PARTS OF YOU...
...WISH I COULD DO THAT FOR MYSELF.

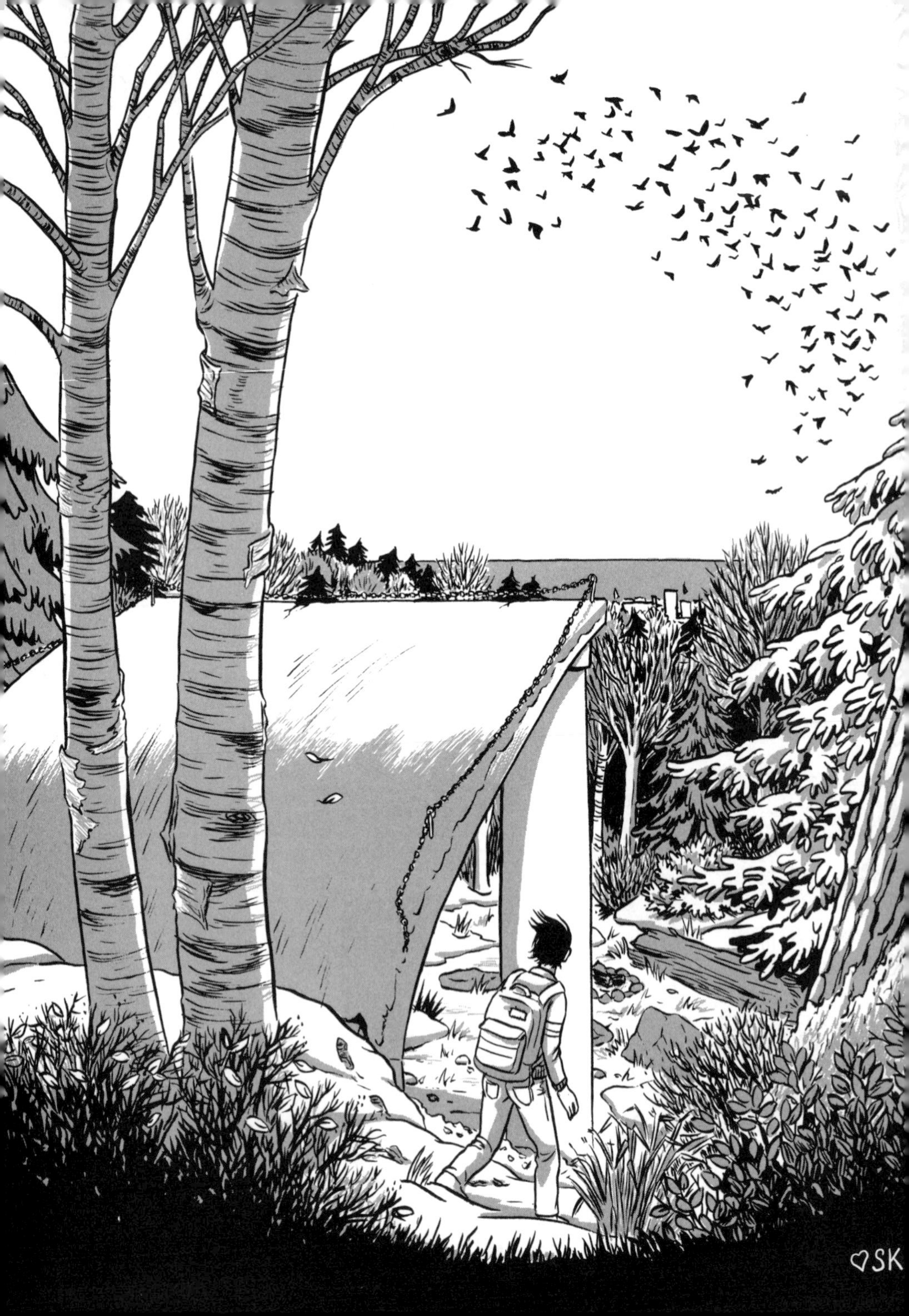
♡SK

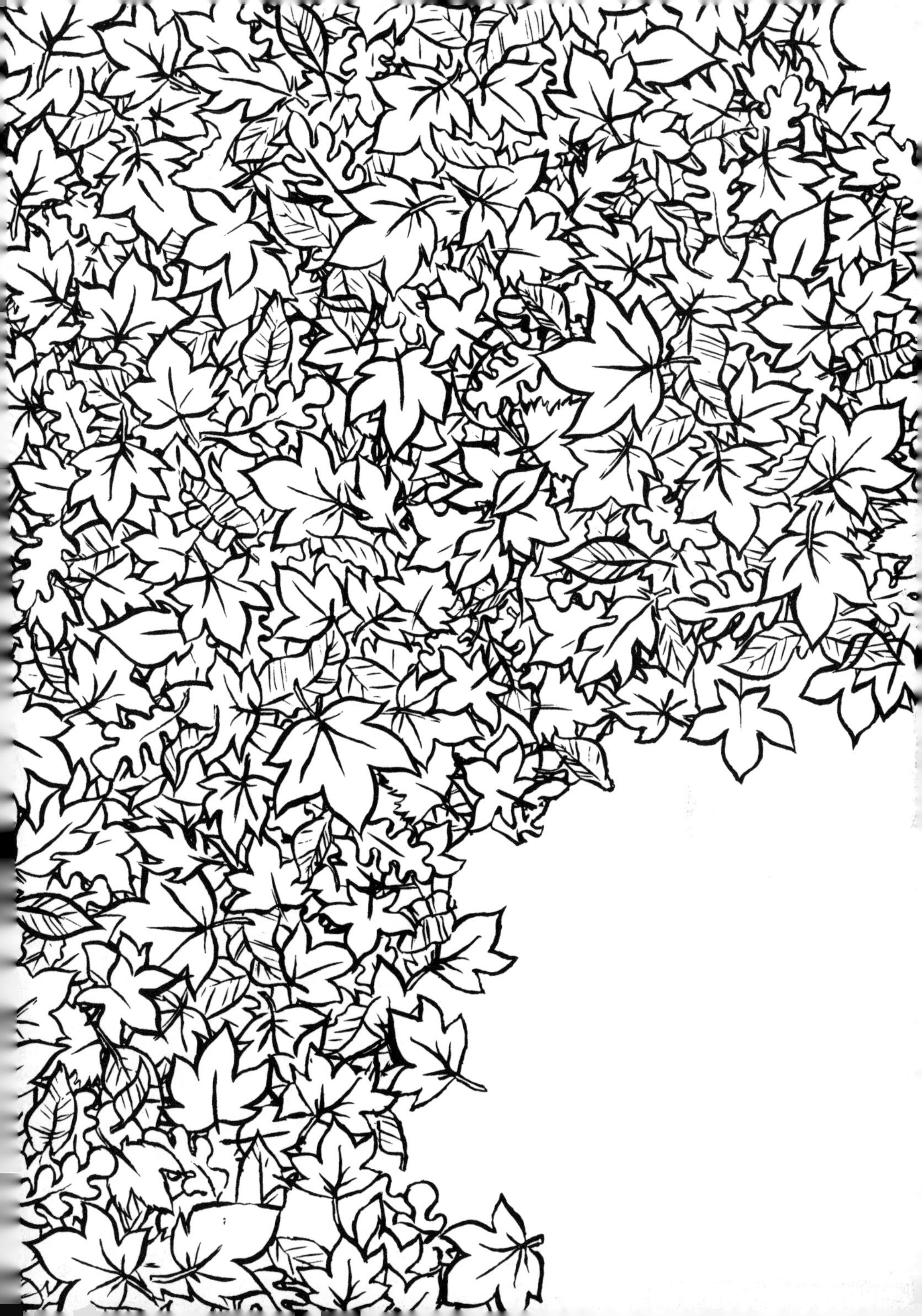

Sarah Oleksyk is an award-winning cartoonist and illustrator dividing her time between drawing funnybooks and tending her tiny urban farm in Portland, Oregon. She believes life should be lived thoroughly and always with style.

saraholeksyk.com

I'd like to thank Douglas Wolk, for years of feedback, conversation and criticism; Steve Lieber, for championing my work and being an incredible resource; Charlie Chu, for being an enthusiastic and detailed editor; my studiomates at Tranquility Base; my family for making me who I am; my friends for their support and insight, especially Heather, Lisa, Lyndsy, Ryland and Sam; the cities of Portland, Maine and Portland, Oregon; and finally, my dear Geoff.

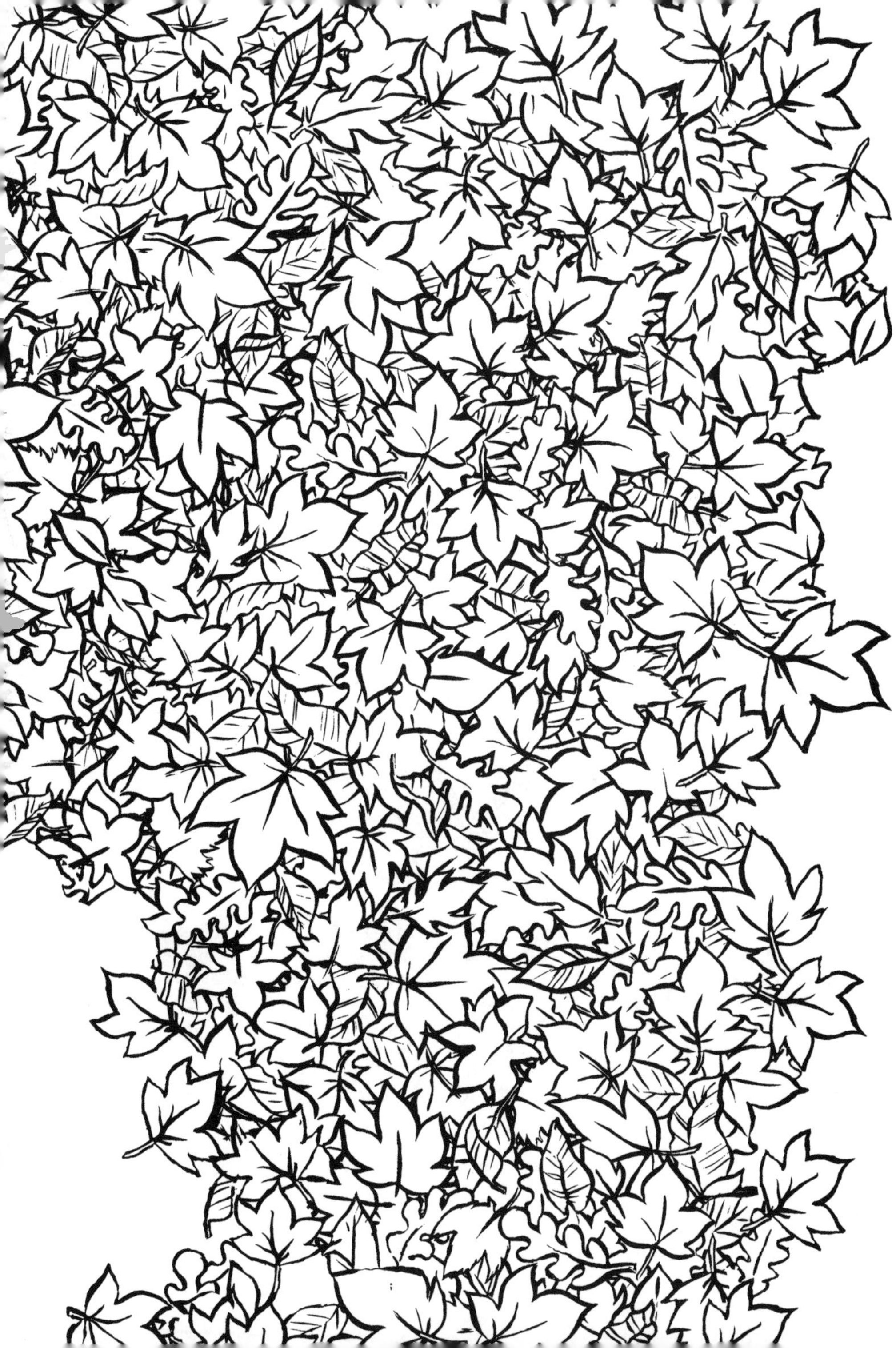

Other books from Oni Press...

wet moon
book 1: feeble wanderings
by ross campbell

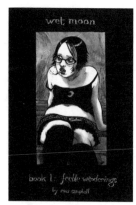

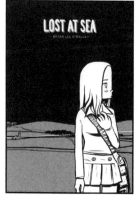

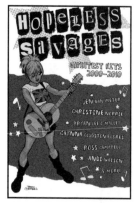

WET MOON, VOL. 1: FEEBLE WANDERINGS
By Ross Campbell
168 pages, 6x9 trade paperback, black and white
$14.99 US
ISBN 978-1-932664-07-2

LOST AT SEA
BRYAN LEE O'MALLEY

LOST AT SEA
By Bryan Lee O'Malley
168 pages, digest, black and white
$11.99 US
ISBN 978-1-932664-16-4

HOPELESS SAVAGES
GREATEST HITS 2000-2010
JEN VAN METER
CHRISTINE NORRIE
BRYAN LEE O'MALLEY
CHYNNA CLUGSTON FLORES
ROSS CAMPBELL
ANDI WATSON
& MORE!

HOPELESS SAVAGES: GREATEST HITS 2000-2010
By Jen Van Meter
392 pages, 6x9 trade paperback, black and white
$19.99 US
ISBN 978-1-934-964-48-4

BRIAN WOOD ★ RYAN KELLY
LOCAL

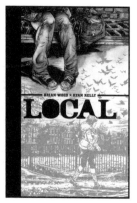

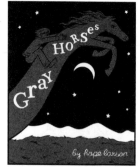

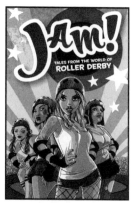

LOCAL - DELUXE HARDCOVER
By Brian Wood & Ryan Kelly
384 pages, hardcover, black and white
$29.99 US
ISBN 978-1-934964-00-2

Gray Horses
by hope larson

GRAY HORSES
By Hope Larson
112 pages, 7x9, trade paperback, 2-color
$14.95 US
ISBN 978-1-932664-36-2

JAM!
TALES FROM THE WORLD OF
ROLLER DERBY

JAM! TALES FROM THE WORLD OF ROLLER DERBY
By Various
192 pages, 6x9, trade paperback, color
$19.95 US
ISBN 978-1-934964-14-9

ONI PRESS

www.onipress.com

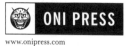

For more information on these and other fine Oni Press comic books and graphic novels, visit www.onipress.com. To find a comic specialty store in your area, call 1-888-COMICBOOK or visit www.comicshops.us.